The State of Our Prisons

CLARENDON STUDIES IN CRIMINOLOGY

Published under the auspices of the Institute of Criminology, University of Cambridge, the Mannheim Centre, London School of Economics, and the Centre for Criminological Research, University of Oxford.

GENERAL EDITOR: ROGER HOOD

EDITORS: TREVOR BENNETT, ANTHONY BOTTOMS,
DAVID DOWNES, NICOLA LACEY, PAUL ROCK,
ANDREW SANDERS

Other titles in this series:

Prison Systems: A Comparative Study Of Accountability in England, France, Germany, and The Netherlands

JON VAGG

Reporting Crime: The Media Politics of Criminal Justice

PHILIP SCHLESINGER and HOWARD TUMBER

Grendon: A Study of a Therapeutic Prison

ELAINE GENDERS and ELAINE PLAYER

Community Policing

NIGEL FIELDING

The State of Our Prisons

Roy D. King and Kathleen McDermott

CLARENDON PRESS · OXFORD
1995

Oxford University Press, Walton Street, Oxford OX2 6DP
Oxford New York Toronto
Delhi Bombay Calcutta Madras Karachi
Kuala Lumpur Singapore Hong Kong Tokyo
Nairobi Dar es Salaam Cape Town
Melbourne Auckland Madrid
and associated companies in
Berlin Ibadan

Oxford is a trade mark of Oxford University Press

Published in the United States
by Oxford University Press Inc., New York

British Library Cataloguing in Publication Data
Data available

Library of Congress Cataloging in Publication Data
Data available
ISBN 0–19–825449–0

Set by Hope Services (Abingdon) Ltd.
Printed in Great Britain
on acid-free paper by
Bookcraft Ltd., Midsomer Norton, Avon

In Memory
Len King, Francis X McDermott and
Paul Grandpierre

General Editor's Introduction

The State of Our Prisons is the fourth volume to be published since *Clarendon Studies in Criminology* was launched in 1994, as successor to *Cambridge Studies in Criminology*.

Clarendon Studies in Criminology, which is published under the auspices of the Cambridge Institute of Criminology, the Mannheim Centre for Criminology and Criminal Justice at the London School of Economics and the Oxford Centre for Criminological Research, provides a forum for outstanding work in all aspects of criminology, criminal justice, penology, and the wider field of deviant behaviour. It welcomes works of theory and synthesis as well as reports of empirical inquiries and aims to be international in its scope.

It is widely recognized that the prison system has been passing through recurrent crises; crises of purpose, of resources, of security and control, of staffing and management, of accountability, and ultimately of its legitimacy. It is not surprising, therefore, that there has been a renewed spate of empirical research and theoretical reflections on the state of the prisons and that three of the four books so far published in this *Series* concern aspects of imprisonment. *The State of Our Prisons* follows Jon Vagg's valuable comparative study of accountability in European prison systems and Elaine Genders and Elaine Player's positive evaluation of the therapeutic prison at Grendon.

Roy King and Kathleen McDermott skilfully weave together their wide-ranging empirical studies of the realities of imprisonment in a variety of penal institutions during the past decade and interpret their findings in the context of changing policies and practices, including the Prison Service Agency's new 'key performance indicators'. By painting an authentic picture of prison conditions in the late 1980s and early 1990s, they have provided both an analysis of changes over that period and a benchmark against which subsequent developments can be evaluated. King and McDermott have also provided a powerful analysis and critique of recent developments in penal policy in the wake of the *Woolf*

Report, the White Paper, *Custody, Care and Justice*, and the Home Secretary's subsequent call for more austere prison regimes. *The State of Our Prisons* will be read with particular interest precisely because it is informed by such a detailed knowledge of the dynamics of prison life.

The authors' articles arising from their research, which have already been highly praised and widely quoted, have raised high expectations for this book. The editors warmly welcome it to the *Series*. This remarkable anatomy of the prison system will be studied and quoted from for many years to come.

Roger Hood
Oxford, February 1995

Preface

This monograph seems to have been an unconscionable time in the writing. Most of the primary data on which it is based are drawn from three pieces of research supported by the Economic and Social Research Council. The first, a study of *Dangerous Prisoners in Maximum Security Custody in the USA*, was carried out in 1984 by Roy King at Oak Park Heights in Minnesota. The second, and much the largest, study on *Security, Control and Humane Containment in the Prison System of England and Wales* was carried out by us jointly under a grant to Roy King which formed part of the Council's Crime and Criminal Justice Research Initiative. It involved a systematic comparison of five representative prisons for adult males in what was then the midland region of the prison service. That work was carried out between 1985 and 1989. The third study, on *Coping with Custody: The Survival Strategies of Prisoners and their Families*, followed immediately on from 1989 to 1991 and involved several prisoners who had participated in the earlier research. Although we were joint principal investigators on that study, Kathleen McDermott had to return to the United States before the end of the research grant, and this inevitably had an impact both upon the original research design and our plans for writing it up.

Several papers covering many aspects of these studies have, of course, already been published—a full list is given in Appendix II—but there remain many central matters which have not, till now, seen the light of day. Almost all of the material presented here is new. It had always been our intention to use this volume to bind our work together. The tragic death of Kathleen McDermott's son, Paul Grandpierre, and the burden of new commitments for us both, however, produced further delays during which we have been all too conscious of the extraordinary changes which have occurred to the prison service since our work was completed. On the wider canvas, these involved the reorganization of management structures and operational directorates within the service, the publication of the Woolf Report and the subsequent White Paper, the move to agency status and the growth of contracting out. More narrowly, the functions of two of our research prisons have also changed.

In these circumstances we are extremely grateful to our publishers, Oxford University Press, and especially to Richard Hart and his colleague, John Whelan, for their tolerance and understanding. Richard carefully reinforced our belief that it was important for our work to stand as a bench-mark against which the effect of these recent changes might subsequently be judged. We had, after all, in one of our published papers (King and McDermott 1989), been able to demonstrate the deterioration in prison regimes which had taken place between 1970 and 1987, in spite of a massive increase of resources, by comparing the preliminary results from our first ESRC study with those from the *Prison Regimes Project* which one of us (RDK) had carried out many years earlier under a grant from the Home Office. In view of the high profile given by Michael Howard at the 1993 Conservative Party conference to the proposition that 'prison works' our data may one day be useful in answering the questions he begs—'in what sense?' and 'at what cost?'. At the same time Richard Hart artfully encouraged us to piece together what we could from whatever sources would enable us to update our materials and to put them in a contemporary perspective. We are particularly grateful to Ian Dunbar, until recently Director of Inmate Administration on the reorganized Prisons Board, for his assistance in that endeavour; and also to Veronica Wilsdon, Secretary to the Prisons Board, and to Philippa Drew, Director of Custody.

We are especially grateful to Anthony Langdon, who was Director of Operational Policy at the time our initial research proposals were submitted. He had already argued the case for independent research on aspects of the prison system in *The Report of the Control Review Committee* and he was undoubtedly instrumental in helping us get these studies off the ground. It might reasonably be suggested that he could guess the likely outcome of any research and gambled that it would draw attention to the need for changes which he (and others) wanted. Be that as it may, it is important to state that he never once sought to influence the nature or direction of our study, but on more than one occasion persuaded his colleagues to overcome their natural disinclination to have their areas of activity subjected to independent scrutiny. This level of disinterest did not entirely survive his departure from the

Prison Department. Whilst we continued to receive support at some delicate moments in the research process, this was strictly within the existing commitment. When we sought to extend the research into the women's prison at Holloway (at that time, at least, we were running ahead of schedule!), permission was not forthcoming. Nevertheless, we should make it clear that at no time have we been asked to submit manuscripts to the prison service for vetting, nor have we offered them.

If Anthony Langdon smoothed our path at the higher levels, Rick Evans steered us into some interesting avenues, introduced us to the mysteries of regime monitoring, and helped us out of one or another tight corner on the ground. Mark Williams was also helpful at a number of points in our research.

Our debts to the governors—Peter Buxton (Birmingham), Richard Tilt (Gartree), Henry Reid (Nottingham), John Dring (Featherstone), Ron Curtis (Ashwell), and Frank Wood (Oak Park Heights)—and the staff of our research prisons, and to all the prisoners and their families who became involved in our work, are obvious but they should not go unremarked. We hope that our writings are worthy of the co-operation and friendship that has been extended to us over the years. This brings us to a consideration of the title of this book. The echoes of John Howard are self-evident. When we discussed the title with one colleague he said, 'Well they may be your prisons, but they are not mine'. This, we suppose, raises the issue of whether prisons could ever be legitimate. We have never quite felt able to permit ourselves such a sense of distance: prisons are assuredly not going to go away. In the large, of course, we feel no sense of ownership, although our tax pounds, like everyone else's, help to pay the ever-expanding bills. More than that, though, we are painfully aware that whatever happens in prisons is done in our name, however much we may feel that Home Secretaries take that for granted. But at the more local level, there is a sense in which, without invoking ownership, these really are 'our' prisons: one way or another working in them significantly changed our lives.

Those closest to us probably feel they now know more than they ever wanted to know about prisons, but without their help we would never have carried these projects through. Our children had to tolerate, by turns, our protracted absences on fieldwork and our intrusive presence as we discussed the analysis and writing up in each other's homes. But they perhaps also reaped some benefit, sometime vicariously and sometimes directly, from amazing discussions and the occasional prison visit. Those now lost to us are missed more than we can say and are remembered, inadequately, in our dedication.

Circumstances have dictated that the updating of the research, and the writing of this monograph, have been undertaken entirely by Roy King. In other respects this has been a joint enterprise and we share responsibility for what is written here, just as we shared most of the fieldwork. We must record our appreciation to Stephen Shaw and his colleagues at the Prison Reform Trust for allowing Kathleen McDermott to use their offices as a base during part of the fieldwork—which also, of course, meant being able to use them both as a sounding board and a necessary source of support. Stephen also gave generously of his time and his knowledge in helping us to understand the sometimes bewildering changes that have occurred in the last couple of years. We owe a special debt to John Borland. If he had not taken over the reins as Head of the School of Sociology and Social Policy at Bangor, the time would never have been found to write this book. He has also helped with parts of the analysis in spite of onerous duties elsewhere. Brenda Clare prepared the diagrams with good humour on each occasion that we changed our minds as to how they should be presented. Several people have read the manuscript in whole or in part and we are particularly grateful to Rod Morgan and David Faulkner for their detailed, helpful, and carefully considered critiques. Their comments contributed to numerous improvements in the text pointing us to errors, omissions, problems of analysis and interpretation. Only occasionally did we fail to heed their advice and we exonerate them from all blame for the deficiencies which remain. Jan King has read most of this at least twice. Her comments on style and presentation have been invaluable, if not inviolate. But her support for this enterprise has inevitably gone a great deal deeper than that.

RDK, KMcD.

Bangor, May 1994

Contents

List of Figures and Tables

Figures

Tables

1

The Prison System in a State of Change: Making Sense of Our Research

AT THE time that the research reported here was carried out, the prison system was a rather different animal from the one we see today. It seems important, therefore, to set out as clearly as possible the context in which the research was planned and conducted, to give a brief outline of the research programme, and then to review the changes which have taken place since, so that the reader can bear these in mind when considering its implications.

As far as reasonably possible we have tried to update our work to take account of subsequent developments, both for our research prisons and more generally for the system as a whole. It has not been an easy task. The number of changes has been great and the pace at which they have been introduced has been accelerating. Moreover, the flow of information about them has been, by prison standards, prodigious, reflecting a new and welcome openness. However, official information on prisons has always needed careful deconstruction before it can be properly understood. That may be even more the case now that it is presented in glossy, user-friendly packages, which also serve to demonstrate the pride of the service and its belief in its mission statement, than it was formerly. Finally, throughout the writing of this volume from November 1993 until April 1994, the Prison Service has once again moved to the centre of the political stage and new battles are being fought over the meaning and legitimacy of those changes. In the circumstances we have sometimes been able to do no more than give a few signposts as to what might be their likely effect and what they may portend for the future. Time, and subsequent research, will be needed to tell whether the most recent and apparently dramatic developments amount to a mutation or some more gradual process of evolution.

The Contextual Background

On 6 July 1981, at the suggestion of David Faulkner, the first meeting of an informal discussion group comprising senior members of the Prison Service and academics took place at NACRO headquarters in Clapham.[1] The venue was significant, a place where it was possible, after hours, for officials to talk and listen to their critics on neutral ground. It would have been hard to imagine such discussions taking place during working hours at Eccleston Square, then the headquarters of the Prison Department.

Those were difficult days for the Prison Service. There was a profound sense of disillusion on the part of some officials about the outcome of the May Committee of Inquiry into the United Kingdom Prison Services (Home Office 1979a). It was not just that the service's attempt at finding solutions to the prison officers' shift and complementing systems—the intractable industrial relations problem which had been at the heart of the Committee's terms of reference, but which had understandably been handed straight back to the Prison Department to resolve—was falling apart. By no means all of them could accept May J's formulation of the concept of 'positive custody' as a serious goal for the Service that would overcome the legacy of 'treatment and training' or do anything about the urgent need to address the question of how standards might be improved. In spite of the widening of the Committee's terms of reference, the nettle of the dispersal system and the spiralling costs of high security provision had not been grasped; and the question of how to improve conditions for remand prisoners had largely been ducked. Even the vast expansion of the prison building programme—anathema to most academics and penal reform groups who had pleaded for a reductionist stance towards the prison population—was regarded by some officials as a mixed blessing. No administrator, of course, can turn down the gift horse

[1] The group came into existence following discussions between David Faulkner, Roy King, Rod Morgan, and Vivien Stern. As it began to take off, the official side came to include Margaret Clayton, Ian Dunbar, Arthur de Frisching, and Jenny Hughes, then a non-executive member of the Prisons Board: and the academic side was expanded to include David Downes and Andrew Rutherford. Tim Flesher acted as secretary.

of additional resources, especially when alleged lack of them had figured so strongly in their official evidence (Home Office, 1979b): but whilst they welcomed the opportunity for directly improving conditions in the dilapidated local prisons through a programme of refurbishment, they were also concerned that, taken together with the other recommendations, the building programme signalled a drift towards growth without any real sense of direction—in short, more of the same. Even the independent inspectorate, eventually to become the May Committee's lasting legacy, had got off to a slow and cautious start. Though it had been opposed by some members of the Prisons Board, others had seen the potential importance of an independent inspectorate in legitimating a more defensible prison system. The question was, in the light of the criticism, how might it be made more defensible?

There had not been a great deal of external evidence to the May Inquiry—but what there was from academics and penal reform groups was extremely critical not just of prisons policy but of most aspects of prison management as well. The Treasury evidence also called into question its value for money (Home Office 1979d). The Prisons Board itself was divided between those who wished to address the criticism seriously and those who were inclined to dis-regard it altogether and soldier on. It was against this background that the first feelers were put out by officials to enter into a con-structive and continuing dialogue. From the outset certain ground rules were laid down. It was agreed that the group would not go out of its way to advertise its existence, although there was no need to make it a particular secret. Members of the group partici-pated as individuals without prejudice to their official position. Chatham House rules prevailed.[2] Proceedings were confidential in the sense that no-one would have wished to embarrass another member of the group by repeating things better not said in public, but if discussion stimulated ideas for an article or for an initiative within the Prison Department, so much the better. In spite of its somewhat conspiratorial beginnings, there came a time when the existence of the group was more openly acknowledged within the Department. At this point consideration was given to mechanisms for publicizing areas of agreement, including the development of research programmes, the writing of papers, and the briefing of

---

[2] Chatham House rules observe the convention that nobody may be directly quoted outside the framework of the meeting without having given explicit consent.

journalists.[3] Virtually no subject was excluded from the agenda of
the meetings, and as the members of the group developed understanding and mutual respect so there was an unprecedented sharing
of data and ideas, with opinions vigorously and freely expressed.
In large part the initial topics for discussion were set by the arguments displayed in King and Morgan's (1980) critical analysis of
the deliberations of the May Committee in *The Future of the Prison
System*, which had been published a few months earlier.

In their evidence to the May Committee, King and Morgan
(1979) had argued that the philosophy of treatment and training of
offenders then enshrined (and for that matter still enshrined) in
Rule 1 of the Prison Rules 1964 (S I No. 388)—'the purpose of the
training and treatment of convicted prisoners shall be to encourage
and assist them to lead a good and useful life'—had been largely a
rhetorical device that was little more than a sham. Embracing the
doctrine of treatment and training had clothed the punitive functions of imprisonment in a more palatable guise for the liberal conscience, but it had at times encouraged the use of prison sentences
rather than alternatives, and longer sentences rather than shorter
ones, in the belief that scientific methods offered a cure for crime
which needed time and the right conditions of control in which to
work. It had also played an important part in establishing a parole
scheme which linked release to response to treatment, just at the
time when such procedures were being discredited in the United
States and elsewhere.

True, the treatment and training philosophy had allowed reform-
minded administrators to smuggle in many humanizing elements
over the years, but there was a yawning gap between the rhetoric
and the reality. Actual programmes of treatment or training were,
to say the least, thin on the ground (King 1972; King and Elliott
1978) and there was precious little evidence that imprisonment had
any beneficial outcomes compared to other, less expensive, sentences even in the United States, especially California, where the
treatment philosophy had been most well tried (Lipton, Martinson,
and Wilks 1975; Brody 1976). However, the real damage of the
treatment and training philosophy, they argued, was inflicted
through the very organization of the prison system on a basis that
assumed the philosophy actually worked. Although security had for

[3] Several articles appeared in the press as a result and on one occasion Bill
Hamilton of the BBC sat in on the discussion for background.

several years been the real driving force behind the classification of offenders, institutional provision was predicated largely on the belief that more so-called training prisons were needed and that they should be protected from crowding in order to provide the best possible facilities for effecting the rehabilitation of offenders. The cost of this, however, was that crowding was deliberately concentrated in local prisons, which as a matter of policy were starved of capital investment. Yet the Prison Department came quite shamelessly close to describing the facilities and conditions it actually provided in them as constituting 'humane containment' (Home Office 1969, paras. 165–71; 1977, paras. 13 and 202; 1979b I, IIA2, para. 18). One consequence of this was that remand prisoners, those to whom the presumption of innocence still applied, actually experienced the worst conditions of any in the system. Perhaps the most debilitating problem, however, with the treatment and training philosophy was that although it allowed administrators and staff to justify what they did on grounds of good intentions, it gave no measures of outcome for their activities that would do other than reinforce a sense of failure to achieve objectives.

What King and Morgan had advanced instead of treatment and training was that the prison system should actually take seriously the notion of humane containment and turn *that* into a reality. Humane containment might not fire the imagination, but its very practical and prosaic quality might help avoid some of the excesses that had been associated with the apparently lofty ideals of treatment and training. Above all, it demanded specification of what constituted a humane regime which might then form the basis for a new set of Prison Rules that would cater for the unconvicted and the unsentenced, as well as sentenced prisoners, in terms that would be consistent both with emerging international norms on human rights and with what had come to be called the justice model of corrections in the United States. King and Morgan, however, did not elaborate at any length on how the justice model would work in the British context. They did not, for example, specify in detail the rights and entitlements that prisoners should expect. Although some such standards were sketched in and others were implicit, the task of fleshing this out was subsequently picked up to some extent in the discussion group, but more especially by NACRO and the Prison Reform Trust and finally by Woolf LJ and the Prison Service Code of Standards Steering Group established after the publication of the White Paper on *Custody, Care, and Justice*. King and Morgan's advocacy of humane containment was directed largely towards developing a more sensible framework for the utilization of resources within the prison system: there being no further justification for training prisons as such, it would be possible to redefine many of them as more local, multi-functional establishments, thereby easing the burden of overcrowding without having to embark on a major new prison building programme.

In a separate piece of evidence to the May Committee, King (1979) had mounted a closely argued attack upon the wastefulness of the dispersal system which had been introduced in 1969. The Government had then chosen to accept the advice of the Radzinowicz Committee (ACPS 1968) to disperse high security risk prisoners amongst lower security risks around several maximum security prisons rather than follow Mountbatten's recommendation to concentrate such prisoners initially in one, but perhaps eventually in two, specialist prisons (Home Office 1966). Whilst no prisoners had ever escaped from dispersal prisons, King argued that the dispersal system had grown in size far beyond most people's wildest expectations, partly in response to the repeated riots and disturbances which occurred in them. Ironically, it had largely been fears about the difficulties of control in Mountbatten's fortress that had originally led to the dispersal alternative. But, by the time of the May Committee, concerns about security and control had become inextricably conflated in official discourse, and together they absorbed a wholly disproportionate amount of the service's resources. Paradoxically, far more prisoners than necessary were kept in costly high security prisons. Yet those same prisons were deliberately kept below capacity because of staff fears about loss of control, whilst elsewhere in the prison system there was gross overcrowding. Having rejected, ten years earlier, the building of one prison to concentrate such prisoners, the government was now apparently prepared to add two purpose-built dispersal prisons to the already huge system of maximum security accommodation.

Bringing these ideas together King and Morgan argued for a system that would have the difficult task of providing *genuinely* humane containment for all its charges and which would be underpinned by three principles:

the *minimum use of custody*—that imprisonment should be used only as a last resort, when other forms of sentence have been exhausted, or are clearly inappropriate having regard to the nature of the offence . . . [and] . . . should be used for the minimum length of time consistent with public safety (King and Morgan 1980, 34);

the *minimum use of security*—that prisoners should be subject to only that degree of security necessary to safeguard the public against any realistic threat, and to ensure that prisoners complete their sentences in the prisons to which they are allocated (*ibid.* 37);

the *normalization of the prison*—that as far as resources allow, and consistent with the constraints of secure custody, the same general standards as govern the life of offenders in the community should be held to apply to offenders in prison (*ibid.* 37).

In truth these ideas were hardly new. The justice model of corrections had been gaining ground in the United States for several years (see, for example, American Friends Service Committee 1971, or Von Hirsch 1976); governments regularly committed, and recommitted, themselves to the minimum use of custody; the expressions 'humane containment' and 'minimum use of security' fell all too easily from the lips of administrators and appeared in numerous official reports; and the principle implied in the ugly phrase 'normalization of the prison' had received much more elegant expression in Rule 58 of the European Standard Minimum Rules for the Treatment of Offenders, itself a version of Alexander Paterson's famous dictum that criminals go to prison *as*, and not *for*, punishment. The Rule was quoted in full and it is worth re-stating here:

Imprisonment and other measures which result in cutting off an offender from the outside world are, by the deprivation of liberty, a punishment in themselves. Therefore the prison system should not, except as incidental to justifiable segregation or the maintenance of discipline, aggravate the suffering inherent in such a situation. The regime of the institution should seek to minimize any differences between prison life and life at liberty which tend to lessen the responsibility of the prisoners and the respect due to their dignity as human beings (Rule 58, Council of Europe, 1973 [rewritten as Rules 64 and 65, Council of Europe, 1987]).

The problem was to find ways in which these concepts could be turned into a reality, and to find agreed standards against which performance could be measured and below which it should not be allowed to fall.

King and Morgan's advocacy of humane containment did not convince the May Committee. Whilst the Committee expressed sympathy with King and Morgan's 'impatience with wishful thinking' (i.e. of the treatment and training model), it feared humane containment 'may throw out the good with the unattainable'; that it was a 'means without an end'; that it 'can only result in making prisons into human warehouses'; that it would require staff 'to operate in a moral vacuum and the absence of real objectives can in the end lead only to the routine brutalization of all the participants' (Home Office 1979a, paras. 4.24 and 4.28). The Committee agreed that the notion of treatment and training had outlived its usefulness (*ibid.*, para. 4.27), but in its denial of humane containment as 'a fit rule for hopeful life or responsible management' (*ibid.*, para. 4.24) it proposed the following alternative Rule 1:

The purpose of the detention of convicted prisoners shall be to keep them in custody which is both secure and positive, and to that end the behaviour of all the responsible authorities and staff towards them shall be such as to:
(a) create an environment which can assist them to respond and contribute to society as positively as possible;
(b) preserve and promote their self respect;
(c) minimize, to the degree of security necessary in each particular case, the harmful effects of their removal from normal life'
(d) prepare them for and assist them on discharge (*ibid.*, para. 4.26).

Moreover, the May Committee was sceptical both about the extent to which a policy based on humane containment would allow a redistribution of resources towards the local prisons and about the case King and Morgan had made for dismembering the dispersal system in favour of a modified form of concentration for high security risk prisoners. In both cases it preferred to rely on the rebuttal evidence supplied by the Home Office (Home Office 1979b, c). Nevertheless, the May Committee only preferred the dispersal policy to concentration '*in present operational conditions*' (*ibid.*, para. 6.72, emphasis added). It was not satisfied that the Home Office had 'struck the right security balance' and it did not believe that the Home Office had 'convincingly answered' the question of how many category B prisoners needed to be in dispersal prisons and why they needed to be there (*ibid.*, para. 6.70).

That the May Committee was so emphatic in its rejection of the idea of humane containment suggests that King and Morgan failed sufficiently to distinguish their use of the term from the complacent, yet essentially negative, way it was used by the Home Office. Certainly other commentators from inside and outside the Prison Service (Dunbar 1985, Stern 1987, and Bottoms 1990) were subsequently to voice much the same doubts as had been expressed to the Committee in consideration of the then prevailing Home Office version. In a vigorous defence of humane containment King and Morgan argued that the May Committee was wrong in regarding it as a means without an end, pointing out that few prison systems had yet achieved genuinely humane containment; that all the supposed benefits of treatment and training could be better justified under the rubric of humane containment; that it was as well to recognize that all prison systems were in fact, and of necessity, human warehouses and that the point was to prevent them from becoming *inhuman* warehouses, whatever their lofty ideals. Positive custody, they argued, suffered from the same defects as treatment and training: it imposed no obligations on the authorities and conferred no rights upon prisoners; and it would still allow administrators to justify their activities by reference to their good intentions rather than by results. In short it was yet another rhetorical device, devoid of real meaning, aimed at manipulating hopes rather than specifying achievable objectives (King and Morgan 1980, 28–30).

In the event positive custody had, if anything, even fewer takers than humane containment. Whilst it was never explicitly rejected by the Home Office it was never explicitly accepted either: the proposed change to Rule 1 was never adopted and positive custody was quietly forgotten. For many people the May Report was 'received with an overwhelming sense of disappointment, anger, and betrayal' (Fitzgerald and Sim 1980, 74–5) because it merely legitimated the existing prison crisis. As Rutherford (1980) summed it up, in a characteristically acerbic manner, the May Report provided 'a salutary reminder of what is likely to happen when ten well-intentioned persons, guided by a Home Office secretariat, take a hasty journey through the complex and . . . unfamiliar quagmire of penal policy'.

With whatever uncertainties about just how to describe the purposes of imprisonment set to one side, the underlying principles of minimum use of custody, minimum use of security, and normalization of the prison seemed to provide a necessary, if not a sufficient, agenda for the meetings of the new working group. To these were added a range of other important questions brought to the meetings by officials and others which had not figured prominently in the considerations before the May Committee—they had to do with grievance procedures, the disciplinary system and the role of Boards of Visitors, the status of Prison Rules, circular instructions and standing orders and their enforceability, and the nature and organization of staff roles at all levels throughout the service.

Not surprisingly, a great deal of the discussion centred upon the implications of all these matters for the use of resources. From the official side came a concern, at times almost despairing, with the problem of staffing as Prisons Board grappled with what had become known as the essential task list (ETL), which formed the basis of determining the staffing complements for prisons. The industrial relations disputes which had bedevilled the system for years, and which gave rise to the May Committee in the first place, showed no sign whatever of going away. Indeed, if anything, they had begun to take on a new form. Increasingly, prison officers linked their restrictive practices to prison conditions, arguing that they could not be expected to allow prisoners more time out of cells, for example, when the courts were sending to prison more prisoners than the accommodation was certified to take. Whenever consideration was given to changing a given policy or procedure, the better to bring into effect improvements to regimes or to the management of prisons, prison officers were able to point to the need for additional staff, given that present numbers were predicated upon the need to complete the agreed existing tasks on the ETL. The threat by staff to 'drop tasks' was an ever-present reality for most prison governors on the ground and surfaced time and again at top level policy meetings. That the staffing situation had been driven by the poorly thought-through concerns with security and control generated by the policy makers themselves made this a particularly difficult hook from which officials needed to remove themselves. In June 1982, Denis Trevelyan, the Director General, asked the Prisons Board to form a 'clear comprehensive view of the realities facing the Service', and by September he was being urged to develop a strategy that would generate the necessary political will to address improved use of staffing, improved systems for managerial control, and the demonstration of better value for money through the development of improved regimes. All this, of course, reinforced the need to think hard about ways of controlling the size of the prison population, of establishing minimum standards, and of monitoring the effective use of resources.

Some indication of the political atmosphere under which the group worked can be gained by recalling that, less than six months after it first met, the then Home Secretary, William Whitelaw, was hounded from the platform at the Conservative Party Conference. His attempt to persuade the conference to support the minimum use of custody principle through an extension of parole at the lower end of the sentencing spectrum was unsuccessful, even though it was carefully balanced by the familiar resort to tougher sentences for more serious criminals (see Bottoms 1977 for a discussion of this process of bifurcation in penal policy). The continuing divisions within the Prisons Board and the reluctance of some of its members to contemplate further opening up the system were revealed by the fact that proposals, by members of the discussion group, for research into the operation of the dispersal system and the wide regional variations in categorization procedures, were met with the response 'that the time is not right'. In the longer term, though, whether attributable to the influence of the discussion group or not, there were signs that the climate had begun to change. Thus, much of an important conference on the purpose of the prison system held at the Wakefield Staff College in October 1982 was devoted to consideration of the justice model, under which broad rubric were gathered many workshop discussions about improving the dignity of prisoners and the accountability of staff. Another sign was that the question of minimum standards was now being taken up by the All-Party Penal Affairs Group, the new Chief Inspector of Prisons, and, apparently, ministers too. On 17 December 1982, Patrick Mayhew, Minister of State at the Home Office, in a reply to Robert Kilroy-Silk announced his intention to produce a draft code of minimum standards for prisons during 1983. But by then David Faulkner was moving on to the Criminal Policy Division, and the group had lived out its natural span.[4] So far as we are aware, the Faulkner group was unique. Certainly the Prison Service has never repeated the experiment of having continuing informal discussion groups, although the Control Review

[4] David Faulkner then established a rather different group with a different membership and a wider brief to look at the criminal justice system as a whole (see Windlesham 1993).

Committee set up a formal Research and Advisory Group in 1984, and from time to time independent consultants have been retained for particular projects.[5]

Anyone who thinks the path of prison reform runs smoothly should note that, by the end of 1983, the Home Office had not delivered its promised draft code of standards, and the commitment was officially withdrawn the following year. Three years later a new Minister of State, John Patten, replied to a parliamentary question with the bald statement that: 'We do not consider that a code of minimum standards for prisons would advance the programme the Government has in hand for improving prison conditions' (Hansard, 21 July 1987). While this book was being prepared a code of standards was finally published—in April 1994—just in time for us to refer to it at various points in our account. It is not quite what had been expected, but that is to run ahead of our narrative. With the withdrawal of any official commitment to standards, the task of drawing up such a code was taken up first by NACRO (Casale 1983, 1985; Casale and Plotnikoff 1989) and then by the Prison Reform Trust (Plotnikoff 1986), with gradually increasing public support from the Chief Inspector of Prisons, the Prison Officers' Association, and the Prison Governors' Association, and occasional papers from senior members of the Prison Service itself (Dunbar, 1985).

The commitment to standards went off the official agenda after 1982 for several reasons. For a start there were serious disagreements internally. Some influential governors considered that the discussions of prisoners' rights and staff accountability at the Wakefield conference constituted a profound challenge to their authority. They received support from some regional directors and the service retreated from its flirtation with the justice model. In any case, the Prisons Board recognized that there was at that time no realistic prospect for large parts of the system of meeting any standards that would not be too humiliatingly low to publish. Moreover, without some dramatic change in the working practices of prison officers, not to mention a sea change in the management of the service, they could scarcely relish the prospect of a public struggle to reach whatever standards they might publish with the Prison Officers' Association using a code of standards as a stick to

[5] Most importantly Sylvia Casale who worked with Ian Dunbar on *A Sense of Direction* and subsequently served on the Code of Standards Steering Group.

beat yet more staff out of them. There was a profound realization that it was first necessary to put better management procedures in place and meanwhile to fend off external pressures until they had made real headway in that process.

However, in part it was also because attention was once again diverted to trouble in the dispersal system. In the summer of 1983, major incidents occurred in Albany and in Wormwood Scrubs, while at the Party Conference in October that year Leon Brittan announced changes to the parole system which dramatically altered the balance between the long-term prisons and the rest of the system. For the first time in the history of the service, a situation was created in which some long-term prisoners felt they really did have little to lose. The Home Secretary, accentuating still more the process of bifurcation in penal policy, 'balanced' the halving of the qualifying period for parole for shorter-sentence prisoners by making it plain that those serving over five years for violence or drug trafficking would not normally get parole at all, and that ministers would set a minimum tariff period to be served for lifers, which for some categories—those convicted of the murder of police or prison officers, sexual or sadistic murders of children, murder by firearms in the course of robbery, or acts of terrorism—the minimum period would be twenty years. As a result of these ill-judged decisions, opposed by officials who were either not consulted or whose advice was ignored, the parole system had eventually to be reconstructed by the Carlisle Committee (1988) and the position of mandatory life sentence prisoners remains a matter of controversy (see Richardson 1993; Lane 1993). More immediately, it was left to the newly established Control Review Committee to consider the practical implications for the dispersal system and to make recommendations.

Meanwhile, with pressure from the Treasury-led Financial Management Initiative reinforcing the critical comment from academics and reform groups, the Prisons Board embarked upon a strategy designed to lift itself up by its own bootstraps. In 1984 the Prisons Board issued a new Circular Instruction (55/84) setting out a *Statement of the Task of the Prison Service* together with a *Statement of the Functions of Prison Department Establishments*. The Director General introduced the new statements at a governors' conference, and his conference address and the circular instructions were reproduced in Train (1985). These new statements, stripped of any inspirational language, listed the four main tasks of the service as a whole and then grouped twenty-two main activities of prisons under six headings: custody of unsentenced prisoners; the court commitment; custody of sentenced prisoners; security, safety and control; services and facilities for prisoners; and community links and preparation for release. None of the statements contained any commitments to standards of performance—although the third task of the service required that prisoners be provided with 'as full a life as is consistent with the facts of custody', the seventeenth function of establishments required them to 'occupy prisoners as fully as possible', and the eighteenth to 'enable prisoners to spend the maximum possible time out of their cells'. Elsewhere there were expectations that security, for example, would be 'appropriate'. Such terminology was familiar from the existing Prison Rules, and always offered the possibility of release from any implied obligation whenever circumstances required it. Nevertheless, it was at least a reasonably clear delineation of activities, and for the first time it was accompanied by a managerial procedure that was intended to ratchet up performance on a prison by prison basis. Instead of an aspirational frame of reference setting out desirable standards of performance, the service had decided to try to identify where each prison currently stood and to set it yearly targets for improvement. These targets were to be set in annual negotiations between prison governors and their regional directors.

There had, in fact, already been some experimental work on the development of accountable prison regimes which had begun in 1981 (Chaplin 1982; Marriage and Selby 1983; Marsden and Evans 1985). This work was to prepare the way for the development of an internal management reporting system—*regime monitoring*—which was to give individual governors a better sense of levels of performance within their establishment, and regional directors and Prisons Board a mechanism for specifying targets, and measuring aggregate performance for the system as a whole (Evans 1987).

Contrary to expectations, the Control Review Committee was able to go a very long way towards defusing the alarming situation which had been created in the long-term prison system by Leon Brittan's changes to the parole scheme. Nothing, of course, could be done about the changing balance between long-term and short-term imprisonment—the numbers serving long-term sentences of four years or more had grown only gradually during the 1970s, whereas they doubled in the 1980s—but the Committee was able to produce a report (Home Office 1984a) that avoided both the appearance and the reality of a crackdown in control terms. Indeed, for the first time it acknowledged clearly and publicly that there was a real distinction between security and control issues, that the dispersal system was a creaking mechanism for carrying the hopes of the service through to the next century, and that steps should be taken immediately to reduce it. This would be possible because the numbers genuinely needing high security amounted to no more than 500 or so prisoners (thus repudiating the earlier Home Office evidence to the May Committee and substantially accepting the figures put forward by King and Morgan). Moreover, they argued ingeniously, it was no longer necessary to choose between dispersal and concentration as such because American 'new generation' prison design seemed to offer ways of keeping more security-risk prisoners in fewer prisons without running the risks to control which had frightened the authorities in the past. They proposed that the perceived problem of troublesome prisoners be dealt with through the development of a range of small units with varying types of regimes, but which were very carefully distanced from the old and ill-fated control units of the 1970s. Perhaps most importantly, Anthony Langdon, who had succeeded David Faulkner as Director of Operational Policy and who had chaired the CRC, argued publicly for the establishment of a joint research and advisory group comprising officials and academic advisors to be involved in the implementation of the small unit strategy.[6]

It was in this climate that the research into *Security, Control, and Humane Containment*, proposals for which had been submitted to ESRC some months before the publication of the CRC report, came into being.

The Research Programme

Security, Control, and Humane Containment

The main aim of this research programme was to get a clearer sense of the extent to which considerations of security and control

---

[6] Three advisors were appointed: Professor Tony Bottoms from the Cambridge Institute of Criminology, Professor John Gunn from the Institute of Psychiatry at the Maudsley Hospital, and Professor Roy King.

had impacted upon the ability of the prison system to provide humane containment for prisoners, and where those concepts traded off against one another in the mid and late 1980s. In an attempt to summarize the position towards which official thinking was tending, the proposals referred to the justification of prisons as follows:

Prisons may protect the public by incarcerating offenders for defined periods of time: if they should no longer expect to be agents of reform, sending out prisoners as better men and women than they came in, then at least efforts should be made to minimize harm, so that, as far as possible, prisoners are not sent out worse. Prisons should offer a range of educational training, industrial and treatment facilities which prisoners who wish to try to rehabilitate, or usefully occupy, themselves may use. (King 1984)

This change in the justification of imprisonment—consistent with a broader shift from a treatment model to a justice-based model of corrections—suggested:

that the effectiveness of prisons should be evaluated rather more by the extent to which they meet certain standards of current performance, and rather less by the measured 'success' or 'failure' of their charges on release. Those standards would include:

   i the security and safety of the prisoners and staff
   ii the physical, social and psychological conditions appropriate to humane containment
   iii the provision of appropriate opportunities for self improvement and preparation for release. (King 1984)

In order to get proper leverage on the impact of security and control upon prison regimes it was essential that a representative group of prisons serving local and training functions at all security levels be included in the study. It was decided initially that the study should be restricted to prisons for men, although the possibility of using spare research capacity to extend the study in a variety of ways, including to prisons for women, was built into the proposals.[7] In view of the controversies surrounding the proper dis-

---

[7] In the event fieldwork progressed with very few hiccups, and we did ask permission to extend the study to Holloway prison, but this was not granted. Instead, the Home Office offered a number of alternative prisons for women, some of which had figured as possibilities in our original proposals. Had it been possible to research Holloway we would have followed that course, because of its centrality to the women's system. However, given the relative marginality of the women's

tribution of resources within the Prison Service, especially as between local and training prisons, it was further decided that all the prisons should be chosen from a single administrative region. It was hoped that in this way it would be possible to regard the region as a microcosm of the whole system and to understand something of its systemic qualities, particularly the inter-relationships between prisons. This decision was reinforced by the Control Review Committee's repeated questioning whether the system contrived to send the right signals to prisoners in terms of rights and privileges as they passed from prison to prison, and the problems this could produce for maintaining order if it did not: as a partial solution the CRC pointed to the need for sentence planning (Home Office 1984a, paras. 22–35).

After some negotiation we agreed that the following research sites, which between them probably offered the best and worst of the prison system, provided as representative a group of establishments as it would be possible to get.

HM Prison, Birmingham, usually known as Winson Green, was a typical large Victorian local prison, built in 1845 as a city gaol, whose 570 places of certified normal accommodation were populated on average in 1985–6 by 1,023 prisoners, making it the second most overcrowded prison in the country after Leeds (Home Office 1986, Appendix 4). It had been in the forefront of public attention on a number of occasions: in July 1976 when fourteen prison officers were found not guilty of beating up the Birmingham Six (*The Times*, 16 July 1976); and, perhaps even more controversially, in March 1982 when three prison officers were found not guilty of the murder of Barry Prosser in Winson Green prison hospital on 19 August 1980 (Coggan and Walker 1982; Sim 1990). The Prosser family continued to maintain a weekend vigil outside the prison during the currency of our research. It had also been the site of seminal research (Sparks 1971) which first drew attention to the parlous plight of the local prison.

HM Prison, Gartree, a category B dispersal prison, had achieved a reputation no less notorious than Birmingham's. It was opened in 1966, a purpose-built low security category C prison in the style of Blundeston, one of eight such prisons to come on stream in the wake of the White Paper, *Penal Practice in a Changing Society*

prisons offered we decided that it would be better use of research time if we returned to our original research sites to explore the impact of Fresh Start.

(Home Office 1959). Like its sister prison, Albany, Gartree under-
went massive strengthening and upgrading to its security before it
was added to the growing dispersal system in 1969. Nobody had
yet escaped from Gartree—or any of the other dispersal prisons—
but on several occasions there had been major losses of control.
The most dramatic incidents were in 1972 when eighteen officers
and five prisoners were injured following an escape attempt, and in
1978 when serious damage was done to the fabric in a riot during
which eight officers were trapped for a time on A wing before their
release was negotiated. Following this incident two wings were
taken out of commission. Prison officers, who were described by
Canter and Ambrose (1980) as having developed a 'siege perspective', refused to reopen the wings until additional safety exits were
provided, and the prison operated at half capacity for several
years. For a time, officials considered taking Gartree out of the dispersal system, especially as the closed-circuit television and other
security systems needed renewal, but in the end new access towers
were built and the security systems were renewed. Though surely
the most serious, the 1978 riot was by no means the last incident
in Gartree's chequered history. In a protracted protest one prisoner
gained access to the roof on 24 November 1983 and did not come
down until 21 February 1984. In 1985–6 Gartree had a CNA of 315
and an average daily population of 307.

   HM Prison, Nottingham, had originally been built as a city gaol
in 1890 but had undergone substantial reconstruction in 1912.
There had been few changes since then, apart from the recent
installation of improved washing and toilet recesses. It was now in
use as a category B non-dispersal training prison. Although
Nottingham was not built in the radial style of many Victorian
prisons, it nonetheless shared many of their architectural characteristics, including galleries of cells on four levels. It had just two
wings, but because its cells were larger and because it was the only
category B non-dispersal prison in the region, it was one of the few
training prisons to be regularly overcrowded. In 1985–6 it had a
CNA of 215 and an average daily population of 297. It had the
reputation of being a friendly, and somewhat laxly supervised,
prison and, although staff told us that it had once been the 'happi-
est prison in the system', they were always careful to use the past
tense.

   HM Prison, Featherstone, was the pride and joy of the midland regional director who had once been its governor. Opened in November 1976 as an industrial prison with vast workshops, it had been designed as a category C training prison and was still operating in that capacity. It enjoyed a good reputation and had been the subject of in-house research on accountable regimes by Marsden and Evans (1985). In 1985–6 it had a CNA of 510 and an average daily population of 542. This overcrowding was largely confined to dormitory accommodation in a short term unit (STU) for category D prisoners who worked outside the prison. (For most purposes we have excluded the STU prisoners from our analyses, because although their inclusion was inclined to distort the Featherstone results they did not seem a sufficiently significant group to warrant reporting separately.)

HM Prison, Ashwell, had been an army camp which was brought into use as an open prison in 1955. As such it operated as a training prison for category D prisoners who were still housed, for the most part, in the same poor quality hutted accommodation which had been first used in the Great War. During the 1960s it had provided the setting for what then seemed an adventurous experiment of giving recidivists access to open conditions. In 1985–6 it had a CNA of 300 in dormitories and an ADP of 367— the only open prison in the country at that time in excess of CNA.

From the outset the study was conceived as one which would lay down some bench-marks so that, at least in a limited way, the Prison Service could be given a clear statement of where it stood in relation to the delivery of certain crucial aspects of what were defined in Circular Instruction 55/84 as its tasks and functions. Our objective was to establish baseline descriptions and, where possible, measurements of those tasks and functions which fell reasonably within our remit. For convenience, the Statement of Tasks and Functions is reproduced in Appendix I.[8] At much the same time as the Statement of Tasks and Functions was issued, the Service began to give attention to the provision of management information systems that would be useful in monitoring performance. Indeed, what became known as regime monitoring sheets were first piloted in the midland region, and rather than risk duplication we decided that it would be better to leave the service itself

[8] The statement of tasks and functions was in fact an elaboration upon a little-known statement which had been developed by the former controller of operations, Alan Bainton, many years earlier.

to develop quantitative measures of the extent of provision in different establishments. We would concentrate our research efforts on the more qualitative aspects of performance evaluation—how what was provided was seen by staff and prisoners. However, we did collect sample regime monitoring sheets during our research and we have been supplied with more recent regime monitoring data for our prisons which have enabled us to make some assessment of the changes which have taken place since our research was completed.

After an extended period of pilot work in Stafford prison—a category C training prison, then considered to be something of a dumping ground for 'nuisance' prisoners in the midland region— the research team spent at least three months in each prison observing virtually all aspects of the functioning of the establishment. The researchers were present at weekends as well as weekdays, and in the evenings and sometimes through the night, as well as during the day. The aim was to become a sufficiently familiar part of the furniture over a sufficiently long period of time for neither staff nor prisoners to feel the need to 'perform' for our benefit. In a 'macho world' we were determined to show that we could 'hack it', to demonstrate that we were willing to work whatever hours it took to get to the bottom of whatever it was we needed to find out, and that we were not prepared to be 'snowed'. Access was permitted to all areas of the prison, though this was in part conditioned by considerations of gender.[9] Virtually all documentary sources of information were made available to the researchers, except for some concerning vital security considerations. In every prison it was possible to attend all important meetings, including that of the Boards of Visitors. All told, literally thousands of hours of observation and conversations were logged, and summarized in field notes. More formally, over 300 prisoners and staff were interviewed, often on tape, and 1,220 prisoners and 226 members of the uniformed staff returned valid and at least partly completed questionnaires, which were only distributed at the very end of the fieldwork in each prison when both the researchers personally, and the

---

[9] The initial fieldwork in Ashwell and Featherstone was carried out by Kathy McDermott and Loraine Gelsthorpe, with some assistance from Ian Rowe. The work in Birmingham, after loraine Gelsthorpe had left the project, was done largely by Kathleen McDermott, while that in Gartree and Nottingham was shared jointly by the present authors. The final phase of fieldwork, to assess the impact of Fresh Start, was carried out by Roy King.

aims of the research, were well known.[10] Several publications which derive essentially from the observational and interview data have already appeared (King and McDermott 1990a; McDermott 1990: McDermott and King 1988) and a full list of the publications arising from these research studies is given at Appendix II. Much of the material presented in this book, however, comes from our prisoner self-completion questionnaires to which only fleeting reference has been made in previous publications. It provides a substantial basis on some matters for comparison with data from the national prison survey (Walmsley *et al.* 1992). It will be helpful, at this point, if we give some basic descriptive detail about our prisoner respondents.

Tables 1.1 to 1.5 set out criminological and social data about our prisoner respondents in each prison. Although the questionnaires were anonymous, and we took great care both to distribute and collect them personally, after which they were immediately removed from the prisons, a number of prisoners chose not to complete the more personal aspects of the questionnaire apparently because they could not rule out the possibilities that the documents would fall into staff hands or be seen by other prisoners and that they would be identified. Since a great may prisoners wrote frankly about their experiences in all the borders and blank spaces of the form once they had completed the precoded questions, we understood their anxieties. The missing cases in these tables are thus typically more numerous than on the more substantive areas of our inquiry.

Table 1.1 demonstrates, not surprisingly, that a high proportion of our sample in Gartree were in custody for offences of murder and robbery, whereas in Ashwell persons convicted of burglary, theft, handling of stolen property, and fraud predominated. Elsewhere prisoners were more evenly distributed across the offence categories.

In Table 1.2 it can be seen, again not surprisingly, that with each increment in the security level of the prison the proportion of our sample with longer sentences rises.

The prisoners in Gartree were noticeably older than those elsewhere, as can be seen from Table 1.3. In Ashwell and Birmingham

---

[10] In the training prisons we attempted to survey all prisoners in custody on the day in question. In Birmingham we distributed forms to every second cell. For staff, we targeted those on duty in the prison on the designated day.

Table 1.1. Main current offence: percentage distribution

	Birmingham Conv. (n = 179)	Gartree (n = 144)	Nottingham (n = 151)	Featherstone (n = 236)	Ashwell (n = 157)	Total (n = 867)
Robbery	11.2	26.4	10.6	25.4	2.5	15.9
Burglary	20.7	0.7	11.9	16.1	28.7	16.0
Theft, handling, fraud	21.2	0.0	18.5	9.3	31.8	15.9
Drugs	8.4	10.4	8.6	16.1	5.1	10.3
Sex	3.9	4.2	2.0	7.2	0.6	3.9
Murder	1.7	43.8	15.9	7.6	4.5	13.3
Other Violence	16.2	2.8	14.6	10.6	4.5	10.0
Other Offences	16.8	11.8	17.9	7.6	22.3	14.6
	100.0	100.0	100.0	100.0	100.0	100.0

Note: Columns do not always add up to 100 because of rounding.

Table 1.2. Length of sentence: Percentage distribution

	Birmingham Conv. (n = 188)	Gartree (n = 154)	Nottingham (n = 155)	Featherstone (n = 259)	Ashwell (n = 155)	Total (n = 911)
6 months or less	11.7	0.0	0.0	0.4	18.1	5.6
7–18 months	21.8	0.0	0.0	1.9	32.9	10.6
19–36 months	33.0	0.0	13.5	23.9	34.2	21.7
3–4 years	11.2	0.6	20.0	23.6	5.8	13.5
4–7 years	13.8	16.2	41.9	34.4	3.9	23.2
Over 7 years	6.9	37.7	5.8	7.3	0.6	11.0
Life	1.6	45.5	18.7	8.5	4.5	14.4
	100.0	100.0	100.0	100.0	100.0	100.0

Note: Columns do not always add up to 100 because of rounding.

Table 1.3. Age: Percentage distribution

	Birmingham Rem. (n = 208)	Birmingham Conv. (n = 200)	Gartree (n = 155)	Nottingham (n = 154)	Featherstone (n = 248)	Ashwell (n = 169)	Total (n = 1134)
18–25	40.4	39.0	18.1	29.9	20.6	36.1	30.7
26–29	21.6	17.0	17.4	22.1	23.8	18.3	20.3
30–35	19.2	18.5	27.7	19.5	19.4	17.2	20.0
36–45	15.9	18.5	25.8	22.7	25.8	18.3	21.2
46–55	2.9	5.5	8.4	5.2	7.3	6.5	5.9
56+	0.0	1.5	2.6	0.6	3.2	3.6	1.9
	100.0	100.0	100.0	100.0	100.0	100.0	100.0

Note: Columns do not always add up to 100 because of rounding.

Table 1.4. Ethnic origin: Percentage distribution

	Birmingham Rem. (n = 208)	Birmingham Conv. (n = 198)	Gartree (n = 156)	Nottingham (n = 152)	Featherstone (n = 253)	Ashwell (n = 166)	Total (n = 1133)
Afro-Caribbean	7.2	4.0	5.7	2.0	4.8	1.8	4.4
Asian	4.8	5.1	10.3	2.0	10.3	3.6	6.3
Black British	9.1	6.6	10.9	6.6	5.5	2.4	6.8
White British	69.7	75.8	64.7	82.2	73.9	88.0	75.4
Other	9.1	8.5	8.4	7.3	5.6	4.2	7.1
	100.0	100.0	100.0	100.0	100.0	100.0	100.0

Note: Columns do not always add up to 100 because of rounding.

by way of contrast, well over a third of the prisoners were 25 years of age or younger.

In terms of ethnic origin, our sample in Gartree had higher proportions of Afro/Caribbean, Asian, and Black British prisoners than anywhere else except Featherstone, which had a similar proportion of Asian prisoners. The details are given in Table 1.4.

Ashwell had the highest proportion of prisoners who were married or in other stable relationships. Gartree and Nottingham had remarkably similar profiles on this variable, as shown in Table 1.5.

Just over two fifths (41.4 per cent) of our total sample claimed that they had been employed at the time of their arrest. Whether employed or not 72.7 per cent described their normal work as manual. Just over one in ten (10.7 per cent) described their normal employment as crime, and in Gartree such prisoners accounted for 16 per cent of the sample. More than two thirds (68.7 per cent) had left school without any formal qualifications—one of the very few variables on which there was no statistically significant difference between our prisons.

Other Studies

The proposals for the above research in the ESRC initiative on crime and criminal justice were slightly modified to take account of the Report of the Control Review Committee, so that a direct comparison between the balance of security, control, and humane containment that had been struck in Gartree could be made with what was achieved in the new generation prison at Oak Park Heights in Minnesota. This had been the subject of earlier research, supported by the then Social Science Research Council to one of us (RDK), which had been carried out in 1984.[11] Care was accordingly taken to include questions in Gartree that would permit a replication of the Oak Park Heights study (see King 1987, 1991a). It was hoped in this way to offer some assessment of the relative merits of the new generation solution which had been favoured by the Control Review Committee, and the dispersal strategy in dealing with the problems posed by high security risk prisoners—even though the systems operated in different cultures.

[11] The research was conducted under research grant E00 23 2030. Support for a study of maximum security custody in the US was sought when it became clear that 'the time was not right' for undertaking research into the dispersal system in England and Wales.

Table 1.5. Marital status: Percentage distribution

	Birmingham Rem. (n = 210)	Birmingham Conv. (n = 199)	Gartree (n = 157)	Nottingham (n = 152)	Featherstone (n = 253)	Ashwell (n = 165)	Total (n = 1136)
Married	49.0	50.8	32.5	33.6	44.3	55.8	44.9
Single	31.9	29.6	38.2	39.5	30.0	30.9	32.8
Separated Widowed Divorced	19.0	19.6	29.3	27.0	25.7	13.3	22.3
	100.0	100.0	100.0	100.0	100.0	100.0	100.0

Note: Columns do not always add up to 100 because of rounding.

One spin-off from this research design was that it would also permit a direct comparison of regime developments in England and Wales over a period of between fifteen and eighteen years. From 1968 to 1972 one of us (RDK) had directed a study funded by the then Home Office Research Unit into prison regimes—the *Prison Regimes Project*. That study had similarly looked at five representative prisons for adult males, albeit not all from the same region. These were Winchester local prison, Albany dispersal prison and Coldingley (category B), Camp Hill (category C) and Ford (category D) training prisons. Although the earlier research was originally designed to explore the potential effectiveness of treatment and training regimes, there was inevitably some overlap in the kinds of data collected, and in the event it became possible to demonstrate the extraordinary extent to which prison regimes had deteriorated over the period which had elapsed between the two studies (King and McDermott 1989). As we now show in this volume, in important respects they have not yet recovered.

As it turned out, the potential significance of any bench-marks we might be able to establish was to be put to the test almost immediately. Fresh Start—the major programme of reorganization to shift systems and working arrangements for prison staff, designed to end the dependence of the Prison Service on overtime working by prison officers and to eliminate some of their restrictive practices—was implemented just as we finished the main programme of fieldwork. We discuss the implications of Fresh Start more fully in the next section. Suffice it to say here that we were able to return to each of our prisons after Fresh Start had been introduced in an attempt to gauge some of its initial impact. So far as we are aware, our reports on the effect of Fresh Start on regimes (McDermott and King 1989) and on prison management (King and McDermott 1991) remain the only independent accounts of those matters.

In the course of the study on security, control, and humane containment we became impressed by the importance attached by prisoners to family contacts, and by the problems experienced by families as a result of their custody. Accordingly we submitted proposals to the ESRC for a study on the problems of *Coping with Custody* and with the support of the Council we embarked upon a study of the *Survival Strategies of Prisoners and their Families*.[12]

[12] This study was funded under ESRC Research Grant No R000231401 with the present authors as joint principal investigators. Kathleen McDermott's return to the

A group of some twenty-six long-term prisoners from the first ESRC study agreed to participate in the families study and gave us permission to approach their partners. To this original group we added a further fourteen prisoners (ten of whom were shorter term) and their families on a 'snowball sampling' basis, bringing the total sample to forty families. Over the next two and a half years, from 1989 to 1991, we maintained contact with members of this group, both inside and outside the prisons, in an attempt to understand the nature of their problems and the way they came to terms with them. By this time in the research, we decided to eschew the privileged access normally accorded to researchers in favour of making visits to prisoners in the same way as do families—through the issue of visiting orders, waiting in line with other visitors, and making our way under escort to the visits area.[13] We had originally hoped to develop a separate and larger sample of prisoners and their families whose experience was of short-term custody, whether on remand or sentence. In the event, the logistics of making contact and arranging visits in the immediate aftermath of a court appearance proved to be insurmountable. Although such a sample could have been organized using the official agents of the court, we decided that such a formal intrusion would have been unwarrantable and would have unduly associated with those agencies what we wanted to be seen as independent research. Some additional understanding of the problems associated with maintaining relationships in short sentences of imprisonment, however, was gained from talking to others on visits and in a programme of fieldwork with the Information and Advice Centre run by the Bourne Trust at Wormwood Scrubs. In the course of the research, contact was also established and maintained with all the major voluntary organizations working with and on behalf of prisoners' families at that time. A preliminary account of this study was reported in McDermott and King (1992) and in Chapter 6 we use additional data from that research to provide a picture of the

US in Sept. 1990, some six months before the scheduled end of a two-year study, led to a number of modifications to the original research design and a renegotiation of the period of the research. Fieldwork prior to Sept. 1990 was carried out by Dr McDermott and subsequent fieldwork by Roy King.

[13] In some cases this meant that a prisoner and his family agreed to forgo a family visit. In such cases it was usual for there to be some reciprocity, whereby we provided transport or child care or some other service on another occasion.

maintenance of family links and preparations for release from both sides of the prison wall.

Changes Since the Research Began

With regard to some of the changes which have taken place since our research began, sufficient time has elapsed for us to comment on them with reasonable confidence. For the most recent changes, however, we do little more than note some signposts here although we reflect on their implications more fully in our concluding chapter.

Fresh Start and the Reorganization of the Prison Service

One of the most important changes to the Prison Service to which reference has already been made above took place during the course of the research. On 13 May 1986, the then Home Secretary, Douglas Hurd, announced the publication of the report of the joint study by the Prison Department and PA Management Consultants. on the complementing and shift systems worked by prison officers (Prison Service 1986). He claimed that the report presented 'a telling indictment of . . . [existing] . . . working practices' and made 'recommendations for new systems which would release large amounts of now unproductive capacity which ought to be used for other purposes'. Thus was ushered in the package of reforms known as Fresh Start, for which a target introduction date was set at April 1987.

The attempt to forge a common working agreement between the Prison Service and the Prison Officers' Association, following the Report of the May Committee, had ended in bitter failure. In spite of Trevelyan's call to the Prisons Board in June 1982 to face up to the realities, neither the Board nor ministers could summon the political will to take on the POA. By 1986 their successors steeled themselves for a confrontation that would enable them to put their house in order. It fell to Eric Caines, the Director of Personnel and Finance, to devise, and then drive through, a package that would buy out prison officers' overtime working and what had come to be called their restrictive 'Spanish' practices, whereby staff could be allocated to supervise areas where there were no prisoners to be supervised, and whereby tasks were dropped from the essential task list for the alleged want of staff to carry them out in safety (see Morgan 1983).

The amount of spare capacity identified by the joint study was estimated to be of the order of 15–20 per cent, and this was to be translated into a combination of:

—enhanced regimes for prisoners;
—reduced hours of work and less overtime for staff;
—reduced manning levels;
—reduced forward recruitment;
—reduced costs to the taxpayer.

Other benefits could include:

—greater job satisfaction for prison staff;
—improved management control and accountability;
—better working practices and more efficient manpower utilization;
—improved industrial relations in the prison service.

(Home Office Press Release, 13 May 1986)

There can be little doubt that Fresh Start, or something like it, was long overdue. At the time of the May Committee prison officers could be required to work ten hours of overtime a week and the average was twelve hours, although in local prisons where lucrative escort duties were also required, some officers contrived to work thirty hours of overtime a week. By the time of Fresh Start, average overtime had grown to sixteen hours a week.

Nonetheless, the negotiations to introduce it were fraught with difficulties and recriminations, and in the end, in spite of an overwhelming vote in favour by the prison officers, it neither satisfied them nor fully met the aspirations of their managers for better control or improved regimes. Given the obvious importance of Fresh Start, we decided to take advantage of the contingency period built into the research design (in case there had been problems in gaining access to our prisons), to return to our five research sites for a period of a week some three to six months after they had been 'fresh started'.

We asked staff whether they thought regimes had improved as a result of Fresh Start: the response was overwhelming, with the great majority of respondents in each prison claiming that regimes had worsened. Only a handful of staff reported any improvements. When we compared regimes on more objective data we found that, although there had been some gains in some areas—improvements in physical education in Featherstone and Ashwell and evening education classes in Nottingham and Featherstone, for example—

these were offset by losses in others; in hours unlocked and hours at work in Nottingham, and in the numbers of prisoners in employment everywhere except Featherstone. In so far as there was a pattern it was that the prisons with the better regimes to start with—especially Featherstone—enjoyed most improvements, whilst some with worse regimes—Gartree and Nottingham—suffered further deterioration. Birmingham, which had little scope for getting worse, just about held its own after Fresh Start. The importance of these results, though far from conclusive, should not be lost. Fresh Start was seen as something of a watershed. Its introduction coincided with the bedding down of the new system of regime monitoring which was to form the new official basis of measuring what the service was achieving. It should be remembered, therefore, that any improvements post-Fresh Start may be measured from an artificially low baseline because, on balance, it looks as though in many regime areas the situation was immediately made worse by the introduction of Fresh Start (see McDermott and King 1989 for a fuller account).

The Fresh Start package on which prison officers were balloted was an inordinately complex one. It was set out in a twenty-eight-page document known as Bulletin 8 (Prison Service 1987b), which at the risk of over-simplification addressed three themes: (i) new working arrangements and management structures; (ii) the unification of the previously separate governor grades and uniformed officers into a single continuous structure; and (iii) the introduction of new pay scales and conditions of service. For uniformed staff this last involved the ending of hourly pay and overtime working in favour of monthly salaries 'conditioned', in the curious parlance of the service, to a thirty-nine-hour week. As the hours were reduced from the current forty-eight-hour week over a five-year period, staff were to suffer no loss of pay but were expected to maintain existing workloads with increases in staff limited to the equivalent of half the hours lost each year. The other half constituted the 'efficiency gain', of which part would finance improvements to the service and part be returned to the Exchequer.

The new working arrangements and management structure were essentially predicated upon the notion of 'group working' in a system that was intended to make 'everyone accountable to someone'. At the top the governor was designated the 'overall manager' and 'operational commander in emergencies'. Effectively this meant a withdrawal from old style 'management by walkabout' and the delegation of most executive duties to a management team that covered six functional areas of activity—operations (including security), residential, inmate activities, medical services, management support services, and works.[14] Prison officers were assigned to duty rosters by group managers and no longer by the central detail office, and it was for group managers to make sure that their group would secure predictable hours of duty, proper periods of staff training, planned holidays, and so on. When we asked about how these new arrangements were working, we generally found that lines of management responsibility had become clearer as a result of Fresh Start, with a better sense of vertical accountability. However, it seemed as though this had been won somewhat at the expense of lateral integration, as staff identified more narrowly with the interests of their groups and less with the needs of the institutions as a whole.

There were, however, three important ways in which Fresh Start failed. Certainly the most astonishing failure, and perhaps immediately the most important, was that Fresh Start was introduced without the proper staff complements for each prison first having been agreed. With no agreed baselines, the meaning of Bulletin 8 has been endlessly disputed since, and the most basic source of disagreement between the POA and the Prison Department—manning levels—has remained unresolved. At a more symbolic level, the original intention to unite the service by having prison governors in uniform was never carried through. In spite of the overwhelming support of prison governors for the change, the matter was seen as something for the Home Office as a whole to decide and not for the Prison Department alone. Although the Prisons Board accepted the proposal, the view taken at Deputy and Permanent Secretary level was that putting governors in uniform would have unwelcome militaristic overtones, and though it might unify governors and officers it might exacerbate divisions between them and other staff. In the end the Home Secretary was advised not to proceed with the change. But perhaps the greatest missed opportunity was

[14] A seventh functional area was also identified in Bulletin 8, namely inmate services. These were intended to include centrally organized services, such as kit change, canteen, and so on. In practice none of our prisons developed this specialism and instead redistributed those matters either to residential or inmate activities, which already included workshops and education.

that Fresh Start was implemented without any serious analysis of the professional content of prison officers' work. It remains one of the mysteries of the Prison Service that, during its period of incorporation into the Home Office, it has seemed unable to discuss the professional task of prison officers in anything approaching the way those issues were addressed by the former Prison Commissioners in the days of Paterson or Fox. The retreat from the justice model after the Wakefield conference had similarly reflected this crippling incapacity. The idea of a professional approach to the treatment of prisoners was simply overshadowed by concerns with security, control, and tactical management of the system.

Be that as it may, the staff who completed our Fresh Start questionnaires were nearly unanimous that, whilst they greatly enjoyed the improved pay and conditions, they had lost interest and satisfaction in the job. Instead of a new breed of professional officers, a new spectre began to haunt the service: whereas once there were said to be 'overtime bandits' who sought to maximize their take-home pay by manipulating the staff detail to work an eighty-hour week, it was now reported that 'the new fiddle is to see how much time you can get off'. Under the new system it was possible to contrive six consecutive rest days a fortnight, although the result of this was that staff lost touch with what was happening in the prison (King and McDermott 1991). Moreover, sickness rates began to rocket, and governors now found it necessary to make housecalls to check whether absent staff were genuinely ill.

On 10 August 1989 the joint Prison Service and PA Management Consultants review team published a further report which concluded that the major changes which CI 55/84 and Fresh Start had introduced now needed to be matched by a radical overhaul of top management (Prison Service 1989). It recommended that the old regional structure which left regional directors with too wide a span of control and which duplicated many headquarters functions in confusing ways, should be abolished and a new and more effective line of command established between prison governors and the Prisons Board.

The conventional, but awkward, distinction between policy divisions headed by civil servants and operational matters which were overseen by a former field man who occupied the office of deputy director general was to be abandoned. Instead, three new directorates were proposed which would combine operational and policy responsibilities. The *directorate of custody* would be responsible for security, tactical management, contingency planning, and the future needs of the prison estate: the *directorate of inmate administration* would deal with inmates' rights and conditions, release arrangements, and parole;[15] and the *directorate of inmate programmes* with regime development and sentence planning. Three other directorates would cover *prison medical services, building,* and *personnel and finance,* and the heads of all six directorates, together with two non-executive members, would comprise a slimmed-down Prisons Board under the chairmanship of the Director General. The role of deputy director general would be abolished (Prison Service 1989).

In place of the regional structure the system was to be divided into fourteen geographical areas, with *area managers,* each responsible for some nine or ten establishments. There was to be no pretence that these establishments constituted functional sub-systems of the whole: they were merely convenient groupings providing a manageable span of control. The new area managers, some of whom would be ex-governors and some administrative civil servants, would be accountable to one or another of the three new operational directors. In the words of the Director General this would provide 'a direct link' between the Prisons Board and establishments (Prison Service 1990), although it would appear this was less of a direct link than when governors were responsible to regional directors who had a seat on the Prisons Board. Each operational director would have a senior management team comprising his or her area managers and the heads of policy divisions.

The review team recommended that the whole headquarters organization, from the Director General downwards, be moved out of London to a new location in the midlands. It was argued that this would bring the organization under one roof, provide better access to and from establishments, and reduce costs. It was further proposed that there should be a wide-ranging debate whether or not the service should become an agency under the government's 'Next Steps' initiative. The Home Secretary announced his general approval for these organizational changes in January 1990 and, apart from the move to the new location, they were implemented

---

[15] The *Briefing* document which described these new arrangements (Prison Service 1989) is intriguing because it explicitly enshrines the notion of prisoner rights within the organizational structure of the service.

on 25 September 1990 (Prison Service 1990). In the interval the number of geographical areas had been increased from fourteen to fifteen, and in the event all of the first appointees to area manager posts had previous experience as governors of establishments. There was some surprise at the timing of the decision to implement the changes because, by then, the Woolf Inquiry into the disturbances at Strangeways and elsewhere was fully into its public phase. At the seminars organized by Woolf, many participants felt that the decision effectively pre-empted anything he might have to say on those matters. No doubt it did—but it also has to be said that the decision in principle had been taken some months before the events at Strangeways, and by September a great deal of planning and preparation had been done. At the time of implementation no decision had yet been taken on the site for the re-located headquarters, and the Director General found it necessary to reassure staff that the move was not in doubt. Precisely one year later, though, on 25 September 1991, the Home Secretary announced that the move to the midlands—a site in Derby having by then been agreed—was cancelled as part of the drive to limit public expenditure! For some observers and participants the planned move was one of the more misguided aberrations to come out of the service's apparent obsession with unity. They believed that relocation would distract the Prison Service from more important tasks for several years, would tear the rest of the Home Civil Service apart, and would create an inward-looking enclave of prison managers just at a time when it would benefit most from external influences.

The main effect of these organizational changes from the point of view of our research, of course, was to render nugatory any analysis we intended to make of the systemic qualities of the Prison Service at regional level. Although we spent many weeks carrying out fieldwork at Calthorpe House, trying to understand the regional structure and its use of resources, there has seemed little point in presenting any serious analysis of those materials. Suffice it to say here that we would have advised strongly against the continuance of the regional system, which had so unfortunately been endorsed by May J in 1979, in favour of better tactical management nationally with regard to the use of resources and the functions of establishments; and for more devolution of responsibility to local levels for day-to-day matters. We are not sure that we would have recommended the system that was adopted—but it had

similar objectives to those we would have proposed, and like Lord
Woolf we took the view that it should be given a chance to show
how ell it works. It has, of course, since undergone further change
and we return to consider the new pattern of organization in due
course.

Strangeways, the Woolf Report, and Custody, Care and Justice

When the news broke of the serious disturbance at Strangeways on
the morning of 2 April 1990 it was profoundly ironic that the
British criminological establishment was on its way to York to take
part in a conference on the special units for difficult prisoners
which had been introduced by the Control Review Committee.
Throughout the 1970s and the first half of the 1980s, serious riots
and disturbances had been confined to the dispersal prisons, and
official discourse on these matters had insisted on attributing the
causes to a small group of troublemakers and ringleaders rather
than seeking any kind of sociological understanding of the circumstances in which riots and disturbances take place. Even the
Control Review Committee had been unable to free itself from
such strait-jacketed thinking entirely, although as noted earlier,
given the circumstances in which it was born, it was remarkable
that it was able to shift the political mood as much as it did.
Nevertheless, the special unit strategy depended upon the doubtful
capacity of the service to identify the trouble-makers who needed
such units (King and McDermott 1990a).

Since then there had been a spilling over of such troubles into
lower security training prisons (Home Office 1987a), but it had
seemed that prisoners in local prisons and remand centres who
spent virtually all of their time locked up had little or no opportunity for concerted action. It is true that the disturbances of
29 April–2 May 1986 involved both Bristol local prison and Lewes,
part of which had a local function. But there is a sense in which
those disturbances took place in very special circumstances: they
cannot be disentangled from the widespread industrial action by
the POA at the height of the propaganda war between the Prison
Department and the unions on the eve of the announcement of
Fresh Start. Indeed, the Report by the Chief Inspector on those disturbances (Home Office 1987a) dwells at length on the industrial
relations problems, and the fact that he noted that none of the dis-

persal prisons was involved and that most of the old and overcrowded locals remained trouble-free perhaps emphasizes this
point. Be that as it may, events in Risley Remand Centre (Dunbar
1989) the previous year had begun to show that keeping prisoners
locked up provided no guarantees against disorder, and now
Strangeways had shown that no establishment was immune. Whilst
the world's media were focused on Manchester the York conference nevertheless proceeded to address yesterday's problem
(Bottomley and Hay 1991).

There were further ironies that the first local prison to blow
should have been Strangeways. Just six months before the riot, on
28 September 1989, the governor of Strangeways, Brendan O'Friel,
had shared the platform with us at the annual Perrie Lectures. We
gave a general review of many of our findings, including the rather
depressing results from our research prisons in the wake of Fresh
Start (King and McDermott 1990b). Brendan O'Friel, by contrast,
gave a very upbeat account of the positive opportunities that Fresh
Start gave, especially for the impoverished regimes of local prisons.
He indicated that the staffing problems we had described had
either not arisen, or been overcome, in Manchester and went on to
talk of the regime improvements that he had been able to introduce. Powerful support for O'Friel's position, moreover, came just
two days before the riot began in the Chief Inspector's favourable
report of an inspection at Strangeways which had actually been
carried out just before the Perrie Lectures. The Chief Inspector
found 'Life at Manchester is a great deal nearer what it should be
. . . than it was some two years ago . . . The imaginative education
programme and the increased use of workshops are examples of
the improvements for inmates. But there is a long way to go'
(Home Office 1990a, preface). There was some ribald comment in
the popular press, both at the unfortunate timing of the Chief
Inspector's Report and at the words of praise he gave without a
hint, apparently, of what was to come, but there is no necessary
inconsistency between regime improvements and riots. Far from it.
Although prison disturbances may more often be associated with
the closing down of opportunities (see Thomas and Pooley 1980;
King and Elliott 1978; and the review by Ditchfield (1990), originally undertaken for the Control Review Committee), most sociol-
ogists would probably expect that a situation in which prisoners
emerge from something approaching lock down, which for so long

had been allowed to characterize our local prisons, would be fraught with danger. Prisoners will not simply welcome such changes as so much largesse, but will have important questions to ask about them as well: if it can be done now, why could it not have been done earlier? If we can have this small amount of work and education, why can we not have more? In short, it raises expectations, and those expectations are considered against just such a context of fairness or justice that was to form the centre-piece of Woolf LJ's programme for reform. There was indeed implicit recognition of this in Judge Tumim's report of the inspection, not just in his statement that there is a long way to go, but also in his observation that the increased hours in the workshops really presented 'an opportunity for association rather than for useful work'. The unspoken message there is that the opening up, however modestly, of the local prison regime provides the same opportunities for concerted action as prevailed in the training prisons *if it is not constructively used*.

Although not everyone greeted Woolf LJ's report on Strangeways (Home Office 1991a) with equal enthusiasm (see, for example, Sim 1994 for an alternative view), it commanded a quite remarkable degree of consensus amongst officials, academics, and penal reform groups, a consensus which had been utterly lacking in its predecessor, the May Report (Home Office 1979a). There are two important reasons why that should have been so. First, there was a consensus, as it were, ready and waiting to be found. The ideas that King and Morgan (1979) had hastily put together in six weeks as their evidence to the May Committee, and which, though carefully considered, were largely dismissed had nevertheless been influential elsewhere. It would be outrageously self-serving to suggest that these were simply ideas whose time had come, but perhaps not too much to suggest that they had stimulated a sufficient level of debate and criticism from all quarters such that they had to be reckoned with. Academics (Bottoms 1990), high ranking prison officials (Dunbar 1985), and leaders of reform groups (Stern 1987) had all chewed over the concept of humane containment and found it wanting—but none dissented from the need for measurable standards of regime delivery, the need to balance out the emphasis on security and control, the need to reduce the gap between prisons and the community, or the need to reconsider the distribution of resources within the prison system so that all prisoners got a fairer deal. Indeed, what debate and criticism had produced was a wealth of important refinements. While it would be idle to suggest that the more than 170 written submissions to the Woolf Inquiry (well over twice as many as there had been to the May Inquiry) were merely variations on a theme, most addressed more than one of these issues.

The second reason is that Woolf single-mindedly went out of his way to capture the consensus, and, where it was not yet fully formed, to lead the interested parties towards it. He began by calling upon expert advice—in the form of two assessors (Gordon Lakes and Rod Morgan) who were extremely knowledgeable about the system, albeit from different viewpoints, and another (Mary Tuck) whose professional task daily involved making judgements on the basis of research evidence—and to these he added the experienced Chief Inspector (Stephen Tumim). By choosing a path that eschewed the role of omnipotent arbiter, and yet also avoided his becoming the creature of the great and the good, Woolf gained immediate and substantial credibility amongst most of the *cognoscenti*—and put the old guard in the Home Office on notice. Indeed by this time it might actually have been difficult to identify the old guard. Home Office administrators in Queen Anne's Gate, as distinct from Prison Service officials in their new headquarters at Cleland House, were probably merely sceptical about the prospects for change rather than resistant to it. However, the same conservative elements within the Prison Service which had forced the retreat from the justice model were still represented upon the Prisons Board and it was important that opportunities be created for internal debates to be aired in public and not left to be decided by the usual secretive manœuvres. Woolf's strategy involved insisting on public hearings and a series of public seminars, at which officials were said to speak in their personal capacities rather than on behalf of the service or of ministers (Morgan 1991). In the event officials were probably more cautious than they need have been. Nevertheless, Woolf contrived a dialogue about prisons that had not hitherto been seen in British public life. It was, by any standards, a *tour de force*. As Vivien Stern (1993) expressed it, Woolf's Inquiry 'became, in all but name, the much needed and long overdue Royal Commission into prisons in England and Wales'.

Woolf's recommendations are well-known and hardly need a

detailed recapitulation here: closer integration of the Prison Service with the rest of the criminal justice system; more visible and more directly accountable leadership from the Director General; increased responsibility for governors; an enhanced role for prison officers; a contract or compact for prisoners setting out their legitimate expectations; a system of accredited and ultimately enforceable standards; a cap on the crowding of prisons; an end to slopping out by February 1996; community prisons emphasizing links with families; sub-division of prisons into smaller, more manageable units; separate facilities and a lower security categorization for remand prisoners; and improved standards of justice with the abolition of the adjudicatory role for Boards of Visitors and the appointment of an independent complaints adjudicator or ombudsman. What tied most of these recommendations together, according to Woolf, was a sense of justice, fairness, and humanity. A proper balance between these and the traditional emphasis on security and control was the *sine qua non* for stability in prisons. In an alternative formulation, given at a seminar at All Souls some months after the report had been published, Woolf LJ confided that he had at one time thought of using the word 'relationships' as a unifying theme— better relationships between the Director General and ministers, between the Prisons Board and prison governors, between governors and the officers who staffed their prisons, and between staff and prisoners: all needed to know where they stood, and that it was on justifiable ground.

What is more at issue is the extent to which those recommendations have been taken up. Woolf was at pains to make it clear that the recommendations had to be seen as an integrated, total package (para. 1.12). It therefore seemed like opportunistic 'cherry picking' when Kenneth Baker, on receiving the report in February 1991, announced a small clutch of immediate reforms on letters, telephone calls, visits, and home leave and then somewhat upstaged Woolf and Tumim by dramatically bringing forward the date for the ending of slopping out to December 1994. Cynics could argue that this was an easy commitment to make: Woolf's proposal merely reiterated what the Chief Inspector had proposed two years earlier (Home Office 1989a), the programme for refurbishment was already well advanced, and the prison population projections still offered the prospect of accommodation and population coming into balance over the next two years.[16] In any event it was to be some time before there was a fuller ministerial response. In the summer of 1991 the Home Secretary was one of the principal speakers at a conference organized by the Prison Reform Trust. The audience had been on tenterhooks ever since the report was published, wondering what an eventual White Paper might include. Mr Baker kept them in suspense: the first part of his speech made no reference to Strangeways or the Woolf report, but talked of the past achievements of the service, before finally indicating that Woolf had mapped out an agenda which would occupy the service for the next twenty years. The audience left very little wiser but generally pessimistic.

In these circumstances most commentators were considerably surprised at the extent to which the White Paper (Home Office 1991b) actually took that agenda on board. Indeed, it is arguable that the very title of the White Paper, *Custody, Care, and Justice*, better characterizes the intentions behind the Woolf Report than did Woolf's own words of *security, control, and justice*. But while much of the thrust of Woolf was incorporated into the policy statement, with the exception of the commitment on integral sanitation, the timetable for implementation was left very vague. Often the commitments were also rather carefully qualified, and in some important areas ministers had clearly decided to hold back. One of these concerned the proposed lower security categorization for remand prisoners (Morgan 1994), but perhaps the most important of these was in regard to Woolf's proposed new prison rule intended to cap individual prisons at the level of their certified normal accommodation. In support of this proposal Woolf had tellingly quoted the oral evidence of the Director General, Chris Train. He had said:

that the life and work of the Prison Service have, for the last 20 years, been distorted by the problems of overcrowding. That single factor has dominated prisoners' lives, it has produced often intolerable pressure on the staff, and as a consequence it has soured industrial relations. It has skewed managerial effort and it has diverted managerial effort away from

---

[16] In fact the Home Secretary's announcement of an advanced date for the introduction of integral sanitation seems to have involved a quicker and cheaper method of putting sinks and toilets in cells. It also involved losing less accommodation than the model which had thus far found favour of converting every third cell into a bathroom to be shared between the cells on either side—see Casale (1994).

positive developments. The removal of overcrowding is, in my view, an indispensable pre-condition of sustained and universal improvement in prison conditions . . . for improvements to be service-wide, the canker of overcrowding must be rooted out (quoted in Woolf Report, para. 11.135–6).

Woolf and Tumim unreservedly endorsed the Director General's assessment of the effect of overcrowding and noted his prognostication that the service would, at last, move from a shortage of accommodation to a surplus of accommodation by 1993. But they wrote: 'Even if overcrowding is banished in accordance with the Director General's timetable, it is necessary to ensure there is no return to the present situation. Once banished, it must not return. Inmates and staff must in future be protected from the corrosive consequences of overcrowding' (para. 11.140). It was precisely because the solution to the crowding problem was so fundamental to the implementation of their package of reforms, and thus in their view to the stability of the prison system, that Woolf and Tumim proposed a rule that would impose narrow and binding limits upon the Home Secretary, non-compliance with which could form the basis for an application for judicial review.

However, in regard to this recommendation the White Paper simply said, 'once the system comes into equilibrium, it will consider the possible substance of a Prison Rule and of any formal procedure to notify Parliament of any significant instance of overcrowding' (Home Office 1991b, para. 6.13). It now seems peculiarly hollow, in the light of subsequent developments, that the Home Office concluded that paragraph as follows: 'It would be necessary, however, to ensure that any formal procedure did not unintentionally appear *to institutionalise a return to overcrowding*' (Emphasis added).

Meanwhile the Council of Europe's Committee for the Prevention of Torture found that the overcrowding in Brixton, Leeds, and Wandsworth, when coupled with the lack of integral sanitation and the lack of out-of-cell activities, constituted 'inhuman and degrading treatment'. They, too, proposed an enforceable ceiling on the population which could be held in each prison (Council of Europe 1991a). To this the Home Office replied that 'the Government does not think it would be right to impose a ceiling on the number of prisoners any particular establishment should hold. This is because the Prison Service has an absolute obligation

to hold accused and sentenced persons committed by the courts'
(Council of Europe 1991b).

It is important to recognize that, at the time of these pronounce-
ments about prison population and overcrowding, the Government
still adhered to a parallel agenda on criminal justice matters which
led to the Criminal Justice Act 1991. A stable prison system had
been one of Douglas Hurd's objectives since resuming at the Home
Office after the general election of 1987. This was to be achieved
through, amongst other means, a consistent and principled sentencing policy. In place of 'alternatives to custody' a new rhetoric of
strengthened community-based sentences and parole supervision
was introduced, intended to bring about real change in the probation service that would raise its credibility in the eyes of the judiciary, thus paving the way for a better and more rational balance
in sentencing decisions. The introduction of unit fines and the
reduction of maximum penalties for some offences was to be tem-
pered by increased powers for dealing with serious violent and
sexual offenders and important changes to the arrangements for
parole recommended by Carlisle's review. Achieving consistent and
principled sentencing would require much closer links between the
various parts of the criminal justice system and a more knowledgeable and sympathetic understanding of their respective roles and
contributions without compromising judicial independence (see
Windlesham 1993, Von Hirsch and Ashworth 1992). After informal
discussions between the Home Office and the higher judiciary, a
seminal country house weekend in September 1989 was hosted by
the Home Secretary, the Lord Chancellor, and the Attorney
General, and attended by the Lord Chief and Deputy Chief Justice
as well as leading members of the magistracy and operational services. What they discussed were the principles underlying the
embryonic Criminal Justice Bill. When Woolf LJ proposed the
establishment of a National Criminal Justice Consultative Council
and area criminal justice committees, he was building upon developments that had already gone some way down that road.[17]

By the time Chris Train gave his evidence to Woolf there were
real grounds for optimism because these policies seemed to be
working. Had they continued to do so the Director General or his

---

[17] I am grateful to David Faulkner for allowing me sight of his as yet unpublished paper on *Policy, Legislation, and Practice* which discusses these matters in
greater depth and on the basis of hands-on experience.

successor might have seen the small surplus of prison accommodation he expected by 1993. However, it was precisely because Woolf
and Tumim were aware that such a precarious balance could be
easily upset, and because they were concerned at the likely frailty
of ministerial response to political moods, that they made their
proposals fora new prison rule to cap the population in establishments. Such a rule was never going to be popular with ministers.
Although officials who had an input into the drafting of *Custody,
Care, and Justice* discussed the possibility of such a rule, none of
them pressed the case. With the prison building programme nearing completion, a prison population then actually in decline, and
the prospect of maintaining stability through the provisions of the
Criminal Justice Act 1991 and the operation of the about-to-be-
established consultative councils, it must have been easy to persuade oneself that such a rule was not necessary and certainly not
worth a confrontation. No-one could then reasonably have fore-
seen the turn-around in criminal justice policy that would produce
such a rapid flight from the 1991 Criminal Justice Act by Kenneth
Clarke a mere eight months after its implementation; and still less
the extraordinary positions taken by his successor, Michael
Howard, in furtherance of his contention, adumbrated at the
Conservative Party Conference in October 1993, that 'prison
works'.

The system did briefly come into balance in the winter of
1992–3. In December 1992 the prison population fell to a low of
40,722 and in the annual report for 1992–3 it was noted that the
last prisoners left police cells in February 1993 (Prison Service
1993g). But overcrowding, on the verge of disappearing, did not go
away entirely even then and it has since become a prominent feature
of the system once again. On 30 April 1993 the prison population
stood at 43,391, some 2,820 fewer than the then 46,211 places—an
occupancy rate of 94 per cent overall. But the local prisons, which
had always borne the brunt of overcrowding, remained 13 per cent
above capacity, necessitating substantial cell sharing. Six months
later, on 31 October 1993, the population was 46,886, some 597
above the CNA of 46,289 places. Although this produced an overall occupancy rate of only 101 per cent the crowding in the local
prisons had risen to 122 per cent. The latest published statistics,
for the end of September 1994, show a population of 49,812 prisoners, which represents 102 per cent occupancy of the 49,014 certi-

fied normal accommodation, with some 258 prisoners once again held in police cells. In the local prisons the occupancy rate was 114 per cent. A few weeks later it was reported that the prison population had broken through the 50,000 barrier.

The opportunity provided by the Woolf Report to control the prison population crisis while the memory of Strangeways was still fresh in the minds of ministers has been lost, if not irretrievably then probably for many years. Certainly the events at Wymott on 6 September 1993, though they were occasioned in part by the tactical management of crowding elsewhere in the system, seem to have inflamed desires for greater austerity in prison regimes and rekindled the embers of old disputes between management and prison officers, rather than refocus attention on the need to cap the growth in prison population. The 249 prisoners received into Wymott category C training prison in the space of just three weeks immediately before the disturbance were decanted rapidly from Liverpool, Preston, and Risley, where overcrowding was particularly acute. These transfers, at twice the normal weekly rate, were cited by the Chief Inspector as a factor in accounting for the riot (Home Office 1993a paras. 3.15 and 3.36). Two months later, prison officers, in a return to the tactics of the pre-Woolf era, sought through industrial action to limit the prison population at Preston—with occupancy at 172 per cent of CNA then the most overcrowded prison in the system. The Home Office was granted an interlocutory injunction restraining the POA from pursuing industrial action, on the basis of the argument that prison officers were technically enjoying the office of constables and so not entitled to engage in trade disputes.[18] When the POA then sought to limit population at Preston to CNA, this time in furtherance of its members' obligations as constables to prevent a possible breach of the peace, the Home Office was again granted an injunction pending a full court hearing which was set for November 1994. The Government took steps under clause 103 of the Criminal Justice and Public Order Bill, to establish by statute that prison officers have the powers of a constable for whom it is unlawful to take industrial action, except on pain of being sued for any losses

---

[18] This interpretation of the 1952 Prison Act was apparently quite well known within the Home Office and had been brought to the attention of the Prisons Board in the early 1980s, although it had never been publicly deployed and official evidence to the May Committee recognizing the POA as a union was allowed to stand.

incurred as a result. Under clauses 102 and 104 prison officers would have the same employment rights as other Crown servants, with the Secretary of State being empowered to determine pay and conditions.

One of the first casualties of the renewed rise in the prison population was the much-trumpeted date for the ending of slopping out. In February 1994 Michael Howard announced that resources were being diverted to create an additional 2,000 prison places. As a consequence the date for ending slopping out was put back from December 1994 to February 1996, the date originally suggested by the Chief Inspector and adopted by Woolf.

Many of the other Woolf proposals, however, have been or are being introduced, at least to some extent, and wherever possible in the chapters which follow we refer to their impact on our prisons and more generally. At the Prison Reform Trust conference on Woolf, Roy King, speaking just before the Home Secretary arrived and fearing that acceptance and implementation of Woolf would be construed 'as having been part of existing policy—and thus legitimately subject to the kinds of priorities already determined within the Department', urged the penal reform groups 'to establish their own shadow task forces to monitor the implementation' themselves (King 1991b). One product of that was a PRT questionnaire to which over a hundred establishments responded. The results from the PRT study suggested that most governors were committed to implementing the Woolf reforms wherever possible. But 'the most significant finding was an enduring lack of confidence in the relationship governors have with Prison Service Headquarters' (Prison Reform Trust 1992). The seasoned observer of the prison scene and the close reader of the Woolf Report would not be too surprised at that.

The continuing lack of confidence in the relationship between governors and headquarters may have prompted the determined and well-received stance adopted by Joe Pilling, briefly the Director General of the Service after Chris Train's departure. As Sparks has noted, Pilling's Eve Saville Memorial Lecture (1992) took up Woolf's sub-text of relationships and, in its emphasis on resonant concepts like respect, fairness, individuality, care, and openness, did much to further the process of re-legitimating the Prison Service. But by then further reforms were in the offing. Sir Raymond Lygo had been appointed in August 1991 to undertake yet another review of the managerial effectiveness of the service, and in December his report was published. It recommended, amongst other things, that the Prison Service become an executive agency and this was accepted by the Home Secretary in March 1992. And the process of contracting out prisons and prison services to the private sector, first mooted under Douglas Hurd but about which little had been done before the events at Strangeways, was gathering pace.

Contracting Out and Agency Status

Contracting out of court escort services and the running of remand prisons had been part of the agenda for criminal justice which Douglas Hurd had discussed with officials on his return to the Home Office in 1987. Woolf gave it scant attention, referring to it only once in his report (paras. 12.164–66) in the context of escort duties and then only to say it was not necessary for the Inquiry 'to be drawn into the argument'. Although the Home Office had contracted out the administration of its immigration detention centres and escort services associated with them to Securicor since 1970,[19] serious attention to the involvement of private contractors in prisons was not given until the ideas of the Adam Smith Institute (1984) received the enthusiastic (and not entirely disinterested) support of Gardiner, the Chair of the Home Affairs Committee (1987). Since then there have been few arguments more divisive. The penal reform groups have been universally condemnatory of what they choose to call privatization and what the Government insists on calling contracting out. In this they have been supported by many academic voices, partly on moral grounds that it would be wrong for private profit to be made out of publicly inflicted misery, partly on historical grounds that private prisons had been abandoned (and with good reason) so long ago that imprisonment had come to be seen as an intrinsic function of the state, and partly on grounds that there would be dangers of a penal–industrial complex, with a vested interest in filling up prisons, becoming unduly influential in criminal justice policy (see Logan 1990; Lilly and Knepper 1992; Ryan 1993; McDonald 1994; and Sparks 1994 for recent reviews of most of these issues).

Others had taken a more encouraging (McConville and Williams

---

[19] In January 1989, Securicor lost this contract to Group 4 Total Security.

1985), or at least a more pragmatic (Taylor and Pease 1987; Morgan and King 1987) stand on the issue, not least because it would be hard to see how any kind of private contract could be drawn up which did not include a higher specification of service than was already provided in the public sector. Morgan and King argued that the contracting out of services rather than whole prisons would offer opportunities entirely congruent with their prospectus for the normalization of the prison. In an attempt to bridge the gap between evolving Government policy and the rejection of the profit motive by penal reform groups, they also floated the possibility that non-profit bodies such as NACRO, already heavily involved in devising standards, might actually engage in the process of implementing them by bidding for a contract—but this was an idea not well received.

Although private prisons figured little in Woolf's deliberations, hardly had the report appeared before the Government issued invitations to tender for running The Wolds as a remand prison. The White Paper also made it plain that the Government proposed a rolling programme to contract out court escort services (Home Office 1991b, para. 3.9). As the tender documents for The Wolds made clear, the Woolf agenda had greatly heightened the validity of the argument that the Home Office would insist that private contractors provide standards considerably higher than those in the public sector and unlike anything previously experienced by remand prisoners (Home Office 1991c). The award of the contract for The Wolds to Group 4 in November 1991 was followed by a competition for Blakenhurst, a 650-bed local prison, which was won by UK Detention Services, a consortium of Corrections Corporation of America, John Mowlem, and Sir Robert McAlpine, in 1992. In September 1993 Michael Howard announced that: '[the] private sector must be large enough to provide sustained competition and involve several private sector companies—a genuinely mixed economy' (Prison Service, 1993b). The strategy was clear— to proceed quite quickly to contract with private sector firms for about 10 per cent of the prison estate, both new prisons and existing prisons, especially those which had most room for improvement, which would be 'market tested'. In this way, without becoming unduly dependent upon any one private sector company, considerable pressure could be exerted on the public sector prisons to become more economical and efficient, if not also more effective. It should be said that pressure has also been maintained on the private sector by the Government's determination to ensure that there will be several players in the field—as evidenced by the award of the third contract for Doncaster to Premier Prisons, a subsidiary of the American security company, Wakenhut.

It was probably always the case that one of the main planks in the Government's platform on contracting out prison services was the pressure that this would bring to bear on the Prison Officers' Association. Fresh Start had eliminated some opportunities for restrictive practices by prison officers, but opened up others. And one of the great failures of Fresh Start, as noted above, had been not first establishing appropriate staff complements for each prison. It was always evident that any savings which were to be made by private contractors would be in the area of staffing. If The Wolds could be seen to staff residential units with a ratio of one officer on duty to fifty prisoners, for how long could comparable public sector prisons continue to operate such units with a minimum of one senior and three basic grade officers? The contracting out of escort services, initially for East Midlands and Humberside in 1993–4, the Metropolitan Police District in 1994, and three further areas now identified as East Anglia, Transpennine, and North East, would remove what once had been a most lucrative perk for prison officers.

The mechanism for making sure that all public sector employees took these lessons to heart was 'market testing' which was pioneered at the rebuilt and refurbished Strangeways. In contrast to the competitions for The Wolds and Blakenhurst, the Prison Service was permitted to bid for the Strangeways contract. As Kenneth Clarke, who had succeeded Kenneth Baker as Home Secretary, put it:

Market testing will, I believe, cause the Prison Service to examine its own performance in the light of the competitive pressure and encourage the spread of those reforms across public sector prisons much more quickly than would otherwise have been the case (quoted in McDonald 1994).

The Prison Service (1992) got the message:

A bid sticking to every detail of a central agreement dating back from 1987 [i.e. Fresh Start] is unlikely to beat the competition . . . Any agreements that hinder the chances of constructing an effective bid will have to be reconsidered in consultation with the unions.

It also got the contract. It is unlikely that it was the lowest bid. But, as Derek Lewis, who by then had become the Director General, made clear, it represented 'levels of performance and value for money that we have not previously seen in the public sector (Prison Service 1993a). From the Government's point of view, the real measure of the success of The Wolds, therefore, may lie as much in the effect it may have had on Strangeways and other prisons subject to market testing, as it will in the normal application of what now have to be called performance indicators. Nevertheless, targets for cost savings in the public sector set for 1994–5 apparently take account of performance so far in the contracted-out sector.[20]

In September 1994 the Prisons Board informed governors that twenty-one prisons with the poorest performance during 1993–4 were under consideration for market testing. None of our prisons was on the list, which excluded dispersal and local prisons. However, it seems unlikely that the lessons would have been lost on Birmingham but short of specific market testing quick improvements there will have been difficult to establish. Of somewhat greater import from the point of view of the research reported here may have been the effect of moving towards a purchaser rather than a provider of health care services, and the contracting out of education. It is by no means clear how far the first of these has proceeded, although on 1 May 1992 the Prison Medical Service was relaunched as the Health Care Service for Prisoners and the annual report for 1992–3 refers to the replacement of three medical officer posts at Belmarsh by psychiatric registrars on secondment from the NHS (Prison Service 1993g, para. 104). Initial findings from inquiries by the Prison Reform Trust suggest that the most immediate consequence of changes in the education service has been the loss of many of the positive features that had previously prevailed (Prison Reform Trust 1993).

On 1 April 1993, three years to the day after the prisoners took over the chapel at Strangeways, HM Prison Service became the third largest executive agency to have been formed since the 'Next Steps' programme was launched in 1988. Woolf had criticized the Prison Service's statement of purpose, adopted in 1988 and displayed in all establishments and virtually all official documents

[20] Personal communication from Philippa Drew.

ever since, because it failed to take specific account of remand prisoners, it failed to make explicit that prisoners should be treated with justice whilst in custody, and it failed to relate the role of the Prison Service to the criminal justice system generally (Home Office 1991a, paras. 10.14–16). In spite of that the mission statement of the new agency remains unchanged: 'Her Majesty's Prison Service serves the public by keeping in custody those committed by the courts.

Our duty is to care for them with humanity and to help them lead law abiding and useful lives in custody and after release'.

Three key documents have set out the basis on which the newly formed agency works. The *Framework Document* (Prison Service 1993c), has a foreword by the then Home Secretary, Kenneth Clarke, and describes the procedures for accountability and the 'stand-off' relationship whereby the Home Secretary allocates resources and approves the corporate and business plans, and the Director General is responsible for day-to-day management of the service. It also declared six goals of the Prison Service and the key performance indicators against which success is to be evaluated. The *Corporate Plan* (Prison Service 1993d) has a preface from the Director General, Derek Lewis, and sets out strategic proposals for achieving the goals over a three year period, whilst the *Business Plan* (Prison Service 1993e) sets targets and action plans for the immediate financial year. Between them these documents replace the Statement of Tasks and Functions introduced under Circular Instruction 55/1984. It has made sense for us, therefore, to present our data under the rubric of the new goals even though they were collected in relation to the earlier statement of tasks and functions; and throughout this volume we refer repeatedly to these three basic documents of the agency. Since each of our succeeding chapters, like those of the new-style annual reports of the Prison Service, is organized around one of the six goals and its key performance indicators, we reproduce the official formulation of them in Table 1.6.

In April 1994 HM Prison Service Agency celebrated its first birthday and ushered in yet more change. With the retirement of Ian Dunbar, his post and the Directorate of Inmate Administration was abolished as part of a review intended to produce a smaller strategic headquarters with a group of Central Services units supporting establishments in which governors will have greater

Table 1.6. Goals and performance indicators of the Prison Service: 1993–4

Goal	Key Performance Indicator
Keep prisoners in custody	Number of escapes from prison establishments and from escorts
Maintain order, control, discipline and a safe environment	Number of assaults on staff, prisoners and others
Provide decent conditions for prisoners and meet their needs, including health care	Proportion of prisoners held in units of accommodation intended for fewer numbers Number of prisoners with 24-hour access to sanitation
Provide positive regimes which help prisoners address their offending behaviour and allow them as full and responsible a life as possible	Average number of hours a week prisoners spend in purposeful activity Proportion of prisoners held in establishments where prisoners are unlocked on weekdays for a total of at least 12 hours
Help prisoners prepare for their return to the community	Proportion of prisoners held in establishments where prisoners have the opportunity to exceed the minimum visiting entitlement
Deliver prison services using the resources provided by Parliament with maximum efficiency	Average cost per prisoner place

devolved powers for budgets, contracts, staff recruitment, and regimes. Under this latest revision line management above establishment level now reports to just two directorates—Custody and Programmes—via a regrouped force of area managers. It is too early to say what effect this reorganization may have but it is possible to take brief stock here of some of the lessons from the first year of agency status.

The first months of agency status seem to have passed fairly smoothly. Derek Lewis and the Prisons Board had set out an agenda in the *Corporate* and *Business Plans* and Kenneth Clarke had agreed it in accordance with the *Framework Document*. Troubles quickly surfaced, however, after Clarke moved to the Treasury and Michael Howard was appointed to the Home Office.

One of the earliest warning signs concerned the appointment of Woolf's proposed complaints adjudicator, now known as the Prisons Ombudsman, which had been promised in the *Business Plan* by the summer of 1993 (Prison Service 1993e, 7). By the autumn it became known that Michael Howard had vetoed the appointment of any of the three highly qualified candidates, whom he refused apparently even to meet, put forward after the usual selection procedures.[21] The appointment of the ombudsman, of course, falls properly within the Home Secretary's acknowledged responsibilities and would not therefore indicate a breach of the new 'stand off' relationship implied in agency status, although it scarcely speaks well of his attitude towards the Civil Service Commission. In the circumstances it cannot have been easy for Sir Peter Woodhead, whose appointment to the post was announced on 20 April 1994, to establish a credible independence which Woolf rightly regarded as essential to the role (Home Office 1991a, para. 14.351). However, before considering any cases, Woodhead has recruited a strong team, insisted on having an office outside the Prison Service headquarters, and embarked on a programme of consultations and discussions which has done much to establish his credentials with academics and penal reform groups (*Observer*, 23 October 1994).

Another sign, and one which perhaps suggested a more directly interventionist stance about the nature of the agenda, came with the leaked memorandum of 30 July 1993 from Michael Howard's private office which indicated that 'the Home Secretary wanted a rather different paper . . . from the one originally provided by Mr Lewis'. The Home Secretary wanted 'to take a more radical look at the nature of the prison experience': prison regimes were described as 'lax', and he took the view that prisoners should 'spend more time working' and less on leisure, outdoor, and sporting activities. The Home Secretary also expressed 'grave concern about the use of temporary release and home leave' and asked for a reappraisal of that policy. In short, what the Home Secretary wanted from Mr Lewis was a 'paper setting out the ways in which prison might be refocussed to become a more austere experience while minimizing the risk of control problems arising from too sudden a change of direction'. The Home Secretary also wanted an

---

[21] It became widely known through press reports that the candidates were Professor Sean McConville, Professor Rod Morgan, and Dr Stephen Shaw.

'assessment of the savings that could be made from a change in policy, recognizing that this represents quite a departure from some of the commitments set out post-Woolf'.[22]

Perhaps the most important signal has come with the publication in April 1994 of the Code of Operating Standards for the Prison Service. The Government had given a rather vague commitment to the introduction of a code of standards in *Custody, Care, and Justice* which left open the question whether there should be a single set of standards for the service as a whole or different standards for different types of institutions and categories of prisoner; how prisons should be accredited; and if and when standards should become legally enforceable. When the consultation documents on standards were circulated in March 1992 they envisaged dual standards, and at the London conference chaired by Ian Dunbar there seemed to be a real danger that the service would enshrine a lower standard as quite acceptable for local prisons and a higher standard to which training prisons might aspire—thus perpetuating the indefensible differences that King and Morgan and others had argued against for more than a decade. This was one of many controversial matters with which the standards steering group, chaired by Dunbar, had to deal over the ensuing months. However, by July 1993 the steering group and its eleven task forces had produced a draft single code of standards 'which all prisons and young offender institutions are expected to achieve'. In a brief introductory paragraph, directly echoing Woolf, it was made plain that 'the aim of the Code is to balance the needs of security, control, and discipline within prisons, with decent conditions and a fair and just system for dealing with prisoners' problems and grievances'.

The *Business Plan* included a commitment to publish the code by 31 December 1993 (Prison Service 1993e, 7), but December came and went and rumours circulated that Michael Howard was insisting upon changes. When the Code was finally published in April 1994 it was under the low key title of *Operating Standards* (Prison Service 1994a) and governors were merely 'expected to work towards them over time'. The phrase 'with decent conditions' had been expanded to 'with decent but austere conditions, active and demanding regimes'. Moreover, the document spells out that in

---

[22] All quotations are from the leaked memorandum.

individual cases the application of the standards will 'be conditional upon prisoners complying with the obligations placed upon them' and that certain standards 'represent privileges which may have to be earned' and which may be subject to 'forfeit'. At several points it is emphasized that the 'standards are not intended to be legally enforceable' although the possibility of making them so, once standards are met more consistently across the system, is not ruled out. There were also a number of differences between the published version and the July draft in the specification of particular standards including, crucially, the deletion of the space standard for existing accommodation which was apparently removed by the Prisons Board and the rights of convicted prisoners to wear their own clothes and to have some meals in association which were removed at the request of Michael Howard. To these and other aspects of the new code we will need to refer at various points throughout the book. Meanwhile, one senior prison governor has told us that, given the recent dramatic rise in the prison population, for him, and most of his colleagues, the new Code of Operating Standards will remain on the shelf.

Some indication of the nature of the new austerity measures, and the anxieties they have provoked amongst senior managers and prison governors, was given at the annual conference at the end of October 1994 (*Guardian*, 28 October and 1 November 1994). The measures so far announced include the earning of privileges, the introduction of compulsory random drug testing, and restrictions on the home-leave and temporary-release schemes, as well as access to telephones. These policy changes signal a deliberate, albeit partial, reversal of the Woolf agenda and have been foisted upon reluctant officials and governors. Whether they can be sustained, and at what cost, remains to be seen. Inevitably the conference was overshadowed by the attempted escape from Whitemoor by five IRA terrorists on 9 September 1994 and the subsequent discovery of Semtex explosive at the same prison. Both matters were investigated by Sir John Woodcock whilst a more extensive review of security, subsequently extended to take account of the escape from Parkhurst, was entrusted to Sir John Learmont. There must now be a risk that a renewed emphasis on security will further undermine the balance between security, control, and justice which Woolf tried so hard to promote (see King, 1994c). However, we have now said sufficient about the main policy and organizational changes to put our research in context and we return to the likely impact of the changes in our concluding chapter.

Changes in Use of Our Research Prisons

There are two final, and more specific, changes since our research and one planned change to which we have to refer. With effect from 1 November 1987, just before we returned to evaluate the impact of Fresh Start, Ashwell ceased to be an open prison and became a 'low' category C training prison. In April 1992 Gartree was finally taken out of the dispersal system and became a category B training prison catering predominantly for life-sentence prisoners. It is expected that Nottingham, where about a fifth of the population were lifers at the time of our study, will in future become a prison exclusively devoted to life-sentence prisoners.

Plan of this Book

The plan of this book is essentially very simple. In Chapters 2 to 6 we present data from our various researches carried out from 1986 to 1991. Each chapter relates to a separate goal of the Prison Service: security (Chapter 2), maintaining order (Chapter 3), providing decent conditions (Chapter 4), providing positive regimes (Chapter 5), and helping prisoners maintain contact and return to the community (Chapter 6). Most chapters follow a common format whereby we first discuss the goals and key performance indicators set out by the Prison Service before presenting our own data. Wherever possible we make comparisons between our results and those obtained in the national prison survey. We then proceed to an examination of more recent developments in our research prisons on the basis of regime-monitoring data, the internal reports of prison governors, and the external reports of HM Chief Inspector of Prisons. Finally we try to assess what seems to have happened more generally through the system in regard to the performance indicators on the basis of published data and materials supplied to us by the Prison Service at the end of its first year of agency status. Chapter 7 is somewhat different from the rest because we did not collect data directly pertaining to costs and the efficient use of resources—the sixth and final goal of the Prison Service. Although we examine the performance indicator and present some materials on staffing, always the biggest element in operating costs, we use

Chapter 7 for a broader discussion which tries to make sense of the prison system, as we understand it today, from the point of view of not just economy, efficiency, and effectiveness but also justice and humanity, and this serves as our conclusion.

We are uncomfortably aware that this sounds like a big prospectus. It is, and we should therefore issue two health warnings. First, although our data touch on all the main areas of Prison Service activity—as seen through our five prisons at least—each of those areas could have warranted a research project in its own right. We bit off a lot. We hope we have got beneath the surface, but at times our approach necessarily resembles open-cast rather than deep-shaft mining. Secondly, the scope of changes in the Prison Service in recent years has been quite bewildering. We have tried to allude to most of those that have a bearing on our data but we have not caught them all. Perhaps the most glaring, albeit deliberate, omission relates to parole, where the changes following Carlisle were so great that there seemed little point in doing anything with our data. No doubt there are many others.

2
Keeping Prisoners in Custody: Security

It is in the nature of things that prisons are about security. A prison that consistently failed to hold its prisoners in custody would be a contradiction in terms: whatever else prisons may also be about, they are certainly about keeping people in custody. Since it is their raison d'être, it should not be surprising that the first goal of the Prison Service Agency specified in the Framework Document (Prison Service 1993c) should be set out so simply: *to keep prisoners in custody*; nor for the key performance indicator to be *the number of escapes from prison establishments and from escorts* (Key Performance Indicator 1).

While the key performance indicator focuses upon the number of escapes, it has always been the quality of escapes rather than their quantity which has driven the security scares which have periodically beset the Prison Service. Thus, it was not an increase in the number of escapes as such which led to the setting up of the Mountbatten Inquiry in 1966 but the fact that the escapers included some of the 'great train robbers' and the spy, George Blake. Although the *Business Plan* expresses its immediate target as ensuring that the number of escapes will be fewer in 1993–4 than in 1992–3 (Prison Service 1993e, 4) the *Corporate Plan* also makes it plain that its priority is to ensure that no category A prisoner escapes and that nobody escapes from any category B prison (Prison Service 1993d, para. 5.7). In a further attempt to put security into perspective, however, the *Corporate Plan* also explains (*ibid.*, para. 5.1) that the service nevertheless wishes to *ensure that prisoners are not held in a higher level of security than is necessary*, for that would cut across the fifth goal: helping prisoners *prepare for release into the community*.

As is apparent from these statements, not all prisons need be equally secure. Moreover, there are profound cost implications of security which have to be taken into account when considering the achievement of the sixth goal, namely *delivering prison services using the resources provided by Parliament with maximum efficiency*. In the late 1960s and early 1970s at the time of the *Prison Regimes Project* there were no published data on costs for individual prisons, and Prison Department officials privately admitted there was no way of working them out. At the beginning of our present study the published data indicated that it cost £24,284 to keep a prisoner for one year in Gartree; £13,312 in Nottingham; £9,724 in Featherstone; and £9,256 in Ashwell. In Birmingham the unit cost was £11,024, but that was an artificially low figure maintained only through gross over-crowding. Privately, officials still admitted that the figures remained subject to considerable margins of error. Today, of course, all those cost are considerably greater—according to the most recently available *Annual Report and Accounts* for 1992–3 (Prison Service 1993g) they had increased, on average, by 81 per cent: to £38,636 in Gartree;[1] £31,044 in Nottingham; £18,148 in Featherstone; £15,340 in Ashwell; and £19,916 in Birmingham. Clearly, to keep all prisoners in the hugely expensive conditions of maximum security would be as wasteful as the keeping of all prisoners in the relatively cheap-to-run open prisons would be foolhardy. It is obviously important to get the balance right.

How secure, then, should prisons be? When the call sign of *rogue elephant*[2] went out over the short wave radios at Gartree on 10 December 1987 prison officers could scarcely believe their ears; when the videotape from the CCTV cameras was shown on television a month later the general public could hardly believe its eyes. A helicopter had landed in the enclosed games field during the afternoon exercise period in full sight of staff, and within thirty seconds Kendall and Draper had effected the most public escape in the history of the prison system.[3] Both were category A prisoners, and this was the first ever escape from any of the country's most secure dispersal prisons. These facts must have embarrassed politicians and frightened some members of the public. But they must also have sent a surge of hope through the hearts of prisoners everywhere. There

[1] Even though for most of that year Gartree had been reduced from dispersal operation to category B training status.

[2] There has been for several years an elaborate system of reporting to the emergency control room in high security prisons using easily recognized call signs to identify both callers and events. 'Rogue elephant' was the call sign to identify an escape in progress assisted by helicopter. Most thought it would never have to be used.

[3] Kendall was recaptured on 31 Jan. 1988 and Draper on 24 Feb. 1989.

were certainly cheers to be heard on the wings in Gartree that night.

Paradoxically, though, it was about the only type of escape from a maximum security prison for which the governor's head need not roll.[4] A year earlier the governor had told us:

As far as escapes are concerned the buck stops here. I am absolutely account-able. If an A man escapes my job is on the line. I would not get it if a heli-copter came down and took someone away because that could hardly be laid at my door. But an identifiable lapse in security would be the end if it led to an A man escaping.

It was accepted there was no actual defence against a helicopter attack. All that the radio call sign was supposed to do was to alert the RAF to make an interception. In the event the RAF response was said to be 'Rogue what?'

The repeated demands by the POA for the installation of wires over the playing field area which would foul the rotor blades of a helicopter appear to have been dismissed at headquarters either as so much paranoia or as the final abuse of the security arguments so often used by the union to ratchet up manning levels. The inquiry by Gordon Lakes, then still Deputy Director General, was a compara-tively low-key affair and was not published. The Home Secretary, however, made a brief statement in the House of Commons on 21 January 1988, dismissing staffing levels as a factor in the escape but pointing to the predictability of exercise periods and the absence of physical barriers to prevent helicopters landing or taking off again. He announced changes which, when we returned to Gartree to examine the impact of Fresh Start, were already being put in place. A large new wire cage, which had anti-helicopter wires over it, had been constructed for the exercise of category A prisoners. There had also been wholesale changes to the staffing of the security section, and some of the officers we had known best from the main study had been moved to other duties or other prisons. The new post of 'helicopter spotter' was just about the least popular job in the prison, not surprisingly, since it involved staring at the sky through field glasses from a hastily constructed hut on the roof; staff assigned to it felt that it was pointless activity and had to endure teasing and even ridicule from fellow officers.

---

[4] Indeed the then governor became Director of Services and a member of the Prisons Board.

The escape from Brixton in July 1991 of McAuley and Quinlivan, two remand prisoners who were charged with terrorist offences and so held on provisional category A, was an altogether different matter.[5] They escaped using a gun which had been smuggled into the prison concealed in a training shoe: the kind of security lapse which ought not to occur, and could not easily be excused, in any prison. The Chief Inspector of Prisons was asked to inquire into the Brixton escape, and Gordon Lakes, now retired and fresh from his role of advising Woolf, was invited, together with Ron Hadfield, Chief Constable of West Midlands Police, to undertake an audit of security in prisons where category A prisoners were housed, as well as the operation of DoC 1, the headquarters division primarily concerned with security matters and the management of category A prisoners. The Chief Inspector's report (Home Office 1991d), the details of which remain largely secret, was profoundly critical. The Chief Inspector found that information warning of the likelihood that these prisoners would try to escape had been largely ignored. There had also been a failure to block the way through the perimeter to an insecure works yard, failure to ensure the speedy process of communications through the control room, and failures in searching and escorting procedures. Hadfield and Lakes in their interim report recommended a review of contingency arrangements with the local police, more stringent attention to circular instructions regarding the use of telephones by category A prisoners, and the installation of X-ray equipment similar to that used at airports for the detection of weapons (Prison Service 1991a).

We return to the more general findings of Hadfield and Lakes at the end of this chapter when we consider changes that have taken place since our research, but the fallout from the débâcle at Brixton could not be managed without someone being held to account. While Kenneth Baker accepted responsibility, 'as the Home Secretary must', he made it clear that his responsibility was limited to policy and that 'administration, development, and the running of the prisons are the responsibility of the Director General and of individual prison governors'. Not surprisingly, it was the governor of Brixton and some of his staff, together with the head of DoC 1, who actually carried the can in this case.

But there has to be some limit to the concern with security. Like

[5] Quinlivan was re-arrested in County Tipperary on 4 Apr. 1992. McAuley was re-arrested in Dublin on 9 Apr. 1992.

it or not, people in custody inevitably fantasize about escaping. The possibility of escape, however remote, provides a kind of safety valve—as the cheers in Gartree and countless prisoner-of-war films seem to show. Unless we really want prisons in which we insist 'Abandon hope, all ye who enter here' (Dante 1307) it is probably important to keep a sense of proportion about security, because prisoners without a sense of hope may well feel they have less and less to lose. The Chief Inspector hoped that his recommendations would not lead to tougher conditions generally, as indeed had just about every inquiry into prison security since Mountbatten's (Home Office 1966). It should not be forgotten that Woolf devoted considerable attention to technical security and control policies and procedures—although he will be best remembered for his insistence that it is vital to get the balance right. Nevertheless, it seems to be very hard for prison systems to resist the tendency towards security overkill. It is unfortunately the case that administrators, such as the Director of the Swedish Prison System, who, when faced with an escape of notorious prisoners from his most secure prison, was bold enough to say *in public* that he did not actually wish to be the man in charge of a system from which no one could escape, are very rare indeed (quoted in Morgan 1992a).

One of the keys to getting the balance right is the process of categorization and allocation of prisoners, but one of the problems that leads to getting it wrong is the tendency for these decisions to be confounded by considerations that properly have to do with good order and discipline rather than security.

The Categorization and Allocation Process

Assessing prisoners for the purpose of determining or recommending (a) an appropriate level of security, and (b) an allocation to an appropriate prison, is a very inexact science. It is carried out for the most part by relatively junior staff in the Observation, Classification, and Allocation (OCA) Units in local prisons.

As is well known, the Mountbatten Report (Home Office 1966) introduced a system whereby prisoners have been classified into one of four security categories:

> *category A* prisoners being those whose escape would constitute a danger to the public, the police, or the security of the State;
> *category B* prisoners—those for whom escape should be made

very difficult but without recourse to the highest security conditions;

category C prisoners—those who lack the resource and will to make serious escape attempts but would abscond from open prisons and should be kept in semi-secure closed custody; and

category D prisoners—those deemed suitable for open conditions.

The classificatory symmetry between prisoners and prisons which Mountbatten would have imposed with the building of a single maximum security prison for category A prisoners, and graduated reductions of security in the prisons for each of the other categories, was deliberately eroded following the Government's decision to implement the recommendations of the Radzinowicz sub-committee of the Advisory Council on the Penal System (ACPS 1968). Since then category A prisoners have been dispersed amongst prisoners of lesser security risk—though the range of other categories amongst whom they are dispersed has varied over the years (see King and Morgan 1980). As a result the security terminology relating to prisons can be somewhat confusing: the maximum security prisons to which category A prisoners may be dispersed are technically described as category B dispersal prisons. Category A prisoners, however, face a number of additional restrictions within the dispersal system which concern cell location, frequency of moving cells and of cell searches, and the conditions under which visits may take place. They will normally also be 'on the book', a system which requires prison officers to accept responsibility for prisoners' whereabouts by initialling a book which follows each category A prisoner around the prison. However, it has been common practice for governors in some dispersal prisons at some times to take some category A prisoners 'off the book'.

The implementation of the dispersal policy was based upon a belief that lower security risk prisoners would somehow offset the control problems that were assumed to follow if high security risk prisoners were all housed together. This led inexorably to a conflation of security and control issues as the Prison Service sought both to answer the question of who 'needs' to be in the dispersal system and to justify why they need be there. The confusion between security justifications and control justifications for the use of dispersal policy has taken many years to unravel and is still far from being resolved (King 1979, 1987; King and Morgan 1980; Morgan 1983;

Home Office 1979a, 1979c, 1984a, 1991a). By definition the dispersal policy provided many more places in maximum security conditions than strict security risk criteria would demand. However, the Mountbatten categories themselves remained essentially unchanged until 1987, at least on paper. In that year, following the escape of Kendall and Draper, new sub-classifications of category A prisoners into *exceptional risk*, *high risk*, and *standard risk* were introduced.

Most other prisoners who are serving sentences long enough to be transferred out of the local prisons are allocated to category B (non-dispersal) or category C training prisons, which are both closed establishments, or to category D training prisons which are open. All local prisons are expected to provide category B security, many of them with special cells to house category A prisoners either direct from the courts or on periodic transfer from the dispersal system. The category B security for local prisons is justified on grounds that they have to receive whoever is sent to them by the courts. Traditionally, prisoners on remand were not categorized for security purposes unless there were grounds for considering them as provisional category A prisoners.

Once prisoners have been allocated it is the responsibility of each prison governor to keep the security category and allocation of prisoners in his or her establishment under review. The governor is also required to maintain a level of security appropriate to the prisoners who are or may be held there. In theory, the process of categorization and allocation in the local prisons, in conjunction with the operation of the category A section at headquarters where appropriate, and the discharge of the monitoring and review of security by governors in the receiving prisons, should serve to keep prisoners in custody with the minimum use of security. In practice this is by no means assured. Security categorization involves important matters of human judgement, and it would hardly be surprising, given the political hue and cry that can surround escapes, if at all levels in the process decision-makers decided to 'play it safe'. The same outcry does not ensue for false positives (those allocated to high security who do not need it) as it does for false negatives (those allocated to low security, who escape and commit further serious offences). As a result, the natural processes of caution could lead to prisoners being held in conditions of higher security than they need and for longer periods than necessary. In England and Wales the decision to implement the dispersal policy, as we have seen, effectively guaranteed such an outcome.

The concern about 'over-categorization', as it has come to be called, is by no means confined to this country. In the United States during the 1970s, where large numbers of prisoners were being held in expensive high security prisons, many jurisdictions argued that prisoners were 'over-categorized'. They sought to develop more 'objective' systems of categorization to help overcome the problem. The best known, and best researched, attempts to reduce the dependence on maximum security through better systems of classification were carried out in the US Federal Prison System (Levinson and Williams 1979; Levinson 1980, 1982a, 1982b; Kane and Saylor 1982), although the National Institute of Corrections, California, New York, Florida, Illinois, and Minnesota, developed somewhat similar systems, as did Canada.

The May Committee, as we have seen, was not satisfied that the Home Office had struck the right security balance, and instead placed its hopes for a better system in the deliberations of an internal Prison Department Working Party on Categorization (Home Office 1979a, para. 6.70). The Working Party reported in August 1981 (Prison Department 1981) but showed no knowledge of American developments and did little more than tinker with existing arrangements, although it did suggest the adoption of a simple algorithm to introduce greater uniformity of security categorization. It admitted that not all category B prisoners were in the right kind of prison (*ibid.*, para. 99) but then, nevertheless, re-affirmed the official commitment to the amount of accommodation provided in the dispersal system (*ibid.*, para. 100). Three years later, however, the then Chief Inspector, James Hennessy, produced a thematic review of security categorization (Home Office 1984b) calling for much greater conceptual clarity on the issues of security and control which too often clouded the minds of those responsible for categorization and allocation (*ibid.*, paras. 3.2–3.4). He made it plain that, in his view, 'for many of the 2,000 or so category B men in the dispersal system such elaborate precautions are probably not necessary to prevent their escape'; and that there appeared to be 'several thousand category C and D men needlessly held in ordinary category B establishments' (*ibid.*, para. 3.26). He called for the development and use of more low security accommodation because it was not possible to 'justify the expense of keeping prisoners, whose escape would be a nuisance rather than a threat, in a high security category just in case they do try to get away' (*ibid.*, para. 3.5). While the Chief Inspector was aware of the Federal classification system it was left to the Control Review Committee to call for a systematic review of classification systems and their possible applications in this country; and it was, of course, the Control Review Committee (CRC) which first officially called into question the very future of the dispersal system itself.

At the time of the CRC report the dispersal system comprised eight prisons: Albany, Gartree, Hull, Parkhurst, Long Lartin, Wakefield, D Hall at Wormwood Scrubs, and Frankland, of which the last was ostensibly designed specifically for the purpose, together with two special security units at Leicester and Parkhurst. A ninth dispersal prison, Full Sutton, was due to open in 1986. The designs of Frankland and Full Sutton were soon to be stringently criticized by the National Audit Office because they were even more 'manpower intensive' and expensive to run than existing dispersal prisons (National Audit Office 1985, para. 3.9). By then, of course, the CRC had already advocated the reduction in the size of the dispersal system and spoken of its possible replacement by a much smaller high security system based on perhaps two 'new generation' prisons. As a step in this direction, they proposed the removal of Wormwood Scrubs and one other prison (subsequently identified as Hull, which assumed the role of a local prison in February 1986) from the dispersal system.

The CRC recommendations on dispersal were not wholly welcome within the Prisons Board. Although the possible application of new generation designs, like that at Oak Park Heights in Minnesota, was considered a viable alternative to dispersal by the Home Office study of new generation prisons in the USA (Home Office 1985a), the report made no firm recommendation to proceed in that way. In part, it is true, attention simply had to be given to the more pressing need to provide local prison accommodation, but there seems little doubt that the Department used this to cover a retreat from the CRC proposal which was viewed as too radical. By the time of the Cropwood Conference on long term imprisonment, which had been organized in conjunction with the CRC-inspired Research and Advisory Group, Anthony Langdon, principal architect of the CRC report, had left the Prison Service, and other representatives rather pointedly refused to enter the debate over new generation prisons (see, for example, Platt 1987).

All prison systems face a similar dilemma. They are likely to have a changing prison population, but, at any given time, a very fixed stock of prison accommodation. Should they simply categorize prisoners so that they fill up whatever spaces they have got? Or should they use the categorization process as a guide to the future shape and structure of the prison estate? In the absence of clear-cut policy guidelines, such matters are largely pre-empted by the practical decisions made by ordinary prison officers on the ground in the OCA units.

As we have seen, the OCA units do not have a free hand at the highest security level. The category A section in DoC 1 is charged with confirming both the initial category A recommendation, which is made by the local prison governor, and any subsequent changes to category A status after appropriate consultation with the Home Office police advisors' section, which is headed by a Metropolitan Police Commander. The category A section also deals with allocation and transfers of such prisoners so that the dispersal prisons effectively form a national system which, as far as category A prisoners are concerned, operates outside the normal allocation network. But the CRC noted that OCA units had 'not been given consistent advice on the important question of whether or not they should allocate prisoners who present control problems to dispersals' and concluded that 'the decision to allocate a prisoner to one establishment rather than another is a disturbingly arbitrary one' (Home Office 1984a, para. 25).

Outside the maximum security system the Home Office Working Party on Categorization, the Chief Inspector, and the Control Review Committee all gave some attention to the problems of the OCA unit staff in the local prisons, whom they thought were given too little appropriate guidance in carrying out their tasks of security categorization and allocation. They were broadly in agreement that a more stringent evaluation of category B and category C was required, with a view to recategorizing prisoners and allowing them to 'cascade' down into lower security prisons. One obstacle to that, recognized by both the Chief Inspector and the CRC, was that long-term prisoners were able to obtain better privileges in higher security prisons than would be available to them if they were transferred to lower security prisons, so that there was little incentive for them to seek or accept recategorization. A good range of privileges was essential for maintaining good order in the higher security establishments, but there was an urgent need to improve the conditions in lower security prisons if the system was to 'send the right signals' to staff and prisoners, as the CRC put it (Home Office 1984a, para. 26).

At all levels of security OCA unit staff have to make their day-to-day dispositions within the range of facilities available to them. Sometimes the choices available to OCA staff are very restricted indeed. Thus Nottingham was the only category B non-dispersal training prison within the midland region and north region then had no category B non-dispersal prison at all. The present geographical distribution of the penal estate is a product of past decisions, many of which had little to do with current thinking on security or, of course, the current thinking on community prisons. It would be surprising if such arbitrary factors had not influenced the proportion of prisoners placed within categories in different regions, as indeed Morgan (1983) demonstrated. According to Morgan, the midland region had just 7 per cent of its accommodation in category B training prisons (i.e. Nottingham), and 53 per cent in category C prisons: it categorized 12 per cent of its prisoners as needing B level security and 55 per cent as needing category C. In the South East, where 22 per cent of the accommodation was category B, 25 per cent of the prisoners were so categorized: and with only 34 per cent of its accommodation in category C establishments only 39 per cent of its prisoners were categorized in that way. Morgan estimated that if the other three regions classified their prisoners in the same way as midland region did then many millions of pounds could be saved without any additional harm to the prison community or the public.

The Chief Inspector argued that security categorization should be consistent and objective, and should be assessed separately from allocation decisions (Home Office 1984b, para. 3.28). However, the Home Office Working Party had been sceptical about the extent to which 'objective categorization would provide accurate information from which future building needs could be assessed'. Indeed, they suspected that the categorization and allocation procedures 'would always tend towards the filling of vacancies' (Prison Department 1981, para. 15). They were probably right—but to combat such a tendency there is probably everything then to be said for periodic reviews of the whole process.

Security in our Research Prisons

Categorization and Allocation

It is appropriate to begin by saying something of the distribution of prisoners in different security categories in our research prisons, how they came to be allocated there, and what they and the staff thought about that outcome.

Since the population at Birmingham, like that at other local prisons, turned over fairly rapidly there is probably little point in doing more than note that, as might have been expected, it contained prisoners drawn from all parts of the security spectrum. For present purposes what is of more interest is that Birmingham as the main, though not the only, allocating prison from which the four training prisons in our study received their prisoners. It was in the OCA unit there that the security categorization process was carried out. We spent several sessions talking to OCA unit staff and observing the process in action.

In spite of the various strictures by the Working Party, the Chief Inspector, and the CRC, the local order which gave advice to OCA staff in Birmingham referred them to Circular Instructions 49/67, 97/67, 39/74, and 61/76 and reminded them of the Mountbatten criteria as well as the criteria of the establishments to which they intended to allocate a prisoner, '*before you decide on the inmate's category*' (emphasis in the original). Although 'objective' factors—primarily current offence, sentence length, and, to a much lesser extent, previous convictions and escape history—played some part in determining security categorizations, this was on the basis of a 'logical tree', or simple flow chart, rather than any more sophisticated algorithm. We were left in no doubt that the perceptions of staff in the OCA unit, both of the prisoners they dealt with and the prisons to which they could send them, were profoundly influential in both categorization and allocation decisions. In particular OCA staff tended to distinguish between 'good' and 'bad' prisoners and 'good' and 'bad' prisons when making their dispositions. One element of that judgement as to goodness or badness of prisoners had to do with whether they were perceived as control problems. In the categorization process, questions of security were most obviously blurred by considerations of control when the choice was between category B training or category B dispersal; and between those who could be 'trusted' in category D and those who could not, and so were classified as category C. The goodness or badness of prisons was judged partly on their perceived capacity to deal with control problems and the methods they adopted for that purpose. For reasons of convenience, as well as conceptual clarity, we will be dealing with control issues in the next Chapter but it is as well to be aware that the distinction between security and control has little integrity on the ground.

Birmingham OCA staff saw Gartree as a 'bad' dispersal, in contrast to the available alternative at Long Lartin which was seen as 'good', and allocated 'eligible' prisoners accordingly. We shall return to this more specifically when we come to consider questions about 'good order and discipline' in the next Chapter, but in terms of security proper, 45 prisoners in Gartree, or nearly 15 per cent of the population, were in category A—one of the highest concentrations of such prisoners then to be found in the system. Amongst the category A prisoners a distinction was drawn between those receiving 'high risk' visits under close observation—some ten prisoners, virtually all regarded as 'politicals' involved in Irish or Arab organizations of one kind or another—and the remainder who had normal visits along with other prisoners. The great majority of prisoners, over 83 per cent, were in category B and a further 2 per cent—one of the smallest proportions in the dispersal system—were category C prisoners.

Since Nottingham prison was the only category B non-dispersal prison in the region questions of reputation hardly arose in allocation decisions. Even so it was clear that a group of prisoners involved in an incident in Stafford—a category C prison—had been transferred to Nottingham on control rather than security grounds. Exactly two-thirds of the Nottingham population were in category B with almost a third in category C and just under 2 per cent in category D. In addition there was a hostel outside the grounds which, by definition, catered only for category D prisoners.

Featherstone was undoubtedly seen as one of the best category C prisons for the region. As far as allocation from Birmingham was concerned, it received the 'best' of the category C prisoners whilst Stafford received the 'worst'. Featherstone also had a reputation for quickly 'shipping out' to other prisons any prisoners who misbehaved. All of the prisoners in the main prison at Featherstone— including some forty life-sentence prisoners—were category C security, although many staff claimed that the population was getting 'worse' as they received some prisoners, formerly in dispersals, who had been re-categorized. At the same time the governor was under pressure, in the light of the reports by the Working Party and the Chief Inspector, to recategorize prisoners as category D wherever possible and send them on to open prisons. In his annual report he claimed only a very limited scope for implementing this policy, no doubt in part because of the conflicting demand to maintain the level of activity in the extensive workshops. Indeed within Featherstone, but separate from the main prison, there was also a short-term unit populated by category D prisoners who worked on the prison farm, and it was often difficult to keep this up to strength. For most purposes, in this and subsequent Chapters, we have excluded the short-term unit from the analysis unless otherwise stated.

All of the prisoners in Ashwell, including seventeen life sentence prisoners, were in category D. But, whatever the difficulties in recategorizing prisoners for open conditions, there was a feeling amongst some staff at Ashwell that the prison was ceasing to be a 'true' category D prison. It was perhaps inevitable that, when Ashell received the occasional draft of up to twenty prisoners from a category C prison, staff should see them as not 'really' category D prisoners— not in the way that persons originally classified as such in the OCA units were 'real' category Ds. However, it is important to note that the governor reported no change in the number or quality of incidents in the prison that could be regarded as a consequence of the increase in lifers and 'recats' in the Ashwell population.

We asked prisoners whether they regarded their own current security categorization as appropriate. Somewhat to our surprise, not all prisoners were sure of their own security category. However, of those who were aware, only three-fifth (58.7 per cent) accepted that the way they had been categorized reasonably corresponded to the risk they posed to the public, the police, or the state. Not surprisingly, the higher the security category of prisoners—or more strictly the higher the security of the prison they were in, for that was more important in practical terms—the less likely were they to regard their own categorization as reasonable. There are, of course, well-established 'reasons' why some lower security prisoners are held in higher security prisons—principally because governors wish to have some prisoners who can be given greater freedom to do trusted jobs. Nevertheless, almost seven in ten prisoners (69.6 per cent) in Gartree felt they were held in too high security—a direct indication that prisoners understandably see the elaborate security in dispersals as being essentially in place for category A prisoners. Given that Nottingham was a scarce category B training resource for the region, it might have been thought that prisoners would have accepted that their allocation had been very carefully considered. Yet almost half the prisoners in Nottingham (45.5 per cent) felt that they personally did not require that level of security. In Featherstone a third (33.8 per cent) felt themselves to be over-categorized, whilst in Ashwell only three prisoners made such a claim—presumably on grounds that they need not be in prison at all. The differences between the prisons in this respect were highly statistically significant (chi-square 138.04, df = 8, p < 0.0001).

For most prisoners, as far as they were aware, their security category had not changed in the course of their sentence. However, of our respondents about a third claimed to have been recategorized downwards and nearly one in ten recategorized upwards; for two-fifths of them the change of security categorization had not been explained and did not make any sense. Once again the prisoners in the higher security prisons at Gartree and Nottingham were more likely than others not to be able to make sense of security changes—whether those changes had been upwards or downwards.

In order to get a staff perspective on this we asked officers to say what proportion of the population in their prisons should more properly be housed in higher or lower security prisons. Although staff in Nottingham, and especially Featherstone, where there was anxiety about receiving prisoners who had been recategorized, reported that some prisoners should be housed in higher security prisons, overall these data provided some support for the over-categorization view—and from a surprising quarter.

Thus virtually all our staff respondents in Gartree thought that some of the prisoners in their charge could be safely housed in less secure conditions: 64 per cent of officers said that up to a quarter of the population could be recategorized, and 25 per cent thought that up to a half could be at a lower security establishment! In Nottingham nine out of ten officers felt some prisoners could be downgraded: 71 per cent thought this applied to up to a quarter of the population and 18 per cent thought this applied to up to a half. In Featherstone 83 per cent of staff saw scope for transferring up to a quarter of their prisoners to open conditions. In Ashwell over half our respondents thought that some of their prisoners did not need to be in prison at all: 47 per cent applied this to up to a quarter and a further 6 per cent to up to a half their population. We believe these findings to be an important indication that there is still considerable scope for reducing the emphasis on security through the recategorization process.

We asked prisoners whether the level of security in the establishment in which they were housed was generally appropriate, bearing in mind the *other* prisoners it contained. Just over half (51.4 per cent) felt that it was about right, two-fifths (40.0 per cent) thought it too much, and a little under a tenth (8.6 per cent) thought it too little. Nearly two-thirds (63.2 per cent) of the remand prisoners in Birmingham thought the security there was excessive, although in their case this might well be a response to the restrictiveness of their environment, locked up as they were for most of the day, rather than a precise evaluation of security as such. As far as they were concerned, of course, it amounted to much the same thing. Just under half (49.3 per cent) of the prisoners in Gartree thought the security was more than was necessary, although the great majority of prisoners in Nottingham (72.3 per cent) thought the security there about right for others, in spite of the fact that so many thought themselves to be over-categorized. Most surprising here, however, was that two-fifths (40.7 per cent) of those who responded in Featherstone thought the security there was generally greater than necessary. Once again the differences between the prisons were highly statistically significant (chi-square 110.51, df = 10, p < 0.0001).

Physical Security

Given the importance which is nowadays attached to security, what would be most surprising to an outsider visiting our higher security research prisons would probably be the improvisatory nature of the security arrangements. Birmingham and Nottingham had both been built with security in mind, albeit according to standards appropriate in the nineteenth century. Still, both at least had perimeter walls, and the galleries of cells were distributed according to well-tried principles of supervisability. Gartree, however, like Albany (see King and Elliott 1978), had been designed before—and brought into use immediately after—the Mountbatten Report. It opened as a low security prison with a twelve-foot high chain link perimeter fence, which would hardly have kept curious schoolboys out, let alone dangerous prisoners in. The process of turning it into a high security dispersal prison—if Albany was any guide—must have been rather like trying to fashion a saucepan out of a colander.

Gartree had been massively strengthened in order better to fit it for its high security role—although it remained woefully inadequate in terms of design. The perimeter had been developed from its initial state, first to include two high security fences topped with coiled razor ribbon which also filled the dead ground between them, and then by converting the outer fence into a solid wall topped with a smooth black tube complete with an inward overhanging 'beak', rendering it virtually unscaleable. Geophonic devices responded to noise and vibration when approached and signalled warnings to the emergency control room. The ECR also monitored an array of closed-circuit television cameras situated at critical points both inside and outside the prison. A prison dog section provided constant patrol of the perimeter as well as supervision of prisoner movements to workshops, exercise, and so on. Externally the most obvious sign that security was an afterthought, however, was the housing of the security section in Portakabins, themselves enclosed in an inner secure compound.

However, the main defects of Gartree as a high security establishment were in its internal design, with poor visual supervision of cells, landings, recreation and work facilities. In each of the four wings which comprised the main living accommodation, the ground floor contained offices for the wing discipline staff, for what was then still called an assistant governor but by the end of our research had become a governor V, and a probation officer. From the wing office it was possible to have some visual supervision of the corridor, but not of the two television rooms and recreation room or the bath house. Above were three levels, each separated by solid floors approached by a central staircase. On each level were three spurs or 'legs', as they were known in Gartree. Two shorter legs each originally contained 'nests' of nine cells, together with showers and sanitary recesses, and a longer leg had sixteen cells. Staff had always argued that these areas were difficult to supervise and, following the riot in 1978, during which some staff had been trapped on a landing, Gartree operated for many years at half capacity. 'Escape', or more euphemistically 'access', towers were eventually built which effectively reduced one of the short legs in each wing to what was known as a 'dead' leg because cellular accommodation there was effectively lost behind new riot gates. Staffing levels were also increased so that there were always two officers to supervise each landing, which now contained twenty-five cells, and additional staff in the office and supervising the communal areas on the ground floor. Even so it remained necessary to restrict the possible locations where category A prisoners could be housed, in part because of the structural weaknesses of the original construction. All this contrasted quite markedly with modern, so-called 'new generation' high security architecture of the kind to be found in Oak Park Heights, which served a similar function in Minnesota with regard to similar prisoners as Gartree, and with which it was possible to make direct comparisons (see King 1991a).

Although Birmingham had been built to the highest security standards of its day, like Gartree it had undergone substantial changes to bring it up to late twentieth century requirements. Most noticeable was the addition of the category B security 'beak' to the perimeter wall, and the construction of a new gate complex which was completed during our fieldwork. Inside the prison closed-circuit television was used, primarily to overcome the problems of supervising a crowded urban site in which there had been much infill building. A prison dog section was very much in evidence, and seemed the more threatening because of the relatively confined spaces within which it operated.

Nottingham, too, had been a secure enough prison when it was built in the nineteenth century. However, although it now operated as a category B non-dispersal prison, it did so without benefit of either dogs or closed-circuit television. The wall had a category B beak but was not otherwise characterized by the modern paraphernalia of security in any obvious sense. As at Gartree the belated importance of the security section was marked by a recent move from the cramped gatehouse to a Portakabin in the grounds, although here it was not considered necessary to contain it within a secure compound.

Featherstone was still being used essentially for the purpose for which it had been designed: a semi-secure category C prison with a heavy emphasis on prison industries. Whether the cavernous industrial workshops were the most appropriate match for the potential supply of labour was under scrutiny at the time of our research, but this was not a matter to be judged purely in terms of security. What was remarkable about Featherstone was the spaciousness of the site and the relative freedom of movement allowed to prisoners within it. The sight of prisoners responding to the factory whistle by making their way from the housing units to clock in at the workshops along what seemed like miles of walkways was far removed from the controlled movements in Gartree.

Ashwell, during our fieldwork, was in the process of having its original hutted accommodation, left over from its army camp use in the First World War, replaced by housing units with individual 'cubicular' rather than 'cellular' rooms. Quite properly these were designed to category C standards of security to allow the most flexible use of accommodation, though the expectations of the researchers that this was a prelude to the reclassification of Ashwell as a category C prison were not yet shared by the governor or his staff. Our expectations were fulfilled, however, almost as soon as our fieldwork was completed. Ashwell thus became a victim of the reluctance of OCA staff to categorize, or prison governors to recategorize, sufficient prisoners as category D to keep it full. Nevertheless, during our study security was not a major consideration at Ashwell.

Dynamic Security

Time was in English prisons when the chief officer did a daily tour of the prison, rather like a matron inspecting her hospital, to ensure that his officers had checked locks, bolts, and bars. He would occasionally rattle his baton along them to check for himself. Chief Officers still existed at the beginning of this research, but by the end they had been phased out under Fresh Start. The security function was then transferred to the operations area of functional activity.

In recent years it has become fashionable for prison administrators, such as Dunbar (1985), to speak about 'dynamic security'—a concept which invites all staff to regard themselves as integral members of the security team. Security, it is argued, does not just depend upon physical barriers, restrictions on movements, and the conduct of routine procedures such as searching or inspections of locks, bolts, and bars by specialist teams, although all of these have a part to play. All staff, from the governor to clerical assistants, are encouraged to be vigilant, to be aware of the safety of themselves and others, and to make reports wherever appropriate in an effort to maintain a high level of intelligence about what is going on in the prison. In some versions of dynamic security the level and nature of prisoner activities are seen as a vital adjunct to good security and good order, and constitute a new and more systematic establishment attempt to thwart the devil's propensity to provide work for idle hands. In other versions staff are required to maintain the highest professional standards of fairness and integrity in their relationships with prisoners to minimize the likelihood of trouble. We address some of the wider issues about activities in later chapters: here we confine ourselves to consideration of intelligence gathering, searching, and supervision.

Intelligence Gathering

Under a system of dynamic security all prison staff, but especially discipline officers, were expected to contribute to the security intelligence system by making security information reports—or SIRs as they are known. SIRs might relate to almost anything—incidents, unusual behaviours or alliances, snatches of overheard conversations and rumours—which had come to their attention and might have a bearing on the security or the good order and discipline of the establishment. The reports would be sent routinely to the security section, headed by a security principal officer, who had a duty to investigate and take appropriate action. Prisoners also contributed to this process, usually anonymously by 'putting a note in the box' to security when they posted their letters. We have written elsewhere of the process by which good security officers learn to filter information provided in this way and of the part it plays in the official discourse whereby particular prisoners become identified as troublemakers and subversives (King and McDermott 1990a).

Since security officers are likely to know more about the real running of establishments than anyone else, we tended to gravitate towards them in our fieldwork, touching base with them whenever we were in the prisons. We spent more time 'hanging out' with them than with any other group of staff. The importance given to the security section and security intelligence varied considerably from prison to prison.

Not surprisingly, the security department in Gartree was proportionately larger, and had more influence in the general running of the establishment, than was the case in the other prisons. During the period of our research a new computer system was in the process of being installed, one which could handle all the details of the approved visitors for category A prisoners and store and cross-reference all the security information reports, as well as print out sociograms indicating shifting alliances within the prison community. In his annual report the governor referred to 1,291 SIRs, an average of nearly twenty-five a week which was somewhat higher than the twenty-one a week we recorded during our fieldwork. Gartree had by far the highest staff presence on the ground, and when we were with them we were aware that staff were straining to know what was happening over our shoulders and would break off conversations to 'check things out'. And when we were hanging out with prisoners we experienced this from their point of view. On one memorable occasion, early in the fieldwork, one of us was 'grassed up' to security when a prisoner had handed us some of his poetry on evening association. One of the security principal officers was discreetly waiting for us as we left the wing after the prisoners had been 'banged up'. We refused to hand over the papers, except in the presence of the prisoner who gave them to us. Although we were able to assure security that what we had were innocent poems and not coded escape plans we were summoned to a rather difficult meeting with the deputy governor the following day. The officer who had seen the transaction explained subsequently that he had reported us to test us out.

All this contrasted rather dramatically with the situation in Nottingham where the governor found it necessary to send the following governor's order to his staff:

SIRs

I am concerned with the recent drop in SIRs coming over my desk. Up to August 1985 we averaged 20 per month. Since August our average has been 5 per month. The management team and more specifically the Security Department depend on your eyes and your ears, and on your willingness to keep us advised on the things you see and hear which concern you from a security stand point. The way to do this is by completing an SIR and passing it direct to the Security PO. We need your co-operation in this matter.

In Featherstone there was a small, but effective, security presence, and the governor was able to report a reduction of escapes from seven in the year before our research to just one in the current year, in spite of a number of weaknesses in physical security which gave him continuing cause for concern. In Ashwell, the numbers of absconds had increased, indeed almost doubled from forty to seventy, including two life-sentence prisoners, but it was not possible for the governor to discern any particular pattern. The security demands in Birmingham were, of course, of a totally different order from those in the training prisons. There had been no escapes, but there was serious concern about the numbers of category A prisoners it was required to hold and the problems this caused when its most secure accommodation on D wing was full. Security officers spent as much time liaising with the police forces outside as they did with trying to keep on top of the situation inside. They felt themselves to be severely stretched in terms of resources which were simply not up to the scope of the task, especially in relation to matters such as searching.

Searching

Perhaps the most intrusive security procedures from the point of view of prisoners are cell searches ('spins') and body searches ('strips'). They are also the most problematic to organize and monitor from the point of view of security staff, even though, like most aspects of life in prisons, they are governed by bureaucratic rules. In England and Wales those rules generally require cell searches to take place in the presence of prisoners. According to staff problems arise on several grounds. First, they claim, there are simply not enough of them and not enough time in the day actually to carry out searches with the frequency required by the rules. Secondly, staff are aware that cell searches do not produce results but that more effective methods simply do not figure in the rules. We were told, for example, in Gartree, that it was not physically possible to search all cells with the frequency which dispersal regulations required, given the available staff and the length of time it took to do a proper job. Conversely, security staff were apt to claim that they had their hands tied in their attempts to control drugs by a policy which precluded them from selecting prisoners during evening association—a time when we were frequently offered 'deals' by prisoners once our presence on the wings was accepted—and subjecting them to body searches. But those same staff were well aware, as were all seasoned prisoners, that such matters needed to be handled with extreme caution and sensitivity if they were not to become an occasion for confrontation. And, wisely, nobody wanted confrontation on evening association in a dispersal prison if they could help it.

We have discussed elsewhere (McDermott and King 1988) how, in the circumstances in which the bureaucratic rules cannot actually be implemented, staff and prisoners go through the motions in a kind of symbolic game of 'hide and seek'. Although every prison security section displays its captured weapons, escape materials, and so on, such finds are rare and almost never occur as a result of routine searching operations. Prisoners told us that serious contraband is not hidden in cells, and certainly not their own cells. Such finds, when they do occur, happen as a result of tip-offs or sometimes following assiduous intelligence targeting. Even so, to judge from the data we report in Chapter 4, all of the governors in our research prisons took much more comfort in their annual reports than they probably should have from the relative absence of drug finds and the rare discovery of a syringe.

Cell-searching is bound to be a delicate matter. For the prisoner the cell is, for want of a better word, his home. In Birmingham he usually had to share it with other prisoners, already a considerable invasion of privacy. Such possessions as a prisoner is able to accumulate become peculiarly precious in prison, especially those personal items and photographs that provide a link with a real home outside. From his point of view the presence of a prison officer is an unwarrantable intrusion, and no members of staff are regarded with more contempt than searching officers, who in the ultimate role reversal are known as 'burglars'. It would be surprising in these circumstances if there were not some process of accommodation at work. Staff and prisoners typically manage routine searching situations with an elaborate regard for ritual which serves to minimize the scope for confrontation. There is often a tacit understanding that whilst the very act of searching reasserts the official view that no part of the prison can be regarded as purely private territory, the rules governing possessions, cell decorations, and so on will not necessarily be enforced to the letter.

This is not to say that cell searches and body searches are *always* well managed because clearly that is not the case. We heard many stories of abuse where property was said to have been deliberately destroyed and photographs torn or defaced during cell searches. We had no way of verifying these stories, although it was our impression that such incidents were much more likely to occur in the aftermath of trouble, during lockdowns and the like, than during routine searches.

We asked all prisoners about the frequency with which their cells had been searched over the last three months, or the time they had been in this prison if that was shorter. The results are given in Table 2.1.

It will come as no surprise that over half the prisoners in Gartree claimed to have had their cells searched at least as frequently as once a fortnight Indeed in Gartree only one of our respondents indicated that his cell had been searched less frequently than once a month.

Table 2.1. Prisoner-reported frequency of cell search: Percentage distribution

	Birmingham Rem. (n = 197)	Birmingham Conv. (n = 191)	Gartree (n = 142)	Nottingham (n = 143)	Featherstone (n = 245)	Ashwell (n = 157)
Weekly	17.8	13.6	4.9	0.0	2.0	1.9
Fortnightly	8.1	6.8	49.3	2.1	5.3	2.5
Monthly	10.2	14.7	45.1	4.9	10.2	5.1
Less	23.4	23.6	0.7	52.4	60.8	15.9
Not at all	40.6	41.4	0.0	40.6	21.6	74.5
	100.0	100.0	100.0	100.0	100.0	100.0

Note: Columns do not always add up to 100 because of rounding.
Chi-square 689.99, Df = 20, p<0.0001

This was consistent with what we were told by security staff who recognized that, while it was not possible to search every cell on the required fortnightly basis, they tried to ensure that every cell was turned over at least once a month; and that they found it more effective to target those prisoners whom they suspected of subversive or illicit activities for repeated, but irregularly spaced, spins rather than stick to a predictable routine. Nevertheless, the frequency of cell-searching in Gartree was very much lower than in Oak Park Heights, Minnesota, where 51 per cent of prisoners claimed that their cells were searched on a weekly basis. The design of Oak Park Heights, and the presence of fixed cell furniture, of course, made cell searching there a much easier task. In Birmingham, with much the largest and most mixed population, the frequency of cell searching varied widely. Even more markedly than at Gartree, security staff seemed to make their assessments about risks, and to target prisoners accordingly: about two-fifths of both remand and convicted prisoners were not on the receiving end of cell searches at all, but at the other extreme about one in six remand prisoners and one in seven convicted prisoners claimed to have had their cells searched at least once a week—much the highest proportions in any of our prisons.

What is most surprising, however, from a reading of Table 2.1 is the apparent reversal of position of Nottingham, the category B prison, and Featherstone, the category C prison. We were told, officially, that the main reason searching was not done more frequently in Nottingham was lack of manpower. However, we were well aware that lack of manpower was the official explanation for virtually all the ills of the service at that time, and as we have shown elsewhere (King and McDermott 1989) Featherstone actually had a somewhat worse staff ratio than Nottingham. It is intriguing, therefore, that searching was given a relatively lower priority in Nottingham than Featherstone, for this was just one of the many ways in which the ethos or climate of these establishments differed.

Staff in Nottingham repeatedly told us of its traditional reputation as a 'happy prison'. Certainly from a researcher's point of view it was the friendliest and easiest within which to work. Because of its cramped physical layout, there seemed to be an enforced closeness of relations between staff and prisoners. Moreover, a very high proportion of staff had been in the prison for many years and saw themselves as carriers of its culture (even though many saw it as having been even happier in the past). Certainly staff did not seem to feel that they had a need either to prove themselves through a show of force, or to protect themselves behind an insistence on bureaucratic procedures, particularly when something like searching was a relatively fruitless activity. This is not to say that security was as lax as it was sometimes made out to be: close relations, it was argued, meant that staff were better able to take the pulse of the establishment. There were, in fact, numerous petty incidents in Nottingham that were allowed to bubble up in the expectation that they would quickly deflate again. Staff claimed that they graduated their response to their sense of the tension within the prison. Often this laid-back attitude was extremely effective. Sometimes, however, it had the consequence of triggering heightened tensions especially when a decision was made to take action in a situation where none had previously been deemed necessary.

Featherstone, on the other hand, was larger and more spread out, and staff were conscious of its reputation as a jewel in the region's crown. The then regional director had been the governor of Featherstone when it was first commissioned and was still felt to be keeping a personal eye on its progress. Searching, like other activities, was judged not so much in terms of its effectiveness but as just one among many standards which had to be maintained.

If cell-searching was a delicate matter, body-searching could impose even greater strains and produce no better results. During body searches both staff and prisoners normally sought to disassociate themselves from the activity as far as possible—rather in the manner in which physical examinations take place within the context of the doctor–patient relationship. In the nature of things, given the actual context of prison, this was not always possible to sustain and we heard stories of lack of respect and sometimes abuse including violence, which were neither possible to verify nor completely to discount.

The frequency of strip-searching is given in Table 2.2.

As can be seen from Table 2.2 the pattern of strip-searching follows the security gradient as far as the training prisons are concerned: with virtually all (96.7 per cent) prisoners in Gartree receiving a strip search at least once a month, almost a half (48.6 per cent) in Nottingham, nearly a fifth (18.7 per cent) in Featherstone, and just under a tenth (8.5 per cent) in Ashwell. Although strip-searching was frequent in Gartree it was nothing like so frequent as in Oak Park Heights where 43.4 per cent claimed to have been strip-searched weekly (see King 1991a).

Table 2.2. Prisoner-reported frequency of strip-searches: Percentage distribution

	Birmingham Rem. (n = 182)	Birmingham Conv. (n = 164)	Gartree (n = 151)	Nottingham (n = 138)	Featherstone (n = 237)	Ashwell (n = 153)
Weekly	9.3	6.1	3.3	0.0	3.0	0.0
Fortnightly	6.6	6.7	59.6	31.2	3.0	1.3
Monthly	7.7	7.3	33.8	17.4	12.7	7.2
Less	15.9	12.8	1.3	17.4	48.9	19.0
Not at all	60.4	67.1	2.0	34.1	32.5	72.5
	100.0	100.0	100.0	100.0	100.0	100.0

Note: Columns do not always add up to 100 because of rounding.
Chi-square 599.94, Df = 20, p<0.0001

It is less easy to interpret these data, however, because at least three policy elements were at work to produce these results, and we did not ask our prisoner respondents to distinguish the circumstances under which they had been searched. The biggest influence on these figures certainly concerns the policy in relation to the searching of prisoners after visits, the outcome of which is obviously in turn mediated by the frequency of visits themselves. Local orders in Gartree, for example, required that all prisoners were strip-searched by two officers immediately after visits (including prisoners who had been visited by clergymen, legal advisers, police, and probation officers unless there had been only such 'official' visits going on in the visiting room at that time). These considerations were also deemed important with the predominantly category B population at Nottingham but scarcely figured at all in the lower security prisons. Alongside the visits policy, however, there were also two other considerations: routine random strip searches, and target strip searches which were instituted when security officers felt there was good cause. Although we have anecdotal evidence to suggest that these were much more likely to occur, not surprisingly, in Gartree and Birmingham than in the other training prisons we are not in a position to quantify that. At this level, though, we once again formed the impression that random and target strip-searching was less frequent, and certainly no more frequent, in Nottingham than in Featherstone. In Ashwell about three-quarters of the population had experienced neither cell searches nor strip searches since they had been there.

Closeness of Supervision and Restriction of Movement

We asked prisoners to rate how closely they were supervised within the main areas of the prison to which they had access, and how closely their movements between those areas were restricted and controlled. They were invited to categorize both supervision and restriction of movement on a four point scale: very close, quite close, not very close, or not at all close. Each response was given a weighted score from +2 for very close to −2 for not at all close. The differences between the prisons are highly statistically significant (supervision: chi-square 226.57, df = 15, p<0.0001 and movement: chi-square 676.08, df = 15 p<0.0001) and the results are presented graphically in Figure 2.1.

It can be seen from Figure 2.1 that restriction of movement and closeness of supervision are closely related in prisoners' perceptions.

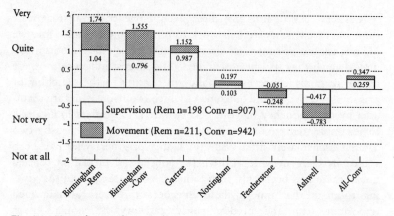

Fig. 2.1   How close is the supervision and how restricted are movements in this prison?—Prisoner perceptions

It appears that the perceived level of supervision operates within boundaries set by the degree of restriction of movement experienced. Two things stand out from an examination of Figure 2.1. The first is that there is comparatively little difference between the levels of restriction and supervision perceived by either remand or convicted prisoners in Birmingham on the one hand, and dispersal prisoners in Gartree on the other. In spite of this the nature of the restriction and the supervision is qualitatively different. In Birmingham, where prisoners spend so much of their day locked in cells and are rarely out of sight or hearing of officers when they are out of cells, both the level of restriction and supervision are self evident. In Gartree it was certainly possible for prisoners to get some distance from the staff, most particularly in the television room and the games room, and to some extent hide in their own or other prisoners' cells. But movement off the wing was grossly curtailed and always accompanied by staff and dog patrols. And, as we have already indicated, the staff presence on the ground in Gartree was far greater than in any other prison, and staff were always straining to hear what was going on. This, combined with the watchful eye of the closed circuit television cameras, offered a high degree of surveillance.

The second is that the four training prisons regularly follow the security gradient. This might not be surprising were it not for the history of the dispersal system with its original rhetoric of providing a relaxed regime within a secure perimeter. In the early days of the system there is no doubt that a serious attempt was made to implement such a concept (see King and Elliott 1978). The present results confirm the extent to which it has been eroded.

In Birmingham as well as Gartree prisoners' perceptions of the closeness of supervision and the restrictions on movement would have been partly conditioned by their awareness of the presence of CCTV cameras and Alsatian dogs. In fact nearly all prisoners will have had some experience of them, even if only briefly, by virtue of having started their prison careers in local prisons. We therefore asked in all prisons whether prisoners found the presence of cameras and dogs unduly obtrusive, or whether they no longer noticed them. We also gave them the opportunity to indicate whether they preferred these proxies to the actual supervision of real staff. Overall only a small minority preferred either CCTV (13.8 per cent) or dogs (11.6 per cent) to staff presence. The remainder were more or less equally split between those who found them obtrusive and those who had go so used to them that they hardly noticed them. Intriguingly, though, in both cases, prisoners in Nottingham, Featherstone, and Ashwell—who were now furthest away from such measures—were more likely to regard these security aids as unduly obtrusive than were prisoners in Gartree and Birmingham—who daily had to cope with their presence (CCTV $p < 0.05$; dogs $p < 0.0001$).

Throughout this chapter we have found that the security measures already in place, and the staff and prisoner perceptions of them, broadly follow the security hierarchy of the training prisons, with Birmingham coming closest to Gartree. In most respects it would have been rather astonishing had it been otherwise—indicating that something was radically wrong with the whole security categorization process. But the security gradient has not been found on all our measures, and on some variables Nottingham and Featherstone have, as it were, changed places, the perceived reality of their security procedures and practices belying their status in security category terms. When we discussed these matters with both staff and prisoners, we found that one way in which they tended to differentiate prisons was according to a generalized notion of 'tightness' in security terms. In an attempt to get an overall perception of the security of our prisons we asked staff and prisoners to rate their own prison according to how tight a prison it was. The results are presented in Figure 2.2.

What emerges from Figure 2.2 (staff: chi-square 48.75401 p,.0001; prisoners: chi-square 497.43735 p<.0001), is that prisoners rate

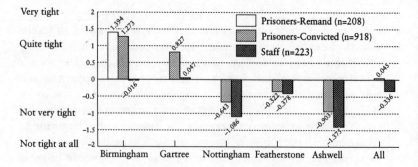

Fig. 2.2   How tight is the security in this prison:—Prisoner and staff perceptions

Featherstone as more security-conscious than Nottingham. Even more strikingly, this was a view that was shared by staff. It is noticeable that hardly any staff in Gartree and none in Birmingham were prepared to say that their prison was very tight in spite of all evidence to the contrary. We were not allowed to ask staff in Birmingham a supplementary question on whether they felt any of their security excessive,[6] although on this evidence it is unlikely that any would have said yes. Indeed only about one in ten staff in Gartree, Featherstone, and Ashwell thought the security excessive, having in mind to the prisoners they housed, and none thought so in Nottingham. About half the staff in each of the training prisons were able to claim that some additional security measures could be provided. Again, we were not allowed to ask this in Birmingham. With what turned out to be impressive prescience, chief among the suggestions for heightened security in Gartree was the installation of wires across the exercise yards to foil helicopter escape attempts.

The Depth and Weight of Imprisonment

Some years ago, in the course of his impressive and pioneering comparison of post-war penal policies in The Netherlands and England and Wales, David Downes (1988) introduced the concept of the *depth of imprisonment*. The length of prison sentences, of course,

[6] Only in Birmingham were we prevented from asking any of the questions we wished to ask. On this occasion a POA representative with whom we were negotiating part of the field work programmes objected to two questions relating to security. The governor ruled that it would be improper to ask them.

had long been a dimension along which criminal justice systems might be compared, but Downes pointed out that 'in a variety of ways, some gross, some nuanced, prison in The Netherlands is experienced as a far less damaging and repressive phenomenon than in Britain'. He characterized this in terms of the relative depth of imprisonment: the extent to which the psychological invasion by the prison was experienced as damaging. It was expressed through 'relations with staff; relations with prisoners; rights and privileges; material standards and conditions; and a sense of the overall quality of life which the prison regime made possible or withheld' (Downes 1988, 166).

Intriguingly, security as such does not figure in Downes' list of the various modalities of the depth of imprisonment—yet it was perhaps in this regard that our prisoners were most likely to use the notion of depth to capture some of the meaning of imprisonment for them. Thus, although prisoners characterized the nature of their prison's security in terms of its 'tightness' they saw their relationship to the system to some extent in terms of 'how deep they were in'. Prisoners in Gartree, and indeed in Oak Park Heights, knew very well indeed that they were in 'deep end custody'; and some of our prisoners, especially those who were serving life sentences from which they probably correctly believed they would not be released for a very long time, if at all, spoke of themselves as being 'in deep'. So, too, did some prisoners who were repeatedly subject to control measures under procedures designed to promote or restore 'good order and discipline'.[7] In their cases they sometimes talked about being 'buried deep'. Although the notion of deep end custody implies there is also a shallow end, prisoners in the lower security prisons were less likely to use that imagery—or if they did we were less responsive to it. However, it was certainly the case that prisoners who were apparently over-categorized felt themselves, and were described by others, to be 'out of their depth' or 'in over their heads'.

With regard to other aspects of imprisonment, including most of those which Downes describes, the imagery used by prisoners related not so much to *depth* as to *weight*. They spoke of these matters as a 'weight on their shoulders', which they found 'heavy and oppressive', and which often 'bore down on them' to the point where there seemed 'little point in getting up in the morning', and sometimes

[7] Rule 43 (GOAD) and CI 10/74 and 37/90 e.g. (see King and McDermott 1990a; and Ch. 3 below).

even to where they felt they could 'no longer cope'. Although several of our prisoners used stereotyped similes involving 'millstones around the neck', and there was the one literary reference to an 'albatross', some old hands recognized the symbolic connection between their current burdens and the convict's traditional ball and chain.

It seems to us worthwhile, therefore, to reserve the use of Downes' concept of the depth of imprisonment for the extent to which a prisoner is embedded into the security and control systems of imprisonment, and to use the concept of the weight of imprisonment to depict the degree to which relationships, rights and privileges, standards and conditions serve to bear down on them. It seems theoretically possible not only that these dimensions of depth and weight may vary independently of one another, but that each is multi-faceted with scope for those 'sometimes gross, sometimes nuanced' variations in their impact to which Downes referred. Much of the rest of this volume is about measuring those variations within English prisons. It is, of course, always dangerous to engage in *ex post facto* interpretations. Nevertheless, if we conceptualize matters in this way it becomes possible to make better sense of the sometimes apparently anomalous switching of positions of Nottingham and Featherstone in our study. Although Nottingham prisoners were 'deeper in', it was sometimes, and in some respects, possible for them to carry the burden more lightly.

Recent Developments on Security Categorization and the Dispersal System

There is comparatively little to be said in relation to subsequent security developments in our research prisons—apart from the obvious changes in security level at Gartree and Ashwell—for the very good reason that neither the annual reports of governors nor the reports of HM Chief Inspector of Prisons are inclined to go into much detail on such matters. For what it is worth, however, the new style annual reports and accounts of the Prison Service publish the numbers of escapes and 'absconds' on a prison-by-prison basis to make more transparent institutional performance in relation to this indicator. In 1992–3 there were no escapes from either Gartree or Ashwell; Nottingham had three escapes from escorts and two absconds; Birmingham had one escape from the establishment, two escapes from escorts, and two absconds; and Featherstone had three escapes from the institution, one escape from escort, and eleven absconds (Prison Service 1993g). Overall the service managed to reduce the number of escapes from 473 or 1.04 per cent of the population in 1991–2 to 389 or 0.89 per cent in 1992–3, but the number of absconds continued to rise, from 1,731 to 1,951.

Nor is there any basis for comparison with our data on the perceptions of staff and prisoners about security matters: the National Prison Survey, which was in any case confined to prisoners, apparently asked no similar questions to ours on security issues.

There have, however, been important developments in relation to processes of categorization and the dispersal system to which we must refer.

The Working Party on Categorization, the Chief Inspector, and the Control Review Committee were all very critical of the lack of effective supervision exercised by regional offices over security categorization procedures. Now that the regional structure has been abandoned, the kinds of arbitrary variations in security categorizations shown by Morgan (1983) will be less easy to detect. There is, however, no reason to suppose that they have gone away. Nevertheless, the systematic review of classification which the CRC called for was duly carried out, and it led to a new Circular Instruction (CI 7/88) which, it is claimed, 'has resulted in a net shift of the prison population towards lower security conditions of custody' (Prison Service 1991b, para. 26). We shall review that claim shortly, but arguably much of the debate over categorization in recent years has focused upon its use in relation to remand prisoners.

As we noted earlier, remand prisoners had not been security categorized unless there were grounds for considering them as potential category A prisoners. Woolf LJ was critical of this practice on grounds that it meant too many remand prisoners were housed in conditions of security greater than they needed. He recommended that a more flexible stance be adopted, with the presumption that remand prisoners should normally be in category C, thus allowing them to be held at lower security community prisons unless there was evidence that they constituted a greater risk (Home Office 1991a, para. 12.313). However, although the Government accepted the idea that remand prisoners be security categorized, it was disparaging about Woolf's suggestion that many of them could be housed safely in category C establishments (Home Office 1991b, paras. 5.20–1; and see Morgan 1994). By the time the White Paper, *Custody, Care, and Justice*, appeared, of course, McAuley and Quinlivan had escaped from Brixton. In their subsequent security audit, Hadfield and Lakes reported that, although the sub-classifications of category A into exceptional, high, and standard risks introduced after the Gartree helicopter escape were being used for sentenced prisoners, no unconvicted category A prisoner was classified as exceptional risk, whatever the nature and circumstances of the charge, apparently as a matter of policy. They recommended that, where reliable intelligence indicated a prisoner to be of exceptional risk, he should be so classified and exceptional precautions taken, even if this meant housing them with convicted prisoners, or in a less convenient prison (Hadfield and Lakes 1991, paras. 59–60).

Intriguingly, Hadfield and Lakes also found that standard-risk category A had come to be used in a way that clearly had never been envisaged by Mountbatten. They argued that the introduction of the three sub-classifications to category A in the dispersal prisons had exposed anomalies in the way such prisoners were perceived and dealt with by staff. In particular, Hadfield and Lakes (1991, para. 53) noted that only the exceptional risk prisoners really corresponded to Mountbatten's original definition of dangerous prisoners who are also highly motivated to escape. Prison staff, they said, could see very little difference from a security point of view between standard-risk prisoners, who were placed in category A *solely on the basis of their offence and without reference to escape-related criteria*, and more run-of-the-mill category B prisoners (*ibid.*, para. 54). Having a large proportion of such prisoners—approximately 75 per cent, according to Hadfield and Lakes, among the then 591 confirmed category A population in dispersals—was actually a potential threat to security, for it devalued the significance of category A status and simply swallowed up resources. Accordingly they recommended that such prisoners be redesignated as category B if they did not genuinely warrant a higher risk status (*ibid.*, paras. 53–8). This was an argument and a recommendation very similar to those elaborated by King (1979) to the May Committee and by King and Morgan (1980), except that Hadfield and Lakes continued to identify such category B prisoners as 'needing' at least the level of perimeter security afforded by dispersal prisons, if not the additional paraphernalia associated with category A status, whereas King and Morgan would have been content for such prisoners to be transferred to category B training prisons.

How far can the claim that CI 7/88 had resulted in a net shift of the population towards lower security conditions of custody be justified? Certainly the proportion of adult male prisoners held in category C prisons increased considerably, from 22.1 per cent in 1985–6 to 31 per cent in 1991–2, dropping back slightly to 30.5 per cent in 1992–3. Over the same period there was a much more marginal increase in category D from 8.6 per cent to 9.5 per cent, but this fell back sharply in 1992–3 to 7.8 per cent. However, these changes seem to have happened largely as a result of transfer of prisoners from the local prisons into the various new prisons which have come on stream, as well as changes of use in some prisons, rather than from a reduction in prisoners initially placed in category B, or the recategorization of prisoners held in category B dispersal and non-dispersal prisons, for the proportion of prisoners held in those conditions has also increased slightly from 15.7 per cent in 1985–6 to 16.7 per cent in 1992–3. The growth in non-dispersal category B population from 8.0 per cent in 1985–6 to 10.1 per cent in 1992–3 has more than offset the proportionate fall in dispersal use from 7.7 per cent to 6.6 per cent. The proportion of the population held in local prisons dropped from 53.7 per cent in 1985–6 to 43.8 per cent in 1991–2 only to rise fractionally in 1992–3 to 45 per cent. The switch from local prisons to category C prisons is, of course, very welcome from a security point of view, providing it does not cut across Woolf's desire for community prisons and the fifth goal of the service of helping prisoners to return to the community. There is a further worrying sign which has to some degree offset the benefit of any downward drift in categorization: the category D prisons and category C prisons have themselves become more secure. One of the few things on security matters to be gleaned from reading the later reports of prison governors was that in 1991–2 it was proposed to add Danet wire to the perimeter fence at Featherstone. Although, as we noted at the beginning of this chapter, the discussion in the Prison Service's *Corporate Plan 1993–96* indicated that it was important to keep escapes in perspective and that the priorities related to category A prisoners and category B prisons, there were references to the reinforcement of perimeter fences with sheet cladding and anti-climbing devices at category C prisons (Prison Service 1993d, para. 5.4). The updated *Corporate Plan 1994–97* takes this a stage further, and indicates that plans for the future will focus on the criminally sophisticated prisoners prepared to plan and effect escapes who are now said to inhabit category C prisons (Prison Service 1994b, para. 4.3). This was precisely the kind of development which we feared and about which we warned in our paper some years ago on the ever-deepening crisis in the prison system (King and McDermott 1989, 127).

Like the Control Review Committee before him, Woolf LJ visited Oak Park Heights in Minnesota and, like the CRC, he considered that it had considerable advantages over the dispersal system (Home Office 1991a, para. 12.299). Woolf recommended that one new generation prison be built to maximum security standards and be earmarked for the dispersal system. If it was successful it should be possible, he thought, to reduce the number of dispersal prisons (*ibid.*, paras. 12.303 and 12.305). In 1989 the Prison Service had reiterated the CRC claim that 'prisons capable of holding category A prisoners are very expensive in terms of both capital and running costs' and announced that plans for the future 'size of the dispersal system provide for six maximum security prisons each holding a higher proportion of category A prisoners' (Home Office 1989b, para. 21). This, at last, introduced a greater measure of concentration because category A prisoners who had originally constituted only about 10 per cent of the population in most dispersals might henceforth form up to 20 per cent in some of these prisons. By the mid-1990s the dispersal system was to comprise Frankland, Full Sutton, Long Lartin, Parkhurst, Wakefield, and Whitemoor (which had originally been in the building programme as a category B non-dispersal prison and Woolf mistakenly believed this was earmarked to play the role of a new generation prison within the dispersal system). In the event, Wormwood Scrubs did not leave the dispersal system until 1989, because it took Full Sutton which opened in October 1987, nearly two years to build up to full dispersal operation. Gartree ceased to be a dispersal prison in April 1992 to be followed by Albany in October of that year. Whitemoore opened in October 1991 and received its first category A prisoners in April 1992. At the time of writing the Special Security Unit for category A prisoners at Parkhurst is being refurbished, while the one at Leicester is being used for other purposes. Their functions have been taken over by the SSUs at Full Sutton and Whitemoor. At Belmarsh there is a further and somewhat larger special unit for category A prisoners.

This fell a long way short both of the CRCs proposals and its time-scale for change. However, the number of dispersal prisons has been reduced from what had at one time been a proposed nine to six; and although the numbers and proportion of adult male prisoners held in high security remained much the same at around 2,800 or just over 7.5 per cent from 1985–6 to 1991–2, in 1992–3 the numbers fell to about 2,400 or around 6.5 per cent of adult males in custody. This does seem to signal that an effective cap may at last have been placed on the size of the dispersal system.

The last word has not yet been heard on the policy of dispersal. It was noted in Chapter 1 that, when the May Committee rejected the arguments put forward by King and Morgan for a return to a policy of concentration, they did so because they could not recommend a change *in present operational conditions*. This was interpreted at the time by King and Morgan (1980) to have meant that one of the principal stumbling blocks to a more parsimonious solution to the security problem was the propaganda advantage that would be handed to terrorist groups if they were to mount a successful attack on the one or two high-security prisons where their personnel were known to be housed. Having begun this chapter with a discussion of the successful helicopter escape from Gartree, it is necessary to end it with a brief consideration of the implications of the unsuccessful attempt by five IRA prisoners to escape from Whitemoor.

It is scarcely surprising, given the emphasis in the *Corporate Plan* on the prevention of category A escapes, that the Whitemoor incident provoked widespread publicity and a certain fluttering in the dovecotes at Cleland House. As we noted in Chapter 1, it is possible that Sir John Woodcock's report will lead to the introduction of new restrictions which could seriously undermine the balance between security, control, and justice which Woolf did so much to nurture. It is to be hoped this will not happen—after all the escape attempt *was unsuccessful*, and the Semtex *was discovered*.

However, as we have argued elsewhere (King 1994c; Borland, King, and McDermott 1995), the events at Whitemoor are important for two quite different reasons. First, it shows the security weakness of the design of Whitemoor where, once the prisoners were over the fence of the SSU, every step they took carried them closer to the perimeter wall. By contrast, in an earth-sheltered 'new generation' facility, such as Oak Park Heights in Minnesota—a design favoured both by the CRC and Woolf and shown to be capable of providing safety, security and positive regimes (see King 1991a and Chapter 3) —prisoners escaping from the living units are likely to find their only means of egress draws them inexorably deeper into the interior of the prison. Secondly, the real significance of the Whitemoor escape bid was not so much the security lapse itself but the context in which it took place—namely the peace process in Northern Ireland. In the wake of the Downing Street Declaration of 15 December 1993 we have seen the IRA cease-fire matched by one from the 'loyalist' para-militaries, and there is a real prospect of at least talks about talks before the end of 1994. Any solution to 'the troubles' will lead to a drying up of the supply of terrorist prisoners. After a short but decent interval existing terrorist prisoners will be first transferred to Northern Ireland and then quietly paroled, leaving a high security prison population with a quite different character. The way will then be open for a drastic reduction in the size of the system required.

Postscript

Our manuscript was completed in May 1994. During copy-editing, in November 1994, it was necessary to refer to the Whitemoor escape attempt. By proofs, in January 1995, the Woodcock Report had appeared and the morale of the service had been further damaged by the (also unsuccessful) escape attempt from Parkhurst, and the summary removal of its governor to other duties. Woodcock, as expected, looked at security through a close-up rather than a wide-angle lens. On 20 December 1994 a special conference of governors was addressed by Derek Lewis and his colleagues on Prisons Board. In a notable kite-flying exercise Philippa Drew, by then apparently moved to Director of Inmate Programmes, was reported as saying that the Woodcock inquiry had been 'a missed opportunity' and that it might now be possible to re-think high security custody, perhaps using Oak Park Heights as a model (*The Guardian* 21 December 1994). Sir John Learmont's inquiry into security, announced by Michael Howard a week earlier, presumably has such possibilities under review. It was also reported, however, that the Home Secretary is to be advised by an expert from the United States Federal Bureau of Prisons. In the present climate the crucial question is whether that advice will follow the best American practice, as at Oak Park Heights, or the current American fashion for overly restrictive, 23 hour lock down, 'super max' facilities such as Pelican Bay in California or McAlester in Oklahoma. Such units are mushrooming throughout the United States, including, apparently, the Federal replacement for Marion within the huge prison complex at Florence in Colorado.

3

Maintaining Order, Control, Discipline, and Safety

The second goal of the Prison Service is *to maintain order, control, discipline, and a safe environment* (Prison Service 1993c). The key performance indicator, against which success in achieving that goal will be measured, is *the number of assaults on staff, prisoners, and others* (Key Performance Indicator 2). The *Business Plan* specifies this more closely in terms of a target, over the period 1993–6, to reverse the rising trend of these assaults expressed as a percentage of the average prison population (Prison Service 1993e, 5). In 1989–90 this measure produced an 'assault rate' of 7.7 per cent, in 1990–1 it rose to 8.6 per cent, and in 1991–2 to 9.4 per cent. Shortly before the end of the reporting period the *Business Plan* noted that already 1992–3 looked like exceeding 10 per cent and this was confirmed at 10.2 per cent in the annual report published in November 1993 (Prison Service 1993g, para. 40). No specific target was set for the year 1993–4 on the basis that the increase would continue in the short term: that expectation was also confirmed with an increase over 1992–3 of 21 per cent to 12.3 per cent (Prison Service 1994c). Assaults on staff increased by 27 per cent to 3,192, and assaults on prisoners increased by 15 per cent to 2,437.[1]

It is not immediately obvious why a single measure such as numbers of assaults should have been chosen as the key performance indicator. Of course, assaults can be frightening and may sometimes result in serious injury, but in our experience they cover a very wide range of behaviours. Moreover, those behaviours are likely to be regarded, reported, and recorded differently in different establishments. The

---

[1] When this ch. was drafted, the statistics for 1993–4 had not been published. The Prison Service kindly provided an Annex to a Prisons Board document giving the outturn against key performance targets. When the results were published a few weeks later, there were some significant differences which are referred to in the text. The figures on assaults, however, were not affected.

Business Plan acknowledges these problems and points to the need to support these statistics by other indicators, such as surveys of the extent to which staff and prisoners feel safe. We surveyed both staff and prisoners in the research prisons, and talked to many of our respondents about such matters at great length. Some of our data reported below will presumably be of a kind that the Prisons Board has in mind. The national prison survey (Walmsley *et al.* 1992) has also produced materials on these matters, albeit only with regard to prisoners, with which our data may to some extent be compared.

This chapter falls into two main parts. In the first we consider the formal procedures for maintaining good order and discipline within prisons and the changes which have been introduced since our research, largely as a result of the Woolf Inquiry. We also present briefly some of our data on these matters where they remain relevant to current discussions. In the second part we consider the general question of safety in prisons. After reviewing aspects of the public record and our more private field notes on these issues, especially in relation to Gartree and Birmingham, we then present our data on the perceptions of staff and prisoners on safety issues in our research prisons. Where possible we make direct comparisons with published data from the national prison survey in this country and we also make previously unpublished comparisons with the new generation prison at Oak Park Heights in Minnesota. In a brief concluding section we return to consider the approach to maintaining order in the post-Woolf context.

Procedures for Maintaining Good Order and Discipline

Traditionally the prison system relied on a panoply of measures to maintain good order and discipline in its establishments which were directly targeted on miscreant prisoners. Those who could be demonstrated, under the not-very-exacting standards of prison disciplinary hearings held either before the governor or his nominated deputy, to have infringed one or another of the many subsections of Prison Rule 47 could be punished with one or more 'awards' available to the governor under Rule 50. Where graver offences—escaping or attempting to do so, assaulting an officer, or doing gross personal violence to anyone else—were involved, or where the punishments available to the governor seemed inadequate, the case could be referred to the Board of Visitors which had greater powers under

Rule 51. For especially grave offences—mutiny or incitement to mutiny, or gross personal violence to an officer—the case would normally be dealt with by the Board of Visitors under Rule 52. In very rare circumstances—in just ninety cases in 1989, for example—a prisoner might be charged with a criminal offence and proceedings taken in outside courts.

However, as a Home Office memorandum to the Prior Committee on the Prison Disciplinary System made plain, charging prisoners with a breach of prison regulations or a criminal offence is just 'one of a number of measures which the prison authorities can take, either before an offence has occurred or afterwards, in order to maintain or restore order, control and security' (Home Office 1984c, 5). According to the Home Office memorandum these measures include the confiscation of property (under Rule 41.1); the use of force (Rule 44.1); the use of restraints (Rule 46); temporary confinement in a special cell (Rule 45); segregation (under Rule 43) either for the prisoner's own protection (OP) or for the maintenance of good order and discipline (GOAD); transfer to another establishment, which required no special authorizing Rule, although Circular Instruction 10/74 allowed for the transfer of subversive prisoners from the dispersal system to local prison at short notice for a 'cooling-off' period of up to twenty-eight days; the recategorization of offenders; the conversion of youth custody sentences to imprisonment; placing a prisoner on the escape list, thereby subjecting him to special supervision; as well as many other measures which 'are entirely administrative in character'. In its own memorably frank evidence to the Prior Committee, the Prison Officers' Association referred to these measures, which were not justiciable, as the 'unacknowledged alternative' disciplinary system (POA 1984, 2). To these measures, the Control Review Committee had added a series of special small units, at Parkhurst, Hull, and Lincoln, to which particularly troublesome prisoners might be transferred.

While the official discourse on control problems, as we have written elsewhere, 'sometimes pays lip-service to the capacity of the system to generate its own trouble, [it] falls back time and again on a model that locates trouble primarily in the dispositions of individual prisoners' (King and McDermott 1990a, 449). The Control Review Committee probably went as far as it decently could, bearing in mind the climate in which it was born, to distance itself from past rhetoric on control problems, in recognizing that 'a man who presents intractable control problems in one establishment may be little or no trouble in another' (Home Office 1984a, para. 44) and in pointing to the *system*'s failure to 'send the right signals' for maintaining good order (*ibid.*, para. 22). However, it stopped a long way short of setting problems of order, discipline, and control within their proper context, namely, the very nature and structure of the prison system as a whole. Having taken great care to ensure that the special units it created outside the mainstream of the prison population would be very different from the control units[2] of a decade earlier, the CRC nevertheless became committed to the task of identifying the right kind of troublemakers to send to them.

It took Woolf LJ's inquiry to establish in the official lexicon a clear statement that the maintenance of good order and discipline depended as much upon a deeper sense of justice and fairness in the management of the everyday affairs of prisoners as it did upon the formal procedures of disciplinary hearings and any special measures for dealing with control problem prisoners. Arguably, by then, no other conclusion was possible. The riots and disturbances, which in the 1970s had been largely confined to the dispersal prisons, had spread in the 1980s to lower-security training prisons and by the end of that decade to local prisons and remand centres. It was becoming increasingly hard to pin all this on a few troublemakers. Having asked for an analysis of the common characteristics of the 'leading players' in the rioting and found that there were none to speak of,[3] Woolf became persuaded that there was 'no objective system for identifying potentially disruptive prisoners' (Home Office 1991a, para. 9.48). In a much-quoted paragraph, Woolf wrote that a recurring theme in the evidence from prisoners involved in the riots was that their actions were:

a response to the manner in which they were treated by the prison system . . . If what they say is true, the failure of the Prison Service to fulfil its

[2] Two control units were established at Wakefield and Wormwood Scrubs following the review of dispersal policy carried out in 1973 by the then Director General of the Prison Service, W. R. Cox. The regime in the units involved a first stage of 90 days without any association, to be followed by a second stage of 90 days with associated work, leisure, and education. At the end of 180 days the prisoner would return to normal location, but if there were any breaches of discipline he could return to the beginning of the first stage. The units quickly fell into disrepute, and in 1981 in *Williams v. Home Office (No. 2)* [1981] 1 All ER 121) it was acknowledged that the procedure involved a clear infringement of Rule 43, although this was deemed insufficient to regard Williams' detention as unlawful. The Cox Review also introduced the procedure known as 10/74 transfers.

[3] Personal communication from Rod Morgan.

responsibilities to act with justice created in April 1990 serious difficulties in maintaining security and control in prisons (*ibid*., para. 9.24).

Whether or not Woolf accepted this with regard to the cases of particular prisoners there is no doubt that he accepted it as a matter of general principle: having found 'no single cause of riots and no simple solution or action which will prevent rioting' (*ibid*., para. 9.23), he put forward a package of reforms which touched on almost every aspect of prison life, the whole thrust of which was intended to enhance both the perception and the reality of fairness.

As Sparks (1994) has noted, the Woolf Report constitutes a distinct conceptual development. It offers a decisive break with the rotten apple and powder keg theories of prison riots (Thomas and Pooley 1980) and with the assumptions in most previous official statements which regarded 'the maintenance of legitimate authority in prisons as *essentially* unproblematic, albeit *practically* difficult at times' (Sparks 1994, 20, emphasis in the original). What Woolf made plain was that the whole question of maintaining good order within prisons depended upon getting the right 'balance between security, control, and justice'. He in no way discounted the need for security or control procedures, although he gave considerable attention to ways in which they could be made more defensible and accountable. Instead he was at pains to point out the mutual interdependence of measures to enhance security and control with those designed to promote a sense of justice, fairness, and humanity.

There have been major changes to the formal disciplinary system since the conduct of our research and some lesser ones in the 'alternative disciplinary system' of purely administrative measures. The watershed case of R. v. *Hull Prison Board of Visitors, ex parte St Germain* [1979] QB 425 had already opened up the way for judicial scrutiny of prison disciplinary procedures involving Boards of Visitors.[4] In 1988, shortly after the completion of our main fieldwork, this was extended to governors' hearings in the case of *Leech*

---

[4] In the wake of the Hull riot the decision was taken not to prefer criminal charges but to proceed against prisoners through hearings before the Board of Visitors. A special panel travelled around the country to hear some 500 charges against 185 prisoners who by then had been transferred to other prisons. The prisoners were not allowed to call witnesses or cross-examine even hearsay evidence against them. Most were found guilty and some received loss of remission of up to 720 days. At first the request for judicial review was turned down by the Div. Ct., but this was overturned by the CA.

v. *The Deputy Governor of Parkhurst Prison* [1988] 1 All ER 485.[5] In 1983 criteria had been established for the granting of legal representation in hearings before Boards of Visitors in the case of *R. v. Secretary of State for the Home Department, ex parte Tarrant* [1984] 1 All ER 799, the case that many consider to be the high water mark for procedural safeguards in the prisons field.[6] Although Justice (1983) had reiterated the recommendation of the earlier Jellicoe Report (Martin 1975) that Boards of Visitors should lose their adjudicatory function and henceforth concentrate on their watchdog role, Boards of Visitors were still very much involved in prison justice at the time of our research.

The Report of the Prior Committee (Home Office 1985b) had also endorsed the recommendation that Boards should cease to be involved in adjudications: instead it proposed the establishment of an independent Prison Disciplinary Tribunal as an intermediate tier between governors' hearings and sending cases to outside courts. Some limited support, however, had been given to Boards of Visitors even while the Prior Committee was deliberating. In the case of *Campbell and Fell* (1985) 7 EHRR 165 (Series A No. 80), the European Court of Human Rights. disagreeing with an earlier conclusion of the European Commission of Human Rights in the same case, ruled that Boards of Visitors were sufficiently independent of both the executive and prison management to meet the requirement of Article 6 of the European Convention on Human Rights to guarantee a fair hearing (see Richardson 1993, 154–5). Although the Home Office initially accepted the idea of an independent tribunal, it was clearly not happy about it, not least on the ground of the expense of having legally qualified persons chairing the panels. In the event it opted for the cheapest possible version with lay panels and then abandoned even those in favour of a more limited experiment to use magistrates' court clerks in Boards of Visitors adjudications in selected establishments (see Morgan and Jones 1991 for a review).

[5] In *Leech* [1988] 1 All ER 485 the HL overturned a previous CA decision in favour of the view which Shaw LJ had taken in *St Germain*, namely that since there was no legal distinction between governors' adjudications and those of Boards of Visitors, both should be equally open to judicial review.

[6] Tarrant had been refused legal representation by the Board of Visitors at Albany when charged with mutiny. The Board of Visitors, on Home Office advice, had said that it had no discretion to grant legal representation. The Div. Ct. ruled that, although Tarrant had no right to legal representation, the Board did indeed have discretion to grant it, and set out the circumstances in which that discretion might properly be exercised, which included those in which Tarrant found himself.

Even Woolf J, as he then was, found in R. v. *Frankland Prison Board of Visitors, ex parte Lewis* [1986] 2 All ER 272 that the dual role of Boards of Visitors was not likely to produce unfairness (Livingstone 1994). However, five years later he was ready to do away altogether with any need for an intermediate tier between governors' hearings and the outside courts, finally drawing the clearest possible distinction between internal disciplinary matters on the one hand and criminal proceedings on the other. Governors dealt with about 95 per cent of all disciplinary cases, and it is clear that Woolf had come to regard the Boards of Visitors as having powers of punishment that were disproportionately excessive, bearing in mind the nature of most of the remaining 5 per cent of offences with which they typically dealt. Indeed, he argued that the extra days served by prisoners in lost remission, when cumulated over the system as a whole, constituted 'an astonishing extra burden' which needed to be 'controlled' (Home Office 1991a, para. 14.401). Henceforth, he argued, most of those cases could be dealt with quite adequately by the governor (*ibid.*, para. 14.416). Woolf also rejected any idea that the Boards should have an appellate function in respect of prison discipline (*ibid.*, para. 13.391)—a role which he recommended should go ultimately to a new post of Complaints Adjudicator, once internal appeals to area managers had been exhausted (*ibid.*, para. 14.424). In fact, in that context, Woolf envisaged that Boards of Visitors, consistent with their watchdog role, might actually assist prisoners, if so requested, to make their representations on appeal (*ibid.*, para. 14.429).

Since 1 April 1992 the Boards of Visitors have ceased to adjudicate on offences against prison discipline. Although Woolf had recommended that a president of the Boards of Visitors be appointed by the Home Secretary, a proposal which had the support of AMBoV (the Association of Members of Boards of Visitors), it emerged towards the end of 1993 that this was rejected by their co-ordinating committee because it would jeopardize their independence. As we noted in Chapter 1, Michael Howard found all three initial candidates for the supposedly independent ombudsman—Woolf's Complaints Adjudicator—unacceptable, and after a long delay appointed Sir Peter Woodhead, former Deputy Supreme Commander in the Atlantic, to the post. Furthermore, on 3 November 1993 Howard announced his intention of strengthening the disciplinary powers of governors and, with effect from 10 December, it became

clear that these included the imposition of up to two weeks' segregation (instead of three days'). This provided an uncomfortable echo
of Kenneth Baker's initial response to the Woolf Report, namely his
determination to introduce a new criminal offence of prison mutiny
to carry a possible ten-year sentence.

Prisoners' Experience of Discipline and Control Measures

In view of the changes to the disciplinary system we limit our reporting here on the views of the prisoners about prison discipline to a
few essential points. It is probably sufficient to note that, although
there were statistically significant differences between our prisons in
the likelihood of prisoners being placed on report and in regard to
the offences for which they were reported, there were no differences
between the prisons in the way prisoners who had been adjudicated
perceived the fairness of the procedure, the justice of the verdict, or
the proportionality of the punishment. All told, some 321 prisoners
(27.8 per cent of those who responded on these questions) had been
placed on report in their current prison. Over half the prisoners in
Gartree (54.5 per cent) and nearly a third in Nottingham (31.6 per
cent) and Featherstone (29.4 per cent) had been on report compared
to only a fifth in Birmingham (21 per cent of convicted and 22.2 per
cent of remand prisoners) and only an eighth (12.4 per cent) in
Ashwell.

The pattern of presenting offences probably tells us as much about
the styles of supervision by staff, their thresholds of tolerance for certain types of behaviours, and the formal and informal policies and
procedures which they followed in relation to searching and other
matters, as it does about the behaviours of prisoners. Thus prisoners in Gartree (28.2 per cent) and Birmingham (18.6 per cent remands
and 22.2 per cent convicted) were much more likely to be charged
with assault compared to their counterparts in Featherstone (3.4 per
cent) and Ashwell (nil), with Nottingham (16.7 per cent) occupying
an intermediate position. However, in Gartree and Birmingham staff
were less likely to take action in relation to such matters as prisoners making 'groundless complaints'[7] (Rule 47.16) or petty acts of

---

[7] On 1 April 1989 substantial changes to the Prison Rules eventually came into
force, consequent upon the recommendations of the Prior Report and the Report of
the Chief Inspector on Prisoners' Complaints (Home Office 1987b). These included
the abolition of the charges of making false and malicious allegations, and repeatedly
making groundless complaints.

'wilful damage' to prison property (Rule 47.11). In Featherstone, where it will be recalled from Chapter 2 that searching was most assiduously carried out, 44.1 per cent of all prisoners on report had been charged with having unauthorized articles in their possession (Rule 47.7). The rate for this was also high in Gartree (29.6 per cent) which similarly had a high frequency of searching. In Nottingham the highest proportion of offences (23.8 per cent) were under the catch-all rubric of 'in any way offends against good order and discipline' of the establishment (Rule 47.20). Perhaps most strikingly, however, no matter what the offence, the great majority of those proceeded against by the governor regarded the proceedings as unfair (60.7 per cent), the verdict as incorrect (63.9 per cent) and the punishment as disproportionate to the offence (72.7 per cent).

Although the numbers who had appeared before the Boards of Visitors were much smaller (137 as against 321) their perceptions as to the justice with which their case was handled were either very similar or else even more disillusioned: 60.6 per cent regarded it as an unfair procedure, 61.7 per cent thought the outcome was wrong, and a staggering 80.2 per cent thought the punishment disproportionate.

We have written extensively about control procedures in prisons elsewhere (King 1985; King and McDermott 1990a; McDermott and King 1988) and much of our material on this, as on a great many other matters, was submitted in evidence to the Woolf Inquiry. We have previously concentrated particularly on the use of administrative transfers under what used to be CI 10/74, and especially about its repeated use. In some cases prisoners were transferred from one dispersal prison to a local prison and then returned to a different dispersal prison only for the process to be repeated two or three months later in a determined attempt by the authorities to break down prisoner resistance. The procedure had variously become known as the 'ghost train' or the 'magic roundabout'. Our interest in this procedure had become heightened when one of us was working for several days down in the block in Gartree. During that time a then notorious prisoner, about whom staff spoke in hushed tones, was on the roundabout and doing his stint in Gartree. During the regular visits to prisoners held on Rule 43 segregation which the governor and the Boards of Visitors were required to make, at least three prison officers would open the cell door and then form a human shield between the prisoner and his visitor, over which it was scarcely possible to make eye contact let alone engage in any meaningful discussion. In the course of our fieldwork this prisoner was removed from the roundabout and reintroduced into general population at Long Lartin where he subsequently played a leading role in a series of very successful open seminars to which the press and public were invited.

By the time of the Woolf Report CI 10/74 had been substantially revised as CI 37/90 to give greater procedural safeguards following the Court of Appeal's decision in the Hague case which established that actions taken pursuant to the Prison Rules were susceptible to challenge by means of judicial review (*R. v. Deputy Governor of Parkhurst Prison ex parte Hague* [1991] 3 All ER 733).[8] We had argued in our evidence to Woolf that in most cases it should have been possible for the authorities to proceed with transfers *after* first having brought disciplinary charges, and then to effect the transfer on a planned, rather than an emergency, basis—on the ground that this would reduce much of the perceived unfairness in the use of these measures, as well as their disruptiveness. Woolf considered that, in light of the revisions in CI 37/90 about giving written reasons, and his own endorsement that the measure should be used sparingly, there remained a need for such an emergency administrative procedure (Home Office 1991a, paras. 12.255–6). We also recommended that, given the Boards of Visitors' functions as they then stood, authorization of such transfers should be made by the Board of Visitors. Understandably, given the other changes in regard to the adjudicatory role of Boards, Woolf explicitly rejected that advice (*ibid.*, para. 12.257). Since we would have wanted the other changes with regard to the Boards' functions we are more than happy to accept Woolf's position. However, Woolf endorsed our proposals for further safeguards, namely that a member of the Board of Visitors in the receiving prison should see the prisoner at, or soon after, his arrival (*ibid.*, para. 12.258); and that the prisoner should also be seen before departure and upon arrival by the medical officers in the

---

[8] Hague had been transferred under CI 10/74 from the segregation unit at Parkhurst to the segregation unit at Wormwood Scrubs in July 1988. He sought judicial review on ground that the circular was *ultra vires* the Prison Rules. This argument was accepted by the CA, which held that segregation occurred under Rule 43, and that Rule 43, unlike the circular, required that the decision to segregate be taken by the governor of the prison in which the prisoner was actually contained; and further that the circular implied that the Regional Director, on behalf of the Secretary of State, would routinely endorse the full 28-day segregation period, whereas Rule 43 required a reasoned decision to be taken.

respective prisons (*ibid.*, para. 12.260). Of course, administrative transfers between prisons can take place at any time and without reference to CI 37/90. One form of these is what staff and prisoners have described as 'regional lie downs', whereby disruptive prisoners from lower security prisons could be returned to a local prison for periods of up to six months. Woolf acknowledged their existence with reference to transfers from category C establishments, although they occur in all categories of establishment, and hoped that the need for them would diminish with the phasing out of dormitory accommodation and the implementation of his other recommendations (*ibid.* paras. 12.262–3).

Woolf also proposed that Boards of Visitors should no longer have a role in authorizing the segregation of prisoners under Rule 43 for purposes of good order and discipline, placing responsibility for this instead upon area managers. Here, too, written reasons should be provided for the decision to segregate (*ibid.*, paras. 12.264–71). With regard to prisoners who were segregated for their own protection, Woolf proposed that a new rule be drafted to deal with their needs, without the additional hardships imposed by segregation (*ibid.*, para. 12.203). The Prison Service has since undertaken to allocate sex offenders to one of twenty prisons which will provide special programmes for their treatment (Home Office 1991b, para. 5.25), and we report on those developments in Chapter 5. However, the Prison Service still sees a need to segregate prisoners for their own protection, if only for short periods, whilst recognizing that they should still take part in normal activities as far as practicable, and the Home Secretary has agreed to amend the Prison Rules accordingly (*ibid.*, para. 5.27).

In regard to the special unit strategy introduced by the CRC, Woolf recognized the need for such units, but cited evidence by Bottoms that the lengthy procedures needed to identify and allocate prisoners did not meet very well the operational needs of dispersal prison governors. He also noted, as we have argued above, that their existence continues to imply that control problems are simply the product of 'difficult' individuals (Home Office 1991a, paras. 12.287–8).

Finally, as we reported in Chapter 2, Woolf LJ had followed in the footsteps of the Control Review Committee and visited Oak Park Heights. He was particularly attracted by the capacity of Oak Park Heights to provide several distinctive regimes within a single secure environment, and quoted the evidence provided by one of us (King 1991a) from the comparison between Gartree and Oak Park Heights, particularly in regard to the safety of staff and prisoners in support of his view (Home Office 1991a, paras. 12.297–305). Accordingly, Woolf recommended that the Home Office earmark at least one 'new generation prison' for dispersal prisoners, including those who would probably now be housed in the special units; and he mistakenly believed that the service had such a role in mind for Whitemoor (*ibid.*, para. 12.305; cf. King 1987). The Home Office made no reference to this recommendation in the White Paper, *Custody, Care, and Justice*.

We asked all prisoners about the use of control procedures against them, and about how they viewed the signals the system was sending in terms of incentives and disincentives to good behaviour. By definition all of the prisoners in the training prisons had been transferred at least once in the course of their sentence—from the local prison to their current establishment, and we discussed in Chapter 2 some of the factors, including control considerations, which influenced the decisions made in OCA units. Leaving aside transfers under 10/74, some 22.5 per cent also believed they had been transferred in the course of their sentence as a punishment. By far the highest proportion of such prisoners were to be found in Gartree, where they constituted 48.9 per cent of the sample population, and the next highest was Nottingham with 27.8 per cent. However, these 'negative' transfers were offset by 'positive' transfers: 24 per cent of prisoners having experienced a transfer which they regarded as a reward. Not surprisingly these were concentrated in Featherstone and Ashwell. The differences between the prisons were statistically highly significant. It is not possible to tell, because of the way the question was framed, how many of the transfers resulted from the POA's underground and alternative disciplinary system and how many resulted from normal sentence planning in so far as that term can sensibly be used of the prison system at the time of our research. But there is little doubt from our interview data that many category B prisoners were resentful at their allocation to the dispersal system and also resentful that, if they had to be in a dispersal prison, they were allocated to Gartree.

Just over one in twenty prisoners (5.4 per cent) had been held in segregation on Rule 43 in the interests of good order and discipline (GOAD). There were no differences in the likelihood of being subjected to this on racial or ethnic grounds, but there were wide differences between the prisons. No prisoners in Ashwell reported that they had been held on GOAD and only 0.7 per cent in Featherstone, compared to 9.1 per cent in Nottingham and 16.1 per cent in Gartree. Moreover, almost half of these prisoners in Nottingham and two-thirds of those in Gartree claimed they had been segregated for periods totalling over a hundred days. In Birmingham 5 per cent of remand prisoners and 5.8 per cent of convicted prisoners told us they had been segregated in this way. We had no way of verifying these claims without breaching the anonymity of the procedures under which questionnaires were completed. However, the results are broadly consistent with the respective institutional usages of the measure.

A small group of prisoners appeared to have been singled out for multiple control measures: 4.1 per cent said that they had been placed in physical restraints; 6.4 per cent had been put in strip cells; and 5.2 per cent claimed that they had been given drugs, such as Largactil, not for medical reasons but in order to control their behaviour. Many prisoners in Strangeways made similar allegations to Woolf (Home Office 1991a, para. 12.132). Such prisoners were most likely to be found in Gartree, where some eighteen prisoners (11.8 per cent of our Gartree respondents on these items) had been both given drugs and placed in strip cells: thirteen of them had also been otherwise physically restrained. Such matters hardly occurred at all in Ashwell or Featherstone, but eleven prisoners (7.9 per cent) in Nottingham and twenty convicted prisoners (10.2 per cent) as well as seventeen remand prisoners (8.2 per cent) in Birmingham said they had been on the receiving end of one or more of these measures.

At the other extreme small groups of prisoners reported that they had been rewarded for good behaviour with the granting of special privileges. In some cases these rewards had to be the subject of formal application and a review process—as for the 2.2 per cent who had regained lost remission. The numbers here were small, and the differences between the prisons were not significant. Most of the other privileges seem likely to have been given at the discretion of probation officers, wing officers, governor grades, and workshop instructors on a relatively informal basis and in particular circumstances. Over a quarter of prisoners (26.9 per cent) had thus been granted additional visits; 11.7 per cent had managed to change their cell for a better one; 22.7 per cent had got better jobs; 11.3 per cent had been given additional earnings; and 6 per cent had been given unspecified other privileges. Regaining lost remission obviously depended upon whether it had been lost in the first place and was most likely to occur in Gartree and Featherstone. But for the other, more negotiable, privileges, a prisoner was most likely to be successful in Nottingham and least likely in Ashwell.

We asked prisoners whether they regarded the system of rewards and punishments, in its widest sense, as an appropriate motivator to good behaviour. Almost three-quarters of them (73.7 per cent) thought that the reward and punishment system worked at least reasonably well in this regard, but there were major differences between the prisons which were statistically significant. Nearly everyone in Ashwell (94.3 per cent) thought the reward and punishment system was effective, compared to three-quarters in Featherstone (75.9 per cent), two-thirds in Nottingham (68.8 per cent) and three-fifths in Gartree (60.6 per cent). In Birmingham three-quarters of the convicted prisoners (76.3 per cent) and three-fifths of the remand prisoners (61.8 per cent) thought the system was effective in maintaining good order. In the absence of any comparative bench-marks it is hard to know whether these relatively high figures should be regarded as encouraging or not. On balance we think probably not. Throughout our research we found that prisoners were remarkably accepting of their lot and not easily moved to take extreme positions—as will be clear from many of the data to be presented later in this monograph. When the CRC was commenting on the system's failure to send the right signals it presumably had in mind that minority of prisoners who saw little connection between their behaviour and their prison career. Such minorities are evidently quite sizeable in the high security prisons at least.

Safety

Some Incidents from the Public Record and Private Field Notes

On 30 April 1986 a category A prisoner on C wing in Gartree handed in a pair of scissors to the office and told staff that he had just stabbed a fellow prisoner to death. He had lured a sex offender into a cell where he had 'given him what he deserved'. Staff found the victim stuffed under a bed, his hands bound behind his back, with multiple stab wounds to the neck. A group of London 'gangsters'—

as the staff referred to them—had been conducting a campaign against sex offenders or 'nonces' and had succeeded in winding up the assailant to do their bidding. It was thought that murder had not been intended, but that matters had got out of hand. This incident occurred shortly before our fieldwork began in Gartree. Thankfully such events are comparatively rare in Britain compared with some other jurisdictions (Bowker 1980, 1982). It was nevertheless widely talked about, usually in a context in which staff were berated by prisoners for being unduly protective towards those who had committed sexual crimes or offences against children. It provided a powerful demonstration both of the divisions within the prisoner community and of the fact that one of the worst pains of imprisonment is being with other prisoners (see also Sykes 1966; King and Elliot 1978).

Prisoners are not merely at risk from other prisoners but also from themselves. In 1993, for England and Wales as a whole, one prisoner committed suicide every eight days. During our fieldwork at Gartree another category A prisoner slashed his left arm and was found in his bed, which was saturated with blood, by security staff who had come to enforce a routine cell change. He was rushed to hospital and recovered, but it was a gruesome occasion which was unsettling for staff and prisoners. The prisoner concerned had just received a 'dear John' letter from his girlfriend, but his demeanour had apparently given no cause for concern. Although his file was flagged to denote a potential suicide risk, there was some feeling that the box had been ticked merely as a back-covering exercise, and since he was closely supervised as a category A prisoner anyway no further action had seemed called for. There is considerable debate both about the rates of suicide in prisons compared with those outside and about the meaning of the many suicidal gestures which occur throughout the system (Lloyd 1990; Liebling 1992). Whether or not suicide is more frequent in prisons, it is probably the case that staff and prisoners live more closely with the spectre of suicide than most others. Everyone is acutely aware of the states of desperation that can build up behind the locked cell door, and it is important to recognize that the possibility of suicide can become woven into the complex manipulations that have to do with control and good order in prisons. In the course of our fieldwork, for example, we heard one prisoner say, apparently seriously, 'Right then, I'll just have to top myself, guvnor' when his request for segregation under

Rule 43 for his own protection was rejected. On another occasion a prisoner was being taken down to the block. He was struggling and shouting that he could not stand any more of this, whereupon one of the officers said 'Then why don't you top yourself?'. Suicide prevention devices and procedures, from the stretched wire netting across galleries[9] to inmate watch schemes, provide a constant reminder of what can and does happen, and these have their own impact upon the prison environment and culture.

It is regrettably also the case that prisoners can be at risk from staff. When the Birmingham Six were remanded to Winson Green on 25 November 1974 they were assaulted in the reception area before being taken to the high security cells on D Wing. John Walker had four teeth knocked out which, it was said at the trial of fourteen prison officers charged with the assaults, were then offered to bystanders as souvenirs (*The Times*, 11 July 1976). One of the accused officers made a statement from the dock:

There were a lot of prison officers about and what followed I can only describe as an explosion of physical and verbal assault. I saw officers there that I knew to be quiet and docile men lose control of themselves. I counted eleven officers, including two principal officers, who had no business to be there.

He refused to give evidence on oath because he did not wish to name his colleagues. According to one prisoner witness 'an officer had banged each bomber's head against a wall in turn' (*The Times*, 7 July 1976). One of our respondents, who was on the receiving end of this violence, told us that in the highly charged atmosphere overwrought prison officers unlocked cell doors and encouraged other prisoners to join in the beatings. In the time-honoured way, when the principal hospital officer and the prison medical officer interviewed the six to complete the appropriate paperwork, they reported that one of them 'explained' his injuries as a fall in the police station, two others as falling down the steps of the police van, and the remainder as falling up or down the stairs in the prison (*The Times*, 11 July 1976). On 15 July 1976, after a trial lasting six weeks, all fourteen officers were acquitted. The Birmingham Six were not the bombers they were thought to be—and there were many amongst our contacts in prison, both staff and prisoners, who recognized some of them from their behaviour and demeanour inside as 'ordinary decent crim-

[9] See Priestley (1985, 181) for an historical note.

inals' (odcs) and not 'terrorists'—but it was to be another sixteen years before the Court of Appeal finally released them.

Barry Prosser, however, was never released alive. Prosser was remanded in custody on 15 August 1980 for medical reports after being found guilty of causing criminal damage to a lock valued at £1.62. The magistrates wanted further information so that they could consider sending him to a secure mental hospital, for he was said to be excitable and possibly suffering from hypomania (*The Times*, 20 March 1982). He had already spent a fortnight in Winson Green before trial and he was now returned to the Hospital Wing. Four days later he was dead.

According to the Home Office pathologist his stomach, his œsophagus, and one of his lungs had been ruptured. The ruptured stomach was the cause of death and it could not have been self-inflicted (*The Times*, 16 April 1981). The initial police inquiries led to the prosecution of hospital officer Melvyn Jackson, but in February 1981 the Birmingham stipendiary magistrate ruled that there was no case to answer. At the inquest in April the jury returned a verdict of unlawful killing and there was never any serious suggestion but that Prosser met his death at the hands, or more likely the feet, of prison officers. The coroner wrote to the Director of Public Prosecutions and to the Home Office expressing his concern at the way in which drugs were prescribed and recorded, and in particular the method of recording instances where force was used on prisoners (*The Times*, 16 April 1981). The case made legal history when the DPP again brought charges against Jackson, this time with two other officers. In September, a second stipendiary magistrate ruled that there was insufficient evidence to go ahead. The DPP at first announced that the case was closed, but the then Home Secretary, William Whitelaw, called for a report on the committal proceedings, after which the DPP sought and obtained a Voluntary Bill of Indictment which effectively by-passed the committal stage. Jackson and his colleagues were tried at Leicester Crown Court, after an application by the defence to move the case away from Birmingham. The defence introduced a new pathologist who suggested that Prosser's injuries could have been self-inflicted (Coggan and Walker 1982, 43). The defendants were acquitted when the judge told the jury that it would be unwise to rely on the uncorroborated evidence of the key witness, a prisoner who worked as the hospital cleaner (*The Times*, 20 March 1982).

The three officers were transferred to other prisons in April, and Jackson eventually left the Prison Service. In the interval between the second and third proceedings against the officers, Birmingham was the subject of an inspection headed by the Deputy Chief Inspector of Prisons, W. A. Brister. His Report (Home Office 1982), which Morgan (1985) has suggested was rushed through to meet a need, identified some shortcomings but basically concluded that the hospital at Birmingham provided a high standard of care. The Home Secretary welcomed this conclusion and hoped that 'it will not be overshadowed by the concern about Mr Prosser's death'. In June 1982 the Home Secretary announced changes to the training of hospital officers. By the time of our research, nearly five years later, Mrs Dorothy Prosser and members of her family still held a vigil outside the prison on Saturdays, but the governor was able to report that by then it presented 'no problems other than a nuisance and indeed it is more or less ignored'. Nevertheless, inside the prison, the legacy of the treatment of Barry Prosser still hung heavily around the prison hospital. Amongst prisoners in Birmingham, the block, the hospital, and the various special units were widely feared.

Of course, staff, too, can be seriously at risk from prisoners. Most members of the public, however, would probably be surprised at the relatively low numbers of assaults on staff. For the year immediately prior to our fieldwork Gartree recorded just nine, Nottingham five, Featherstone three, and Ashwell none at all. Even Birmingham, where a large population was held in very confining circumstances, took disciplinary action against only thirty prisoners for assaulting staff—effectively about the same proportion as Gartree. None of these warranted special mention in the body of the governor's report so it may reasonably be inferred that there was no serious injury. On the other hand, we witnessed several near misses. On 29 October 1986, to take one example from our field notes, a prisoner in Gartree threatened his probation officer. The previous day he had asked the probation officer to make enquiries about his wife's health. The probation officer indicated that he would deal with the matter the following week, a delay which outraged the prisoner. 'What kinds of wankers become probation officers?' he asked one of us on evening association that night. 'This one is such a fucking air head every time he farts he becomes thicker'. The next lunchtime the probation officer was taking applications on the wing and the prisoner asked him again. We could not hear what the reply was but the prisoner immediately threatened him. A prison officer quickly got between them and told the probation officer to get off the wing quick. Two other offices provided reinforcements, and the prisoner turned away and threw his tray down to the floor. At this point one of the officers pressed the alarm bell, but the prisoner by then had decided there was nothing for it but to start walking to the block. When incidents such as this occurred in our presence staff always acted with assiduous concern for our safety and we were bundled or motioned into an office to get us out of the line of fire.

By the time we returned to undertake our enquiries about the implementation of Fresh Start, there had been a much more frightening incident: the education officer in Gartree and one of his part-time teachers received knife wounds when they were taken hostage by two prisoners whom they came across in what appeared to be an ill-planned and abortive escape attempt. The teacher was the more seriously injured, with slash wounds to the face which at first were thought likely to endanger his sight. The education officer was slashed on the neck in the struggle but managed to sound the alarm. The prisoners were quickly overpowered when prison officers arrived on the scene. Not surprisingly the education staff were badly shaken by the incident quite apart from the physical injuries caused to them.

The occasions when both staff and prisoners feel themselves to be most obviously at risk, however, are when the prison is in a state of loss of control or riot. Whatever the proximate causes for the disorder may have been, such events also provide opportunities for the settling of scores and what are often seen as justifiable acts of punishment or retribution may take place. It is also important to recognize that whilst riots are nearly always quickly characterized by anarchy they can also bring a real, if fleeting, sense of liberation to people who feel they normally have no control over their lives. The natural history of the riot is insufficiently understood. Gartree had a regrettable history of riot and disorder. In the 1972 riot, which apparently followed an escape attempt by fourteen prisoners, three fires were started in various locations around the prison. One wing remained barricaded overnight, and many prisoners managed to climb on to the roof. By the end some eighteen prison officers and five prisoners had been injured. In 1978, according to the sanitized summary provided in the CRC Report (Home Office 1984a, 65), a riot occurred following rumours that a prisoner had been beaten up and forcibly drugged in the prison hospital. At evening association staff offered to allow two prisoners to visit the hospital to see the prisoner for themselves. This offer was apparently rejected and prisoners began to smash fittings and throw missiles. Three prisoners did then go to visit the hospital but by the time they returned a riot had effectively started. For a short time some eight prison officers were trapped in A wing, although their release was soon negotiated. The riot spread to B and D wings which were evacuated by staff. Prisoners in these three wings erected barricades and successfully repulsed MUFTI[10] teams with boiling water and various projectiles.

The incident ended the following morning, and no staff or prisoners were seriously hurt; but it was an incident that had a profound effect on Gartree. When Canter and Ambrose (1980) carried out their research on prison design and use, A and D wings were still empty, their prisoners had been decanted to other dispersal prisons, and some of their staff detached for duties elsewhere in the system.[11] The staff who remained were said to suffer from a 'siege perspective, a defensive conceptualization which places even greater distance between staff and inmates than is normally present' (Canter and Ambrose 1980, 228). Experience of the riot was said to have permeated every staff evaluation of facilities (ibid., 192). Staff were particularly negative about the attention given to their personal safety, the poor visual contact they had with other officers on the wing, and the difficulties they had in supervising prisoners during recreation (ibid. 189). Canter and Ambrose reported a strong sense of fear among staff that a similar incident might occur again (ibid. 192).

The defensive posture of the staff at Gartree following the 1978 riot kept two wings closed for several years, as staff engaged in a struggle with the Home Office, insisting that they would not reopen the wings until new access towers had been added giving them an escape route should they become trapped. Officials at first refused, and for a long time the Prisons Board considered removing Gartree from the dispersal system altogether, especially as much of its closed-circuit television and other security systems had come to the end of their useful life. But in the event the access towers were built, and

[10] Minimum Use of Force Tactical Intervention (MUFTI) Squads were introduced following the riot at Hull Prison in 1976. The first public awareness of their use came to light in the course of putting down an apparently peaceful demonstration in Wormwood Scrubs in 1979 during which more than 50 prisoners were injured.

[11] Gartree, nevertheless, had a very high staff ratio then, just as it did during the currency of our research.

the security systems replaced, and in 1983 Gartree resumed its full dispersal role, albeit with a much greater leavening of life-sentence prisoners who were thought to have a stabilizing influence on the prison population. The provision of the access towers involved the loss of six cells on each level of each wing, which were effectively cordoned off behind riot gates: a design whereby each T-shaped wing had originally 'one long leg and two short legs' was now described by staff as having 'one long leg, one short leg and one "dead" leg'.

During our research staff and prisoners talked about the riot a good deal. Immediately after the riot when the two wings were closed, staff were able to run a very tight ship, and they felt they were fully in control. They told us: 'for six to nine months after the riot it worked perfectly. Never worked better. After a bit the new governor and the chief said please can we have our gaol back and gradually we gave it to them a bit at a time. But within weeks the incidents were back up again'. In spite of such statements we were intrigued to note, as we shall report more fully in Chapter 5, prisoners actually spent more time out of their cells and at work during the time when Canter and Ambrose were describing staff as suffering from their siege perspective than they did during our research. Nevertheless, as we conducted our fieldwork and watched Gartree staff at very close quarters over a sustained period, it seemed to us that they had fully regained confidence in their abilities. With few exceptions we were generally impressed by their professional competence in most situations. Nevertheless, as we drank endless cups of prison coffee on the wings in the evenings, basic grade officers and senior officers would look back to the riot and tell us how it had sorted the men from the boys. When one of the wings went up, we were told, that the Principal Officer in charge went straight to the toilet: 'some people are regular and take lots of bran, others are caught short unpredictably. Of course, the fact that it happens every time there is trouble must say something'.

Nor did they have much time for assistant governors, as they were still then called, and their like: in times of emergency they were either not there, or else considered to be useless. On the other hand there was a very strong sense of *esprit de corps* amongst themselves, and we lost count of the number of times we were told how important it was to demonstrate that when the alarm bell goes you are not 'running slow to get there last, because next time it might be you who is out on a limb'. Prisoners, also, told us that the time when we should have seen staff was during the riot, but since that was not possible we should watch them when the alarm bells went (as they did with some frequency during our research). What they had in mind was the over-zealous use of force, which staff could more easily get away with in emergencies, and the abuse of property in the subsequent shakedowns and lock-downs.

We have taken our examples here from Gartree and Birmingham with good reason. These were the prisons with a public record of disorder and the public record provided a fair reflection of the levels of aggravation inside. This is not to say that incidents did not occur in the other prisons. In Nottingham, particularly, there was a fairly constant degree of 'aggro' but it was generally at a much lower level of seriousness. While Featherstone and Ashwell occasionally pro- duced their moments of tension there was little that would have attracted a headline in a newspaper. It is probably important to bear in mind that Ashwell, and prisons like it, offered some kind of refuge for staff as well as prisoners who had been victims of assault or other trauma in tougher establishments. The fact that the other prisons in our study were probably unknown, outside the local communities in which they were situated, is probably a reflection of the fact that the media and the public take all too little account of institutional arrangements until something goes demonstrably wrong.

Prisons can constitute frightening environments in which to live and work. When Michael Howard says that 'prison works' because prisoners can no longer prey upon the public, this shows remarkable disregard for the fact that they can still prey upon each other and upon the staff, and that the way in which our prisons are run can make these events more or less likely to happen. It is also, regret- tably, true that on occasion prisoners can fall foul of violence by the staff themselves. It is all too easily taken for granted by the civilian population outside that prisons are maintained in a state of control by a firm but fair body of staff. To the extent that justice may some- times be rough and ready, the public probably takes a rather unsym- pathetic view: once a man gets sent to prison he gets what he deserves or at least he should be able to look after himself. In fact the extent to which the supervision and control of staff reaches dif- ferent prisoners and different parts of the prison varies widely from prison to prison and from time to time in the same prison.

In each of our prisons we asked three series of questions about the experiences and perceptions of staff and prisoners: whether they had been victims or perpetrators of abuse; whom they regarded as a threat to their personal safety or their belongings; and how they perceived the safety or dangerousness of their prison.

Prisoners as Victims and Perpetrators of Abuse

In the first series we asked prisoners whether, during their current stay in this prison, they had been victims or perpetrators of various kinds of abuse: theft of, or damage to, property; sexual attacks; threats and verbal abuse; and violent physical assaults. We are very much aware that the responses to these questions cannot be taken simply at face value: either self-interest or machismo, and sometimes both, will perhaps have served to distort the true extent of these happenings. To the extent that it has, it will almost certainly be in the direction of under-reporting. Nevertheless, it is worth noting that these were by no means 'cold' responses to 'hired hand' research. The anonymous questionnaires were distributed and collected personally, and with a great deal of care, by us and one of our former colleagues. By that time we had spent at least three months in each prison, and we were certainly well known and, we think, quite well trusted by both staff and prisoners. In regard to some of these matters we had also talked extensively to many of our closest respondents. For these reasons we think the under-reporting may be less than it otherwise might have been. There were characteristic differences between the prisons on these matters.

Perhaps not surprisingly prisoners were most ready to report that their property had been damaged or stolen or that they had been on the receiving end of threats or verbal abuse. About a third of all prisoners had found each of these to be a problem. Only about one in eight, however, admitted to being the victim of a violent physical assault, and only one in fifteen to being the victim of a sexual attack or other sexual abuse.

The only comparison which may be made on these variables with the data so far published from the national prison survey concerns victims of assault. Walmsley, Howard, and White (1992, 41) report that 9 per cent of a national sample of some 4,000 prisoners had been assaulted by another prisoner in the previous six months. Walmsley *et al.* do not cite a separate assault victimization rate for adults, but it must be lower than 9 per cent (perhaps around 7 per cent) because that figure presumably includes young offenders of whom, they report, 15 per cent were assaulted. Moreover, it is not clear whether the NPS definition of assault included or excluded sexual attacks or attempts. Our data relate to 1,160 prisoners in five representative adult prisons, of whom 12.5 per cent reported they had been assaulted in their current prison and a further 6.8 per cent that they had been sexually attacked.

We should make it perfectly plain that straightforward comparisons between our data and the NPS data are not possible because of the ways in which the questions were asked. The NPS limited the responses by time, presumably in the hope that recall over a period of six months would be reasonably accurate and would offer some standardization and control. We chose not to time limit the responses to some of our questions, including these, for two reasons. First, we thought prisoners were much more likely to recall accurately whether they were assaulted in this prison as distinct from others they had been in than to recall whether or not the event had occurred within any given time period, because prisoners tend to measure time by reference to when they are transferred. Secondly, and more importantly, it seemed to us more likely that the salience of an assault for prisoners would depend on whether or not it had happened in the prison they were now in no matter how long ago it had occurred. Nevertheless, we cannot rule out the possibility that we may be picking up between two and three times as many assaults as the NPS simply because of differences in time at risk. We do, of course, have data on the length of time each of our prisoners had been in their current prison at the time the questionnaire was completed, the analysis of which reveals that slightly under a third of all those prisoners who reported both assaults (30.7 per cent) and sexual attacks and attempts (31.1 per cent) had been in their current prison for six months or less. But we obviously do not know, because we did not ask, at what points in their stay the remaining two-thirds of our victims had been assaulted. Moreover, although in our questionnaire we did not ask how many times they had been assaulted, we know from our interviews that many prisoners had been victimized (just as others had perpetrated attacks) on many occasions.

One further point needs to be made in considering time at risk. It is not just a question of time, as measured by length of time served, which may affect the risk of becoming a victim of prison assault. Of far greater importance, in our view, will be the length of time daily spent out of cell when that is taken in conjunction with the nature of the regime on offer. A long sentence spent largely behind one's door is likely to involve fewer risks than a short sentence spent in a more 'open regime'. In the comparisons which follow, length of time spent in the prison, length of time out of cell, and the nature of the regime then experienced all play a part. We would want to stress, however, that nothing we have to say here should lead to a reversal of the trend towards having prisoners out of their cells for longer periods, although it may focus attention upon the possible variations of open and active regimes that could be made available. In fact, unravelling what constitutes an assault, who are the perpetrators and who the victims, and what the circumstances are in which it occurs, is likely to be a much more complex matter even than this analysis suggests. All of this seriously calls into question the meaning to be placed upon the key performance indicator of assaults expressed as a proportion of the population and that is a matter to which we return at the end of this Chapter.

The total figures so far published from the national prison survey do not reveal the very large differences which are to be found in assaultive and other behaviours between prisons of different types. Our data are presented in Table 3.1.

More than four in every ten prisoners in Gartree (42.6 per cent) claimed to have been victims of assault or sexual attack and in Nottingham the figure was more than three in ten (33.9 per cent) In Featherstone the proportion fell to 17.2 per cent and in Ashwell to 5.4 per cent. In Birmingham 14.7 per cent of our remand prisoners and 9.5 per cent of the convicted prisoners had been either assaulted or attacked sexually. The highest rates of property abuse were found in Nottingham, but for verbal threats and intimidation the highest rate was once again found in Gartree and decreased with each reduction of the security level of the institution. There seems little doubt that property abuse and threats and intimidation are widespread throughout prisons and form part of the stuff of prison life—as perhaps they also do of the armed services and public schools. However, we did not have any means of distinguishing between greater or lesser threats and there is clearly scope for much more detailed research on these matters. The victimization rates for both remand and convicted prisoners in Birmingham were somewhat lower than we had expected. During the time we spent on the wings and landings in the course of our fieldwork in Birmingham the latent level of hostility and tension seemed, if anything, greater than in the other

Table 3.1. Prisoners who were victims of abuse: Percentage distribution

	Birmingham Rem. (n = 211)	Birmingham Conv. (N = 201)	Gartree (n = 155)	Nottingham (n = 156)	Featherstone (n = 269)	Ashwell (n = 168)	Total (n = 1160)
Property	32.7	26.9	36.1	42.3	33.5	24.4	32.4
Sex attack	5.2	3.0	12.9	11.5	7.1	3.0	6.8
Threats	34.6	26.4	49.0	42.6	35.7	13.7	33.4
Assault	9.5	6.5	29.7	22.4	10.1	2.4	12.5

Property	chi-square 15.83217	$p < .01$
Sex attack	chi-square 23.98231	$p < .0001$
Threats	chi-square 57.48396	$p < .0001$
Assault	chi-square 81.45251	$p < .0001$

institutions. The lower reporting of incidents there almost certainly reflects the reduced opportunities for predatory behaviours given the very restricted periods that prisoners were allowed out of their cells. In all cases the differences in victimization rates between the prisons were statistically significant.

There seems to be little doubt that the risk of being assaulted whilst serving a sentence in the higher security prisons at least is a matter that cannot be taken lightly. It will, of course, be tempting to explain that by reference to the characteristics of the prisoners in those institutions, more of whom may have records of violence and who may be deemed to be more assaultive than those in the lower security prisons. However, it is important in this connection to have regard to some previously unpublished data from the comparison between Gartree and Oak Park Heights. Although there were a number of differences between the prison populations held in the two prisons it could not reasonably be argued that prisoners in Gartree were more violent in their previous criminal behaviour than prisoners in Oak Park Heights. Thus, it is true that Gartree had more people convicted of murder (40 per cent as against 33 per cent) but it is usually argued that life-sentence prisoners are easier to manage within prison—this was why additional lifers were moved into Gartree after the 1983 riot in an effort to stabilize the population. Gartree also had more people convicted for robbery (29 per cent as against 21 per cent). On the other hand Oak Park Heights had greater proportions convicted of assaults and woundings (10 per cent as against 8 per cent) and many more sexual predators (21 per cent as against 6 per cent). Nevertheless, the self-reported victimization in Oak Park Heights was only one third of the level we found in Gartree—4.7 per cent as against 12.9 per cent for sexual attacks, and only 9.3 per cent as against 29.7 per cent victims of assault. The proportionate difference was even greater for victims of property abuse—10.7 per cent in Oak Park Heights as against 36.1 per cent in Gartree. It is important to remember that the same questions were asked by the same researcher in the same way in Gartree and Oak Park Heights, thus eliminating some of the usual sources of error. In fact the victimization rates in Oak Park Heights, with a population and function analogous to Gartree, nevertheless are lower (in the case of property abuse, considerably lower) than those we found for Featherstone. It should further be noted that prisoners were out of their cells in Oak Park Heights for up to fifteen hours a day both during the week and at weekends, longer than in any of the British prisons in our study.

Cultural factors have been suggested to us as playing a possible part in explaining the differences between Oak Park Heights and Gartree. It is argued that American prisons constitute a much more macho environment than British prisons and that Oak Park Heights prisoners might therefore feel less able to report themselves as victims. If that were the case, however, it would be very hard to explain why the same prisoners were also more reluctant to report themselves as perpetrators of abuse than their counterparts in Gartree. Alternatively, it has been put to us that Oak Park Heights prisoners might hold back in their predatory behaviour because they are aware that if they start a fight they might be called upon to 'go all the way' and make it a fight to the finish. But in that case the question simply becomes why should that happen in Oak Park Heights when it manifestly does not in other American institutions (see Bowker 1980, 1982)? In the course of scores of hours of taped interviews with prisoners in Oak Park Heights there are repeated references which indicate that the low levels of violence have to do with the way in which out of cell activities are organized and supervised: thus a frequent complaint was that 'normal' prisoners had to endure having a 'sex case' in a neighbouring cell without their being able to exact the kind of retribution that sometimes happens in Gartree and which we described earlier in this chapter. It seems to us that these differences in victimization rates can only be explained by reference to differences in the design of the facilities, the nature of regimes provided whilst prisoners are out of cells, and the policies and procedures relating to them.

Before leaving these data we should say something about ethnic differences in victimization. Walmsley and colleagues report a higher proportion of Asians than of either white or black prisoners who had been assaulted but cite no figures, presumably because the differences could have been accounted for by chance factors. Our data seem to show a different picture: in our study 18.1 per cent of black prisoners had been assaulted, compared to 14.3 per cent of Asians and 11.6 per cent of white prisoners. This rank order, however, varied from prison to prison with black prisoners being the most frequent victims in Birmingham and in Featherstone, and white prisoners in Gartree and Nottingham. In Ashwell the frequency of assault was so low it can be discounted. However, as with the national prison survey, the differences between assault rates for ethnic groups did not reach statistical significance.

Prisoners were, understandably, somewhat more reluctant to self-report as the perpetrators of these abuses: only 3.7 per cent reported stealing or damaging the property of others and only 1.4 per cent reported making unwanted sexual overtures towards other prisoners. The differences between prisons on these variables were not statistically significant. Rather more prisoners were prepared to admit to using threats and intimidation (18.7 per cent) or actual violence (9.8 per cent) to maintain their position against other prisoners. The pattern of admitted predatory behaviour of these kinds, as between prisons, was the same (albeit at a lower level) as the pattern of admitted victimizations, and again the differences were statistically significant. The details are given in Table 3.2.

The national prison survey offers no data on rates of predatory behaviour, but once again there is an instructive and hitherto unpublished comparison to be made between Gartree and Oak Park Heights: in Gartree 19.9 per cent of the prisoners admitted assaulting others compared to only 9.6 per cent in Oak Park Heights.

Staff as Victims of Abuse and Staff Use of Force

The national prison survey appears not to have included staff. Nor were staff included, because of lack of time, in the study of Oak Park Heights. Our data here are therefore limited to the reported experiences of staff in our five study prisons.

We asked staff whether or not prisoners in the prison where they were now working had tried to bribe or compromise them; whether prisoners had stolen or damaged their property, threatened them or their families, or physically assaulted them. Almost a quarter of our respondents said that prisoners had tried to bribe or compromise them. Nearly a third of Nottingham staff (31.4 per cent) reported this, compared to only one in eight of those in Ashwell (12.5 per cent) but about a quarter of the staff in each of the other three prisons reported such attempts and the differences between the prisons were not statistically significant. Only a tenth of staff reported that they had had property stolen or damaged by prisoners, and again the differences between the prisons were not significant. Nearly half of all prison officers, however, had been on the receiving end of threats either to themselves or their families. By far the highest rate was to be found in Nottingham (62.9 per cent), followed by Birmingham

Table 3.2. Prisoners admitting predatory abuse: Percentage distribution

	Birmingham Rem. (n = 209)	Birmingham Conv. (N = 201)	Gartree (n = 151)	Nottingham (n = 155)	Featherstone (n = 268)	Ashwell (n = 167)	Total (n = 1151)
Property	3.3	3.0	2.6	3.2	7.1	1.2	3.7
Sex attack	1.0	0.5	2.0	3.9	1.1	0.6	1.4
Threats	12.4	14.4	29.8	29.0	20.9	8.4	18.7
Assault	9.1	7.0	19.9	16.8	5.6	5.4	9.8

Property	chi-square 12.38331	p NS
Sex attack	chi-square 9.71200	p NS
Threats	chi-square 43.50209	p < .0001
Assault	chi-square 36.76091	p < .0001

(52.4 per cent), Gartree (39.7 per cent), Ashwell (37.5 per cent), and Featherstone (34.1 per cent), and these differences approached statistical significance (chi-square 0.02747, df = 4, p < 0.07). Actual assaults on staff did differentiate between the prisons in ways that could not have been accounted for by chance. All told, just over a quarter of staff (26.7 per cent) reported that they had been assaulted. In both Birmingham (34.9 per cent) and Gartree (also 34.9 per cent), over a third of staff claimed to have been assaulted, compared to 28.6 per cent in Nottingham and only 9.1 per cent in Featherstone and 6.3 per cent in Ashwell (chi-square 14.80472 df = 4 p < 0.01).

Of those staff who had been assaulted or placed under threat, some 17.3 per cent had to have time off work as a result and a further 2.3 per cent had been moved to other duties. Once again these outcomes were more likely in Birmingham and in Gartree, followed by Nottingham, but the differences between the prisons in this regard did not reach statistical significance.

We also asked the staff how often they had used force on prisoners in the last year. Nearly two-fifth (38.1 per cent) of staff had not used violence at all in the last year, although nearly a quarter (23.4 per cent) had used force on three or more occasions. There were, however, dramatic differences between the prisons (chi-square 39.20087 df = 12 p < .0001). Thus in Ashwell (70.6 per cent) and Featherstone (51.1 per cent) the majority of staff had not used force at all, and only 5.9 per cent in Ashwell and 4.4 per cent in Featherstone had used force more than once. In Birmingham, on the other hand, the use of violence at some time was part of the experience of over three-quarters of the staff. For almost half of them, indeed, it was a regular occurrence: 49.2 per cent had used force on three or more occasions and only 23.1 per cent had not used force at all. Nottingham staff were the next most likely to use force, with 34.2 per cent using it on three or more occasions. In Gartree more than two-fifths (42.2 per cent) of the staff had not used violence and just over a tenth (10.9 per cent) had used it three or more times.

The extent to which staff are regularly involved in the use of force is a product of several factors: these include the general level of incidents in which force may be required, the speed with which certain members of staff respond to alarm calls, whether or not there is a defined 'heavy mob' of staff who are called on in particular circumstances, the stability of staff cultures, and whether staff who are involved in incidents have been trained in control and restraint (C and R) techniques.[12] At the time of our research most staff in Gartree had been trained in C and R 1, using three-man teams to disarm, restrain, and relocate violent prisoners. About a quarter had also undergone C and R 2 (A) training in more advanced self-defence procedures and C and R 2 (B), to deal with small scale disturbances as part of a twelve-man unit. In the other prisons, the proportion of C and R-trained staff varied widely: in the lower security prisons the majority had not yet received training in C and R 1, and elsewhere, although many had received their basic training, hardly any had been trained in C and R 2.

There is no doubt that there was something of a canteen culture of violence in both Birmingham and Nottingham; and in both these prisons there was a core of long-serving officers to carry that culture. When alarm bells go there is a *frisson* of excitement that rushes round the prison like adrenaline. In Gartree this had to a considerable extent been replaced by the more extensive use of C and R-trained staff. More than one of our respondents in Gartree looked back with some nostalgia to the old days when staff would all pile in when the alarm bell went. But they also spoke with some degree of pride about how the existence of C and R obviated the need for the use of actual violence. Thus one principal officer told us:

In the old days when we moved prisoners we often used to end up rolling round the floor and people got hurt. Sometimes there would be so many guys in there you didn't know who you were fighting. You'd grab an arm or a leg and you'd find it belonged to one of your mates. Now that we have C and R it doesn't have to happen. The prisoner doesn't have to resist to prove anything. He can still have his self-respect because everybody knows that it's three against one and we are trained. In the old days, he might end up

[12] C and R techniques were introduced under Circular Instruction 24/1984, the Control Review Committee having identified a need for staff to be 'trained in MUFTI techniques and methods of personal restraint' (Home Office 1984a, para. 115). Initially there were two training syllabuses. C and R 1 covered methods for restraining an individual prisoner and separating and restraining prisoners who are fighting. It also included the use of a 3-man team to disarm, restrain, and remove from a cell an armed and violent inmate. C and R 2 was in two parts: (A) involved self-defence techniques for an officer under attack and (B) the use of a 12-man team in response to a disturbance where prisoners were armed with clubs or missiles and, say, barricading a landing. Under CI 58/1988 it was announced that MUFTI was to be phased out by Mar. 1990 and replaced by C and R 3, which would involve a development of C and R 1 and 2 techniques and deploy a 36-man team (effectively three 12-man units) with refined equipment. Whereas all officers under 55 years who were medically fit were to be trained in C and R 1 and 2A, the intention was to train an elite group of 4,000 officers across the system as a whole in C and R 2B and C and R 3.

having seven bells of shit kicked out of him but he'd bloody well take some of us with him if he could. Nine times out of ten now he'll just put up his hands and go quietly.

However, C and R is not always used on such occasions in all prisons and even when it is used it is sometimes used incorrectly. One cynical officer put it to us as follows: 'What's good about C and R is that now you can stand up in a court of law and say he was restrained using the official control and restraint method. We are not outside the law then, but shielded by the law'. The most likely circumstance in which staff reported that violence was used in Birmingham was dealing with disruptive prisoners, followed by breaking up fights between prisoners, and intervening when staff were being assaulted. These situations accounted for more than two-thirds of the incidents in Nottingham and Gartree as well. As we have reported elsewhere, however, prisoners take a different view of the circumstances in which staff violence is used (McDermott and King 1988; King and McDermott 1990a).

Prisoners and Staff: Threats to Personal Safety

In a second series of questions we asked prisoners to say who they perceived to be the biggest threat to their personal safety and well-being in the prison. Prisoners were invited to indicate whether, in so far as they had problems of this kind, these arose from victimization or grievances with one or two particular prisoners or one or two members of staff; or whether their problems arose from some more general sense of harassment, either from the prisoner community or the staff group as a whole. They were also given the opportunity to say if they had no problems of this kind. The findings are presented in Table 3.3.

All told, 21.9 per cent indicated that they perceived other prisoners, either individually or collectively, to be the main threat to their safety, whilst a further 24.5 per cent considered the staff to be the main threat, and 53.6 per cent had no problems in this regard and presumably felt safe, or at least more than able to take care of themselves.

There were statistically significant differences between the prisons on each of the four sources of threat which we identified. However, several of the findings which are presented in Table 3.3 stand out and deserve further comment. A third (32.9 per cent) of the prisoners in

Table 3.3. Prisoners' perceptions of source of threat to self: Percentage distribution

	Birmingham Rem. (n = 202)	Birmingham Conv. (n = 203)	Gartree (n = 153)	Nottingham (n = 149)	Featherstone (n = 267)	Ashwell (n = 166)	Total (n = 1140)
Few prisoners	9.4	5.4	11.8	13.5	4.9	5.4	7.9
Prisoners generally	15.3	7.9	28.8	32.9	6.7	1.2	14.0
Few staff	17.8	12.8	15.8	18.0	9.7	4.8	12.9
Staff generally	19.3	12.8	11.8	14.8	6.7	5.4	11.6
None	38.2	61.1	31.8	20.8	72.2	83.2	53.6
	100.0	100.0	100.0	100.0	100.0	100.0	100.0

Note Columns do not always add up to 100 because of rounding

Few prisoners   Chi-square   16.66753 $p < .01$
Prisoners generally Chi-square   112.45218 $p < .0001$
Few staff   Chi-square   20.98896 $p < .001$
Staff generally   Chi-square   25.81449 $p < .0001$

Nottingham and more than a quarter of those in Gartree (28.8 per cent) felt themselves to be most under threat simply from the presence of other prisoners generally—regardless of any individual grievances that might have developed with particular prisoners or staff. But surely even more worrying is that just under a fifth (19.3 per cent) of remand prisoners in Birmingham felt themselves to be threatened by the staff generally and with almost as many (17.8 per cent) registering fears about individual members of staff, this meant that 37.1 per cent or nearly two in every five remand prisoners regarded staff as a threat to their personal safety or well-being. Whilst Featherstone and Ashwell were generally safe institutions and seen to be so by the prisoners, only one in five prisoners in Nottingham, one in three in Gartree, and two out of five remand prisoners in Birmingham felt safe from other prisoners or the staff.

These data seem to suggest a much higher level of fear about personal safety than appears to have been uncovered in the national prison survey. So, too, does the recent study by Adler (1994) for the Prison Reform Trust in which she reports that half of all prisoners and two-thirds of prison officers are afraid for at least some of their time in prison. One reason why the national prison survey reports lower levels may be because their researchers seem to have asked only about fears from the actions of other *prisoners*—at least according to the data so far published.[13] Thus Walmsley *et al.* (1992, 41) report that only 18 per cent of prisoners said that they did not feel safe from being bullied or injured by other prisoners. Even that is lower than our figure of 21.9 per cent, and it may be that our prisoners responded more fully because the preceding question had asked them directly about whether they had been victims of abuse. Walmsley *et al.* note that as many as 26 per cent of those already on Rule 43 for their own protection did not feel safe. In our study Rule 43 own-protection prisoners were under-represented, partly because of difficulties we experienced in delivering and collecting questionnaires for this group and partly because those who responded sometimes left crucial parts of the questionnaire blank. Nevertheless, the differences between prisons in our study are greater than the difference between own-protection prisoners and general population prisoners reported in the national prison survey. Very few prisoners were

---

[13] According to Walmsley *et al.* (1992) further work is in progress on the analysis of the national prison survey data, so a more detailed account of its findings may yet appear.

afraid of others in our low-security establishments while substantial proportions were afraid in higher-security prisons.

Another finding from a different part of the national prison survey, however, seems to lend support to our data. When asked to agree or disagree with the statement, 'some prison officers assault prisoners here', apparently 25 per cent agreed (Walmsley *et al.* 1992, 40) and intriguingly this was the question which most sharply differentiated between establishments of different types, with 30 per cent agreeing at local prisons. If the response to that question were taken as a kind of proxy for the responses to our questions about individual staff or staff generally, this would suggest much closer comparability between the findings of the two studies.

Of course, it could be argued that these prisoner perceptions are deliberately misleading about staff and should be treated with caution. Such a view seems to us but a variant of the ideology that kept the provision against making 'false and malicious allegations' part of the Prison Rules for so long. We would have to say that, weighing all the responses from staff and prisoners throughout the whole body of our research, we see no reason for treating prisoners' answers about fears of staff with more caution than, say, staff answers about their fears of prisoners—or indeed than any of the other responses. There seems more force in the possibility that prisoners may have a well-judged fear that staff could affect their well-being through their power over decision-making and that this has become conflated with fears for physical safety. Nevertheless, it would be foolish to ignore the fears which prisoners report in relation to staff. Thus in Nottingham, it was repeatedly drawn to our attention that staff sometimes turned a blind eye to homosexuality and bullying, and it was plain that some staff incorporated this into their recipe for maintaining a 'happy prison'. It was suggested to us, by both staff and prisoners, for example, that 'pretty young boys' were introduced to a well-known life-sentence prisoner, who enjoyed a cell in a secluded part of one of the upper galleries, because staff knew he would 'look after them'.

A few further words of explanation may also be called for in relation to the fears of staff expressed by remand prisoners in Birmingham. It is possible that remand prisoners on C wing responded in accordance with their culturally acquired knowledge about Barry Prosser and other cases as well as their own direct experiences. But there was also a well-defined fear in Birmingham about what went on in nearby D wing. In most prisons there is a well-understood fear which prisoners have of 'the block' where prisoners may spend time under punishment. Rightly or wrongly, the block is widely regarded as a place in which staff use violence against prisoners. Traditionally, taking prisoners to the block has been an occasion for violence which has often had a relatively high visibility. In both Gartree and Nottingham there was an appreciable measure of fear expressed in relation to the block although this was very muted in Featherstone and Ashwell. But it was in Birmingham that fears about staff violence were most widely expressed. Prisoners' fears and fantasies were fed by the aura which surrounded D wing. Whether or not prisoners had actually seen it D wing's reputation was widely known throughout the prison. D4 houses Rule 43 own-protection prisoners; D3 accommodated up to a dozen category A and provisional category A prisoners; D2 contained many prisoners who were regarded as mental-health-problem prisoners and who were often heavily sedated; and D1 had cells used for prisoners segregated under Rule 43 to maintain the good order and discipline of the establishment. Prisoners described being on D wing as 'limboing' or being 'in limbo'. The wing was dark and gloomy, and whenever we visited it was always deathly quiet, although we were told that at other times it could be extremely noisy. It was always locked down tight.

We were particularly concerned to discover whether in any of the prisons our respondents felt themselves to be intimidated by other prisoners who might be seen to be acting as a group, either in concerted gang-like activities or as members of a power elite within the institution. Over a quarter (27.5 per cent) of the prisoners in Gartree and a fifth (20.2 per cent) of the remand prisoners in Birmingham felt that prisoner gangs, cliques, or elites made life especially difficult for them. This was somewhat less of a problem in Nottingham (15.8 per cent), Featherstone (16.5 per cent), and for convicted prisoners in Birmingham (14.1 per cent), and much less in Ashwell (5.5 per cent). The differences were statistically significant (chi-square = 30.74616, p < .00001). When we asked those prisoners who felt intimidated to identify the categories of prisoners who made life difficult for them in this way, the majority of those in Gartree identified London gangsters as the power elite, whilst in Birmingham the problems were seen, by white prisoners, as stemming from black prisoners. In Birmingham, more than elsewhere, we were told by staff and prisoners that trouble inside reflected the troubles outside on the streets of Handsworth with the same gangs continuing their territorial struggles inside (cf. Jacobs 1974). In Featherstone and Nottingham there was less unanimity, with black prisoners and those involved in the drugs scene identified as the main creators of problems. Significant numbers of prisoners in all the prisons regarded sex offenders or 'nonces', grasses, and mentally unstable prisoners or 'nutters' as causing problems, although almost by definition these were not typically involved in gang-like activities.

Staff were asked whether there were any groups or categories of prisoners in their prison with whom they felt particularly vulnerable. We then asked them to rate how severe a threat to the good order and discipline of the prison those groups of prisoners posed. In Ashwell, Featherstone, and Nottingham between two-thirds and three-quarters of staff claimed they had no problem in regard to vulnerability, but drug users and mentally unstable offenders gave some cause for concern to remaining staff in Ashwell and Nottingham, as did sex offenders in Ashwell and Featherstone, and ethnic minorities in Featherstone. In Gartree most staff (59.4 per cent) denied they felt vulnerable to any particular group, but amongst those who did admit some vulnerability the biggest single group they identified was variously described as 'politicals' or 'terrorists' (26.9 per cent), followed by London gangsters (11.5 per cent). In Birmingham more than half (53 per cent) admitted some feelings of vulnerability and identified mentally unstable offenders as their principal anxiety, followed by drug users and ethnic minorities. There seems little doubt that significant numbers of prisoners in Birmingham might more properly have been detained in a mental hospital than a prison.

The data on how severe a threat these groups of prisoners constituted for the good order and discipline of the prisons, as perceived by the staff, are presented in Figure 3.1.

It can be seen that drug traffickers were regarded as a serious threat to good order and discipline in all establishments, regardless of the level of security. For other groups the perceived level of threat to good order largely reflected the allocation policies we described in Chapter 2. Only in Gartree were 'political' groups or 'terrorists' seen as a problem because Gartree was effectively the only prison which held them. In the course of our fieldwork in Gartree considerable anxiety was caused by our expectation that we would have as free access to these prisoners as we did with all others. It is a remarkable testimony to the governor and staff at Gartree that we were allowed

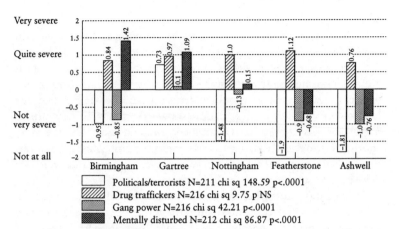

Fig. 3.1   Threats to good order and discipline—Staff perceptions

such access. On one memorable occasion a relatively junior member of a middle-eastern terrorist organization was instructed by his superiors to show us proper hospitality by inviting us for a meal on the wing.[14] The situation was carefully stage-managed by him, knowing that a formal request in advance ran a more serious risk of refusal. Came the day we were on tenterhooks on evening association while he cooked the meal. We then watched with admiration as the request was put 'as a matter of honour' when the security principal officer— a member of staff to whom we were already well known—made his rounds. It was not considered appropriate that we should eat in his cell, but it was fully accepted that it should be a private occasion. The security PO arranged that we use the smaller television room where we could eat in privacy but where staff could see us. A somewhat surprised wing staff joked nervously about us being poisoned, though we proceeded to enjoy one of the best meals we had in nearly eighteen months of fieldwork. On another occasion when the governor told us that staff were worried because Kathy McDermott, an American citizen, might be in particular danger from some of the middle-eastern groups in Gartree, she told him, 'That's all right,

[14] Gartree was the only one of our prisons where prisoners had the wherewithall to cook on the wings in the evenings. It was, in our view, one of the most civilizing aspects of the prison and extremely important in the lives—and of course diet—of prisoners (see Ch. 4).

most of them here think I'm Irish'. The governor gasped, saying 'My God. That's even worse!' Such are the stereotypes to be found in prison (see Borland, King, and McDermott 1995).

Gang power was a threat in Gartree and to some extent in Nottingham, but nowhere else. There was, however, a world of difference between the gangs. In Gartree, what the staff called the London gangsters were, by prison standards, immaculately turned out. They shaved their heads, pumped iron, and controlled the rackets. In Nottingham they were disorganized street gangs. They tattooed their foreheads, their necks, and their fingers, and were not infrequently stoned on cannabis.

The mentally disturbed prisoners—prisoners who were regarded as unstable but not clinically within the terms of the Mental Health Acts—were seen as a problem everywhere except Featherstone and Ashwell. Such prisoners were unlikely to be eligible for open prison on security grounds, and as we saw in Chapter 2 the observation, classification, and allocation unit staff at Birmingham were unlikely to send mentally disordered category C offenders to Featherstone, preferring to keep Stafford as a dumping ground. But if there were mentally disturbed prisoners who met the criteria for category B and might otherwise be bound for Nottingham, they ran the risk of being re-defined as 'needing' dispersal conditions in which case OCA staff sent them to Gartree rather than Long Lartin. There were several occasions in the course of our fieldwork when we had to hold our ground in the face of behaviour by some of these prisoners that was obviously intended to intimidate. We are under no illusions about the disruption that they can cause.

Prisoners and Staff: Perceptions of Safety and Potential Danger

Our third series of questions asked prisoners and staff mainly about the perceived safety or potential danger of particular locations within the prison. On most variables we asked our respondents to make a rating on a four-point scale from very safe (+2) to very dangerous (−2) and we present the results here, comparing staff and prisoner ratings for each location. The data show some interesting universals, or near universals, across the prisons, as well as important and intriguing differences between them.

In general terms it came as no surprise that the place where prisoners felt safest in every prison was behind their doors in their own cells or rooms. Staff, too, felt safest on their own ground in the wing office, but noticeably less safe than did prisoners on their own territory, no doubt because the office is often the location for refusing prisoners' requests and this sometimes results in altercations. The situation is represented in Figure 3.2. The differences between the prisons were statistically significant (staff: chi-square 30.441 p < .01; prisoners: chi-square 47.917 p < .0001).

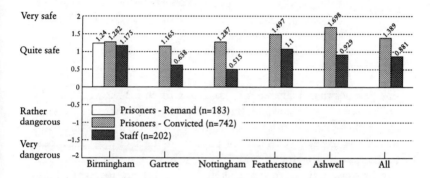

Fig. 3.2 How safe or dangerous is your own cell or office?—Prisoner and staff perceptions of own safety

Prisoners felt noticeably less safe in other prisoners' cells than in their own, but still did not typically regard these as dangerous areas, as is shown in Figure 3.3. Staff in the higher-security prisons clearly recognized prisoners' cells as dangerous territory, especially in Gartree where, in spite of having two staff to a landing and access towers, the memory of the riots still lingered. Once again the differences between the prisons were statistically significant (staff: chi-square 52.037 p < .01: prisoners: chi-square 117.49 p < .0001).

Many assaults on prisoners, both violent and sexual, are reputed to take place in the toilet and shower recesses, partly because prisoners in a state of undress or performing the natural functions are obviously more vulnerable, and partly because these areas tend to be poorly supervised by staff if only on grounds of delicacy, though they are sometimes also accused of turning a blind eye to homosexuality and bullying. In Nottingham it seemed that the recesses were less closely watched than elsewhere. It is one of the celebrated explanations for injuries when prisoners appear before adjudications or on

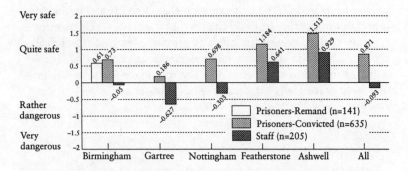

Fig. 3.3 How safe or dangerous are other prisoners' cells?—Prisoner and staff perceptions of own safety

sick parades that 'I slipped on a cake of soap in the showers, sir'. As can be seen from Figure 3.4 there was a marked difference between the higher-security prisons and the lower-security prisons with regard to the perceived safety or potential danger of these locations, on the part both of staff and prisoners. Indeed, in the higher-security prisons, staff were more likely than prisoners to regard these areas as dangerous—perhaps because if they intervened in such situations to protect prisoners they put themselves at risk.

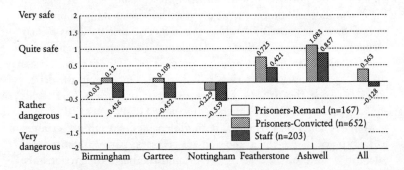

Fig. 3.4 How safe or dangerous are the recesses?—Prisoner and staff perceptions of own safety

It should be emphasized that the presentation of these data in terms of mean scale scores tends to mask the very real perception of danger by substantial minorities of prisoners. Thus, more than one in five prisoners in Birmingham and Nottingham regarded the recesses as very dangerous, and almost as large a proportion felt the same in Gartree. Several prisoners told us in graphic terms that one of the 'very worst things about being in prison is that you can't have a shit or a shower without worrying who is in the next cubicle and who is coming in next'. Shortly before our fieldwork began in Gartree a prisoner was gang-raped on D wing: and in Nottingham a prisoner was knifed while taking a shower. Differences between the prisons were statistically significant (staff: chi-square 44.075 p < .0001; prisoners: chi-square 110.058 p < .0001).

In Figure 3.5 we show how prisoners perceived their safety in a number of more public places: landings, corridors, and staircases; the association rooms; the prison workshops; and the exercise yard.

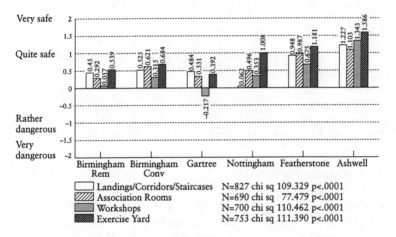

Fig. 3.5 Safe or dangerous public territories—Prisoner perceptions of own safety

In Figure 3.5 it can be seen that prisoner responses on these variables generally follow the security gradient, with these areas being perceived as somewhat less safe in the higher-security prisons. 'Accidents' are often said to happen when prisoners 'lose their balance and fall down stairs' as in the press reporting of the Birmingham Six quoted earlier. It should be noted that one in six prisoners in Nottingham regarded the landings, corridors, and staircases as very dangerous and almost half regarded them as dangerous to some degree. Anyone who has ever seen a prison film will also know that the workshops provide weapons, the possibility of creating diversions to distract staff, and opportunities to get out of the sight of officers and instructors. There is little doubt that the workshops offered these possibilities in Gartree, where 20 per cent of the prisoners regarded them as very dangerous places and a further 35 per cent as rather dangerous.

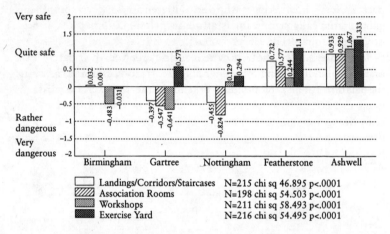

Fig. 3.6   Safe or dangerous public territories—Staff perceptions of own safety

Staff were generally more concerned than prisoners about their safety in public places though this was very much more marked in Birmingham, Gartree, and Nottingham, as can be seen from Figure 3.6. The workshops in Birmingham were seen as especially dangerous by one member of staff in every five (not that they were in operation all that often as we shall see in Chapter 5); and one in ten staff in Gartree took a similar view. A particular problem in Gartree was that prisoners sometimes set delayed incendiary devices in the workshops, and it was routine practice to send in sniffer dogs as soon as prisoners had left to find them.

From a consideration of these diagrams it is apparent that all areas of Featherstone and Ashwell were generally regarded as safe by both staff and prisoners. In Nottingham, prisoners felt reasonably safe except in the recesses and on the landings and staircases, whereas staff felt rather uncertain or decidedly unsafe except in their offices. In Birmingham, prisoners felt least safe in the recesses and in the workshops, and staff only felt safe in their offices. In Gartree, prisoners were most likely to find the workshops positively dangerous, although they also admitted the lowest levels of safety on almost all the other variables, which is important bearing in mind that most Gartree prisoners probably felt some pressure to live up to an image on these matters. Gartree staff felt unsafe everywhere except in their offices or on the exercise field, where there were always dogs on patrol. Some idea of the attitude towards this in Gartree can be gained from the joking banter between staff. Thus the new principal officer told his senior officer in the wing office, 'Right I'm going to the 4s, and I'm going to check the recesses, then I'm going to do that on all the landings, and then I'm going into the TV room and change the channel'. The senior officer replied, 'Yes sir, right sir, it's your wing sir'. Needless to say he did not do any of those things.

By way of trying to summarize this situation we asked staff and prisoners to rate how safe or dangerous their prison was, first of all for the prisoners who lived there and then for the staff who worked there. The findings for the safety of prisoners are presented in Figure 3.7, from which it can be seen that staff always regarded their own prison as more safe than dangerous for the prisoners in their care, albeit with the higher-security prisons as less safe than the lower-security prisons. Prisoners, for the most part, agreed with them, usually rating the prison as even safer from their point of view than staff had done. That pattern, however, falls down in Birmingham and Gartree where prisoners on balance found the prison to be positively dangerous. Nevertheless, in terms of our distinction between the depth and weight of imprisonment developed in Chapter 2, the deeper prisoners were in to the security levels of the prison system, the heavier was likely to be their experience of the system in terms of its potential danger.

In Figure 3.8 we present the summary data for staff and prisoner perceptions of how safe or dangerous each prison was for the staff who worked in it. The pattern is reversed. In each prison the prisoners generally regarded it as a safe environment for staff, albeit that the low-security prisons were seen as safer than the high-security prisons. Staff broadly agreed, but this time reported somewhat lower levels of safety than prisoners. Again in Gartree and in Birmingham the staff perceived the prison to be a dangerous working environment.

We have reported elsewhere (King 1991a) that in Oak Park

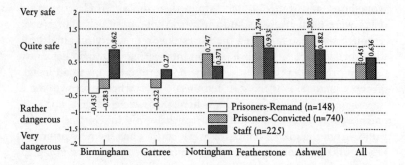

Fig. 3.7 How safe or dangerous is this prison for prisoners?—Prisoner and staff perceptions

Heights, nearly ten times as many prisoners (30 per cent) reported their prison as very safe for prisoners, as was the case in Gartree (3.3 per cent); and nearly three times as many (32.5 per cent compared to 11.1 per cent) thought it very safe for staff. There was a celebrated incident, much talked about in Oak Park Heights, where a prisoner had succeeded in wrenching a handle off the shower-room door preparatory to attacking the prisoner inside—but the incident was easily dealt with. For most practical purposes there were no really dangerous places in Oak Park Heights.

It is difficult to make further comparisons between our data and the national prison survey, because so far there has been only rather

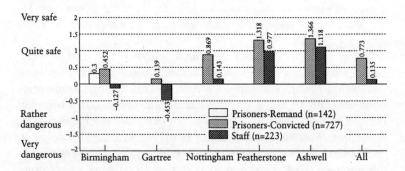

Fig. 3.8 How safe or dangerous is this prison for staff?—Prisoner and staff perceptions

condensed reporting of these matters in the national survey and because our questions were asked in rather different ways. However, the 18 per cent of prisoners in the NPS who had declared that they did not feel safe from other prisoners were further asked about the circumstances in which they felt least safe. Some 35 per cent of this group of prisoners seemed to feel unsafe everywhere in the prison, a further 15 per cent felt least safe in the showers and toilets, 13 per cent in places when they were out of sight of officers, and 10 per cent in their own (presumably shared) cell or dormitory (Walmsley *et al.* 1992, 41). We report much higher levels of perceived potential danger. Some 9.5 per cent of our *total* sample found their cells to some degree dangerous places. The majority of these were in shared cells in Birmingham, though it should be remembered that our main finding is that one's own cell is for most people the safest place. Some 40.2 per cent of our total sample regarded the toilet and shower recesses as dangerous places. These apparent differences are not necessarily incompatible because prisoners in our study could, rather like New Yorkers riding the subway, correctly perceive these places as dangerous, without feeling or admitting themselves to be personally at risk.

One final point worth making is that it is not just a sub-group amongst the vulnerable prisoners identified in the national prisoner survey who feel most at risk whenever they are out of sight of staff. When we asked staff in each of our prisons about other times and circumstances in which they felt vulnerable, this was mentioned by two out of every three staff in our total sample, and was the most important factor mentioned by staff in Gartree, Birmingham, and Nottingham.

Maintaining Order After Woolf

Although our lower-security research prisons may be regarded as safe for prisoners and staff, similar institutions have by no means been immune from disorder. British high security prisons generally have had a troubled history in terms of loss of control and, as we have seen from the data presented here, are not regarded as safe by many staff and by significant numbers of prisoners. It seems possible that our high-security prisons and our remand prisons may be much less safe than so far would appear from the findings of the national prison survey. By contrast, a prison such as Oak Park

Heights seems to have offered safety levels comparable to our lower-security prisons whilst housing a population comparable to our higher security establishments. What prospects are there for a better future in terms of the maintenance of good order for our prisons in the world after Woolf?

As we noted in Chapter 2, Woolf did not neglect issues to do with direct and physical measures for maintaining security and control. Nevertheless, the great achievement of Woolf LJ's Report was that it put the whole question of order and control in prisons, usually considered in narrow, technical terms, into a broader context, linking it both to the quality of life in prison and a moral climate of just and humane treatment. There are, for example, many clear statements in the report (Home Office 1991a) linking riots to regimes:

there is a close link between the nature of the regime, in the broadest sense of that word, and the risk of prisoners behaving in a disruptive manner (*ibid.*, para. 12.228)

The best way of reducing the risk of disruption and disturbance is to improve the regime within a prison and to improve the way prisoners are handled within the prison system. An improved regime will also be the best way of ensuring that, if a disturbance starts, fewer prisoners are inclined to join in (*ibid.*, para. 12.231).

There would be less likelihood of prisoners creating trouble if they:

were content with the location of the prison which is holding them (*ibid.*, para. 12.235)
feel they are part of manageably sized groups (*ibid.*, para. 12.236)
can take part in a regime with as many incentives towards good behaviour as possible and with as few disincentives as is practicable (*ibid.*, para. 12.237)

and where there is 'an effective grievance procedure' (*ibid.*, para. 12.238).

At the beginning of this Chapter we noted, citing Sparks (1994), that Woolf marked a distinct conceptual development in official thinking. It is important to recognize to what degree the change in the penal lexicon brought about by Woolf, and then transmitted through the Government White Paper, *Custody, Care, and Justice*, has found its way into the Prison Service *Corporate Plan*. Woolf was concerned that the Prison Service statement of purpose, introduced in November 1987 during the currency of our research, did not refer to treating prisoners with justice, although he was almost persuaded that this was implied by the duty to look after them with humanity (Home Office 1991a, para. 10.20). The statement of purpose remains unchanged after Woolf, but the expanded expression of the vision, goals, and values makes plain the intention that prisoners 'will be treated with fairness, justice, and respect'. It is perhaps surprising, therefore, that the chapter devoted to maintaining order, control, discipline, and a safe environment in the *Corporate Plan* makes no further mention of the word justice. Nevertheless, the main strategies listed for achieving the goal of maintaining order go far beyond the narrowly technical matters. They are listed as follows:

— creating an environment in which the risk of a breakdown of order or loss of control is minimised, mainly through: good relationships and active regimes; providing decent conditions and meeting prisoners' needs; and good design.

— preventing disorder, by: gathering information; and dealing with disruptive prisoners (if necessary, as a last resort, by segregating or transferring those who are believed to be causing trouble); and protecting vulnerable prisoners.

— responding firmly and effectively to restore order and control when trouble arises, by: using control and restraint techniques when necessary; and bringing criminal and disciplinary proceedings (Prison Service 1993d, para. 6.9).

Moreover, in an important declaration of intent at least, the *Corporate Plan* offers a commitment 'to reduce as much as possible the transfer of disruptive prisoners from one prison to another'. Instead it will 'encourage each prison to contain and deal itself with prisoners who pose control problems'—that is, in prison parlance, for them to 'consume their own smoke' (*ibid.*, para. 6.13). This is a welcome commitment, although it remains to be seen how successful the service will be in this regard and how carefully it will be monitored.

It should, perhaps, be noted that a number of officials within the Prison Service have taken the view that Woolf's recipes for maintaining good order in prisons were a trifle on the optimistic side, and that he under-estimated the potential for disruptive behaviour by prisoners in open regimes. Certainly there has been ample demonstration of what can happen within unduly open regimes, and when those regimes are curtailed, throughout the history of the dispersal system (see King and Elliott 1978, for example). Such a critique of Woolf tends to discount the many recommendations that he made in drawing out the lessons from part one of his Inquiry, some of which are alluded to above. Nevertheless, it is hard not to feel that some such second thoughts were passing through the mind of Judge Tumim when he made his report of an inspection at The Wolds and pointed to the dangers of inactivity on the part of prisoners who were out of their cells for most of the day (Home Office 1993f).

Be that as it may, given the strategy outlined for maintaining order in the *Corporate Plan*, it is the more surprising that the chosen performance indicator should have been the rather restrictive one of the numbers of assaults. For what it is worth the new-style annual reports provide data on assault on a prison-by-prison basis. Taking the data we cited earlier, assaults on staff in Gartree fell from nine in 1985–6 to five in 1992–3; in Nottingham they rose from five to ten; in Featherstone they rose from three to twelve; and in Ashwell they rose from zero to one. In Birmingham assaults rose from thirty to fifty-two over the same period. It should be said that the later figures include assaults on others as well as assaults on staff, and so the comparisons may in any case be inappropriate, but we could not even begin to interpret these statistics without much more information. Since *we*, at least, already know a great deal about the nature of these institutions it is hard to know what anybody else could sensibly make of these lists as a performance indicator.

It is true that the annual report goes on to express these assaults as a proportion of the average daily population, but that is only a minor step towards standardization. The standardized rates for prisoner assaults on other prisoners, which are also published, apparently produces the nonsensical outcome that prisoners in Nottingham (0.5 assaults per 100 population) are 'safer' than those in either Featherstone (1.09 per 100) or Ashwell (0.78 per 100). Indeed, the fact that prisoner assaults on staff are apparently more numerous than those on prisoners suggests these data tell us more about the way such incidents come to light and are processed than they do about the reality on the ground. To understand whether these are statistics that should give rise to comfort or alarm it is necessary to know how serious the assaults were, by what process they came to be defined as assaults whereas other did not get so defined, what punishments they received, and something about the levels and styles of supervision to which prisoners were subject.

More satisfactory 'objective' performance indicators might count and classify injuries requiring medical attention, the numbers of prisoner requests for 'protection' and the numbers of staff days lost from work following incidents. However, it seems unlikely that any easily measured indicator will be adequate as an index of the safety and good order of establishments, and victim surveys of the levels of property abuse, threats, and intimidation, sexual attacks and assaults of the kind reported here will be necessary on a periodic basis to round out the picture.

As we noted at the outset the service is aware of some of the short-comings of the performance indicator on assaults. The *Business Plan*, perhaps anticipating failure to achieve the targeted reduction, seems to seek some insurance by arguing that the rate of assaults may be influenced by the types of prisoners held—a factor over which it has no control—and points out that the proportion of prisoners with records of violence or drugs offences has increased from 51 per cent in 1988 to 57 per cent in 1992 (Prison Service 1993e, 5). To seek refuge in such excuses, however, is to duck the real issues about safe environments which are fully under the control of the authorities, and this is the real lesson from the comparisons with Oak Park Heights. To be fair the Prison Service has at last come to see the need to live up to its responsibilities on these matters. Thus, when the per-formance against targets for 1993–4 was published, reference was made to policy matters as well as to the supposed changes in the quality of the prison population in attempting to explain the rise in assaults. It was noted, for example, that the rising trend might in part be a product of the 'strenuous efforts to stamp out bullying' (Prison Service 1994c) which presumably result in more assaults being reported and proceeded against. There is no doubt that the apparent rise in assaults has angered the Home Secretary and wor-ried the Chief Inspector of prisons. As we have seen the Home Secretary increased the powers available to prison governors beyond those thought necessary by Woolf, but it seems to us unlikely that the service will achieve its aim of reversing the trend 'through the tougher disciplinary powers which governors now have' (*ibid.* 2). It also seems more likely that the clamp-down on drugs through the introduction of random testing, presaged in the *Corporate Plan 1994–7* and fleshed out by Michael Howard at the Prison Service annual conference in October 1994, will increase rather than decrease the likelihood of assaults as shortages of supply increase the pressures on both prisoners and staff. Those fears are shared, to some extent at least, by senior officials (*Guardian*, 28 October 1994).

More hopeful, we think, are the recent attempts in some prisons to segregate bullies and predators rather than their victims, and to create voluntary drug-free wings. We particularly welcome the declared intention of the Prison Service to examine 'the reasons for sharp variations in the levels of assaults [between prisons and to use] the information gathered to develop more effective counter measures' (Prison Service 1994c, 2). We trust that such an examination will fully acknowledge the very real difficulties in interpreting the data on assaults, and consider in particular the way in which assault data may be confounded by performance in relation to other goals. Thus, an increase in hours out of cell might be expected to put more people at risk of assault for longer periods, although heightened levels of constructive activity during out-of-cell time might reduce that risk, and so on. It is to these matters that we turn in the following chapters.

4

Providing Decent Conditions for Prisoners and Meeting their Needs

The third goal of the Prison Service is to *provide decent conditions for prisoners and meet their needs, including health care* (Prison Service 1993c, 5). Two key performance indicators have been selected as the measures for success in achieving the goal. First, *the proportion of prisoners held in units of accommodation intended for fewer numbers*; and secondly *the number of prisoners with twenty-four-hour access to sanitation* (Key Performance Indicators 3 and 4).

Accommodation and Sanitation

The rather clumsy circumlocution of Key Performance Indicator 3 defines a measure of overcrowding. In view of the fact that the Prison Service had already adopted space standards for its new prisons which meet or exceed international guidelines (usually taken to be sixty square feet or 5.5 square metres for single occupancy cells), it is disappointing that the performance indicator for overcrowding has been taken to be the proportion of prisoners sharing accommodation intended for fewer prisoners. On that basis, the *Business Plan* records reductions in the proportion of prisoners held either two or three to a cell from 27 per cent in September 1991 to 22 per cent in April 1992, 17 per cent in September 1992, and 13 per cent in December 1992, though it notes that the figures do not distinguish between enforced and voluntary cell sharing (Prison Service 1993e). The *Business Plan* translates the key performance indicator into a *key target* of no triple-celling by 31 March 1994, subject to the proviso that none are held in police cells unless absolutely necessary. In truth this is a target which could actually have been met at most periods in recent history, had the service been prepared to extend voluntary cell sharing to the training prisons.

There can be no doubt that successive prison administrators and virtually all commentators have attached great importance to finding a solution to the problem of overcrowding, seeing it as the foundation stone upon which decent prison conditions might be built. In Chapter 1 we quoted the remarkable evidence of the then Director General of the Prison Service, Chris Train, to the Woolf Inquiry. He described overcrowding as a canker, the removal of which was an 'indispensable pre-condition of sustained and universal improvement in prison conditions' (Home Office 1991a, para. 11.135–6). In endorsing that view Woolf was determined that the 'corrosive consequences' of overcrowding had to be overcome and that 'once banished, it must not return' (*ibid.*, para. 11.140). We also reviewed the developments, following the rejection of his proposed new prison rule, to prevent the population exceeding CNA except in emergency situations, which have shown Woolf's worst fears to be fully justified. At the end of April 1993, the month when the Prison Service Agency was launched, the prison population stood at 43,391, some 2,820 *below* the total certified normal accommodation. Six months later the prison population had risen to 46,886, some 597 *above* CNA. Even in April 1993, however, overcrowding had not been eliminated, though it had improved. Overcrowding has always been largely confined to the local prisons and remand centres, with occasional bottlenecks elsewhere in the system. In April 1993 the locals were 13 per cent above capacity, and by October this had risen to 22 per cent. Even that level of overcrowding was not evenly spread. The tactical management of the situation in the grossly crowded prisons in the north west, by the rapid transfer of large drafts of prisoners to Wymott, was cited as one of the causes of the riot in September 1993 (Home Office 1993a). Soon afterwards Preston Prison, with overcrowding at up to 72 per cent above CNA, became the scene for renewed confrontation between the Home Office and the POA.

In December 1992 there were only 210 prisoners in triple cells, and in February 1994 Derek Lewis was able to appear on television to reiterate that, in spite of increased pressures, virtually no prisoners had been held in police cells for the last year. However, in order to meet the target by 31 March 1994 it seems that a little massage of the statistics may have been necessary to cover some eleventh (or thirteenth) hour emergency directives to prison governors. According to documents before the Prisons Board the overcrowding target was not fully achieved due to population growth. A projected average prison population for the year of 42,300 had turned out to be 45,900 and the population at year's end was 48,800—nearly 5,000 higher than expected. As a result, there were 492 prisoners in police cells—two thirds of whom were said to be locked out of Liverpool. Some thirty-nine prisoners were held three to a cell in the two remaining prisons still trebling up—Leeds and Leicester—and there were said to be 8,489 [sic] prisoners held two to a cell so that some 18 per cent of the population were held in accommodation for fewer prisoners. In the official statistics published in the Prison Service *Briefing* just a few weeks later it was claimed that 'trebling ceased altogether by 31 March 1994', that those 'held two to a cell which was designed for one has more than halved—from 17,800 (in January 1987) to 8,500', and that the service 'had to resort to a limited use of police cells in recent months' (Prison Service 1994c, 3). The difficult situation in the north west had been relieved by the contracted-out remand centre at The Wolds agreeing to overcrowd its establishment (Prison Service 1994c).

Whilst overcrowding is undoubtedly an important factor likely to colour the experience of both prisoners and staff, it is important to remember that measuring it is not as easy as it might seem. Nor is its meaning to staff and prisoners self-evident and simply to be taken for granted. King and Morgan (1980) pointed out that cells certified for use by one prisoner could vary considerably in size, depending upon when they were built and the regime for which they were intended. They demonstrated that it was possible for two prisoners sharing some Victorian cells to have more space than a prisoner with a single cell in some modern prisons, and that prisoners in open prisons often had the least space where the accommodation was always intended for dormitory use. Without an objective space standard the measurement of overcrowding by reference to intended usage is not very meaningful. Moreover, King and Morgan argued that the *experience* of overcrowding will vary, depending on the regime within which it is embedded: if a prisoner is locked up for twenty-three hours a day then being two, or even three, to a cell might be regarded as preferable to near solitary confinement.[1] In any case it is perfectly

[1] This interrelationship between different aspects of prison conditions is, of course, enshrined in the European Prison Rules and has been at the heart of the campaign by NACRO and others for enforceable minimum standards. It was the basis on which the Council of Europe's Committee for the Prevention of Torture found that overcrowding in Brixton, Leeds, and Wandsworth constituted inhuman and degrading treatment when combined with lack of integral sanitation and out-of-cell activities (Council of Europe 1991a).

possible that many prisoners might prefer to share cells for a variety of cultural and strategic reasons.[2] It is intriguing that Weiler (1992) reports that, whereas the Prison Service drifted into triple-celling just after the Second World War without consulting ministers, indeed without even a minuted discussion at Prisons Board, the development of double-celling was accompanied by much heart-searching over homosexuality and the matter went to the Home Secretary, Henry Brooke, before it was approved in 1964.

In 1980 King and Morgan had argued that there was considerable scope for redistributing the prison population around existing but refurbished establishments before recourse had to be taken to new prison building, especially as new prisons would simply be filled up. However, it would be extraordinary if the expensive investment in the largest prison-building programme since the spate of radial prisons built after the establishment of the new model prison at Pentonville in 1842 had not done something to improve standards of accommodation within the system.

The *Corporate Plan* reported that a census of prisoner accommodation was to be completed by 1 April 1994 which would redefine crowded and uncrowded capacities. Given that standard H1 of the July 1993 draft of *The Prison Service Code of Standards* proposed a minimum of 5.5 square metres for single occupancy, with double-occupancy cells at least 1.5 times that size, and for multiple occupancy units at least 3.5 square metres of *unencumbered* space per prisoner (Prison Service 1993f), it seemed likely that those standards would be used in the census of prison accommodation, so that for the first time the officially recorded figures of overcrowding would take on a known meaning. Elsewhere we reported details of the accommodation available to prisoners in our research prisons, and compared them with those in the *Prison Regimes Project* carried out in 1970–2 (see King and McDermott 1989). The July 1993 standards would have defined the conditions we reported for all the triple-celling arrangements in both sets of study prisons, and most dormitories, as overcrowded, whilst leaving all the double-celling situations we reported as uncrowded. Interestingly, the standards

[2] It is worth noting that in Russia, where prisons are grossly overcrowded by any standard, many prisoners said they would not like to be in single cells even though they would want overcrowding to be reduced. Even prisoners undergoing punishment usually share cells, and juveniles cannot be put in single cells for punishment—see King 1994a.

would have left some of the smallest cells in some post-war prisons on the borderline for acceptable single occupancy, or just below it. Such matters are now purely of academic interest because it seems the service had second thoughts. By the time the official *Operating Standards* were published in April 1994 what was perhaps the single most important baseline standard had simply been removed. The new standard H1 simply requires the familiar, but mysterious and obscure, process of certification to take place as it has for the last forty years under section 14 of the Prison Act 1952. What is more, under standard H2, the minimum size of a refurbished (as distinct from a new) double cell is 1.3 rather than 1.5 times the size of a single cell.

Key Performance Indicator 4 is at least more direct: the number of prisoners with twenty-four-hour access to sanitation. In a world in which the precise formulation of words counts, one notes that whereas the first indicator was expressed in proportionate terms the second is expressed numerically. It is not clear why it should have been expressed in this way. On the face of it a numeric formulation distances this indicator from the preceding one and allows the provision of sanitation to be assessed independently of progress towards accommodation targets. However, since the key target in the *Business Plan 1993–94* of providing '24-hour access to sanitation in at least 4,700 more prison places (excluding new and renovated accommodation)' was presented as part of the wider commitment to give all prisoners access to sanitation at all times by the end of 1994, the two indicators remain inextricably linked.

The key target required either the provision of electronic unlocking to give prisoners access to night sanitation or the installation of simple sanitation (i.e. a lavatory and a washbasin) in each cell. As we noted in Chapter 1, the latter solution offered a quicker, cheaper method of providing access to facilities than had been envisaged in the original programme of refurbishing the old local prisons, and it did not involve any loss of prisoner accommodation. Under the refurbishment programme the preferred method involved converting every third cell to provide a sanitary annex for the cells on either side. The adoption of the new approach was a key factor which enabled the Home Secretary to upstage Woolf and the Chief Inspector by bringing forward their target for the ending of slopping out from February 1996 to December 1994. By saving some cells that would otherwise have been lost to improved sanitation it also helped towards meeting targets to end overcrowding. However, by the end of January 1994 it had become clear that the need to provide additional accommodation to meet the growth in the prison population had diverted funds from even the cheaper programme of sanitary installations: the Chief Inspector of Prisons was quoted as saying that it might be another two years (his original target date) before the end of slopping out could be proclaimed (*The Guardian*, 27 January 1994) and this was confirmed by Michael Howard the following month. The key target for 1993–4 was indeed met with 4,724 places provided, which meant that 91 per cent of the population had access to sanitation at all times—still a very creditable achievement. The service believes that it is on track to achieve the revised milestones of 95 per cent access by the end of 1994 and 100 per cent by February 1996 (Prison Service 1994c).

The commitment to the ending of slopping out had a high symbolic value but, like the preference for single-celling, the provision of integral sanitation can be something of a mixed blessing. In the course of our research a great many prisoners expressed reservations about it. In a setting where prisoners spent a great deal of time locked up, and most ate all their meals in cells, they frequently put the question back to us: 'Would you want to live and eat in a toilet?'[3]

Nevertheless, it would be idle to pretend that there have been other than major improvements in the quality of the prison estate in terms of its physical accommodation and sanitation over the last decade. And this will surely be true for a great many prisoners, whether or not the revised target date for the end of slopping out is met, and even if the present levels of overcrowding continue. Indeed, when we reported some of our results in our research prisons and compared them with those from the earlier *Prison Regimes Project*, we noted that in terms of the ratios of lavatories, washbasins, and baths or showers to prisoners even Birmingham met the then suggested NACRO standards (as a result of an earlier refurbishment programme), whereas the similar prison at Winchester fifteen years earlier would have failed them. The problem in Birmingham was not

[3] There are important cultural factors at work here. American criminologists are puzzled at this reaction by British prisoners. They point out that British hotels still often have bathrooms and toilets two flights down and across the hall, which horrifies American tourists who measure status in terms of the size of the *en suite* facilities. In some Russian prisons there is an unscreened toilet in the corner of a cell shared by up to 40 prisoners: sometimes the toilet facilities for staff are very little better.

so much provision but access, and it is this situation which current programmes are striving to address.

Prisoner and Staff Evaluations of Accommodation and Sanitation

In 1986 and 1987, when the main data for this study were being collected, the debates over the justice model had come and gone, and any commitment to minimum standards had been explicitly rejected in favour of an attempt to set annual targets for improvement based around the statement of tasks and functions of the Prison Service. A good deal of our research effort was therefore devoted to establishing existing levels of performance, and much of the objective data we then collected has already been published (see particularly King and McDermott 1989). We therefore concentrate here upon the more subjective ratings which we asked both prisoners and staff to make of the various facilities in their establishment. In the case of sanitation these data may now be largely of historic interest, although it may be useful to see how far the system has come. In view of the ducking of an objective space standard and the return of overcrowding, the material on accommodation remains highly relevant.

We began by asking prisoners and staff about the cell accommodation and in particular to rate the amount of personal space available to each prisoner on a four-point scale. At the time of our study 77 per cent of the prisoners in Birmingham were triple-celled, 13 per cent were double-celled, and 7 per cent single-celled, with a further 3 per cent in small dormitories. In Nottingham 64 per cent of the population were double-celled, with the remainder in single cells. The remaining prisons had everyone in single cells except for Ashwell where 17 per cent were still in rather decrepit dormitories.[4] The ratings of both staff and prisoners are presented in Figure 4.1.

The subjective ratings of personal space represented in Figure 4.1 relate to what can be thought of as a reasonably 'objective' situation daily experienced by prisoners and daily observed by staff. Cells were of finite size, occupied by an identifiable number of persons, for measurable periods of the day. Birmingham cells were comparatively large but almost all in multiple occupation, and prisoners spent most of their time in them, with remand prisoners locked up for even

---

[4] 5% of the prisoners in Featherstone were sharing cells at the time of our research. They were all contained in the Short Term Unit which has been excluded from the analyses in this volume.

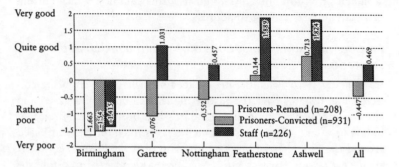

Fig. 4.1   Prisoner and staff ratings of personal space

longer periods than convicted prisoners. Gartree cells were in single occupancy but were the smallest to be found in any of our prisons, and prisoners spent more time locked up there than in any of the other training prisons. Nottingham cells were one and half times the size of Gartree cells—fine for those who were single-celled, but cramped for those who were doubled up—and the prisoners spent only marginally more time out of cells than prisoners in Gartree. Featherstone and Ashwell cells were midway between those in Gartree and Nottingham in terms of size but were all in single occupation, whilst Ashwell prisoners spent even more time out of cells than Featherstone prisoners.

We lay these considerations out in some detail because they serve to show how closely the prisoners' ratings corresponded to the actual conditions prevailing in their prisons (the differences between prisoners' responses across prisons were highly statistically significant: chi-square 487.36 p < .0001). This apparent faithfulness of the prisoners' response to the real situations which they experienced, and which differed widely from one prison to another, was repeated on all variables where some similar 'objective reality' was available against which it could be compared. Time and again we were conscious that prisoners did not express extreme views, and certainly not extreme negative positions, as some observers might have expected. It seemed not only that they were careful to articulate their responses to their actual experiences, but also that they were operating within a set of reasonable expectations of what was realistic given their status as prisoners, the climate on law and order, and the state of the economy.

Staff evaluations of the same phenomena reveal a somewhat different pattern of response from that of prisoners. In the training prisons staff rated the amount of space favourably but seem, perhaps, to have responded more to the question of cell size and cell sharing, taking less account of the amount of time out-of-cell. In each of the training prisons staff rated the space significantly more favourably than did prisoners. But what is most striking in Figure 4.1 is how closely staff in Birmingham agreed with the prisoners in their custody about how poor was the provision of personal space. The differences between staff responses across prisons were all statistically significant (chi-square 240.88032 p < .0001). There is here a tendency, which is much more marked on some other variables but nevertheless runs through most of our findings, for staff to respond in role. Whatever they were asked to rate staff were much more likely to restrict their choice to one or other of the positive evaluations, whereas prisoners were more likely to use the whole range of response and not just confine themselves to the negative evaluations. Even where we knew staff were actually very critical about something, they sometimes preferred to leave a question blank rather than to respond negatively, presumably out of a local sense of *esprit de corps* and because it would have seemed unprofessional to criticize the service publicly. Moreover, staff seemed to compare facilities and services inside prisons with the worst possible case outside, and thus on 'less eligibility' grounds to regard what was offered inside as at least quite good, if not very good. It also seemed that on some matters staff were content to assume that, if a facility or service existed, then this was sufficient, without necessarily asking how well or otherwise it worked. For prisoners, of course, these additional questions were likely to be critical matters governing their response. The conditions in Birmingham, however, on this and many other variables were such as to break through these professional barriers and sometimes to produce near unanimity between staff and prisoners.

In Figure 4.2 we present prisoner and staff ratings of prisoners' access to toilets. Featherstone had integral sanitation (as did a fourteen-cell Rule 43 unit at Gartree). For the rest, of course, the longer prisoners were out of cells the easier it was to attend to calls of nature, although it should not be forgotten that in Nottingham, Gartree, and Birmingham the recesses were sometimes seen as dangerous places, as we showed in the previous Chapter. Birmingham staff were less negative than Birmingham prisoners about the access

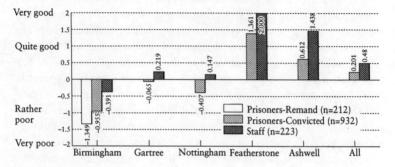

Fig. 4.2   Prisoner and staff ratings of access to toilets

to toilet facilities, presumably seeing themselves as more willing to unlock prisoners for this purpose than they were sometimes seen by prisoners. The differences between the prisons were statistically significant (staff: chi-square 168.79044 p < .0001; prisoners: chi-square 492.55456 p < .0001).

In Figures 4.3 and 4.4 we present the prisoner and staff ratings of prisoners' access to showers and washing facilities. The picture shows that, whereas the situation for bathing was generally regarded as quite good in the training prisons, especially Featherstone, once again both staff and prisoners were agreed that in Birmingham it left a great deal to be desired (staff: chi-square 157.20815 p < .0001; prisoners: chi-square 511.35284 p < .0001). It has perhaps been over-

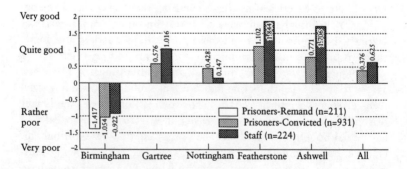

Fig. 4.3   Prisoner and staff ratings of access to showers

looked in most discussions of the problem of sanitation in prisons that, if anything, prisoners are even more concerned about washing and shaving facilities than they are about bathing and showering. With a shortage of sinks, limited time, blunt razors, and sometimes a supply of only tepid water, however, this should not be so surprising. This was much less of a problem in Featherstone, which had washbasins in cells, than it was in all three of the highest-security prisons (staff: chi-square 207.14112 p < .0001; prisoners: chi-square 692.11014 p < .0001). The programme to provide in-cell sanitation, of course, includes facilities for hand-washing as well as toilets.

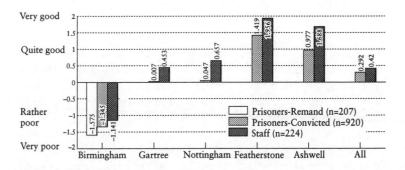

Fig. 4.4   Prisoner and staff ratings of access to wash basins

By way of trying to summarize the situation on the general physical conditions, and in a deliberate attempt to draw both staff and prisoners into extreme positions, we invited them to characterize the conditions into one of four categories which are widely used in popular discussions about prisons—too good for prisoners; decent but not luxurious conditions; meeting basic needs only; and not fit for animals.[5] The results are presented in Figure 4.5.

In spite of the somewhat provocative nature of the categories offered, we were intrigued to see that prisoners continued to differentiate between the prisons broadly in line with the objective differences between the establishments, and within what they regarded as

[5] The House of Commons Social Services Committee, which had recently reported on the Prison Medical Services, had used these very words 'prison inmates are being kept in conditions which would not be tolerated for animals' (Social Services Committee, 1986, para. 11).

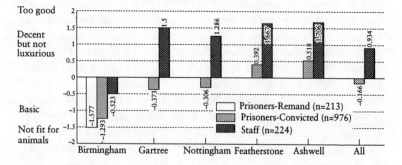

Fig. 4.5 Prisoner and staff evaluation of general conditions

reasonable expectations. However, for the most part the differences between staff evaluations disappeared. The great majority of staff in the training prisons regarded the conditions as at least decent, with about half regarding them as better than prisoners deserved. Only in Birmingham did significant proportions of prisoners (70.9 per cent of remands and 53.7 per cent of convicted) characterize the conditions as barely fit for animals. In this they were joined by one in eight of the staff. Given the tendency for staff elsewhere to draw together and act as a role group, the fact that prison officers in Birmingham were prepared to break ranks in this way must put it beyond dispute that the conditions in Birmingham required dramatic improvement.

Other Conditions: Food, Canteen, and Clothing

The *Corporate Plan* refers to a great many other matters besides accommodation and access to sanitation under the rubric of decent conditions. These include adequate light and ventilation, access to laundry and association areas, adequate nutritious and wholesome food, clean and suitable clothing, suitable facilities such as visiting areas and workshops, and the meeting of health and safety and other statutory requirements. Some of these were beyond the scope of our research. Others, such as association areas, visiting areas, and workshops, seem better dealt with when we come to say something about the circumstances of their use in Chapters 5 and 6. We report here our data on food, the prison canteen, and clothing.

Food assumes enormous importance to prisoners in custody.

When we asked prisoners how important various matters were to them outside prison, some 56.2 per cent mentioned food as being very important. When we asked them how important it was to them in doing their time inside, 72.5 per cent of our prisoners regarded it as very important, and a further 20.8 per cent regarded it as quite important. Only 6.7 per cent said that they were indifferent to it. For most of us in outside society meals break up the day; although family eating patterns are changing, many of us will have been brought up to believe that a good breakfast is vital to start the day, and that lunch and dinner and tea depending on cultural traditions, provide social opportunities for catching up on events with family and friends, for meeting new people, or for getting business done. Occasionally meals become grand or intimate occasions to look forward to and as an opportunity to indulge oneself. Sometimes meals, or components of meals, have particular religious or cultural significance, and both the ingredients and the way they are cooked may be crucial to the ritual experience. At other times it is the abstinence from meals or from certain foods which is important.

For most of us institutional food is an occasional necessity: for prisoners it conditions much of their life in custody. Any individual prisoner is likely to get too little of this, too much of that, and what he does get is likely to be the same week in, week out throughout the whole of his sentence. Many prisoners we interviewed worried about the effect it had on them—constipation, diarrhoea, getting fat, losing weight—and felt that there was little they could do about it. Sometimes they worried that the food was deliberately adulterated by staff or other prisoners or just that it was prepared in unhygienic conditions. If there are cockroaches in your cell, they reason, what must the kitchens be like? One prisoner we knew was convinced that he was being poisoned and built this into what appeared to be a delusional structure about which he repeatedly petitioned the Home Secretary.[6] The days of bread and water punishments may have gone, but for many prisoners nearly all prison food is experienced as punitive.

Twenty-five years ago, in even the most stressed local prison, some

---

[6] This prisoner was sectioned under the Mental Health Acts and transferred to a special hospital shortly after our field work was completed. He had feared that he would be 'nutted off' in this way and told us that it would not happen while we were still in the prison.

attempt was made to get some prisoners out of their cells for meals as a privilege—even though the only place to put the folding tables was on the ground floor between rows of cells. Winchester, for example, had 'diners out' and 'diners in' even with occupancy at 160 per cent of CNA in 1970. Virtually all training prisons were built with communal dining halls, but these have been progressively taken out of use. King and Elliott (1978) recount how one of a series of disturbances at Albany began when a prisoner held up a sack, apparently from the neighbouring Camp Hill prison farm, marked NOT FIT FOR HUMAN CONSUMPTION and convinced fellow prisoners that this was what they were fed on. As a result of that, and other similar incidents, social dining had all but been abandoned in English prisons apart from some lower-security establishments. Instead of going to a dining hall prisoners collect their meals and take them back to their cells to eat—by which time they are often cold and even less appetising than when they were first cooked. Standard L5 of the July 1993 draft of the Code of Standards was designed to reverse this trend. It gave prisoners the opportunity to eat at least one meal each day in association, and the choice of eating in association or in cell. This standard has simply been dropped from the published *Operating Standards*, which contain no reference to where meals should be eaten. Standard L2 further made provision that there should be one hot choice at each meal; that, too, has been deleted from the published code.

Staff are very well aware that mealtimes can be tense occasions. Incidents at the servery are frequent events, and prisoners are sometimes put on report for taking too much or for wasting food. Quite often a prisoner will complain about the food and end up throwing it at staff in frustration. In fairness to catering officers, who often exercised great ingenuity in trying to create varied and interesting menus which provided both appropriate nutrition and met increasingly complex considerations for religious and ethnic minority groups, it has to be said that their efforts were constrained by a total victualling budget in 1986–7 which averaged out at thirty-four pence per prisoner per day. In 1991–2 HM Chief Inspector of Prisons noted that the sum spent on prisoners' food had risen to £1.07 per day, although he contrasted this with the £2.20 spent on a student at the Prison Service Training College.[7]

[7] Attributing costs is a hazardous business. These figures for 1986–7 are taken from the Annual Report on the Work of the Prison Service, App. 6, Table F (Home Office

Mealtimes were often absurdly early. We were constantly confounded in making appointments by the fact that the mid-day meal, the main meal of the day, was sometimes being served by 11am and the evening meal was often over by 4pm. Under the new *Operating Standards* breakfast must be served between 07.30 and 09.00, lunch between 12.00 and 14.00, and the evening meal between 17.00 and 19.30. Only Ashwell had a 'social' dining system with prisoners going to the dining halls in rotation so that each had their turn when the food was hottest and freshest—but prisoners were in and out again in under fifteen minutes, sometimes in under five. In Birmingham the food was cooked in central kitchens. In a depressing, thrice-daily ritual prisoners filed to the basement servery below the centre to collect food and return to their cells. In Gartree and Featherstone the food was cooked centrally and delivered to the wings in heated trolleys. In Gartree hot plates were set up opposite the wing office for serving food. In Featherstone, absurdly, prisoners came to a proper servery in what had been their dining halls only to collect their meals and return to their cells. In Nottingham the food was prepared centrally and then served separately from hot plates in each of the two wings, whence prisoners took it back to their cells.

We asked prisoners and staff to rate the food in their prison. The results are presented in Figure 4.6.

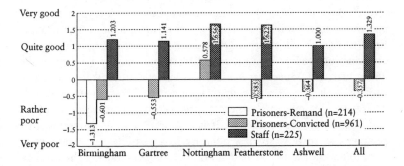

Fig. 4.6   Prisoner and staff ratings of food

1987c). In many prisons there will be farms or market gardens producing foodstuffs which may not necessarily figure in these accounts.

As can be seen from Figure 4.6 there were marked differences between the evaluations placed upon this by staff and by prisoners, although in neither case did the pattern of response follow the security gradient. In Nottingham, prisoners rated the meals considerably more favourably than in any of the other prisons: fewer than one in twenty said the food was very bad, and almost one in five regarded it as very good. There seemed to be three reasons for the better rating of the food in Nottingham: the kitchens were highly accessible so that many prisoners who dropped in to the kitchens saw food prepared and perhaps exercised a kind of quality control; the kitchens were reasonably close to where the food was served and so it was hotter than in other prisons; and the catering staff seemed to show greater ingenuity and flexibility in varying menus. Prisoners elsewhere were generally quite negative, with about one in three rating the food as very bad. Amongst the remand prisoners, whose memories of home cooking were presumably freshest, over half described the food as very bad. It did not seem to make much difference whether or not there were good local supplies of fresh vegetables and other produce from the prison farm or gardens, perhaps because the food was generally regarded as over-cooked and was then kept hanging around in heated containers. The differences between prisoner ratings in the five prisons were statistically significant (chi-square 222.38688 $p < .0001$).

Staff were much more inclined to rate the food as good, taking into account its quantity and nutritional values rather than taste or presentation. Even in Birmingham staff did not break ranks to confirm prisoners' judgements. Of course, they did not have to eat it: and this, no doubt, made it easier for some staff to be censorious about waste, holding that prisoners should be grateful for having 'a roof over their heads, a bed, three meals a day, and no worries'. There is a prison ritual whereby prison governors are required to taste the main meal each day. It is a source of some amusement to prisoners as to how small a quantity it is possible for some governors to get on the tip of their spoon before pronouncing the meal as good. We tried to eat the food in every establishment. We also ate in the staff mess. We could not honestly recommend either experience. More privately, some staff in all prisons were able to appreciate food provision from a prisoner's point of view, but tended then to point out that prisoners did not have to come here. We also asked staff how much the quality of the food service contributed to the maintenance of good order and discipline in the prison: the pattern of response was broadly the same as shown in Figure 4.6. It is possible that some staff misunderstood the question, but even so it is interesting that in each prison staff reported that the food made somewhat *less* of a contribution to good order than might have been expected if it actually were as good as they said it was.

Only Gartree had any facilities on the wings for prisoners to cook. One simple electric cooker on the ground floor of each wing made it possible for some prisoners every night to vary the routine and to take some control over one sector of their lives by cooking a meal for themselves and their friends. This was one of the most humanizing touches in Gartree, and we did not come across—either directly or in the SIR files—any incidents of abuse, for example of prisoners being forced to cook for others. There were sometimes difficulties about whose turn it was to cook, and about keeping the cooker clean, but these seemed to be minor problems. We reported in Chapter 3 how we were guests of one prisoner for a memorable meal.

We could see no reason why cooking facilities should not be extended to all prisons—if only as a valuable incentive that would help to send the right signals, as the CRC put it. Regrettably the *Operating Standards* do not cover such an eventuality, although they point out that where prisoners are able to prepare their own food it should be done in hygienic conditions (Standard L12). In order to make sensible use of a cooking facility, however, it is necessary to be able to buy food either from the prison shop, known as the canteen, or else by special order from outside shops. One problem with this is that it is staff who have to make the purchases: staff sometimes feel it is undignified to do shopping for prisoners and prisoners sometimes think staff deliberately come back with the wrong ingredients. Subject to occasional housekeeping hiccups of this kind, it seemed to work reasonably well.

Prisoners were allowed to go to the canteen twice a week in Nottingham and Featherstone, but only once a week elsewhere. In each prison they could spend their prison earnings on whatever they liked, and up to £104 a year out of private cash on general items although in Birmingham, Gartree, and Nottingham these limits were sometimes breached either inadvertently or as a matter of policy. This could put additional strain on families to provide cash which is a problem we discuss further in Chapter 6. In Featherstone,

Birmingham, and Ashwell prisoners could also spend a further £3 a month on toiletries, and in Ashwell—the only prison which at that time had telephones for prisoner use—they could buy a £2 telephone card out of private cash each month. We asked prisoners and staff to rate the quality of their canteen in terms of the range, quality, and prices of the goods it stocked. It is perhaps important to recognize that going to the canteen was not just a way of getting food and produce but also a social occasion. In Gartree it offered a welcome opportunity to have fleeting contact with prisoners from other wings, and in all prisons it provided opportunities for different types of social contact. Prisoners probably responded to the total experience of shopping, including the service they got from staff. In Featherstone and Ashwell the canteen was already in the process of being civilianized, although elsewhere it was still staffed by prison officers. The results are presented in Figure 4.7.

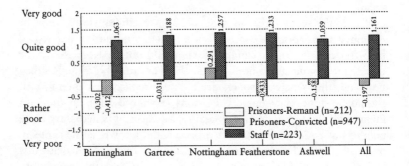

Fig. 4.7   Prisoner and staff ratings of the canteen (shop)

As with food, the differences between prisoner responses with regard to the prison canteen were unrelated to the security level of the prisons, although they were statistically significant (chi-square 61.03731 $p < .0001$). Only in Nottingham was there a favourable rating from prisoners. In Gartree the positive responses of some prisoners were cancelled out by the negative responses from others. Elsewhere prisoners were, on the whole, somewhat negative about this facility, and this was most evident in Featherstone. In marked contrast, however, the staff were almost universally approving of the canteen for prisoners in their prison, and such differences as were found were not statistically significant.

Prisoners placed a rather different priority on clothing. Outside prison 51.2 per cent regarded clothes as very important to their lives. But whereas food increased in importance whilst in custody, clothes decreased, almost certainly because prisoners gave up any serious hope of maintaining appearances in prison issued clothing. Only 40 per cent regarded clothes as very important in their present situation, although a further 38.7 per cent thought them quite important, and 21.3 per cent were indifferent to what they looked like whilst in prison. In Birmingham remand prisoners were theoretically entitled to wear their own clothes, but the vast majority of them soon came to wear prison issue. Fewer than one in four of the remand prisoners whom we interviewed still retained any of their own clothes because there were simply no proper facilities for laundering them. They thus soon fell foul of staff who determined that their clothing was not considered 'suitable, tidy, and clean' (cf. King and Morgan 1976). Not surprisingly, in such circumstances, their interest in clothes waned.

Convicted prisoners in Birmingham and elsewhere were issued with regulation prison uniforms, shirts, and underclothes which could be exchanged, usually on a weekly basis, at the Clothing Exchange Store. Although the training prisons aimed to provide two pairs of clean underpants per week, this was not always achieved. Birmingham was regularly hard put to it to provide even one clean pair of underpants per prisoner per week. Only Gartree had a rudimentary personal kit system in operation, whereby each prisoner's kit was identified by a number so that he kept the same kit throughout his stay. However, it did not work very efficiently, largely because of problems over laundering. The other prisons exchanged clothing according to size, and sometimes the sizings were approximate. The CES in Birmingham was situated next to the bath house, and just as some prisoners did not always get their weekly bath, so they did not always get their weekly kit change. In fact there were constant shortages of clothing, and much went missing. We were told that headquarters refused to provide more clothing supplies, claiming that they worked to guideline provisions which ought to be sufficient. Nevertheless, it was patently obvious on the ground that there simply were not enough to go round and what was available was often in a very poor state (see also McDermott and King 1988).

In the higher-security training prisons it was possible for prisoners to wear some items of their own clothing, for example, tee shirts, sweat shirts, and training shoes. However, regulations limited the circumstances in which they could be worn, restricted the size of logos, forbade headbands, and so on, in ways which might sometimes be justified on security grounds but all too frequently defied logic, exasperated prisoners, and strained good relations with staff. In the lower-security prisons everyone was required to wear prison issue all the time. This caused considerable aggravation in Featherstone where prisoners who had been transferred to lower-security conditions could not understand why they were no longer able to wear the gear they wore in the dispersal system. Thus one of our respondents who refused to accept that he now had to wear uncomfortable prison shoes instead of his trainers was immediately shipped out to another prison. For reasons which eluded us, in Ashwell only life-sentence prisoners were provided with jackets which were sufficiently warm for them to go outside in winter.

We asked prisoners and staff to evaluate the quality of prison clothing. The results are given in Figure 4.8.

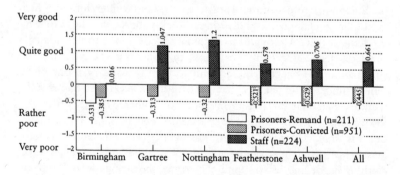

Fig. 4.8   Prisoner and staff ratings of prison clothing

As can be seen from Figure 4.8 prisoners rated the clothing situation negatively in each of our prisons, and such differences as we found were small and did not reach statistical significance.

Staff differences between the prisons, on the other hand, were statistically significant (chi-square 43.63909 p < .0001). It seems likely that the pattern of staff response reflects the greater privileges available to prisoners in Gartree and Nottingham as far as wearing their own clothes is concerned.

Clothing is another area where a major change has taken place between the draft standards and the *Operating Standards*. In July 1993 draft Standard M1, in an extension of Woolf (Home Office 1991a, para. 14.194), indicated that 'prisoners may choose to retain and wear their own clothing, providing it is clean and conforms to specified criteria'. This has been dropped from the published standards, although Woolf's suggestions on prisoners being allowed to wear their own shoes (*ibid*., para. 14.195) are incorporated as Standard M3. Instead the service aims to improve the range of prison-supplied clothing and Standard M2 promises increased quantities such that prisoners may, eventually, be able to change their underwear on a daily basis. Standard M5 provides for better laundry services.

Meeting Prisoners' Needs, Including Health Care

In its *Corporate Plan* the Prison Service gives an overview of what it has in mind about meeting prisoners' needs which ranges from the balancing of security with humanity and justice enshrined in the Woolf Report to the need to define standards of service as laid down in the Citizens' Charter. It talks about good relationships between staff and prisoners; keeping the Prison Act 1952 under review to ensure that the service meets its obligations under various international agreements; the development of the Code of Standards; the appointment of a Prisons Ombudsman; and the elimination of discrimination, particularly through the implementation of its race relations manual. Our data on the development and implementation of the race relations policy have been published elsewhere (McDermott 1990) and so we make no further reference to that here. Some of the needs of prisoners, in terms of work and education for example, are most appropriately considered as part of the development of positive regimes, and we deal with them in Chapter 5. In this section we look briefly at our data in relation to prisoner and staff assessments of three matters: the legal advice, particularly in relation to bail and legal aid, that was available to prisoners; the services provided by personal officer and group officer schemes; and the prison chaplaincies. We then go on to give somewhat more detailed consideration to health care.

Legal Aid and Advice

Although most prisoners are in custody as the outcome of the criminal justice process, a significant minority are held in custody whilst that process is still going on. For those who are remanded in custody the outcome of their trial may well depend upon the access they have to legal advice in prison, which in turn may depend upon the advice they get in relation to legal aid. For some convicted and sentenced prisoners there may well be important questions of whether or not they should appeal. In recent years the possibility of using the legal system as a means of gaining redress for a variety of prison grievances has become more important, both through the process of judicial review and via appeal to the European Court of Human Rights. Some prisoners and their families develop considerable expertise in these areas, often wholly against the odds, as we shall report in Chapter 6. But it has been increasingly recognized that the Prison Service has an obligation to provide some legal advice, both at a personal level and in terms of an accessible library holding basic legal materials.

Standard E1 of the new *Operating Standards* states that establishments should provide information and advice to enable prisoners to apply for legal aid and bail, to arrange legal representation, and to contact their solicitors. The advice should be provided through legal aid officers and other staff trained to deal with legal matters. At the time of our research all of our prisons had at least one prison officer deputed to give advice on legal matters, most usually on making applications for legal aid. In the training prisons the role of giving legal advice was usually vested in the library officer. In Birmingham there was one senior officer for remand prisoners who gave advice at reception, and another for convicted prisoners who was based in the OCA unit (in spite of a recommendation by the Inspectorate five years earlier that the two offices be amalgamated). Although a number of bail information projects had been developed in other parts of the country, the expansion of which was recommended by Woolf, there was no bail information scheme operating in Birmingham at the time of our research.

We asked prisoners who had experience of legal advice to rate the quality of the help they received. Only just over a third of our prisoners had any experience of this, and almost two-fifths of those, not surprisingly, were in Birmingham on remand. Taken over the sample as a whole, prisoners found this service to be neither good nor bad. However, both remand and convicted prisoners in Birmingham (the prison where there was much the greatest experience) found the advice of the legal aid officer modestly helpful. In Gartree, where there were more prisoners concerned to do something, if they could, about many decisions which had already affected them—from long sentences which they wished to appeal, security categorization, and perhaps especially parole knock-backs—there was an enormous sense of frustration and anger which in this instance was focused on the legal advice (chi-square 54.33588 p < .0001). As on so many other variables staff seemed to take the view that if there was *any* provision for advice with legal problems then this was sufficient: there was no need to dig deeper to establish how useful or effective the advice might be. Nevertheless, the differences between the prisons were statistically significant (chi-square 29.29025 p < .01). The details are given in Figure 4.9.

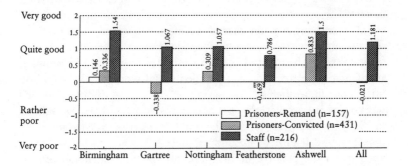

Fig. 4.9   Prisoner and staff ratings of help with legal advice

Personal and Group Officer Schemes

Prisoners might need advice not merely on technical matters relating to the law and legal aid, but on spiritual and a host of practical, personal, and social matters. With regard to the latter, of course, there had long been a welfare officer role associated with the activities of the old National Association of Discharged Prisoners' Aid Societies and the Central After-Care Association. However, following the recommendations of the Advisory Council on the Treatment of

Offenders in 1963, prisoner after-care was reorganized, with the probation service assuming responsibility for the voluntary supervision of prisoners after release and the secondment of probation officers to work in prisons. By the time that parole was introduced under the Criminal Justice Act 1967, the need for what came to be called 'throughcare', covering the needs of prisoners from the time that social inquiry reports might have been prepared for the courts before conviction until their period of licence had expired after release from prison, came to be recognized. In all conscience, as we will be reporting more fully in Chapter 6, it remained a very patchy service more than twenty years after the high ideals had first been expressed.

A number of linked studies, known as the midlands experiment on social work in prisons, explored the role and effectiveness of probation officers in prisons (Shaw 1974; Holborn 1975). Even before the introduction of probation officers into prisons, however, the question was being raised whether some of the traditional tasks done by welfare officers might not be done by prison officers with some additional training and some professional oversight. Such a redistribution of tasks might offer one way in which the role of prison officers could be enhanced from that of turnkey concerned with custody, security, and control, to one that involved more rewarding and professional tasks. It might also offer a more effective use of resources, supplementing professionally qualified social workers who could do little more than offer a 'sticking plaster' service. A Whitley Council working party on the role of the prison officer had been established in 1963, but, as we noted in Chapter 1, the Prison Service for some reason found it difficult to address this issue openly. Thus it shied away from the positive implications for the role of prison officers when it briefly flirted with the justice model, and it did so again throughout the discussions over Fresh Start. Nevertheless, by then a number of prisons, including Featherstone, had participated in local initiatives whereby probation and prison officers collaborated in various shared working arrangements in which the former played a more consultative and advisory role.

In 1984 Jepson and Elliott reviewed nineteen shared working schemes for social work in prisons, or SWIP as it was now called, and their report was considered by the Prisons Board. Jepson and Elliott identified four models involving: (a) the full-time attachment or (b) the part-time attachment of individual prison officers to the prison probation department; (c) assigning specific welfare tasks to individual prison officers; and (d) a fully integrated team based on the wings. In August 1986 guidance was issued under CI 25/86 stressing that the 'active involvement of prison officers in prisoner throughcare should be considered the norm rather than the exception'. In effect this endorsed the integrated wing team approach— even though experience had shown that this model was actually the most difficult to organize and maintain. The political context in which it came about was the run up to Fresh Start, but there was remarkably little discussion of it in the formal negotiations and the implementation of Fresh Start provided neither time nor resources for training of staff in these matters.

There had, of course, also been a long tradition in the Prison Service whereby some prison governors, with or without support from headquarters and with or without co-operation from the probation services, tried to make prison officers more personally responsible for the prisoners in their care. Often this took the form of making prison officers, usually those assigned to residential duties on the wings, responsible for writing reports on a small group of prisoners in their unit, and dealing with their more immediate problems. Over the years such officers have been variously described as case officers or group officers but are now, in keeping with present ideologies of individual responsibility, usually referred to as personal officers. Such schemes have fought against a number of factors that serve to undermine them: a lack of training for staff, a problem of keeping staff allocations sufficiently stable for officers to get to know their charges, and in view of both the foregoing (as well as other factors deriving from prisoner culture and well founded beliefs that adverse reports might not facilitate parole) a credibility deficit that attaches to the 'welfare screw' (splendidly caricatured by Mr Barraclough in the television series *Porridge*).

The notes which qualify Standard P3 on giving advice and help to prisoners in the new *Operating Standards* refer to the operation of a personal or group officer scheme and/or a shared working arrangement. In reality, at the time of our research at least, there was only the most blurred of distinctions to be made between case, group, or personal officers responding to daily problems on the wings, and a specially appointed group of SWIP officers with some additional training working in conjunction with probation officers. Neither system was well understood by either staff or prisoners and neither seemed particularly effective. Staff found they were too often taken away from their welfare duties: prisoners, if they knew who should be responsible for them, felt that he or she was never there when needed. With that caveat in mind we consider the roles of probation officers and SWIP officers specifically in Chapter 6 where we examine throughcare and preparations for release. Here we confine our attention to the service offered by officers on the wings in dealing with prisoners' problems.

When we talked to prisoners on the wings about case officers, group officers, and personal officers the standard response was either 'What is that then?' or, if they knew about the supposed existence of the system, 'Who's my case officer? I've never seen him'. In part this was no doubt an expression of a prisoner cultural value whereby it was difficult to cast screws in a good light, at least publicly (see Wheeler 1958 and Kauffman 1988 for discussions of 'pluralistic ignorance'). There was, however, a real grain of truth in the matter. Birmingham made no pretence of having a case officer or personal officer system, and while in theory there was some such scheme operating in the other prisons, in practice it was often a different matter. Thus, in Ashwell staff were few and far between, in Nottingham there were fears about being able to maintain the limited gains they had made in shared working, and in Gartree there were problems with maintaining sufficient stability of staffing to service the personal officer scheme. Only in Featherstone had there been a reasonably substantial commitment to developing personal officers. This is not to say that there were not many staff whom we met who enjoyed a welfare role, and many prisoners who appreciated it. But they all had difficulties in coming to terms with this aspect of their relationship and especially with the reactions of their respective peers.

Indeed, when asked with whom they would discuss a personal problem 35.3 per cent of all our prisoners said they would keep it to themselves, 34.5 per cent that they would wait to discuss it with relatives on a visit, and only 24.6 per cent that they would discuss it with staff. Given the difficulties experienced by probation officers in discharging their welfare role when they are seen as part of the authority structure of the prison (see, for example, NAPO 1971) it is hardly surprising that prison officers should not fare well in this regard. Prisoners were most likely to be prepared to discuss things with staff in Featherstone and Ashwell and least prepared to do so in Birmingham. It might be some comfort to staff to know, however, that even fewer, 20.6 per cent, felt able to discuss things with their fellow prisoners.

We asked staff, and prisoners who had experience of personal or group officer schemes, to evaluate them. The results are given in Figure 4.10.

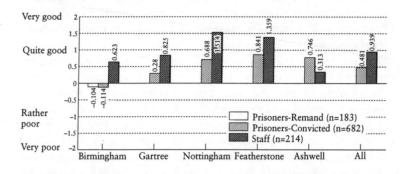

Fig. 4.10   Prisoner and staff ratings of personal officers

It seems likely that some prisoners were responding rather generally to the preparedness of landing officers and wing staff to listen to problems and to try to do something about them, rather than specifically to the operation of a personal officer system as such. That said, prisoners in the training prisons were generally favourable in their ratings, and the differences between the prisons may nevertheless reflect the visibility of the schemes on the ground. In Birmingham, it is hard to see how prisoners could have regarded wing staff in a favourable light. Interestingly, the staff in Ashwell were less likely to regard the personal officer scheme favourably, and this is consistent with the governor's comment in his annual report that his staff were resistant to training in these activities. The differences between the prisons were statistically significant (prisoners: chi-square 94.02454 p < .0001; staff: chi-square 56.22621 p < .0001).

The Chaplaincy

The prison chaplaincy as an institution is as old as the prison itself and used to subsume much more than the welfare role entirely under its spiritual umbrella. As Britain has become a more secular society, so the role of the prison chaplaincy has declined. No longer does the Chaplain General have a seat on the Prisons Board; and the days are long gone when the great houses on either side of the prison gates were occupied one by the governor and the other by the chaplain. Since Fresh Start there has been no seat for the local chaplain on the senior management committees of individual establishments either. Nonetheless, to judge from the statistics of prisoners professing each faith which are still published annually in the annual reports of the Prison Service, it remains the case that in time-honoured fashion, anyone not vigorously proclaiming an alternative religion or no religion is registered as Church of England. The prison chaplaincy appears to have taken some comfort from the fact that church- and chapel-going in prison is proportionately more frequent than it is in outside society. There are a number of irreligious reasons why this should be so. There are precious few alternative things to do on Sunday mornings in prison. Going to the chapel sometimes provides the opportunity to meet prisoners from other wings with whom contact might otherwise be restricted. And going to chapel can provide a prized Sunday bonus of seeing young women who may visit the prison to sing in the choir. In Strangeways, of course, the chapel was the location for the start of the riot.

Of course, there are some prisoners who go to church out of habit, although in our experience few seemed to have been regular churchgoers outside. Indeed, when we asked our prisoners what had been important to them outside, only 12.4 per cent of those who responded (or 10.9 per cent of our total sample of 1,220 prisoners), mentioned religion. It was by far the least important in a list of eight variables. But amongst the churchgoers there were a good number of 'born agains' who had found God in prison and given themselves wholeheartedly to Jesus Christ. It was not unusual to find them clutching a bible wherever they went, and for them to give us a text for the day as we went about our field work. Sometimes they got caught up in religious power plays with other prisoners, from which it could be difficult for chaplains or priests to hold themselves aloof. Such prisoners often found themselves in a familiar double bind: although their religious conversion at one level represented the perfect prisoner response it was not necessarily believed, and the harder they protested their faith the more its genuineness might be called into question.[8] Whilst

[8] This is a fate that commonly besets prisoners whom the American penologist John Irwin (1970) first described as 'gleaners'; prisoners who are determined to use the facilities of the system to improve themselves whilst inside. Their good faith is called into question: might they be dissimulating just to get parole? See also King and Elliott (1978) for a British account of this problem.

the chaplains in one prison described themselves as charismatically evangelical and were happy to embrace the phenomenon, in another prison the chaplain was disdainfully dismissive of 'born agains'.

The secularization of native British society has coincided with an extraordinary growth in the importance of other religious faiths which in recent years have become increasingly evident in British prisons. Brought here by immigrant groups and often kept in a low profile by a grateful first generation, they have burgeoned with second and third generations increasingly more assertive of their rights in a society initially reluctant to recognize them. Amongst ethnic minority prisoners there were many for whom religion was important and who struggled to obtain proper observance of fasts and festivals as well as a place to worship. A particular problem was finding religious leaders from local communities able to come in and conduct services. In these circumstances the chaplaincy has been required to change, to have regard to a more ecumenical and multi-faith approach, and to be proactive in finding shepherds for persons not of their own flock. It cannot have been an easy task, though some have embraced it more readily and with greater success than others. Some religious leaders of other faiths told us that they sometimes did not receive appropriate respect for their faith. It was, they told us, 'as though ours is not a proper religion'. In one prison, which we cannot name because it would identify the persons concerned, the chaplain saw nothing inappropriate in reporting a Sikh for wearing a turban because it then breached the Prison Rules. Prisoners from ethnic minorities also claimed that on occasions the representatives from the established religions spoke unfavourably about minority religions on prison committees.

In *The Future of the Prison System*, King and Morgan (1980) suggested that the prison chaplaincy should cease to be a specialist service within the prison system and instead become fully integrated with services in the local community. Several to whom we spoke in the course of our research endorsed that view. That has not happened. In November 1988 a new *Directory and Guide on Religious Practices* was issued to help chaplains implement the race relations policy. At a meeting in February 1989 the Prisons Board re-affirmed the importance of the chaplain's role in the work of the Prison Service: in meeting the needs of those of non-Christian faiths; keeping alive contacts with the outside world; and in supporting staff.

In each of the prisons the chaplaincies tended to think of them-selves as teams. Birmingham had a full-time Catholic chaplain as well as one for the Church of England, who were supported by a vis-iting Rabbi, and several part-time ministers from other Christian denominations. Separate services were arranged for Sikhs and Muslims, with individual arrangements being made for Buddhists and Hindus. In Gartree there was a full time Church of England chaplain who offered regular combined chapel services for Church of England and free churches on Sundays. Part-time or visiting min-isters provided a Catholic mass on Mondays, a Jewish service on Thursdays, and a service for Muslims and Sikhs on Fridays. Other religious observances had to be by special arrangement. The Nottingham chaplaincy was led by a Church of England chaplain with a Methodist minister providing substantial support, and several other ministers operating in visiting capacities. Featherstone and Ashwell each had a full-time Anglican chaplain supported by other ministers on a visiting basis. The usual pattern was that a single chapel was shared by the various Christian denominations, either in joint or separate services, although in Ashwell Catholic prisoners were allowed to go to outside mass because the priest found it diffi-cult to get to the prison on Sundays. Other rooms, of varying suit-ability, were used for other faiths. The lack of suitable or dedicated accommodation for non-Christian forms of worship often became a serious cause of complaint. Standard T4 of the new *Operating Standards* reinforces the 1988 guidance on religious practices by reit-erating that places of worship should be dignified, clean, and equipped to meet the needs of different faiths.

When we asked prisoners and staff to rate the quality of their respective chaplaincies we found that, apart from prisoners in Gartree, most generally held them in quite high regard. The details are given in Figure 4.11.

It is worth drawing attention to the very high ratings received by the chaplaincy in Birmingham, whose hard work in the most diffi-cult of circumstances did something to mitigate the awful experience that doing time in Winson Green constituted for so many prisoners. Only in Birmingham did the chaplaincy seem to us to approach ful-filment of its ecumenical goals and demonstrate a genuinely tolerant attitude towards social and cultural as well as religious differences. The differences between the prisons were significant (prisoners: chi-square 54.54639 p < .0001; staff: chi-square 21.33836 p < .05).

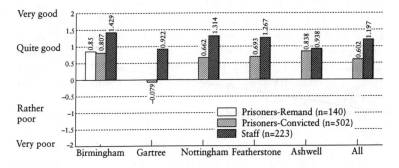

Fig. 4.11   Prisoner and staff ratings of chaplaincy

Health Care

No subject has been more controversial in the recent history of imprisonment than prison medical services and their roles in the care and control of prisoners. Sim (1990), in the preface to his recent book, *Medical Power in Prisons*, makes it plain that his work had been carefully vetted by a libel lawyer and involved a degree of self-censorship. King and Elliott (1978), in the postscript to their book, *Albany*, noted that the burden of the comments they received from the Home Office seemed intended not merely to put the prison medical service in a better light but almost to place it effectively beyond criticism.

King and Morgan (1980) suggested that many specialist services currently provided mainly from within the prison system—medical, educational, and library, as well as the chaplaincy—could be wholly integrated with those services available in the community. This was not the first expression of this view, and since then there has certainly been a much fuller working through of the arguments, not just by outside researchers and reform groups but also by dissenting voices from within. Over the years attention has been focused upon prescribing practices especially with regard to women prisoners (Owen and Sim 1984; NACRO 1986; Genders and Player 1987); the problems of mentally disturbed prisoners (Gunn *et al.* 1978; Smith 1985); the problematic relationship between treatment and control[9]

---

[9] One of us was recently in the embarrassing situation on the Research and Advisory Group on the Long Term Prison System (offspring of the Control Review Committee) of registering a note of dissent concerning the proposal to hold prisoners

(Lee 1983; Smith 1984; Sim 1990); the training, or rather the lack of it, of hospital officers in male prisons (Smith 1984; Shaw 1985; NACRO 1990); the programmes, or lack of them, for alcohol and drug abusers (World Health Organization 1990), for sex offenders (Prison Reform Trust 1990), for the prevention of suicides (Liebling 1992), and for HIV-positive prisoners (Padel 1990; Thomas and Costigan 1992; Young and McHale 1992).

At the time of our research these controversies were coming to a head. The Prison Reform Trust, in a small but influential booklet, *Prison Medicine* (Prison Reform Trust 1985), had recently brought several of these issues together, and the House of Commons Social Services Committee (Social Services Committee 1986) had just issued its report on the Prison Medical Service. Whilst we were conducting our fieldwork the response of the Government to the Social Services Committee's recommendations was eagerly awaited. Since our research there has been a reorganization of the PMS somewhat along the lines of the Committee's recommendations. Our objective here is, therefore, simply to record some of our findings about the problems which prisoners told us they experienced in the health field, and of the evaluations of the available treatment programmes and the medical service by prisoners and staff. They seem amply to justify the level of public concern.

Some 37 per cent of our prisoners said that physical fitness and health had been at all important to them in their lives outside prison. Only religion ranked lower on the list of matters we suggested they might be concerned about. However, 60 per cent now said that they were very concerned about their physical condition deteriorating in prison, and a further 24.3 per cent were quite concerned. Only 15.6 per cent professed not to be worried about this at all. This level of concern about physical condition seems astonishingly high to us for such a young population and seems to demonstrate that whatever their actual state of health, imprisonment sets up circumstances in which prisoners are likely to worry about it. However, there also appears to be a striking correlation between the proportions who described themselves as 'very concerned' in each prison and the time they spent out of cells and the access they had to physical activities, matters on which we report more fully in Chapter 5. Thus, the

under psychiatric supervision in the Parkhurst Special Unit without consent, when this was not considered necessary by the former Director of Prison Medical Services (Home Office 1987d, 40–1).

prison in which the greatest proportion of prisoners was very concerned about their physical well being was Birmingham, where prisoners spent most time locked up in cells and had the fewest sports
and recreational facilities: 77.9 per cent of remand prisoners and 65.8
per cent of convicted prisoners responded in that way. The proportion of prisoners in the training prisons who reported themselves as
very concerned progressively declined the more open were their conditions. In Gartree, where there was a long waiting-list to access the
gymnasium, the proportion was 64.1 per cent, and in Nottingham,
with the next highest waiting-list for physical education, it was 55.8
per cent. There were no particular barriers to the pursuit of physical
activities in Featherstone and Ashwell where the proportions very
concerned dropped to 50.6 per cent and 45.3 per cent respectively.
By and large the longer prisoners spent in cells the more likely were
they to be concerned about their physical condition.

Just as being locked up in one's cell is likely to increase fantasies
about what one is missing—food, sex, and freedom—it is also likely
to give prisoners time to dwell upon and perhaps to magnify signs
and symptoms that they are actually experiencing. It is not hard to
see, moreover, how a vicious circle sets in. Prison doctors have a reputation for dismissing prisoner ailments as hypochondria or lead-
swinging, and to prescribe 'aspirin water' and placebos. The medical
officers in two of our prisons told us, in strikingly similar words, that
in most cases their initial assumption was that the presenting problems of prisoners would turn out to be nothing at all, and that the
onus was thus upon the prisoner to demonstrate that he really was
ill. In such circumstances prisoners become concerned that their
symptoms are not taken seriously and fear that more serious diag-
noses are being missed. They return for a second time or a second
opinion, thereby confirming the doctor's original judgement.

When we asked prisoners more specifically to rate their physical
fitness immediately before their sentence began and then to rate their
fitness now there was a marked decline: 25.5 per cent had seen themselves as very fit before coming in to prison, but only 11.1 per cent
did so at the time of completing the questionnaire. Only 6.1 per cent
described themselves as very unfit before they came in, whereas that
increased to 15.5 per cent by the time of the research. There was
a similar reduction in their reported emotional stability: before
they came into custody 51.9 per cent claimed to be very stable emo-
tionally, but now this had declined to 30.9 per cent whilst those

describing themselves as very unstable increased from 6.6 per cent to 11.7 per cent. Not far short of half our prisoners, 44.7 per cent, were very fearful that in the course of their sentence they would become very depressed, 25.1 per cent were very frightened that they would actually get to like prison, and 21.6 per cent were very concerned that they would not be able to cope with life outside. Once again these differences were systematically related to prison conditions, namely the hours locked in cells and the access to recreational facilities. To our surprise they were not related to the length of time prisoners had already served during their current sentence.

Over three-quarters, 78.5 per cent, of the prisoners in our study had smoked before they came into custody and 75.5 per cent continued to smoke inside. A few had evidently given up since coming into prison, almost certainly on grounds of expense rather than because of any health promotion programme warning of the dangers of tobacco—for such did not exist in any of our research prisons. Most simply switched from 'tailor-mades' to 'roll-ups'. Virtually the same proportion of prisoners, 78.4 per cent, were regular users of alcohol before coming into prison, but this was a much more difficult habit to maintain inside. Nevertheless, one in five of our sample (20.1 per cent) claimed to use alcohol at least intermittently whilst in custody. This was most likely to occur in Gartree where almost a third of the prisoners claimed to have been able to drink alcohol in prison. Nor was this all home-brew: during the course of our research one member of staff was dismissed for bringing alcohol into the establishment for prisoners.

Almost two-fifths (37.4 per cent) of the prisoners admitted to regular use of cannabis before coming into prison. Amongst those on remand in Birmingham just over half had been users of cannabis, as had almost a half of prisoners in Nottingham, about a third of the convicted prisoners in Birmingham, and of the sentenced prisoners in Gartree and Featherstone, and a quarter of those in Ashwell. Somewhat to our surprise both the number and the proportion of prisoners who claimed to use cannabis whilst in prison was actually greater than those claiming to use it outside: 427 prisoners or 38.7 per cent of those who responded to this question (or 35 per cent of the total sample) claimed to have smoked cannabis in their current prison. This was most likely to occur in Nottingham (55.7 per cent) where one of our respondents enclosed the message 'Why drink and drive when you can smoke and fly?' with his questionnaire. Almost half (47.5 per cent) of the remand prisoners in Birmingham and a similar proportion in Gartree (47.1 per cent) claimed to smoke cannabis whilst inside. During evening association in Gartree one of us was regularly offered a thumbnail-sized 'deal' at the going rate. On one occasion it was offered with the following invitation: 'What a way to run a prison, eh? Most of us up there are stoned out of our minds. Want to join us?' In Ashwell, the open prison, where theoretically at least it should have been easiest to smuggle in contraband, self-reported cannabis use was lowest, at 23.8 per cent. There was no doubt that staff were fully aware of the use of cannabis inside and that most staff were content to turn a blind eye on the ground that it made for a more contented population. They were also uncomfortably aware that to intervene might create more problems than it would solve. The current concern to do something about drugs in prison, most recently expressed in the *Corporate Plan 1994–97* and reiterated by Michael Howard in October 1994, under which more rigorous searching and drug testing is to be carried out, will sooner or later come face-to-face with those consequences. We return to this problem at the end of the chapter.

About one in six prisoners claimed to have been users of amphetamines before they came into custody; one in ten used cocaine and barbiturates; and one in twelve used heroin. Fewer prisoners admitted to having used these drugs whilst in custody though 5.8 per cent claimed at least intermittent access to amphetamines, 4.4 per cent to cocaine, 4.8 per cent to barbiturates, and 4.1 per cent to heroin. These figures may be somewhat higher than the authorities would wish to admit, but are not inconsistent with the privately expressed views of security officers, notwithstanding the zero finds of actual drugs and the occasional finds of syringes and equipment reported in Chapter 3.

Although the majority of our prisoners reported regular use of alcohol, and many of these and others reported extensive involvement in drugs, we are not in a position to say how many were clinically dependent on these substances. What we can say is that, if any of them required serious treatment for substance abuse, they would not have found it in any of our prisons. There were occasional meetings of Alcoholics Anonymous and it was always possible to raise questions both of alcoholism and drug misuse with medical officers, but these did not appear to be policy priorities. There were thus no formal screening procedures to identify those prisoners who might benefit from treatment, and no treatment programmes available. Everything depended upon the individual practices of the medical officer concerned. Nor did any of the prisons have any active treatment programmes for sex offenders. There were posters in several of the prisons warning of the dangers of AIDS, but in some cases these were accompanied by cartoons in staff offices which were more likely to perpetuate myths than dispel them. It was possible for prisoners to be tested for HIV on a voluntary basis, but comparatively few came forward for testing, and the annual reports of the medical officers revealed that few cases were discovered. In Gartree it was planned to set aside part of the hospital to serve as a regional AIDS unit, and in Birmingham they were in the process of fitting out a very small isolation unit for hepatitis and HIV patients.

For the most part the Prison Medical Service operated as a kind of general practice, seeing patients either on an appointments basis or at sick parades. It dealt mostly with minor ailments, bringing in occasional specialist help and sometimes referring prisoners to hospitals outside. Each prison included amongst its visiting specialists one or more psychiatrists, dentists, and opticians, although Ashwell had found it more economic to send prisoners out to the optometrist than to have one brought in. When we asked prisoners and staff what they thought about the level of provision of treatment programmes, both were generally pretty negative, with the majority rating them as rather poor. The results are presented in Figure 4.12.

Neither the differences between prisoners nor those between staff reached statistical significance. Although the positive response

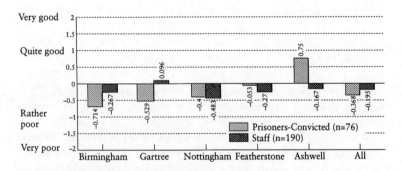

Fig. 4.12   Prisoner and staff ratings of treatment programmes

amongst prisoners in Ashwell could simply be attributed to chance factors it might reflect the greater likelihood that they would be referred to outside specialists. In Gartree the staff were just prepared to give a positive rating—although generally this was the question that evinced the most negative ratings from staff throughout our study.

There was a much greater closing of ranks amongst the staff when we asked them to rate the quality of the medical service, with Birmingham and Gartree getting particularly favourable ratings. Only in Nottingham did the staff evaluate the medical service negatively. Amongst the prisoners the medical service in Gartree was rated least worst and it may be that prisoners had developed more trust in the medical officer there, who was the only one in our research prisons who distanced himself from the control system by not carrying keys. The differences were statistically significant (prisoners: chi-square 52.45734 p < .0001; staff: chi-square 56.55569 p < .0001). The data are presented in Figure 4.13.

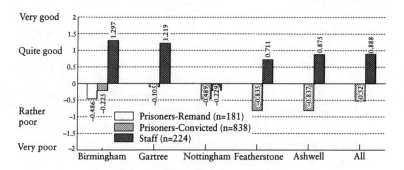

Fig. 4.13   Prisoner and staff ratings of medical service

Making Sense of the Data and Assessing the Situation Today

The materials presented in this chapter provide further evidence of the sometimes complex relationship between the depth and weight of imprisonment. There seems little doubt, for example, that prisoners in deeper-end custody at Gartree and Nottingham carried with them a heavier burden than did those who enjoyed the benefits of confinement at the shallow end in Featherstone and Ashwell. Nowhere was that more evident than in the concerns which prisoners expressed in relation to their physical fitness and emotional stability. Although Birmingham initially receives prisoners from all security categories direct from the courts, its security is geared to that required for the most serious risks and its conditions of confinement are in many respects the most restrictive. Not surprisingly, then, its prisoners expressed even greater concerns about their wellbeing. Whilst the results on many variables followed the security gradient in this way, there were some on which the pattern was reversed. The most obvious example here, perhaps, was in relation to clothing, where in the higher-security prisons concessions had been made about the wearing of own clothes which did not apply in the lower-security prisons. In many respects such concessions are appropriate but they begin to make less sense when prisoners are transferred through the security categories, and it was just in regard to matters such as these that the Control Review Committee felt that the system was failing to send the right signals.

In spite of these more obvious tendencies there were other variables on which prisoners who were deeper into the system nevertheless carried less weight in terms of their custodial experience. Perhaps the best example here concerns prison food, a matter of very high salience to prisoners, where Nottingham scored much more favourably than elsewhere. There were also several other services, particularly those that were dependent upon good staff attitudes, for example, the canteen, the medical service and legal advice—where Nottingham scored more favourably than Featherstone and sometimes more favourably than Ashwell.

Our fieldwork, however, was carried out several years ago and for many the main impact of our findings was in our demonstration that overall, in so many areas of prison regimes, performance had declined over the last fifteen or twenty years (King and McDermott 1989), and had not been improved by Fresh Start (McDermott and King 1989). That realization played some part in restoring standards to the official agenda at the time of the Woolf Inquiry. Although we have referred to the various *Operating Standards* adopted in April 1994, in the foregoing analysis these remain aspirations towards which the service is working. It is important to know in what ways the situation on the ground has actually changed since our research.

We reviewed the extent to which the service had met its targets for 1993–4 at the beginning of this Chapter, but the performance indicators referred to in relation to the third goal only cover accommodation and sanitation and not the various other needs set out in the *Corporate Plan* and the *Business Plan*. We have accordingly looked at the evidence from the national prison survey to get some sense of how typical the responses of our prisoners might be (the NPS, unfortunately, did not extend to staff). We have also scrutinized the latest available statistics on overcrowding, the last of the old-style annual reports to headquarters by the governors of our research prisons which relate to 1991–2, as well as the reports by HM Chief Inspector of full and short inspections to try to bring things up to date.

Overcrowding and Sanitation

The national prison survey, which was carried out in January and February 1991, offers some national statistics on these and related matters. At the time of the national survey the total average daily population had fallen to 45,185 from 47,200 at the time of our research and the certified normal accommodation had risen to 44,270, an increase of 4,070 places, so there might be a reasonable expectation that things would have improved. Unfortunately NPS questions were asked in rather different ways from ours and so the outcomes are not directly comparable. Walmsley and colleagues report that some 43 per cent of all adult male prisoners wanted to see a reduction in overcrowding and 55 per cent wanted to have lavatories in their cells, but in the local prisons where overcrowding continued, some 86 per cent wanted to see improvements in their cell conditions (Walmsley *et al.* 1992, 34). Of the male prisoners interviewed, 65 per cent had unlimited access to baths or showers, 16 per cent had received one bath or shower in the previous week, and 2 per cent had not been able to bath or shower at all. Of those with restricted access virtually all said they wanted more.

In his annual report for 1991–2 the governor of Birmingham noted that the occupancy rate was virtually the same as when we had studied the prison nearly five years earlier. However, the most recent figures available, for 31 July 1994, show that Birmingham with 780 prisoners was a much less crowded prison, with occupancy at 139 per cent of its certified normal accommodation of 562 places, than it had been during our study when the official occupancy rate was 190 per cent of CNA. How brief a respite this will prove remains to be seen because just nine months earlier, at the end of October 1993, the prison was only 21 per cent overcrowded. The main physical development at Birmingham has been the building of a new wing with integral sanitation which has increased the certified normal accommodation, but also served as a decanting wing whilst others were refurbished. The programme of providing integral sanitation has suffered several delays, because of lack of finance, and in 1992 only two wings had been completed. The governor considered it 'most unlikely' that it would be completed by 1994, and was disappointed that 'a more effective and imaginative use of the staff resource' had not been brought about in the units where in-cell sanitation had been provided. The Chief Inspector expressed reservations about two prisoners sharing a normal size cell in which integral sanitation had been installed, because of the resulting cramped conditions and the fact that prisoners were forced to eat food next to the toilet (Home Office 1992c).

In Nottingham overcrowding appeared to have been eliminated with an occupancy rate at 95 per cent of CNA at 31 October 1993 and 94 per cent at 31 July 1994, compared with 146 per cent of CNA during our research. Compared with Birmingham the improvement in Nottingham has been longer sustained, the last time the prison had overcrowding of the same general extent as during our research being in 1990–1. In spite of repeated cuts in budget, moreover, the governor was able to report that Nottingham was ahead of schedule in installing integral sanitation. This was confirmed at an unannounced short inspection carried out in November 1992 when the Chief Inspector reported that integral sanitation would probably be completely installed by March 1993 (Home Office 1993b).

There were no major changes in the level of overcrowding in the other three prisons: CNA had increased in Ashwell and in Featherstone as a result of new building, some of which was under way during our research, and declined in Gartree where accommodation was taken out of use for the installation of toilets and washbasins. In Gartree one wing had been refurbished by the end of 1991–2 reporting year, but the governor's hopes that this would have included low-voltage electricity in cells had not come to fruition. The Chief Inspector considered the refurbished cells adequate though small (Home Office 1993c).

Other Conditions

Woolf was concerned about the standards of food preparation in often inadequate kitchens, the lack of variety in diets, and the fact that so many prisoners ate in cells without the option of social dining at times which were dictated by staff duty hours and thus widely out of step with normal practice outside. He did, nevertheless, sympathise with catering officers and prisoners working in the kitchens, recognizing they had a near impossible task (Home Office 1991a, paras. 14.198–219). Woolf was also scathing in his comments about the supply of prison clothing and the notorious gap between what was said to exist and what was seen to exist in the local prisons. He argued that there was no reason why personal kit systems, by then introduced into fifty-five training prisons, should not be extended to local prisons. He decried the undue restrictions on the wearing of personal clothing and argued that the provision of washing machines in the wings would greatly facilitate the extension of prisoners' use of their own clothes (*ibid.*, paras. 14.177–97).

According to the national prison survey, which was being carried out at the time that Woolf reported, only 13 per cent of prisoners thought the food good whilst 51 per cent thought it bad, with as many as 36 per cent recording no opinion. The findings are not directly comparable with ours, but we are surprised that so many should have expressed no opinion to the national survey team. Only forty-five of our 1,220 prisoners failed to express an opinion, and we had proportionately both more prisoners who approved (33.7 per cent) and who disapproved (62.5 per cent). Nevertheless, the single improvement which most NPS prisoners wanted to see was better food, mentioned by 89 per cent of the total sample. When asked which of all the improvements they had mentioned prisoners rated as the top priority, better food again came equal first (along with more visits), with 15 per cent rating this as the most important. Clothing appears not to have been mentioned in this part of the national survey, even by women prisoners, or if it was presumably it was so low down the list of priorities that it was not worth reporting. Elsewhere, the NPS reports that 68 per cent of prisoners were dependent upon prison underwear, including 44 per cent of male unconvicted prisoners who were entitled to wear their own clothes, and 78 per cent of male convicted prisoners. In 1990 the Prison Service reviewed inmate clothing, and Angela Rumbold, then the

Home Office minister responsible for prisons, announced an increase in the supply of underpants to allow a minimum of four changes a week, although this was to be phased in during 1991. At the time of the NPS the target remained two pairs a week.

When we searched the Inspectorate Report on Birmingham for 1990 to see if any improvements had been made, we learned that the kitchen conditions were better than the Inspector had found a year earlier, but he looked forward to the building of a complete new kitchen, although the Home Secretary indicated this could not begin until the work to end slopping out was completed. There were continuing problems with kit losses, and prisoners continued to get a weekly kit change next to the bathhouse which, like much of the prison, was infested with cockroaches, rats, feral cats, and pigeons (Home Office 1990b). Two years later, in spite of the new regulations on underwear, prisoners were still receiving only two pairs of pants and two pairs of socks a week, and meals were still served too early with lunch at 11am and the last meal of the day served shortly after 4 o'clock (Home Office 1992c).

In Gartree the Inspector found, as we had done, that the personal kit system was still not working effectively, that many items went missing, and the system was over budget. The food was thought by the Inspector to be good, although he sympathized with the catering officer's desire to have an additional allowance of 50 pence per prisoner per week so that the diet for long-term prisoners could be made more varied. The Inspector criticized Gartree for allowing staff to make purchases from the prisoners' canteen (Home Office 1990c). By 1992 the Chief Inspector was able to record that in the refurbished A wing in Gartree provision had been made for social dining on each landing so that prisoners no longer had to eat in the small cells now fitted with integral sanitation (Home Office 1993e). In Nottingham the Chief Inspector was told in November 1992 that the governor intended to introduce cooking facilities so that prisoners could prepare hot snacks, although prisoners continued to eat all their meals in cells. Launderette facilities had been introduced on both wings (Home Office 1993b). Featherstone continued to have prisoners eating in cells, although the Inspector recommended they switch to social dining. A personal kit system had been considered in Featherstone but it had not been introduced (Home Office 1989c). In Ashwell the Chief Inspector commented adversely on the extent of provision within the personal kit system, and the fact that prisoners were not allowed to wear personal clothing apart from trainers (Home Office 1993c).

We could find little further information from the annual reports by the governors of our research prisons for 1991–2 about the food, canteen, and clothes. In the case of Birmingham these matters were not mentioned at all. In Gartree an audit of the kitchen areas had taken place, necessitating further action to ensure that outside clothes were not worn in the kitchen and to provide more accessible washbasins at the servery points. In Nottingham it was reported that a more sensible pattern of meal times was being introduced and that there had been an increase in the use by prisoners of their own clothing. In Featherstone there had been some upgrading work in the kitchens, and procedures to monitor the use of private cash at the canteen and the operation of the kit exchange system had been improved. However, the introduction of a personal kit system was still being inhibited by problems with laundering. There had been many complaints about the food in Ashwell during the early part of 1991, but the situation was said to have improved dramatically with the drafting in of a new catering officer, a point confirmed by the Inspectorate.

The White Paper, *Custody, Care, and Justice*, referred to improvements already made to prison kitchens, and in the dietary allowances and greater choice of meals for prisoners. It promised greater budgetary freedom for catering officers and more associated dining for prisoners at more social hours (Home Office 1991b, paras. 6.32–4). With regard to clothes the White Paper referred to improvements in the provision of underwear and it promised greater use of own clothes for convicted male prisoners, but linked this to security, laundry, and other problems, and noted that change would have to take place over a period of several years (*ibid.*, paras. 6.27–31). The *Corporate Plan* (Prison Service 1993d) and the *Business Plan* (Prison Service 1993e) both contain commitments to improve the quality of food. Neither document seems to mention prison clothing, but the *Corporate Plan* lists prison canteens as amongst the services presently provided to be market-tested.

Meeting Needs and Health Care

The national prison survey makes no reference to the chaplaincy or to the prison medical services or to the mental health, drug dependence, and extent of HIV/AIDS amongst prisoners. The latter omissions were partly on the ground that Gunn, Maden, and Swinton (1991) had recently completed a Home Office-commissioned survey on mental health amongst sentenced prisoners, and because of the delicacy of tackling such matters in a general survey. The NPS does report, however, on the preparedness of prisoners to confide in staff which touches on issues similar to those we have discussed above in relation to personal officers. Only 13 per cent of the national sample said they would be able to talk to most staff, with a further 33 per cent able to talk to one or two staff. Unfortunately, the NPS questions on this contained some ambiguities which led Walmsley and colleagues to suggest that these results might be less of a reflection upon staff than appears at first sight. However, only 24.6 per cent of our prisoners said they would be prepared to confide in staff about a personal problem. To suggest that this is a reflection on staff, one way or another, is rather to miss the point. It is much more likely to be a reflection of the social structure of the prison and the acknowledged power differentials it inevitably contains. The fact is that no matter how sympathetic and well-intentioned prison officers may be, confiding in staff is likely to carry costs for prisoners, both because staff may feel bound to use that information in reports which in the end may not help a prisoner's case, and because prisoners may at best lose face with fellow prisoners or at worst be suspected of grassing. Staff might take some comfort, however, from our finding that prisoners were even less likely to confide in each other.

Woolf had little or nothing to say on the chaplaincy and offered fairly brief comment upon the medical services, apart from noting that they failed to deliver services comparable to those in the National Health Service and warning of the dangers of over-medication (Home Office 1991a, paras. 12.131–4). Woolf kept his comments so brief presumably because the results of an efficiency scrutiny were already being considered by the Prison Service. Later he broadly endorsed the recommendations in John Gunn's report of his research into mentally disordered offenders (*ibid.*, para. 12.253) which suggested that 'drug dependence is the commonest psychiatric problem in sentenced prisoners' and that, with few exceptions, 'prison doctors regarded drug and alcohol abuse as being outside their area of concern' (*ibid.*, paras. 12.340–1). Woolf was also critical of the procedure whereby prisoners tested positive for HIV were placed under a Viral Infectivity Restriction (VIR) and recommended a complete review of policy in relation to HIV (*ibid.*, paras. 12.354–73).

According to Gunn's evidence to Woolf, 8.6 per cent of sentenced adult male prisoners had a primary diagnosis of alcohol dependence, and a further 10.1 per cent a primary diagnosis of drug dependency or abuse (excluding cannabis). We could, of course, lay no claim to our data substituting for a clinical diagnosis of dependence—our questions on alcohol and drugs were included in a comprehensive questionnaire and related to 'regular use' without further definition. Clearly, amongst our 78.4 per cent who regularly used alcohol there were many who were social drinkers without being dependent. We are, however, intrigued to see the close correspondence between our data for regular drug use and those found by Gunn and colleagues. Many of our sample were users of several substances, of course, but we set out our data here separately for each substance, giving figures for remand prisoners, which were higher in all cases, in brackets: 13.3 per cent of sentenced prisoners (19.1 per cent of remands) used amphetamines; 9.3 per cent of sentenced prisoners (15.3 per cent of remands) used cocaine; 8.7 per cent of sentenced prisoners (12.6 per cent of remands) used barbiturates; and 7.4 per cent of sentenced prisoners (10.5 per cent of remands) reported using heroin. This correspondence, especially upon such delicate matters, gives us further confidence about our findings generally. It is much harder to comment about the use of drugs in prison, although our data suggest that between a third and a half of those reporting regular use of 'hard' drugs outside had at least some access to them inside, including injecting. Use of cannabis apparently went up.

The *Corporate Plan 1993–96* acknowledged the history of criticism of the quality of health care much more directly than had the Government White Paper two years earlier. By then it was no longer merely a question of adverse comment by academics or outspoken members of the service itself: there had to be a response to the Social Services Select Committee (1986), the findings of the Chief Inspector of Prisons, the comments of Woolf, and the findings of the 1990 Efficiency Scrutiny (Home Office 1990d) and a joint review by the Prison Service and the IHSM Consultants of the Directorate of Prison Medical Services. In 1992 the Prison Medical Service was relaunched as the Health Care Service for Prisoners, and in accordance with the recommendations of the Efficiency Scrutiny was to become more closely aligned with the National Health Service, with a greater emphasis on prevention of illness and health promotion, and should move to becoming primarily a purchaser rather than a provider of services for prisoners. Pilot projects were to be established in a number of prisons beginning in 1993, none of which involved any of our research prisons.

On scrutinizing the Inspectorate Reports and the annual reports of prison governors since our research we find no significant developments to report in these areas, apart from a heightened awareness of the need for more effective suicide prevention procedures to be put in place. On his short inspection of Birmingham the Chief Inspector commented that there was still no personal officer scheme and that SWIP was undertaken by untrained instructors in the textile shops (Home Office 1992c). On a similar short inspection of Featherstone (Home Office 1992b) the extraordinary contrast was noted between the well equipped, but empty, hospital facility at Featherstone, and the deplorably overcrowded hospital at Birmingham, which the medical officer noted in his annual report was often illegally overcrowded. A new hospital for Birmingham is planned but no start is expected until after 1996. Sadly the prison hospital at Birmingham had been the setting for another tragedy when, on 8 July 1989, John Ryan, who had lost nearly 20lbs in weight during his eight-week stay, died from dehydration three days after being transferred to the hospital wing. The inquest returned a verdict of death through lack of care. It remains to be seen how far the proposed changes will go towards improving the level of confidence in the medical service that was expressed by our prisoners.

In October 1994 Michael Howard announced a random urine-testing programme, as well as the regular testing of known drug users, in an attempt to clamp down on the use of drugs. Prisoners who test positive, or refuse tests, will apparently face disciplinary charges with penalties of up to twenty-eight days to be added to their sentences in addition to loss of privileges and earnings. It is a pity that the undoubted drug problem in prisons is to be dealt with as a law-and-order issue rather than a medical matter, thus repeating the mistakes so often made in drug-control policies outside prisons. As we noted in Chapter 2 staff believed that, if one really wanted to find drugs on the wings, then a policy which targeted known users and dealers during association periods, when deals were openly made, would be more effective than routine cell searches which turned up very little. However, they also knew only too well that to introduce such a policy would raise tensions to unacceptable levels, and make the staff who had to implement it more vulnerable to assault and attempts to corrupt them. They argued that it was better to be aware of what was going on and arrange the occasional transfer of known traffickers—who, as we reported in Chapter 3, were seen as a serious threat to good order and discipline—whenever matters looked to be getting out of hand.

There are welcome signs that senior managers in the Prison Service are well aware of these kinds of dangers. In a briefing document presented at the annual conference later in October, Philippa Drew and Tony Pearson, respectively Directors of Custody and Inmate Programmes, argued that 'simply punishing those who test positive runs the risk of creating serious disorder or staff collusion with prisoners'. The document noted that clear incentives were necessary if prisoners were to be persuaded off drugs, and argued for a 'broader treatment strategy' in which those who have tested positive could be offered counselling: 'mandatory testing should not be introduced without treatment or rehabilitation programmes in place' (*The Guardian* 28 October 1994). As we have seen in this chapter no such programmes were on offer in any of our research prisons. Although in recent years some prisons have experimented by developing drug-free wings on a voluntary basis, it is clear that drug treatment programmes are still very much in their infancy in the prisons of England and Wales.

It remains to be seen what will be the effect of the new testing programme which is to be introduced into eight prisons in January 1995 on a pilot basis. It is to be hoped that those prisons, at least, will have drug-treatment programmes in place by then. As on so many other matters we also hope that the process of implementing this policy change will be rigorously and independently researched. Finally we think it important that ways be found to develop performance indicators for the many other aspects of prison conditions and the needs of prisoners which go beyond the current measures of accommodation and sanitation.

5
Providing Positive Regimes

The fourth goal of the Prison Service is to *provide positive regimes which help prisoners address their offending behaviour and allow them as full and responsible a life as possible* (Prison Service 1993c, 5). Two key performance indicators against which success is to be measured are, first, *the number of hours a week which, on average, prisoners spend in purposeful activity* (Key Performance Indicator 5); and secondly, *the proportion of prisoners held in establishments where prisoners are unlocked on weekdays for a total of at least 12 hours* (Key Performance Indicator 6). The *Business Plan 1993–94* translated these performance indicators into specific targets: respectively to ensure that prisoners spend, on average, at least 3 per cent more hours a week in purposeful activity resulting in an average of 24.9 hours per week per prisoner; and that by 31 March 1994 at least 34 per cent of prisoners are to be held in establishments where prisoners are unlocked for a total of at least twelve hours on weekdays. These improvements are to be secured through greater efficiency (Prison Service 1993e, 8).

At the end of the first year of agency status the Prison Service (1994c) was able to claim that it met the first performance indicator but not the second. On the one hand, the actual average time spent in so-called purposeful activity during 1993–4 was 24.7 hours a week, marginally below plan; but since the actual hours achieved in 1992–3 turned out to be only 23.7 hours, somewhat less than had been anticipated when the target was set, it was possible to claim success on grounds that the increase was 4.1 per cent instead of the 3.0 per cent which had been targeted. On the other hand, only 29 per cent of the prison population was held in establishments where prisoners are unlocked for twelve or more hours a day. This was, proportionately, half way between the performance the previous year at 24 per cent of the population and the target of 34 per cent, but the growth in the prison population had long since put paid to hopes of meeting the objective set. However, as we shall argue in this chapter, whilst KPI 6 is rather rough and ready, time out-of-cell is a relatively unambiguous concept. This cannot be said for KPI 5 on purposeful activity: it does not mean what it appears to mean, and it is beset by methodological difficulties. Unfortunately, KPI 5 is likely to become the most important touchstone for evaluating the extent to which the service implements the Woolf agenda.

It is important to note at the outset that there are two major differences in the formulation of the goals as set out above from the statement of tasks and functions enshrined in CI 55/84 (reproduced in Appendix 1) which prevailed at the time of our research. While the task of the Prison Service referred to providing prisoners with as full a life as is consistent with the facts of custody, it was not specifically either a task of the service or a function of establishments to address *offending behaviour* or to promote *responsibility* among prisoners. Although Function 18 was to enable prisoners to spend the maximum time out of cells, no targets were specified; moreover, under Function 17 activities were simply construed as occupying prisoners as fully as possible in a balanced and integrated regime. It was precisely in these areas of time spent out of cells and in purposeful activities, of course, that we were able to show (King and McDermott 1989, 1990b) how far standards of service had deteriorated in the Prison Service on the basis of comparisons between our five current prisons and the earlier study of five prisons as part of the *Prison Regimes Project*. We were also able to show that Fresh Start, at least initially, had done little to fulfil its promise of enhancing regimes (McDermott and King 1989; King and McDermott 1990b). We are now able to point to the beginnings of a reversal of that trend, although there remains a very long way to go. But there are also signs, since our research was carried out, of interesting developments in tackling offending behaviour and promoting a greater sense of personal responsibility amongst prisoners.

In this chapter we begin with a reminder of the extent of the decline in prison regimes and then present further data, which have not previously been published, about the way in which both prisoners and staff evaluated the quality of the activities available in their prisons. We then try to determine the extent to which things have actually moved on since our research, using four main sources of data. First, and perhaps most importantly, we obtained regime monitoring data for our prisons for the month of November 1992 with which we were able to compare the regime monitoring materials we routinely collected five years earlier. Secondly, we obtained the annual reports of the governors of our research prisons for 1991–2, which usually also included the reports of the various middle managers covering specialist areas. Thirdly, we scrutinized the Inspectorate reports on our research prisons, both of full inspections and short inspections on the basis of unannounced visits, which often also contained valuable descriptive material. Fourthly, we looked at the findings from the national prison survey to see to what extent the evaluations expressed by our respondents still strike a chord nationally. In the course of our analysis we offer a critique both of regime monitoring and of the key performance indicators and suggest a more meaningful measure of purposeful activities. Finally, we try to assess the prospects for accomplishing the aspirations enshrined in the Woolf Report and the latest venture into addressing offending behaviour and promoting prisoner responsibility through sentence planning and the provision of appropriate programmes.

The Deterioration of Prison Regimes

When we summarized our initial comparisons between the findings from our current research prisons and those from their matched pairs in the earlier *Prison Regimes Project* at the Perrie Lectures in 1990, we characterized the most important change to have occurred in the Prison Service over the intervening period as 'the astonishing shrinkage of the unlocked day' (King and McDermott 1990b, 32). The 'best' modal time[1] out of cells in Gartree in 1986–7 was just nine hours on a weekday compared with 14.25 hours in Albany in 1971. In Nottingham it was 9.5 hours compared with fourteen hours at Coldingley. The deterioration in the lower-security prisons was less marked, but still significant: Featherstone prisoners were unlocked for eleven hours compared with thirteen hours in Camp Hill, and Ashwell prisoners for fourteen hours compared with fifteen hours at

---

[1] In calculating the 'best' modal response we took the most favourable normally operating circumstances which applied to the largest group of prisoners rounded to the nearest quarter of an hour. Normally this related to prisoners in workshops when the workshops were fully operational. Some prisoners, e.g. kitchen workers, may spend much longer out of cells whilst others, notably those without work or on punishment or Rule 43, spend much less. Many other calculation methods could be used, which would have produced different results. The best modal response seems to us the fairest reasonable method of comparison. In the training prisons it probably produces a figure quite close to the mean hours out-of-cell. In Birmingham it almost certainly presents a more favourable picture, where 36% of the convicted prisoners had no work, education, or training to occupy themselves at all.

Ford. Convicted prisoners in Birmingham spent only 5.5 hours a day out of cells compared with nine hours enjoyed by their counterparts in Winchester fifteen years earlier. Only for remand prisoners had the situation not worsened: but, as we pointed out, when prisoners already spend twenty-two hours a day locked up there is not much scope for deterioration. In Birmingham remand prisoners spent two hours a day out of cells, including exercise, slopping out, washing and shaving, collecting meals, and so on, just as their predecessors had in Winchester.

Not surprisingly, with prisoners spending less time out of cells they had less time for constructive activity. When we compared the hours spent at work, for example, again using the best modal response, Gartree now managed only five hours a day compared with the eight hours Albany had provided and Nottingham only 4.5 hours compared with eight hours at Coldingley. In the lower security prisons the reductions were smaller, but nevertheless important: thus Featherstone provided at best six hours of work a day compared with 7.5 in Camp Hill, and Ashwell 6.5 hours compared with 7.5 at Ford. Once again the higher-security prisons in the late 1980s resembled the local prison regime in the early 1970s. However, convicted prisoners in the local prisons appeared to have suffered the worst proportionate decline in hours of work. In Birmingham they now only managed 2.5 hours a day whereas Winchester had actually provided 5.5 hours.

Not only had the amount of time out of cells and the amount of time in work been reduced, but the size of the modal group experiencing the 'best' conditions had significantly reduced in all but one case. Gartree had only 48 per cent employed in industry compared with 61 per cent in Albany; Nottingham had only 36 per cent compared with the 70 per cent in Coldingley; Ashwell had only 30 per cent compared with 47 per cent in Ford; and Birmingham a mere 24 per cent compared with 59 per cent in Winchester. Only Featherstone had a higher proportion employed in workshops (55 per cent) than its counterpart prison, Camp Hill (37 per cent) of fifteen years earlier, although this is probably not a fair comparison: Featherstone had been established as an industrial prison whereas Camp Hill had no such pretensions.[2] However, further important caveats have to be

---

[2] The real comparator for Featherstone was Coldingley which was the flagship industrial prison of the 1960s. However, for most other purposes our comparisons have been based upon security categories and it would be confusing to switch the basis for comparison here.

entered here. The description of this as 'best' modal response refers strictly to the product of numbers of prisoners involved in work-shops and the amount of time they spent so engaged: i.e. it got the biggest single group of prisoners out of cells for the longest time. It takes no account of the fact that most prisoners regarded the work activity provided as pointless, soul-destroying, and demeaning. Nor had industrial work fulfilled the hopes of either the Advisory Council on the Treatment of Offenders (ACTO 1961, 1964) or the Prison Service Industries and Farms of becoming economically viable, let alone profitable and capable of sustaining real wages, compensation for victims, support for families, and savings for release. Wages were at the most derisory pocket money levels to be found anywhere in the prison systems of the western world.[3] Recognizing these issues, the Prison Service had hugely reduced its reliance on prison industry, with a reduction of 60 per cent in workshop hours over the preceding decade and the closure of forty-two workshops in 1986–7 alone. Moreover, the 'padding' of workshops with prisoners who had no real work to do but would otherwise remain in cells was increasingly frowned upon even though it had not been eliminated. The same approach was taken towards works parties and domestic cleaners, which nevertheless still accounted for 28.4 per cent of all the prisoners in our prisons. As a consequence there were increases in the numbers of prisoners who were openly unemployed: these amounted to 15.4 per cent of all the convicted prisoners in our prisons, rising to 36 per cent of those in Birmingham.

To offset the decline in importance of prison industry the service sought more balanced regimes by providing alternative activities such as daytime education classes and vocational and industrial training courses. In Gartree about one in six prisoners (16 per cent) were engaged in day time education, with 12 per cent in Nottingham, 7 per cent in Featherstone, 14 per cent in Ashwell, and even 7 per cent in Birmingham, although the system there mostly involved open learning packages in cells rather than classroom teaching. There had been no daytime education available for adults in the prison system at the time of the earlier *Prison Regimes Project*, but since prisoners

---

[3] Woolf described prisoners as the 'poor men of Europe' when it came to wages (Home Office 1991a, para. 14.164). At the time of his report average wages were still only £2.65 which he proposed should be increased to £8 a week at a cost of £13.4m a year. Woolf still regarded that as derisory by any normal standard (*ibid.*, paras. 14.168–9).

were then out of cells for so much longer most prisons ran a full programme of evening education classes during association periods. By
contrast, evening education had been substantially curtailed in the
prisons by 1987, in part because of the reduced amount of time on
association in the evenings. Ironically the end result appeared to be
that, in spite of the welcome growth in daytime education, fewer
prisoners actually participated in education of one kind or another
in the current study than had been the case fifteen years earlier. The
one real gain, no less ironic in its way, was that there had been a
genuine increase in the proportion of prisoners engaged in some
formal vocational or industrial training programmes in three of the
training prisons—Nottingham, Featherstone, and Ashwell, compared with their counterparts Coldingley, Camp Hill, and Ford—in
spite of the greater emphasis given earlier to the rhetoric of treatment
and training of offenders. There was no difference over time between
the dispersal prisons in this regard, neither having any programmes
at the time of the research. What little training there had been in the
local prisons had completely disappeared.

In spite of massive increases of staff which had far outstripped the
growth in prison population, it was evident that regimes had grown
substantially worse. Indeed the unthinkable seemed to have happened. High security prisons had deteriorated to the point where, in
several important respects, their regimes resembled what had earlier
been on offer in the local prisons. Those very conditions in local prisons had then been widely regarded as completely unacceptable—
what the Home Office itself described as mere humane containment
(or, as we argued in Chapter 1 where we tried to take the notion of
humane containment *seriously*, what would better have been
described as *in*humane containment). Meanwhile those same local
prison regimes had become still more impoverished, at least for convicted prisoners. It seemed evident that the obsession with security
and control had a limitless capacity not merely to absorb additional
resources but also to curtail existing regimes.

The first publication of these findings attracted the attention of the
Chief Inspector, who quoted them in the report of his inspection of
Gartree in 1989 (Home Office 1990c). By the time of the Woolf
Report it was also possible to take on board the fact that Fresh Start,
which was in part intended to draw a line under the past and,
through efficiency savings, plough back monies to enhance regimes,
had made little impact upon these matters. The only change in hours

unlocked was at Nottingham, and that was for the worse. As far as hours spent in work were concerned, Nottingham had further deteriorated although Featherstone had improved. Some planned and long-awaited training courses had, at last, come on stream in Gartree, but fewer people were engaged in training at Nottingham, Featherstone, and Ashwell than had been the case before Fresh Start. Although there had been further improvements in the numbers on daytime education in Featherstone, the situation had got worse in Gartree, Nottingham, and Ashwell.

Prisoner and Staff Evaluations of Regimes

Work

Work might be expected to be the centrepiece of any prison regime, just as work continues to be the centrepiece of most people's lives outside prison. For most people it not merely offers the means of sustaining life and providing some comforts and perhaps a few luxuries, but is also crucial to creating and maintaining identity. What we do, to a considerable extent, determines who we are, not just in our own eyes but the eyes of others. Although unemployment and social security provisions impact upon this at the margins, both in present fact and future prospect these are just the margins from which most of those who pass through the criminal justice system and end up in prison are drawn. This does not mean that work should be less important in prison. Quite the contrary. If people are going to spend time in custody there would seem to be everything to be said for using that time in ways that show not merely the dignity of work but its potential for conferring rewards.

Prison work is an area in which there are intriguing international variations. In Russia today there are often-expressed anxieties stemming from the history of slave labour in the GULag about whether it is appropriate to compel prisoners to work. It is a problem that is rapidly going away of its own accord as unemployment hits Russian society and, inevitably, its corrective labour colonies. Meanwhile, for those still in work, Russian prisoners are engaged in similar activities with similar pay and subject to the same health and safety regulations as those outside. They pay for their keep, compensate their victims, support their families, and save for their release (King 1994a; Mikhlin and King 1994). In Britain our Prison Rules still require prisoners to work, albeit for not more than ten hours a day. However, historically we have exercised considerable ingenuity in making prison work deliberately punitive and expressly useless in nature. Overcoming this legacy proved so intractable that by the mid-1980s the Prison Service was signalling a substantial retreat. By contrast, prison labour in the United States has always been directed towards productive and profitable activity, at least for some prisoners— although there have properly been fears about private exploitation that mirror the former Soviet state exploitation of prisoners. Unemployment and the massive growth of prison populations in the United States over the last decade or so have understandably made considerable inroads into those pockets of industrial activity which once flourished there.

There were fourteen workshops in our prisons at the time of our study, employing some 37.3 per cent of all the convicted prisoners. Six of them were textile shops, either heavy (mailbags) or light (prison uniforms and army bandoliers); three were making knitwear (mostly tee shirts), and one was a laundry. All of these, rightly or wrongly, were deemed to be 'women's work' by prisoners. Of the remainder, one involved simple assembly work of the most tedious nature, two were making shoes and other footwear for prisoner use, and one involved simple engineering work in the manufacture of parts for convector heaters. Though these shops were free of the stigma of women's work, only parts of the footwear and engineering operations were at all skilled or interesting in terms of their content. With wages ranging form £2.22 a week as a learner in the workshops to £4.50 as the top rate for the most skilled shop-worker, it is hardly surprising that prisoners felt that workshop employment gave them little dignity, sense of purpose, or financial reward. In spite of the best efforts of industrial managers and workshop managers, closures of the workshops were not uncommon, and much time was lost to interruptions for a variety of reasons. In Birmingham 51 per cent of available time was lost to closures or interruptions; in Gartree it was 32 per cent, Nottingham 31 per cent, and Featherstone 17.5 per cent. Only Ashwell maintained a reasonable record in this regard, losing 5 per cent of available time, although to the constantly voiced disappointment of the governor the workshops operated well below their true capacity because of the inability of PSIF to supply raw materials and machinery. Not surprisingly, the experience of prisoners in the workshops merely served to reinforce the negative feelings about work they brought with them from outside. It certainly did nothing to turn these feelings around.

There were, of course, other work opportunities in all of the prisons, as cleaners, orderlies, kitchen staff, and members of various work parties. Some work parties offered both variety and skilled work as well as some freedom of movement. Kitchen work offered perks in exchange for long hours. Some of the activities of orderlies and cleaners brought prisoners into positions where they might gain access to useful information as well as some perks. But the biggest single form of employment in each prison was in the workshops and so this dominated the perception of work opportunities for prisoners. We asked all staff and those prisoners with direct experience of work in each prison to evaluate the work programmes. Only in Ashwell were the prisoners even mildly favourable in their evaluation, although in Featherstone it could be said they were only mildly negative. Elsewhere the work programmes were roundly condemned by prisoners. In Birmingham and Gartree prison officers broke ranks and joined prisoners in almost as severe a condemnation. Only in Featherstone and Ashwell were staff able to assert that the work programmes were good, offering much more favourable ratings than prisoners. All the differences between prisons were statistically significant (prisoners: chi-square 78.62337 p < .0001; staff: chi-square 81.27254 p < .0001). The details are given in Figure 5.1.

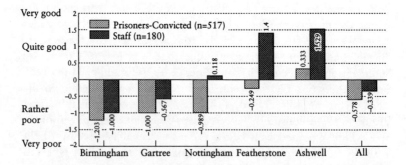

Fig. 5.1   Prisoner and staff ratings of work programmes

Training

Some 230 prisoners out of our total of 1,220 responded to our question which invited them to evaluate the training courses on offer in their prison. We intended the rating to be one of quality based upon direct experience. However, although the question was framed with that in mind, some thirty prisoners in Birmingham responded even though there were no courses there which they could have experienced. Elsewhere the response was somewhat higher than the number of places available, and included a substantial number of prisoners who had received a training course in the past and some who were on the waiting list for courses. Gartree had made great efforts to create a furniture-making course and a micro-engineering vocational training course but there had been funding difficulties and staffing problems, and neither was established until we went back to the prison to evaluate the impact of Fresh Start. In Nottingham there were popular courses on radio and television maintenance and repair as well as the more usual bricklaying, plastering, and decorating courses. During the year of our fieldwork fifty Nottingham prisoners received City and Guilds qualifications. However, staff retirements meant that the radio and television course had closed by the time of Fresh Start. Featherstone had a precision milling vocational training course during our fieldwork, but that, too, had closed by the time we returned after the implementation of Fresh Start. It retained its well-liked courses in grinding, capstan setting, and welding, and a somewhat less well-appreciated course in industrial cleaning. Ashwell was seeking to restore a plumbers' course which had formerly operated at the prison but without success, although it did have several other small construction industry courses (CITs) for painting and decorating, carpentry, electrical, and bricklaying, as well as a health and safety course.

Where courses existed they were nearly always oversubscribed. Prisoners for the most part found them interesting and reasonably enjoyable. It was not so much that they saw this as a training for what they wanted to do outside, although some did. It was more that this gave something credible to do with one's time inside, would provide a plausible basis for parole applications, might just offer something to do immediately on release, and would possibly come in handy around the home anyway. Being on a course was much less soul-destroying than being in a workshop, and relationships with instructors were likely to be on a different basis from relationships with other staff. For several prisoners, however, there would have been considerable loss of credibility had they sought to join such a course. The results are presented in Figure 5.2.

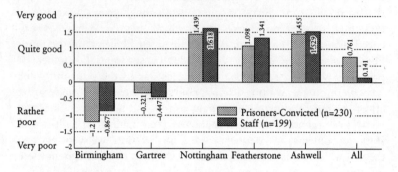

Fig. 5.2 Prisoner and staff ratings of training programmes

In Nottingham, Featherstone, and Ashwell prisoners who had experienced these courses were highly favourable towards them, as were the staff in those establishments. In Birmingham prisoners seemed to be expressing their anger at the absence of courses, and in Gartree the negative response seems to have come from frustrated prisoners hoping for the promised VTCs to get under way. Once again staff took much the same view as prisoners. All the differences were statistically significant (prisoners: chi-square 108.76543 $p < .0001$; staff: chi-square 101.56224 $p < .0001$).

Education and Library Services

Some 208 prisoners, or about one in ten of all convicted prisoners in our research prisons, were accommodated on daytime education courses at the time of our research. All of the prisons had an education department which operated five days a week. In Nottingham the education day was somewhat shorter, at 4.5 hours, than elsewhere, but this was compensated for by an evening programme that ran for an hour and a half on four nights of the week. Elsewhere, the education department operated for five hours a day, but in Birmingham, in practice, this was reduced to about half that because of the frequent cancellation of classes. Gartree and Birmingham had evening classes for one and a half hours on two nights each week, Featherstone had evening classes of two hours on three nights a week, and Ashwell had no evening classes at all.

The education departments varied considerably in their facilities but were all much of a muchness in terms of size, accommodating between thirty-five and fifty full-time students each. Because of the very different populations in the prisons, however, this accounted for just 7 per cent of convicted prisoners in Birmingham and as many as 16 per cent of those in Gartree. Education officers were appointed to the service by local education authorities, usually on a secondment basis from local colleges of further education, with one or two full-time teaching appointments and other teachers coming in on a part-time basis. The courses ranged from basic remedial education in literacy, English, and mathematics to a variety of craft-based and more academic courses, including a number of Open University courses. Birmingham was also in the process of developing an extensive open learning programme whereby prisoners pursued private study in their cells with occasional tutorial support.

Education gave real opportunities to several groups of prisoners. To some of the more thoughtful and articulate it provided a chance to develop and stretch themselves in ways that could not have happened in the workshops or even on training courses. Sometimes this led them to address their own offending behaviour. To many others it offered the opportunity to retrace the faltering and painful steps they had taken in a school system to which, for one reason or another, they had been unable to relate. To all it offered an oasis away from the pressures on the wings and the futilities of the workshops, a chance to experience an alternative set of values and a different set of institutional constraints. It was not, of course, possible to distance oneself entirely from the realities of the prison whilst at education. Often there were more discipline officers than seemed strictly necessary to supervise the process. Just as prison work has traditionally been regarded as punitive, so the possibility that prisoners might escape its rigours in education was punished by disincentive 'wages' which were kept deliberately low.[4]

[4] The inequalities in pay between those taking education and those employed in workshops and elsewhere were taken up repeatedly by Judge Tumim in the public seminars during the Woolf Inquiry and Woolf committed himself to the principle of commensurability between them in his report (Home Office 1991a, para. 14.110). This

Some measure of the importance given to education by prisoners can be gained from the fact that rather more than twice as many prisoners from our sample replied to this question as could be accommodated on the existing daytime education programme. All, however, claimed some experience either of the full-time education programme in that prison or the evening education programme. This was one of the very few variables examined in our study where the prisoners ratings were, on average, favourable in all prisons—even in Birmingham. Not surprisingly, they were more favourable in the training prisons, notably in Nottingham and Featherstone where the provision was most extensive, especially in the evenings. Staff broadly followed the pattern of response of prisoners here, although as might be expected their ratings were even more favourable. The differences between the prisons were statistically significant (prisoners: chi-square 60.02129 p < .0001; staff: chi-square 43.41519 p < .0001). The details are given in Figure 5.3.

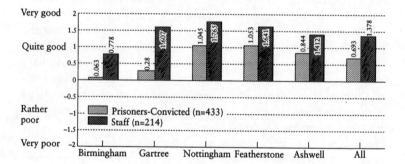

Fig. 5.3   Prisoner and staff ratings of education programmes

Education is somewhat dependent upon library resources, although libraries also serve an important function in prisons, as they do outside, in providing recreational and other instrumental forms of reading. Libraries were stocked by the local library service, but staffed by prison officers and prisoners, with some overseeing from

was roundly rejected in the White Paper in exactly the same way that guilty and not guilty pleas are treated in the courts: you cannot be punished for exercising your right to plead not guilty, but you can be rewarded for pleading guilty. So it is apparently to remain for prison education and prison work (Home Office 1991b, para. 7.31).

civic librarians. In the training prisons the library was open during evening association: Nottingham and Ashwell for five evenings a week, Gartree for four evenings, and Featherstone for three evenings. In Birmingham, where there was precious little association, there were separate facilities for convicted and remand prisoners. The library for convicted prisoners was open, in theory though not always in practice, for thirty-six hours a week and prisoners could visit up to twice a week. For remand prisoners the service was more irregular. The stock of books varied widely, being best in Nottingham and Ashwell, followed by Featherstone and Gartree, with the poorest facilities in Birmingham, especially for remand prisoners. The vast majority of prisoners used the library facility to some extent, and their ratings are presented in Figure 5.4.

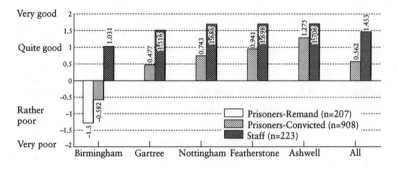

Fig. 5.4   Prisoner and staff ratings of the library

As with the canteen, the library seems to be one of those facilities that, if it exists at all, the staff are happy to regard it as good, although the differences in staff ratings between prisons were nevertheless statistically significant (chi-square 29.84209 p < .005). In the training prisons most prisoners seemed to rate the library quite highly, although much less so than staff. In Birmingham both remand and convicted prisoners rightly regarded the library facilities as poor (chi-square 491.79071 p < .0001).

Physical Education and Recreation

Opportunities for some kind of physical activity, in the form of organized physical education, supervised weight training, or just working out or engaging in handball, badminton, five-a-side football, or similar games, were at a premium in the higher-security prisons. In Gartree the gymnasium was available for 35.5 hours a week, including weekday evening association periods, but there was a long waiting-list of prisoners who wanted some or more access. The situation was the same in Nottingham except that there the waiting-list was somewhat shorter. The gymnasium in Featherstone was available for a total of forty-eight hours including four evening association periods and this was sufficient to accommodate all the prisoners who wanted to use it, albeit not as often as some of them would have liked. In Ashwell both the demand for physical education and the availability of the gymnasium were much lower—a mere twenty hours and this included weekend use as well as two evenings a week. Both remand and convicted prisoners in Birmingham had access to the gymnasium which was open for forty-three hours a week, including two evenings, but no prisoner was able to go more than once a week. In Birmingham the gymnasium, like the workshops, education classes, the library, and so many other activities, could be closed unpredictably as the demands of the exigent day took over.

It is hard to over-emphasize the importance of physical activity in prison. It will be recalled from our discussion in Chapter 4 that the proportion of prisoners seriously concerned about their health generally, and their physical fitness and their emotional stability in particular, was directly related to hours locked in cells and to opportunities for physical activity.

Physical education, like education generally, as well as being valued for itself offered opportunities for different kinds of relationships with staff. PE instructors were often able to gain the respect of prisoners in ways that other officers could not, and there was often a noticeably more agreeable atmosphere in the gym than elsewhere. Prison staff valued the gymnasium too, not merely for their own occasional use but because it was thought that giving prisoners the chance to burn off their energies in that fashion made it less likely that they would release their tensions in other, more disruptive, ways. In Gartree, however, the demands of security were ever-present, and whenever prisoners were in the gymnasium an officer—known locally as 'Jim Bell'—was situated outside, whose sole job it was to ring the alarm should trouble arise. When the Chief Inspector visited in 1989 he suggested that this post might be dispensed with since no one could recall the bell being rung (Home Office 1990c, para. 3.89).

When we asked our prisoners to evaluate the opportunities for physical education, almost all of them responded. Only in Featherstone and Ashwell, however, where the existing demand could be met, were their replies favourable and then only modestly so. In Nottingham and Gartree prisoners were generally somewhat dissatisfied, primarily because they did not get enough time there. In Birmingham, where demand far outstripped the available facilities, prisoners rated the opportunities as very poor. As with other physical facilities in Birmingham, the staff came quite close to the evaluations made by prisoners, endorsing their very poor rating. But in the training prisons staff generally described the opportunities as at least quite good. The differences were statistically significant (prisoners: chi-square 464.580997 p < .0001: staff: chi-square 161.11201 p < .0001). The mean scores are presented in Figure 5.5.

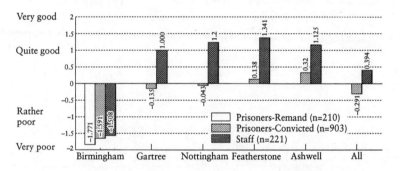

Fig. 5.5   Prisoner and staff ratings of physical education opportunities

The opportunities for other forms of recreational activity were obviously limited both by the remaining hours that prisoners were unlocked and the facilities then available to them. In Birmingham there was no prospect of any outside activity apart from ritual exercise periods when prisoners filed around in concentric circles in time-honoured fashion. Nor was there much prospect in Birmingham, for that matter, of indulging in recreational activities inside: prisoners were either locked in cells or unlocked for specific purposes—slopping out, meals, work, exercise, visits, sick parade. Not surprisingly, when we asked them to evaluate recreational possibilities, both remand and convicted prisoners in Birmingham were extremely negative. Elsewhere it was possible for prisoners to spend time on the field, weather permitting, and regular exercise periods did not have to be slotted into the daily routine. But this is not to say access was unrestricted, and there were many resentments, especially in Gartree (even before the escape of Draper and Kendall by helicopter), about the limited time prisoners could spend outside. Indoor recreation for those prisoners who were not attending evening education classes or the gymnasium largely took the form of watching television and a weekly video, or playing table tennis or pool. Prisoners in the training prisons expressed mild approval, except in Ashwell, where the design of the physical plant offered fewer places for prisoners to come together. Staff were generally more approving of the facilities than prisoners although Ashwell staff appeared to have taken note of the relative poverty of the regime in this regard, and Birmingham staff once again stepped out of role in assessing these opportunities for prisoners as rather poor. The differences were statistically significant (prisoners: chi-square 538.05958 p < .0001; staff: chi-square 115.42906 p < .0001). The ratings are presented in Figure 5.6.

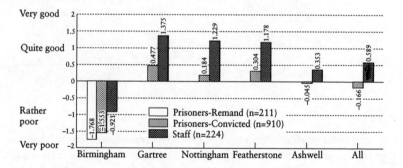

Fig. 5.6   Prisoner and staff ratings of opportunities for recreation

Turning Things Around

On most of the regime activities we have just discussed the differences between the prisons followed the security gradient: the deeper into the system in security terms the heavier was the experience likely to be. There was some evidence, however, that for some prisoners at least in Nottingham—those who were able to attend training courses and education—the burden of imprisonment was marginally lighter than in Featherstone or even Ashwell. But the overriding cause for concern was the extent to which all prison regimes had declined over the years.

Recognizing that something was wrong with prison regimes and that a halt had to be called to their continuing decline was a necessary first step towards change for the Prison Service—just as acknowledging that there might be something wrong with their behaviour is considered a prerequisite for the rehabilitation of offenders. However, in both cases recognition of the malaise is one thing, but finding appropriate and effective strategies for doing something about it is another.

The Control Review Committee took a managerial leap forward by recommending that a clear central responsibility be taken for regime matters at headquarters and by reconceptualizing regimes more flexibly than hitherto: as a series of activities or programmes that might be offered to prisoners in different combinations in different prisons rather than each prison being thought of as having a particular type of regime. In the belief that an industry-centred regime might no longer be practicable the CRC argued for the development of education and training programmes so that as many prisoners could be engaged in purposeful activity as possible, and that these activities should be organized around coherent sentence planning procedures and then monitored so that progress could be measured (Home Office 1984a, paras. 89–100). Circular Instruction 55/1984 facilitated this process by setting out the possible functions of establishments in rather detailed and prosaic terms, on the basis of which regional directors might negotiate specific aspects of those functions with individual prison governors. By the time our research began prison governors were being given annual targets by their regional directors that were intended to ratchet up performance. These could sometimes be rather vague—'to identify two ways in which socially useful work in the community could be expanded'; and were sometimes concerned with managerial minutiae—'the governor and the administration officer should routinely scrutinize the books kept by the officers' club and officers' tea room'. It was not always clear what would happen if the targets were not met, but the very formalization of the process, which might give individual prisons thirty or forty targets, sent an important signal that attention was being given to such matters. However, the evidence from our research seemed to show that these internal efforts had not got very far, if anywhere, in halting the decline: regime activities operated very much below levels which had obtained nearly two decades earlier.

Part of the justification for Fresh Start was making savings that would be ploughed back to enhance prison regimes, but we have argued elsewhere that regime enhancement took a progressively lower profile as the negotiations developed and as the package of reforms was implemented (McDermott and King 1989). We indicated above that there were as many losses as gains in the pattern of regime activities in our research prisons following Fresh Start. Nevertheless, Fresh Start saw the reorganization of local management structures as giving a clearer responsibility for inmate programmes which the CRC wished to see, and this was subsequently reflected in the representation of inmate programmes at Prisons Board level with the reorganization of headquarters and other management structures introduced in September 1990. By then the Woolf Inquiry was well under way, and its deliberations and subsequent recommendations about a code of enforceable standards (Home Office 1991a, paras. 12.98–119) gave enormous impetus to the need to raise the level of service delivery. The agreements over targets reached between governors and regional directors were, of course, the embryonic basis for what Woolf was subsequently sometimes to call 'compacts' and sometimes 'contracts' between area managers and governors (ibid., paras. 12.88–97), an idea he extended to embrace the relationships between the Home Secretary and the Director General of the Service (ibid., paras. 12.43–7), and ultimately between prison governors and the prisoners in their custody (ibid., paras. 12.120–3). The emergence of contracting out raised the extraordinary prospect of writing in conditions for private contractors which set much higher standards than those currently obtaining generally within the prison system, but there can be no doubt that it was the Woolf Inquiry that provided the fuel to drive the engine of change.

Shortly after Joe Pilling delivered his well-received Eve Saville Memorial Lecture—somewhat unfortunately titled, or so it seems in retrospect, *Back to Basics*—the Director General sent out a glossy, but nevertheless important, package of documents on regimes to each establishment (Home Office 1992d). A covering letter of 9 June

1992 set the package up, indicating that it derived from the White Paper, *Custody, Care, and Justice*, and sought to give governors a clear overall picture of proposed developments. In this letter Joe Pilling also looked forward to the publication of a model regime for local prisons and remand centres, which in fact appeared in November that year (Home Office 1992e); the development of a model prisoner compact—the name preferred by the Prison Service precisely because it seemed not to carry the legal connotations of a contract—and about which consultation documents also appeared in November; and the work on the code of standards which eventually came to fruition in March 1994. A further letter of 17 June 1992 gave guidance on the development of balanced regimes and set out the criteria which governors should use in making decisions about regime activities in their institutions.

The first document in the regimes package was prepared by the Regimes Research and Development Unit. It sought to show, on the basis of a reporting of some recent research, that:

after many years spent believing that nothing that happened in prisons would affect future reconviction, there is ample evidence to show that *some things work*: well designed and well implemented programmes can have a statistically significant impact on reconviction (emphasis in original).

This set the scene for information about programmes designed to address offending behaviour—on anger management and an update on the sex offender core treatment programme which had been introduced the previous autumn and which now extended to thirteen prisons.

Another document in the package announced that, with effect from 1 October 1992, sentence planning, using standardized documentation, would be introduced for all sentenced category A prisoners, all life-sentence prisoners, and all newly received prisoners sentenced to four years and over. Further documents addressed the introduction of quality work projects, including one at Featherstone, and the accreditation of workshops to British Standard 5750, and invited governors to consider setting up businesses where these offered good value for money. The introduction of National Vocational Qualifications for prisoners in workplaces and on training courses, for which some 300 schemes had already been funded, was to be further extended in 1992–3. New statements of the importance of education and physical education were included in the package, although no mention was then made of contracting out education which was not decided until the following month. Finally, a new pay scheme for prisoners was to be introduced in December 1992 which would give governors greater flexibility in providing incentives, and allow prisoners to earn an average of £6 a week—some 75 per cent of what Woolf had proposed.

During much of the period that the Prison Service was the Prison Department of the Home Office it had seemed to operate on the belief that a circular instruction issued from headquarters saying that something should be done was for all practical purposes a guarantee that whatever had been decreed was actually carried out. Such communications from headquarters were usually poorly typed, poorly set out, and poorly reproduced. No doubt prison governors dutifully read them and duly added them to their burgeoning files, but it must have been extremely hard for them to convince themselves that anyone much cared about the outcomes. The real function of such communications in the past must have seemed to provide the appropriate cover for bureaucratic backs. Ever since the Control Review Committee had visited the United States, and been impressed by the professional appearance of Federal Prison Service manuals, there had been a growing awareness of the need for upgrading the image of the service and improving the nature and quality of its communication. Some of those concerns were rehearsed in the communications about Fresh Start. The package on regimes took these standards of communication to new heights and that gloss has been further developed since the service became an agency. Nevertheless, it would be unwarrantably cynical to regard the new documentation as merely public relations. For one thing, whereas historically communications flowed out from the centre, transmitting messages that were not infrequently contradictory, there had now for several years been a concerted attempt to think things through in a consistent fashion and the documentation on balanced regimes makes that clear. For another, whereas historically there simply were no systematic mechanisms for checking whether instructions were acted upon until something went wrong, it was now becoming more and more clear that results might actually matter.

If there were to be any serious attention given to the improvement of prison regimes, then central to that endeavour was the need to develop an effective management tool for monitoring those regime activities on the ground. Only then could the achievement of standards and the maintenance of those standards be measured. In fact, much of the early work on regime monitoring arose out of the attempt to develop what was then called an accountable regime at Featherstone between 1981 and 1984 (Marsden and Evans 1985). By the time our research began regime monitoring forms were being piloted in several prisons and were more or less in place across the system by the time of Fresh Start. The system was revised somewhat in March 1992 to take better account of out-of-cell association activities and to give better recognition to the fact that in local prisons whilst prisoners were at court they could not be engaged in activities and should not be counted as doing nothing.

Regime Developments in the Research Prisons: 1987–92

In what follows we use a combination of our original research data and regime-monitoring data to try to evaluate the nature and extent of the changes in regime activities that had occurred in our five research prisons over the five-year period from November 1987 to November 1992. We already had reasonably complete regime-monitoring data for November 1987 and we therefore asked for regime-monitoring summaries for November 1992 so that at least we could eliminate seasonal variations as an explanation for any differences.[5] To round out the analysis we have also scrutinized the information contained in Inspectorate reports and the annual reports of the prison governors concerned. Where appropriate we have also drawn some comparisons with data from the national prison survey.

We should enter some caveats about the analysis at the outset. To state the obvious, since our analysis stops in November 1992 it takes no account of the developments set out in the regimes package introduced by Joe Pilling. At the end of this chapter, however, we try to make some provisional comments about sentence planning and the revived concern with offending behaviour, and their prospects for success. More importantly, there are serious methodological problems with regime monitoring which we note here, but return to from

[5] In the original inquiry we routinely obtained regime-monitoring data for the first week of each month but we were often given much fuller information by staff who were glad that someone shared an interest. On subsequent investigation we had nearly complete information for the whole of Nov. 1987. In Featherstone and Ashwell, however, our data are averages for the available weeks in Nov. plus the first week in Dec. We are grateful to Veronica Wilsdon for arranging to supply data for Nov. 1992 and to Mark Williams for explaining changes to recording procedures.

time to time in what follows. Developing foolproof regime monitoring systems is an impossible task. There is no simple litmus test that can be applied. Monitoring involves collecting very elaborate and detailed information on a daily or weekly basis, even to capture very simple quantitative parameters of what is happening. The more meaningful the information sought the more complex the procedures become for collecting it and the more counter-productive is the process likely to be as the providers of information become irritated and even alienated by the demands made upon them. There are built-in sources of error which are well known inside the service. First, different prisons adopt different practices in recording at the so-called 'reporting points' which are usually, though not always, the sites at which the activities take place—workshops, education centres, and so on. The most important problems are likely to be that gross hours of activity are recorded, simply using the supposed start and finish times and the number of prisoners involved, although some reporters may use net hours and take account of late starts and early finishes, and perhaps even temporary absences or interruptions for one reason or another. To our certain knowledge the same activity in the same prison has been recorded in different ways at different times depending upon who is on duty. In current measures of other out-of-cell activities, that is time spent on association rather than purposeful activities, there is evidently even some confusion whether some prisons include time so spent at weekends, whereas others record only weekday association periods. Secondly, there is a problem of entry-recording errors, which most likely take the form of staff simply completing the forms in the same way each week, repeating earlier figures even though the situation may have changed.

Morgan (1992b) has noted that during the Woolf Inquiry the investigators found it impossible to reconcile 'objective' regime-monitoring data with the subjective reports of their regime by staff or prisoners. He further observed that the Inspectorate rarely, if ever, used regime-monitoring data in its reports. Morgan suggested that it would make more sense to use prisoners as the monitors of regime performance since they had an interest in the outcome and the time to complete the forms. It seems unlikely that any heed will be paid to such a suggestion. As we have noted elsewhere (McDermott and King 1989), in any hierarchical system where performance is being monitored there is likely to be a tendency towards 'apple polishing', whereby subordinates may strive to say what their superiors wish to hear. It is perhaps only natural that representatives of the system at all levels will wish to present their activities in the best possible light by concealing, or not drawing attention to, poor performance or at least trying to explain it away. In the process of negotiating annual targets between governors and area managers there may be an understandable tendency to bring targets and performance more realistically into line, by lowering targets as well as raising performance. Such developments may well be perfectly proper, although when trying to make an evaluation of performance against targets it is as well to be aware what has happened—a higher percentage achievement of a lowered target may *feel* better without actually *being* a better performance. The more there is riding on the outcome the more likely is such a system of self-evaluation to become what we called a 'paper massage parlour for stressful facts'. The commitment to key performance indicators by the Prison Service Agency, which in part are to be judged through regime-monitoring data, is likely to have heightened this kind of strain in the system, although there is a very real danger that the more such statistics are actually used in this way the less they will be questioned.

Some periodic adjustment of baseline targets will, of course, be necessary to take account of planned, or at least known, changes in the population, otherwise there would be a danger of making quite unrealistic evaluations of performance. In fact, three of our research prisons, Birmingham, Gartree, and Nottingham, were operating with somewhat lower populations during the November 1992 regime-monitoring period than had been the case at the time their plans for the year had originally been set. Gartree, in particular, had a much lower population because of the disruption caused by the installation of integral sanitation. These reductions in population, paradoxically, might have made it harder to achieve some targets which had been set for higher numbers. In several cases, however, the targets appear to have been reduced to take account of this. It needs to be remembered that the reverse may also be true; that in times of overcrowding it may actually be easier to achieve some targets unless the baselines are adjusted accordingly. We return to these matters when considering the appropriateness of particular performance indicators below. It would be wise, however, to regard regime-monitoring outcomes as showing the best possible construction that can be put on what is happening on the ground. They are certainly unlikely ever to underestimate performance. This is not in any way intended to discredit the process, nor to suggest that it has not been important, but simply to note that it needs to be used with due caution and for what it is—a tool developed to enable managers to monitor regimes and not a research instrument designed to evaluate them. From this point of view it has been a useful way of keeping performance in the forefront of the attention of those who deliver the service.

It is, of course, possible to use regime-monitoring data for descriptive research purposes as well as for management purposes, and we do so below. It will be helpful, however, to begin by setting out the changes which seem to have occurred in the occupational profiles of our prisons.

The Occupational Profile

In an earlier paper (King and McDermott 1989) we presented an occupational profile for the prisoners in our research prisons. In Table 5.1 below, we have reworked that profile so that we could make direct comparisons with the occupational profiles agreed with area managers in 1991–2 which formed the baselines for planned activities against which performance is measured under regime-monitoring.[6]

In considering Table 5.1 it has to be borne in mind that data for 1987 represent the actual occupational breakdown on a given census day during the research, whereas the figures for 1992 represent planned baseline targets of attendance in the various occupations. We have given two sets of figures for Gartree: the main figures are those which applied at the time of the regime-monitoring data for November 1992 and which had been in force for two months, taking account of a lower population as wing refurbishment was undertaken. They are presumably intended to be temporary. The figures in parenthesis were those in operation from the beginning of the financial year in which Gartree changed its function from dispersal category B training and, presumably, the ones to which it will return when refurbishment is complete.

It is clear from Table 5.1 that there have been several major changes in the occupational profiles. First, the flight away from prison industries has continued apace in Gartree (although

---

[6] In order to facilitate the comparison we have (i) amalgamated the short-term unit with the main prison at Featherstone; and (ii) reclassified those who worked outside the prison on Featherstone farm as well as those in other community employments under industry.

Table 5.1. Occupational profile for prisoners 1987–92: Percentage distribution

	Year	No	Industry	Education	Training	Works	Domestics	Unemployed	Total
Birmingham	1987	606	26	7	0	9	22	36	100
	1992	405	27	15	4	6	47	0	100
Gartree	1987	306	48	16	0	8	21	7	100
	1992	225 (311)	36 (23)	19 (19)	11 (29)	8 (5)	26 (23)	0 (1)	100
Nottingham	1987	295	37	12	17	6	16	12	100
	1992	194	20	21	29	7	24	0	100
Featherstone	1987	499	58	6	12	4	14	6	100
	1992	564	56	9	14	4	16	2	100
Ashwell	1987	363	33	14	18	16	16	3	100
	1992	399	26	16	25	11	21	2	100

Notes:
Rows do not always add up to 100 because of rounding.
Industry includes prisoners working on farms and other jobs outside the prison.
Training includes prisoners on induction programmes and pre-release courses.
Works also includes gardens party.
Domestics includes orderlies, redbands, storemen, as well as kitchen workers and cleaners.

temporarily abated there), Nottingham, and, to a lesser extent, in Ashwell. In Featherstone, which was designed as an industrial prison, the proportion (of a substantially larger total population) engaged in industries has remained much the same. In Birmingham the proportion employed in industry (of a substantially smaller convicted population) has marginally increased, although the planned shop and laundry opening hours there have gone down. The reduced emphasis on prison industry has been offset by increases in the proportions of prisoners attending full-time education classes or undergoing vocational or construction industry training courses. In Birmingham the proportion on education has doubled (though most of these were on open learning programmes); in Nottingham it has risen by about 75 per cent, in Featherstone by about 50 per cent, and in Gartree and Ashwell by about 15 to 20 per cent. The proportions on training courses rose dramatically in Gartree from none to nearly a third—although this was the area of activity hardest hit in the temporary adjustments. In Nottingham and Ashwell training increased from around a sixth of the population to a quarter or more. There were modest increases in Featherstone and a welcome start to these activities in Birmingham, though as we shall see it was a rather fragile plant in that environment. However, a rather worrying trend is the apparent transfer of quite large numbers of prisoners from their unemployed status to the substantial army of domestic workers around the prisons. It looks as though, in its attempt to meet targets for prisoners to be engaged in purposeful activities, the service has abandoned its earlier strictures about not padding domestic parties. As it happens, we share the view that it must be better for prisoners to be out of cells doing something, rather than sitting in cells doing nothing. However, it would be a pity if the phenomenal growth in domestic activities in Birmingham were regarded as unequivocal evidence of an increase in purposeful activity there, even though, as we will show, there are some grounds for applauding the improved performance in Birmingham on more meaningful measures.

Purposeful Activities and the Unlocked Day

The occupational profiles discussed above relate to the numbers of individual prisoners to be catered for in the main work-like activities of the prison. These numbers formed the basis for setting targets for planned activities and the subsequent measurement of actual performance against those targets. Most individual prisoners, however, are

likely to be engaged in more than one activity in the course of the
week, and so regime-monitoring is not directly about individuals but
about the total number of inmate hours spent in each of a series of
measured activities. The key performance indicator which we cited
at the beginning of this chapter, *the number of hours a week, on
average, prisoners spend in purposeful activity* (Key Performance
Indicator 5), is calculated on the basis of fifteen such activities, the
first twelve of which correspond to the occupational profiles: daytime education, vocational training courses, construction industry
courses, works, PSIF workshops, farms, gardens, kitchens, other
domestic, induction, other (specified), and all others. The remaining
three activities—physical education, chaplaincy, and evening education—are rather different: physical education, in part at least, is
likely to occur at the same time as other occupations, prisoners being
taken from their main activity to the gymnasium. The same may
happen to some extent for chaplaincy activities, although both PE
and chaplaincy may take place outside work hours, as does evening
education by definition. For each activity the number of inmates
involved is multiplied by the number of weekly hours they spend so
engaged. The figures are then added together to produce the total
activity hours for the establishment and divided by the average daily
population to produce an average figure of activity hours for each
inmate which, when applied to the system as a whole, offers in a single statistic the key performance indicator of *average weekly hours
spent in purposeful activity.*

There are many different ways in which one might seek to represent the performance of the prison system as a whole and that of particular institutions within it. Each may be useful for some purposes
though none taken by itself can capture the complexity of the situation on the ground. One way envisaged in the regime-monitoring
process is through the proportion of planned hours in any activity
which were actually achieved. But while this may be useful managerially for pointing to particular problems in a particular prison at a
particular time it is not much use as a comparative measure of performance over time because, as we have seen, the targets themselves
can and do change, and whether or not they are achieved can depend
upon changes in the prisoner population. Another is by displaying
the proportion of total activity time which is spent on different activities through a series of pie charts: these could be averaged for the
service as a whole or for types of prisons or for individual prisons.

This can effectively demonstrate changes in the balance between different regime elements, and is extensively used in annual reports of the Prison Service and official documents including the White Paper, *Custody, Care and Justice*. However, unless the proportions also take account of unoccupied time—which they rarely do—the method does not show real changes in the actual level of each activity over time which is what is really required as a measure of performance. There is at least one further issue which none of the measures so far devised has successfully tackled, and that concerns the distribution of activities amongst different categories of prisoners: thus it may well be the case that certain groups of offenders, for example those on Rule 43 for their own protection, are much more likely to be unemployed than others, and that this situation may persist throughout much of their sentences.

The choice of what the Prison Service calls *hours prisoners spend in purposeful activity* as a key performance indicator has a number of important merits. Since it adds together the actual amount of time that any prisoner spends in all identifiable activities it provides the most comprehensive and understandable basis for comparisons between establishments over time. Moreover, since that total figure is then divided by the average daily population in each establishment it permits comparisons between establishments which are not contaminated by population differences. Lastly, it does not involve needlessly complicated considerations about changing targets and focuses straightforwardly upon accomplishments. As a result, apart from the thorny problem about what information is actually entered at the recording points, it should yield data which are capable of showing real changes on the ground. However, in our view, it is quite misleading to call this an indicator of *purposeful* activities because it includes too much and it regards all activities as equally purposeful. It would be far better to regard it for what it is, a measure of *total* activity, and to use it in conjunction with a more discriminating measure of purposeful activities which would be more in keeping with the rhetoric and intentions of the Control Review Committee, Dunbar's paper A Sense of Direction, and the *Corporate Plan* of the Prison Service Agency.

As it stands many of the activities measured by regime-monitoring and included in the performance indicator, such as gardens, kitchens, other domestic, works, and the numerous parties and odd jobs that are classified under 'other' activities, are jobs that *have* to be covered in any prison. In that limited sense, at least, they *may* be regarded as purposeful. They may, of course, in individual cases *actually* be purposeful in a real sense. But they distort any measure of performance, precisely because they are not the kind of activities that the prison management has to work at in order to provide. Nor does it have to think them through in relation to the sentence plans of prisoners. Moreover, they are just the sort of activities in which it has always been possible to 'make' work for 'extra' prisoners to do and thus to pad out performance. We have already argued above that it is better to have prisoners engaged in almost any activity than to leave them locked in cells, but it borders on self-deception or cynicism to regard activities which are open to such discretionary manipulation as *purposeful*.

In the sections which follow we use the regime-monitoring data to describe in detail the changes which have occurred in our prisons on six activities which might more appropriately be regarded as actually or potentially purposeful—workshops, vocational and construction industry training programmes, daytime and evening education classes, and physical education. We include physical education because of its constructive and purposeful role in offsetting the debilitating effects of custody: thus, as we showed in Chapter 4, difficulties of access to physical education and longer hours locked up seemed to be directly related to the concerns of prisoners about their physical and emotional well-being. These activities lend themselves much better to the task of measuring institutional performance, not merely because of their more obviously purposive nature but because none of them is necessary for the smooth running of the establishment. They are all prisoner-oriented activities for which the institution has to plan. At the end of our discussion we use the actual hours spent in these activities to calculate our own performance indicator of *genuinely purposeful activities*. We found the results of our analysis surprising. Clearly, other and better indicators might be developed, but these data are readily available as a subset from within the present regime-monitoring process.

We must first, however, say a few words about the current outcome on the official key performance indicators. For what it is worth (i.e. as a measure of average hours spent in total activity) the official performance figures on KPI 5 for our prisons in November 1992 were as follows: Birmingham 17.99 hours; Gartree 30.77 hours; Nottingham 25.08 hours; Featherstone 26.48 hours; and Ashwell

34.96 hours. We have obviously not thought it worthwhile to calculate comparable figures retrospectively from our 1987 data but we
offer the following interpretive comments. Birmingham's total 'purposeful' activities have been considerably inflated by the hugely
increased proportion of domestic workers, some of whom 'worked'
long hours, but who in 1987 would have been classified as unemployed. No fewer than 7.2 hours of their total of 17.99 hours were
produced by the single category 'other domestic'. The figure for
Gartree is higher than we would have expected, and occurred in spite
of a decline in workshop activity. The increase arises in part because
of the transfer of unemployed prisoners, and others, to the new VTC
courses but also because of increases in education and other activities which were available for longer periods than in 1987. On the
other hand Featherstone's performance is considerably worse than
we would have predicted. In part this is because of its continued
reliance on workshops which were open for two hours less a week
than had been the case five years earlier. In fact most of the activities we could compare in Featherstone were operating for shorter
periods than when we had known them. Nottingham and Ashwell
seem broadly in line with what we would have predicted.

The paucity of activities which we found in our research prisons
in 1987 compared with those in the early 1970s was in part attributable to what we called the astonishing shrinkage of the unlocked
day. Key performance indicator 6, *the proportion of prisoners held in
establishments where prisoners are unlocked on weekdays for a total
of at least twelve hours*, recognizes the importance of reversing this
trend. We tried to get regime-monitoring data in relation to hours
out of cells for our prisons in November 1992 but were told that they
were not available. There seems to be some ambiguity in the way this
is officially calculated for regime-monitoring purposes. To calculate
this for ourselves, we therefore turned to the daily routines which are
usually published as an appendix to the Chief Inspector's reports and
the information available in the annual reports of governors. Such
published routines formed the starting point for our earlier calcula-
tions of hours out-of-cell for the best modal response which we
described earlier. It has to be said that such a measurement is somewhat rough and ready, and in the present usage we did not have the
opportunity to ask questions or to test out the stated routine against
actual practice. Nevertheless, it looks as though there had been some
major improvements in this most important indicator. Time spent

out-of-cell in Birmingham for convicted prisoners had increased from 5.5 hours to eight hours a day during the week, and although the Chief Inspector was critical that remand prisoners spent only three hours a day at best out of cells during January 1992 that was a 50 per cent improvement on the two hours achieved in 1987. It was, of course, a long way short of the twelve hours soon to be held out as an eventual prospect in the model regime for local prisons and then to be adopted as the operating standard. Time out-of-cell had also gone up in Gartree from nine hours to 10.5 hours; and in Nottingham from 9.5 hours to eleven hours. Important as these are, *none* had yet returned to the levels achieved for convicted prisoners by their counterpart prisons twenty years earlier: convicted prisoners in Winchester had been unlocked for nine hours, Albany had been unlocked for 14.25 hours, and Coldingley for fourteen hours. With regard to the lower-security prisons, Ashwell had held its ground at fourteen hours, although that was still less than the fifteen hours achieved twenty years ago at Ford in the *Prison Regimes Project*. However, to our great surprise Featherstone had actually fallen back to below its 1987 level, unlocking prisoners for only 10.5 hours compared with eleven previously. This gave considerable concern to the Chief Inspector on his short inspection in 1992, not least because, at the time of his full inspection in 1989, prisoners had been out of cells for 11.5 hours (Home Office 1992b, para. 6.10).

We now turn to an examination of the performance of our prisons in 1992 compared with what they had achieved in 1987 over those areas we have described as offering genuinely purposeful activity. For convenience we preface each section with the standard now held out for that activity in the *Operating Standards* published in 1994, so that our 1987 and 1992 results can be seen in their current context. Inevitably, setting out the findings from several different sources is a laborious business. In trying to capture the complexity of the regime-monitoring data, for those interested in the finer print, we perhaps provide too much detail for other readers, who may prefer to pass on to the section where we try to make sense of the data and propose a more realistic measure of purposeful activity.

Workshops

Operating standard U5 makes no particular reference to workshops as such, but requires establishments to provide sufficient workplaces for prisoners who are required to work, so that work should be the normal daytime activity for the majority of convicted prisoners. In a nuanced change from the July 1993 draft, work should also be provided for other prisoners (i.e. the unconvicted) who should be 'encouraged to work' (Prison Service 1994a), rather than 'given the opportunity to do so' (Prison Service 1993f). Standard U6 requires the working day to reflect that operating outside prison, and U1 that this should be part of a structured programme of activities covering a minimum of forty-two hours a week.

When we examined planning baselines and regime-monitoring data for 1992 it was clear that the continuing flight from prison industries was most marked in the high-security prisons. Indeed the 1994 re-emphasis on work may now require bringing back workshops into commission.

In Gartree the number of workshops had further declined from four to three, and the planned total number of prisoners employed in them had halved from 144 to seventy-two, although the workshops were open for six hours a day instead of five. But whereas in November 1987 the workshops operated for 82.3 per cent of planned hours, in November 1992 only 63.7 per cent of the greatly reduced planned hours was actually met. In Nottingham the three workshops operating in November 1987 had been reduced to just one light textile shop. It planned to occupy forty-two prisoners instead of the 105 originally catered for, although the shop was open for one hour longer at twenty-four hours a week. The performance in November 1987 was aberrant at a mere 18.5 per cent of target hours, but the performance in 1992 was only 58.3 per cent, much the worst of the training prisons. In Featherstone there had been much less by way of planned change. The two large workshops in textiles and engineering continued, with a planned 287 prisoners which was some thirty-four more than in November 1987, although this was offset by a shorter working week, down from thirty-two hours to thirty hours. However, for reasons we were unable to discover, the regime-monitoring sheets for November 1992 were working towards lower targets than planned. Moreover, performance was somewhat down also, from 89.5 per cent to 82.8 per cent, even in respect of these lower targets. Ashwell had continued to struggle with problems of supply and organization over its industries, but by November 1992 both its tailoring and footwear shops were operating again much as they had done five years earlier. They planned to employ 105 prisoners, five fewer than previously, and the working week had been reduced by one hour to thirty-one hours a week. However, Ashwell met 87.5 per cent of its planned hours compared with 82.4 per cent five years earlier, and this was the best performance of any of the training prisons.

Birmingham still retained two heavy textile workshops and the prison laundry, although between them they were now intended to employ 110 prisoners rather than 122. The shops were open for 17.5 hours compared with twenty hours earlier and the laundry for twenty-two hours compared with twenty-five hours a week. These changes meant a substantial reduction in the planned hours, and whereas in November 1987 Birmingham reached only 57.5 per cent of its target hours, in November 1992 it achieved 103.3 per cent of its target. Without data from the reporting points it is not clear how that can have happened, but the most likely explanation, if record-ing error is ruled out, would be that on some occasions additional prisoners were sent to the shops for some reason.

Workshops accounted for just 14 per cent of all time spent in activities at Birmingham in November 1992. In Gartree they accounted for 18 per cent, in Nottingham a mere 10 per cent, in Featherstone 41 per cent (including the farm), and in Ashwell 22 per cent. Whether or not it would have been practicable to continue with industries at the centre of prison regimes there seems to be little doubt that their role has been hugely diminished. Even at Featherstone there had been substantial reductions in November 1992, though these may well have been temporary. It has to be hoped that what remained after such massive reductions over the years would be the more interesting, higher quality, more profitable, and better paid work. If that were so, work could play its full part as an incentive in the lives of prisoners, enabling them to gain some job satisfaction and to exercise some responsibility for themselves, their families, and their victims.

Regime-monitoring was not designed to provide qualitative infor-mation about any of these matters, although the Regimes Research and Development Section of the Prison Service (which has just been disbanded under the 1994 reorganization at headquarters) had been considering possible ways in which it might do so in future (Prison Service undated). However, the annual reports by the governors and their industrial managers, as well as those of HM Chief Inspector of Prisons on both his full and short inspections, contain some useful value judgements. Broadly speaking, the workshops seemed to be offering much the same kind of work as they had earlier—light engineering, textiles, and footwear—although some of the worst heavy textile and assembly shops seemed to have gone. The shops seemed also to experience much the same problems of continuity in supply as they had during our research, and the Chief Inspector drew particular attention to problems of time-keeping in Nottingham (Home Office 1993b, para. 2.5), but there appeared to be a greater concern with paper evaluations of quality of output than was previously the case. Both Ashwell shops, for example, were in the process of being assessed under British Standard BS 5750, and the textile shop in Featherstone was said to be the most successful in the system in terms of sales, whilst its engineering shop was said to produce consistently high-quality work. Moreover, several shops in the training prisons had become accredited for the award of National Vocational Qualifications (NVQ) although the education officer in Featherstone noted that the NVQ levels in respect of some shops and training programmes were pitched so low that they involved de-skilling existing programmes. Wage levels had been improved but they remained considerably below those which Woolf had proposed. In Featherstone it was already possible to earn up to £6 a week in the tailor's shop but the Chief Inspector noted that prisoners still did not like working there, and instructors reported that it was difficult to recruit and keep workers. None of the other prisons seemed to match that level. Worst off were prisoners in Birmingham who received between £2.45 and £3.85 a week, depending upon their occupation.

The national prison survey included a number of questions about work, although few findings have so far been reported, and those that have are not always directly comparable with our own data. Some 59 per cent of the NPS sample said that they currently did some work in prison, excluding education and training activities. Of those who worked, 23 per cent were cleaners, 20 per cent were in workshops, and 14 per cent in kitchens (Walmsley *et al.* 1992, 29). These findings seem broadly consistent with what we would have expected for our research prisons based on the occupational profiles given above, bearing in mind that whilst our research sites were chosen as being representative of the *types* of prisons for adult males our study over-represents prisoners in training prisons at the expense of those in local prisons.[7] According to the NPS, however, those who did

[7] In 1992, e.g., our training prisons contained about 78% of the prisoners in our research prisons compared to abut 57% in training prisons nationally. Unfortunately

actually work in the week preceding the interview claimed to be employed for an average of thirty hours (Walmsley *et al.* 1992, 30), with sentenced prisoners in local prisons working the longest, at thirty-six hours. Both these figures would seem to be implausibly higher than could have been predicted from planned targets if our prisons are at all representative of the system as a whole.[8] About a fifth of those in work thought it would be useful upon release. More than nine out of ten prisoners interviewed wanted to be paid more so that they could save for their release, and nearly eight in ten wanted to earn more so that they could send money home. About nine in ten prisoners wanted to have proper work to do whilst in prison. When asked to rank these, some 16 per cent thought more pay to enable them to send money home the most important, 15 per cent thought being able to save the most important, and 8 per cent that they should have proper work to do. These laudable attitudes were somewhat more common amongst older prisoners than younger prisoners.

Education

Operating standards U7 and U8 require establishments to provide an education programme, based on a needs assessment, which provides classes in the mornings and afternoons five days a week for fifty weeks a year and on at least five evenings a week for forty-two weeks a year. Under standard U9 opportunities for part-time education have to be provided, and compulsory education of at least fifteen hours a week for juveniles is required under U10. The July 1993 draft standards envisaged compulsory education of two hours a week for 17 to 20-year-olds, but that does not appear in the published code.

The developments in our training prisons with regard to education since our research was completed present a very mixed picture. As we noted earlier, Pilling's letters of June 1992 made no mention of contracting out, but in July 1992 ministers accepted the recommendation of consultants that education should be bought from further

the NPS classification of occupations does not appear to correspond with those used in the planning process of baseline profiles, and it is difficult to comment further on the employment of the remaining 43% of employed prisoners in the national prison survey.

[8] In fact 4 of our prisons out-performed the average for their group in this regard according to the regime-monitoring data supplied to us and this reinforces our reservations about the NPS figure for hours in work.

education providers selected on the basis of competitive tendering. Although it was expected that services would continue to be provided in many cases by the existing further education colleges, albeit on a more formalized contractual basis with prison governors, by November 1992 many education staff were understandably anxious about their future.

In Gartree the number of planned places in education had gone down from eighty to forty-two, although part of this reduction reflected the reduced population during refurbishment. The time devoted to education, however, had gone up from 23.75 hours a week to twenty-seven hours and there was a dramatic improvement in meeting the planned hours, from a mere 52 per cent in 1987 to virtually 100 per cent in 1992. Evening education was more vulnerable than daytime education, but here, too, there had been improvements. In 1992 the planned inmate hours had doubled to 360, and 50 per cent of those were actually achieved compared to 38 per cent in 1987. The Chief Inspector found the education programme at Gartree to be working satisfactorily, although he noted that the limited opening hours of the library which he had criticized in an earlier report had not been addressed (Home Office 1993e, para. 3.25). The end result, though, was that education in Gartree had a greatly enhanced role for its smaller population. In Nottingham planned places in full-time education had increased from thirty-five to forty prisoners, and the available time devoted to it had increased from twenty-two to twenty-four hours a week. This produced an increase in planned hours from 770 to 960, but performance had declined disastrously from 89 per cent achievement in 1987 to 69 per cent in 1992. Just as he had complained about poor time-keeping in the workshops in Nottingham so the Chief Inspector commented on the problems of getting prisoners to education on time (Home Office 1993b, para. 3.17). A similar pattern was to be found in regard to evening education in Nottingham. In a very modest programme planned hours had increased from 100 to 120, but performance had fallen from 115 per cent in 1987 to 67 per cent in 1992. According to the Chief Inspector the evening programme had been affected by budgetary cuts (*ibid.*, para. 3.13). Overall the total number of hours actually spent in education in Nottingham had marginally fallen over the period, but, as at Gartree, its role within a prison with a smaller population than before had somewhat increased.

In Featherstone, although the planned places in education had increased from forty-seven to fifty-two prisoners, the classroom hours had fallen dramatically from thirty-six to thirty hours a week, and so the total planned inmate hours fell from 1,692 in 1987 to 1,560 in 1992. Moreover, the performance level had declined from almost 95 per cent to just under 80 per cent. When the Chief Inspector visited Featherstone in July 1992 evening education had stopped for the summer (Home Office 1992b, para. 4.5). As far as we could tell from a comparison of the regime-monitoring sheets, by November 1992 evening education was operating slightly above the 1987 levels, but this was not enough to offset the decline in daytime education.

In Ashwell, like Gartree, there were real increments in time devoted to education in spite of a rather poor performance rate. The planned number of prisoner places increased substantially from forty-six to sixty-five, and although the number of available classroom hours decreased from thirty-three to thirty-one hours a week, there was a big net increase in the total planned hours from 1,495 to 2,170. Whereas in 1987 Ashwell had achieved 94.8 per cent of its total hours in education by 1992 this had fallen to 71.7 per cent. Nevertheless, this still produced more hours in the classroom for more prisoners than it had five years earlier. Even more marked was the fact that by 1992 Ashwell had at last got a programme of evening education off the ground, and it was hugely oversubscribed. The Chief Inspector noted there were divisions, even factionalism, amongst education staff in Ashwell which had to some extent been evident during our research, but he also noted that it did not appear to affect the satisfaction of prisoners (Home Office 1993c, para. 4.17). He was also complimentary about the library facility in Ashwell (*ibid.*, para. 4.24).

It is a great deal more difficult to make sense of the changes in education in Birmingham, because the situation there in 1987 varied so widely from week to week. For what it is worth, the regime-monitoring sheets for November 1987 provide total planned and actual hours for education but give no meaningful information about the numbers of prisoners involved. In 1992 Birmingham planned to provide nearly 18.5 hours of education a week for sixty-two prisoners, giving a total of 1,145 hours. This was actually slightly lower than the 1,637 planned hours in 1987, but an improvement in performance from 62.4 per cent to 79.2 per cent produced an increase from 1,022 to 1,236.5 hours actually achieved. Whereas there was no evening education in Birmingham in 1987, by 1992 it was achieving

333 hours a week out of its planned 388 hours. In 1989 the Chief Inspector had been critical of the inadequacy of the educational programme (Home Office 1990b, para. 3.80), and of the library facilities (*ibid.*, para. 3.87), but expressed some optimism in regard to the further development of open learning (*ibid.*, paras. 3.81–2). His short inspection in 1992 drew attention to the shortfall of education classes for remand prisoners and the more general need for constructive out-of-cell activities for the convicted population (Home Office 1992c, paras. 3.12 and 3.23).

Daytime and evening education together accounted for just 7.2 per cent of all prisoner activities in Birmingham; 17.5 per cent in Gartree; 13.7 per cent in Nottingham; 9.4 per cent in Featherstone; and 16.7 per cent in Ashwell.

According to the national prison survey 95 per cent of prisoners were aware of the existence of prison education or training classes, and of those who knew about them 47 per cent attended classes of one kind or another. Of those who did not attend, 46 per cent said they would like to do so. The average time spent in education by those who had attended education in the week before the interview was fourteen hours a week (Walmsley *et al.*, 1992, 27). Some 68 per cent of those attending thought that the classes would prove useful to them after release. The NPS does not distinguish between education and training courses, of the kind we discuss separately below. Nor does it distinguish daytime education from evening education and so it is not strictly possible to make comparisons with either our original data or the regime-monitoring materials. However, the education participation rates which we reported separately for each of our study prisons (King and McDermott 1989) would produce an average participation rate of 43 per cent in 1987 compared with 60 per cent in the earlier *Prison Regimes Project* study prisons. A participation rate that embraced those prisoners who had attended either education classes or training programmes at some point during their stay in our research prisons in 1987 would have been 62.6 per cent compared with 65 per cent in the early 1970s. Bearing in mind methodological differences, and the fact that our research prisons in both studies over-represented prisoners held in training prisons at the expense of those in local prisons, the NPS figure of 47 per cent suggests that the decline in participation rates since the early 1970s has been halted and to some extent reversed, but is still some way from being fully restored.

Contracted-out education services were supposed to have been in place by April 1993 on the basis of tenders returned in November 1992. In practice it was impossible to meet the timetable, largely because of uncertainties about whether the safeguards, contained in the Transfer of Undertakings (Protection of Employment) Regulations (known as TUPE), which applied to employees during the takeover of one firm by another, would apply to prison teachers. By July 1993 the Prison Reform Trust reported that in sixteen prisons education had been handed over to new providers. In a further twenty-one, the old providers were seeing out their last few months before handing over to new providers on 1 September. Some fifty-eight prisons did not yet know who would be providing the education service and in only thirty-one was there continuity of provision. The PRT, not surprisingly, described the outcome as one of confusion and waste (Prison Reform Trust 1993). In Ashwell and Gartree the education contracts were eventually awarded to a private firm called Mill Wharf Education Services with effect from September 1993.

Training

Operating standards U17 and 18 simply refer to the provision of tuition for recognized certificates of achievement and encouragement to pursue National Vocational Qualifications. Although the published standards do not refer to construction industry training as did the draft standards, this is probably because such courses can simply be subsumed under the more general rubric.

The reduction in the population in Gartree during the installation of integral sanitation in 1992 seemed to have its biggest impact upon the training programme. Earlier that year it had planned to have ninety prisoners, some 29 per cent of the population, on its furniture-making and micro-engineering vocational training courses for just over twenty-seven hours a week. By November these plans were down to twenty-four prisoners or 11 per cent of the reduced population. It is to be hoped this was a temporary phenomenon. Even so this was a major improvement over the days when it had still been a dispersal prison. In 1987 there had been no training programmes at all, however hard the governor had tried to get them established. There were evidently difficulties in maintaining even this level of operation, because Gartree achieved only 53.7 per cent of planned hours, but either this situation did not apply two months earlier at the time of the Chief Inspector's short inspection, or else it passed unnoticed. The Chief Inspector broadly approved of the intention to make Gartree about 50 per cent dependent upon education and training and 50 per cent on work and production (Home Office 1993e, paras. 3.07 and 3.12). In Nottingham there continued to be a mixture of VT and CIT courses in 1992 which catered for about the same number of prisoners as in 1987. The hours of the VTC had been reduced, however, from 26.5 hours to fewer than twenty-one hours a week; and the operating hours of the CIT programmes had also dropped from just over twenty-six hours to just over twenty-two hours a week. This resulted in a reduction in the total planned hours of training from 1,347 in 1987 to 1,123 in 1992. However, attendance at the VT courses had greatly improved from 56 to 98 per cent, and while there had been a decrease in the attendance at the CIT courses, from 86 to 66 per cent, the total of 900 achieved hours in training was not far below the 968 achieved in November 1987. In a prison which had many fewer prisoners than in 1987 training assumed a much higher profile.

In Featherstone there had been a net reduction in the total achieved hours attributable to vocational training courses from 1,404 in November 1987 to 1,154 five years later. This was largely brought about, according to the governor's annual report, because the original sixty places in 1987 had to be 'restructured down' from the intended sixty-four to forty-eight in order to save on materials. The opening hours of the course had already been reduced from twenty-nine hours to twenty-seven hours, although in 1992 89 per cent of planned hours were actually achieved compared with 82 per cent earlier. As we noted earlier in our discussion of workshop provision it was regrettably the case that the introduction of NVQ standards in some cases actually reduced the skill levels of the courses that had been provided.

Unfortunately it is not possible to reconcile the planned places and planned operating hours for either the VT or the CIT courses which are given in the agreed baselines for Ashwell, with the total planned hours which appear to have been accepted for regime-monitoring purposes. Nor do the Inspectorate reports throw light on what actually happened, although the Chief Inspector noted that there was need for greater co-ordination between those responsible for activities in Ashwell, and for them to act upon the outcome of regime monitoring returns (Home Office 1993c, paras. 4.38–9). It seems likely that for unspecified reasons targets had been revised down-wards, so that some twelve prisoners were engaged in vocational training and about forty-five prisoners on CIT courses for about twenty-seven or twenty-eight hours a week. If those assumptions are correct, this involved a reduction of about ten prisoners on CIT courses since 1987. The performance level in terms of the proportion of hours actually achieved was about the same in 1992 for both types of courses as it had been in 1987, but the end result was nevertheless an effective reduction from 1,475 hours of training to about 1,190 hours.

Birmingham started with no training in 1987 and had acquired very little by 1992. There were modest plans for ten prisoners to spend 22.5 hours a week on a painting and decorating course. In November 1992, which may just have been a bad month of the kind it all too frequently had in 1987, Birmingham achieved only 8.1 per cent of planned hours, a mere eighteen hours of training activity. Neither the Inspectorate reports nor the governor's annual report makes specific reference to this CIT course, but the poor perfor-mance may have been attributable to industrial action by the POA which was blamed for other problems in the Birmingham regime.

Training accounted for just 0.1 per cent of all prisoner activity hours in Birmingham compared with 4.26 per cent in Gartree, 16.6 per cent in Nottingham, 8.0 per cent in Featherstone, and 9.0 per cent in Ashwell.

Physical Education

One of the most serious differences between the published operating standards and the draft standards of July 1993 concerned physical education provision. The July 1993 draft specified a programme of at least eight different activities, which operated for fifty-two weeks a year with morning, afternoon, and evening sessions during the week as well as sessions at the weekend. Prisoners should have access for at least six hours a week (to include the stipulated minima of two hours for young offenders and five hours for juveniles). The com-mentary also made it clear that cancellation of PE classes was to be regarded as unacceptable. The published standard U13 simply states that a range of PE facilities be provided to which young prisoners should have access for at least two hours a week and juveniles for at least five hours a week. This downplaying of physical education is, no doubt, in keeping with Michael Howard's expressed views according to the leaked memorandum of July 1993, in which it was said:

Although he can see that there may be a case for some outdoor activities, particularly to develop a sense of responsibility or to help others (such as disabled children), he does not think sporting activities undertaken purely for fun should be a prominent part of the custodial experience.

However, it does seem unfortunate, in the light of the apparent relationship between such activities and the feelings of physical and emotional well-being expressed by prisoners which we discussed earlier.

In fact, of all the activities it was possible to monitor, physical education had changed least in our prisons over the period from 1987 to 1992. In part, no doubt, this was because the gymnasium constituted a very fixed plant which in most cases was used as extensively as possible given the other exigencies of the regime. In Birmingham, Gartree, Featherstone, and Ashwell the total number of hours spent in physical education had moved only marginally from the picture we had found in 1987. In Nottingham there appeared to have been a substantial reduction, which we are at a loss to explain. The report of the most recent inspection carried out in November 1992, the same month to which our regime-monitoring data relate, mentions that few PE classes had achieved their maximum attendance level in recent weeks (Home Office 1993b, para. 3.19) and it may be that self-selecting factors in the changing population account for much of the reduction. The annual reports of governors shed no further light on the matter. In the absence of a more convincing explanation, our assumption is that the regime-monitoring sheets for Nottingham in November 1987 exaggerated both target hours and achieved hours in the manner we discussed earlier and that the reduction is more apparent than real.

The findings published so far from the national prison survey appear to make no mention of physical education or the use of the gymnasium. Given the salience this had for many prisoners in our study we wonder whether the absence of reported data from the NPS may reflect the absence of a direct question in the survey. To judge from the annual reports of prison governors and the Inspectorate, however, physical education continues to be a valued activity for prisoners and one which is also welcomed by staff.

Making Sense of the Data: A More Realistic Measure of Purposeful Activity

How might we make sense of the complex changes which we have set out in the preceding sections in what might have seemed tiresome detail? As we noted above the official key performance indicator (KPI 5) is best regarded as a measure of *total* activity rather than of *purposeful* activity. That is useful in its own right but it needs to be used in conjunction with a more precise measure, tailored to evaluate the performance of prisons in providing genuinely purposeful activities. The indicator we propose uses the six activities we have just described—workshops, VTCs, CIT courses, daytime and evening education, and physical education.[9] We have taken these from regime-monitoring sheets and, just as is done for the official KPI, calculated the total amount of inmate hours spent on each activity and divided it by the average daily population for the period in question. In Table 5.2 we present the comparison for our prisons on these variables from 1987 to 1992.

In interpreting the findings in Table 5.2 there are, inevitably, some important caveats to bear in mind. First, our investigation has necessarily been confined to a comparison of the regime-monitoring sheets for a single month in 1992 with those for a single month in 1987. We did not have the opportunity to check the most recent results against experience on the ground as we did during the course of our original research. It is entirely possible, therefore, that the findings reflect special circumstances which applied in the month in question and that a comparison conducted over a longer period of time might reveal a different pattern. In an attempt to eliminate that possibility we sought in every case to reconcile the regime-monitoring data with the baseline targets for each prison, and we searched the Inspectorate reports, as well as the annual reports of the governors and their respective heads of departments, for information that would cross-validate the findings or otherwise put them in perspective. Where we have been able to identify special circumstances we

[9] Two other activities could be added from the present regime-monitoring data. Farms are monitored separately from workshops and could form an activity in their own right, although since only Featherstone had a farm we have included it here under workshops. Similarly the indicator could include chaplaincy activities, but these were unreliably measured in 1987 and so there seemed little point in including them here. In any case we would suggest that chaplaincy might better be taken together with activities designed to address offending behaviour in a separate measure.

Table 5.2. Average weekly hours in purposeful activities 1987–92

	Year	Workshops	Training	Day Education	Evening Education	Physical Education	Total
Birmingham	1987	2.03	0.00	0.86	0.00	1.01	3.90
	1992	2.52	0.23	0.87	0.43	1.39	5.44
Gartree	1987	9.42	0.00	3.16	0.22	2.57	15.37
	1992	5.53	1.31	4.65	0.73	3.43	15.65
Nottingham	1987	1.52	3.28	2.31	0.39	3.76	11.26
	1992	2.86	4.64	3.42	0.42	2.62	13.95
Featherstone	1987	15.13	2.61	2.96	0.20	2.77	23.67
	1992	10.81	2.12	2.28	0.23	2.67	18.11
Ashwell	1987	8.06	4.10	3.93	0.00	2.45	18.54
	1992	7.56	3.16	4.13	1.73	2.60	19.18

Notes:
Training includes both vocational training and construction industry training courses.
Featherstone workshops for this table includes the farm in both years.

have already referred to them in the text, for example, the disruption caused by the installation of integral sanitation in Gartree. However, there could well have been some which we were not able to discern. Secondly, it will be necessary to give due weight to the facts that Gartree changed from a dispersal to a category B training prison in March 1992 and that Ashwell was already in the process of becoming a category C prison in November 1987. Thirdly, the population in Birmingham, Gartree, and Nottingham was significantly lower in November 1992 than it had been five years earlier.

With the above cautions in mind Table 5.2 nevertheless reveals some apparently striking developments with regard to purposeful activities. Thus Birmingham, helped by the decline in its average daily population, seems to have made improvements in each of these areas of activity with the exception of daytime education. Indeed, the total of 5.44 hours represents a 40 per cent increase over the period which is much the biggest improvement for any of our prisons. Of course, when one starts from such a low base as Birmingham did, comparatively large increments may be relatively easy to achieve. The fact is that even this improvement means that, on average, prisoners in Winson Green get little more than an hour each weekday of these activities. In 1989 the Chief Inspector of Prisons declared that in Birmingham 'it cannot sensibly be said that HM Prison Service is fulfilling its duty to look after prisoners with humanity' and that the prison 'had become content with its low level of functioning (Home Office 1990b, Preface and para. 4.5): by 1992 he saw momentum for change which nevertheless needed to be accelerated (Home Office 1992c, para. 4.7). The enormity of the task that still confronts a prison like Birmingham is undoubtedly daunting.

Nottingham made the next largest gains, with improvements in workshop activities, training programmes, and daytime education. The change in evening education seems too close to call, and as we have already noted there was a significant reduction in the take-up of physical education. The improvement from 11.26 hours in really purposeful activity to 13.95 hours represents an increase of 24 per cent over the position in 1987. Although the position in Gartree appears to have changed little overall—a modest increase of 2 per cent from 15.37 to 15.65 hours—what is remarkable is that this was achieved in spite of a reduction in workshop hours of more than 40 per cent. This huge deficit was more than made up for by improvements in all other spheres of purposeful activity. Ashwell appears more or less to have marked time, with falls in both workshop and training activities, offset by improvements in daytime, evening, and physical education programmes, to produce a modest improvement of 4 per cent from 18.54 to 19.18 hours. However, the most startling result, albeit presaged by some of the earlier analysis, is the apparent decline in the performance of Featherstone. Featherstone seems to have suffered a major reduction in average hours spent in the workshops as well as more modest falls in training, daytime education, and physical education programmes. The only area where it appears even to have held its own is in regard to evening education activities. The overall outcome as far as Featherstone is concerned is a reduction in purposeful activity hours from 23.67 to 18.11, a fall of 24 per cent which actually takes it to below the operating level of Ashwell. Featherstone, in effect, has lost half an hour a day in time unlocked and an hour a day of purposeful activity compared with the situation in 1987.

Some years ago we made a tentative report on the impact which Fresh Start appeared to have had upon our research prisons (McDermott and King 1989). There, too, we entered a number of caveats because we could not pretend to have conducted a full evaluation of Fresh Start. We described it as a preliminary look at the impact of Fresh Start but we were concerned to publish it precisely because we feared there might otherwise be no evaluation. So far as we are aware, no serious alternative evaluation has yet appeared. What is of interest here is that in our preliminary look at Fresh Start we used the same variables we have used here—workshops, training courses, and daytime, evening, and physical education programmes—as well as the number of hours out-of-cell. When we compared our prisons pre- and post-Fresh Start on these variables we found that there had been almost twice as many examples of regime deterioration (twelve) as we did of regime improvements (seven) with a further nine cases where there had been no change and two where the pattern was somewhat up and down.[10]

If we make the same comparisons now between 1992 and 1987 from Table 5.2, with the addition of time out-of-cell reported earlier, we find an almost exact reversal of the pattern: twice as many cases of improvement (sixteen) as of deterioration (eight) with a fur-

[10] In the original we reported 16 deteriorations and 8 improvements but we included the numbers employed as a further variable. We have excluded that from our comparison here precisely because it is capable of being padded.

ther six in which there had been no real change. What is more, the pattern whereby the improvements and deteriorations were distributed has also been reversed. In 1989 we reported that most of the improvements had occurred in Featherstone which already had the best regime and most of the deteriorations had occurred in Gartree, Nottingham, and Birmingham where the regime was very deprived. It seemed to be a case of 'for unto every one that hath shall be given, and he shall have abundance: but from him that hath not shall be taken away even that which he hath' (Matthew 25, 29). Now it is the other way around: most of the improvements seem to have been concentrated in Birmingham, Gartree, and Nottingham, whilst the main deterioration has been in Featherstone.

Tackling Offending Behaviour and Promoting Responsibility

We pointed out at the beginning of this chapter that there are major differences in the ways the goals of the new Prison Service Agency have been formulated when compared to the earlier statement of tasks and functions. In the new formulation positive regimes are supposed to address offending behaviour and to promote the responsibility of prisoners, rather than merely occupy their time.

The key instruments for the delivery of a regime which addresses offending behaviour and a sense of responsibility are sentence-planning, on the basis of which prisoners may be allocated to regime activities, and the notion of prisoners' compacts, which are to be agreed during the induction phase. As envisaged by Woolf (Home Office 1991a, paras. 12.120–9) the contract or compact would set out what facilities the prisoner could legitimately expect from the prison in return for honouring his obligation of good behaviour. These compacts might specify incentives and disincentives, which might be provided or withheld contingent upon prisoner compliance. Compacts were thus conceptually distinct from the accredited standards which the prison would, over time, be obliged to provide. That conceptual distinction has been eroded by Michael Howard, first in the leaked memorandum of 30 July 1993 which called for a shift to make prison 'a more austere experience . . . recognizing that this represents quite a departure from some of the commitments set out post-Woolf'; and secondly, in the last-minute deliberations over the code of standards, effectively making the status of the whole code of standards much more ambiguous. As Derek Lewis states in his letter which introduces the *Operating Standards* (Prison Service 1994a): 'The standards are not entitlements for prisoners. Increasingly the delivery of standards in individual cases will be conditional upon prisoners complying with the obligations placed upon them, as for example outlined in local prisoner compacts'.

Just what difference these changes of emphasis might make is inevitably hypothetical. Some indication of the way things will go, however, was given by Michael Howard at the Prison Service conference in October 1994. Although he belatedly acknowledged that accounts of high security-risk prisoners sending out for lobster thermidor whilst others continued to run their businesses from prison pay-telephones were isolated examples blown up by the media at the time of the Whitemoor escape attempt, he nevertheless insisted they would not be tolerated. Core privileges such as additional visits, access to private cash, the wearing of own clothes, and extra time out of cells would have to be earned through good behaviour (*Guardian*, 1 November 1994). It is possible that a clearer connection between prison behaviour and commitment to work or training on the one hand, and prison conditions and the availability of facilities on the other, might send just the right signals to prisoners which the Control Review Committee had called for ten years earlier. It is certainly easy to see how such a linkage is attractive to politicians and the public alike. Unfortunately, it is just as likely that the fallible process of implementation will open the way to the arbitrary use of powers by staff, leading to non-accountable decision-making and discrimination. Unless the new ombudsman is able to deal promptly with the ensuing complaints of unfairness, then the sense of justice, which Woolf considered to be necessary if future disorders were to be avoided, will be undermined. Changes in the access to telephones and to the operation of the home-leave scheme may be particularly damaging to the prospects for maintaining community links.

It is too early to assess what impact the introduction of standards or prisoner compacts might actually have on the ground, although it has been reported that Feltham and Deerbolt already have a system of awarding points to prisoners for good behaviour. At Feltham, prisoners may earn or forfeit privileges depending upon the state of their points account: at Deerbolt, prisoners can buy their way into a wing with an enhanced regime (Prison Service 1994c). Such schemes are hardly new, for the history of imprisonment is littered with similar examples. In the past many have foundered, in part, because the supply (of privileges) has failed to meet the effective demand (from well qualified candidates), thereby creating justified perceptions of unfairness. Be that as it may, it is worth addressing a few remarks at least to the problems associated with sentence-planning and the prospects for promoting personal responsibility and the confrontation of offending behaviour.

Sentence-planning which addresses offending behaviour depends upon having some kinds of programmes available which could plausibly be regarded as actually addressing such behaviour. The activities which we have counted as purposeful, far fewer than those the service regards as purposeful, could only be regarded as addressing offending behaviour in a very indirect way but this was clearly not what the drafters of the *Corporate Plan* had in mind. The regimes package distributed by Joe Pilling referred to the core sex offender programme, which had by then been introduced to thirteen prisons, and the development of six assessment centres where an extended sex offender programme was being piloted for the most serious risk offenders, as well as to anger-management programmes, all of which, on the face of it at least, seem to be much more finely focused upon the specifics of some criminal behaviour. Such programmes are not entirely new. In Gartree during our study the psychologists had begun to develop anger-control programmes which they also offered on a peripatetic basis in other prisons. There was also a certain amount of work with sex offenders. We have not dwelt on such activities here, not because we think they are unimportant but because they captured so little of the time of so few offenders that they would not have registered at all on any measure of time that was ultimately divided by the average daily population.

The *Corporate Plan 1993–96* called for the development of programmes to tackle sex offending, anger management, cognitive skills, and social skills so that by March 1996 they could be offered to at least 1,000 high-risk offenders a year (Prison Service 1993d, paras. 8.11–19). It also looked forward to the monitoring and evaluation of such programmes, although we are not aware of how it is proposed to carry this out. We believe that it is important that some routine performance indicator be developed for these activities which captures the number of prisoners who are thought to need the programmes, the numbers actually involved in them, for how long and with what result. Conceivably such a measure might also include chaplaincy activities as well as alcohol and drug dependency programmes where they exist. Indeed, we regard it as a major omission that the new focus on offending behaviour in the Corporate and Business Plans pay so little attention to drug dependency and substance abuse. As we noted in the previous chapter, a 'law and order' approach to the use of drugs inside prisons is likely to be counterproductive and is a poor substitute for voluntary drug-free zones, counselling, and drug rehabilitation programmes. The Prison Reform Trust has been concerned that, because of resource pressures not all those who needed the sex offender programme would receive it (Sampson 1992). Brown (1994) has also argued that the programme as administered leaves out of account important work with families and is in any case needlessly bureaucratic in its constant form-filling before progressing to the next stage. Meanwhile, we can report that during 1993–4 some 438 prisoners had passed through the core sex offender programme which was said to be running in eighteen establishments: staff from forty-five establishments had so far been trained to run anger-management courses: and a Canadian cognitive skills package on reasoning and rehabilitation had been piloted in ten establishments.[11] We obviously welcome the commitment to evaluation as well as monitoring and express the hope that it will be carried out independently of the service-providers.

Of course, by no means all offenders require such programmes and it is much less clear what sentence-planning is supposed to offer them. The *Corporate plan 1993–94* committed the service to extending the process of sentence-planning to include all prisoners serving sentences of twelve months or more by 1996. To those of us who have kept an eye on the doings, as well as the aspirations, of the Prison Service over the years a more important consideration than the sentence-planning process is the extent to which sentence plans may ever actually be read once they have been written, let alone acted upon. The idea of sentence-planning was not newly born with the Control Review Committee. It had been mooted many times over many years and many prisons actually claimed to have something like it in place—at least for the duration of a prisoner's stay in that prison. But, as one of us recorded many years ago (King and Elliott 1978), it was a system with form but devoid of content and both staff and prisoners regarded it with some cynicism. Thus, in Albany the

---

[11] Data supplied in a personal communication from Philippa Drew, Director of Custody.

sentence-planning process in the end came down to requiring that staff annotate the files of each prisoner with a 'minimum of three entries a month', whereas for prisoners the end of this process was that they were allocated to the soft toys class.

Since its advocacy by the Control Review Committee sentence-planning has come to assume hugely ambitious proportions. Linked to the notion of throughcare it aspires to sensible planning across the entire system from a prisoner's reception through to the expiry of his licence after release. Moreover, it is intended that the process is operated in such a way that the prisoner comes to accept some responsibility for his actions in prison. Although the possibilities for monitoring sentence plans have been revolutionized by the extraordinary growth in information technology in recent years, it is important to recognize that the old barriers to implementing sentence plans have not gone away. Thus it is by no means clear how many forms of offending behaviour should or could be addressed within the context of prison; even if it is clear, the appropriate means for addressing that behaviour may not be available within the service when they are needed; even if they are available, other needs for security or control may take precedence; and so on and so forth. In fact, for most prisoners it is unlikely that much of the process will have anything to do with offending behaviour, although it could have an important bearing on his sense of responsibility; and the prospects of being closer to home and engaging in interesting work or training programmes could well be important factors in rehabilitation or at least mitigating the effects of custody.

In view of the hopes expressed that prisoners will take a more responsible attitude it is unfortunate that the introduction of sentence-planning in England and Wales is a markedly more bureaucratic and managerial process than seems to be the case in Scotland where a much more participative approach has been taken (see King 1994b). In Scotland prisoners are invited to complete a personal development file which is intended to form a starting point for the sentence-planning process. This bottom-up approach contrasts markedly with the situation in which sentence plans are 'provided for' or 'prepared for' prisoners by staff south of the border. Although the sentence plans are said to be 'open' documents 'designed to be disclosed to the prisoner' there is a deal of difference between openness and participation, and the extent and manner of consultation with prisoners probably varies widely. The completion of the standardized documentation depends upon the co-operation of prisoners in providing information that may, or sometimes may not, have a bearing on the sentence-planning process and it is good to learn that prisoners have not entirely lost their sense of humour. Thus, when asked if he had any religious targets, one prisoner is said to have replied: 'Yes, by the end of this sentence I want to be a fucking saint' (quoted in Pilkington 1994).

Of all the tasks the service has set itself, developing and implementing meaningful sentence plans which will transcend the facilities available in any one prison is by far the most difficult. It is perhaps in this light that a recent intervention by the Prison Inspectorate should be seen. In a report entitled *Doing Time or Using Time* (Home Office 1993d) the Inspectorate sought to push the Prison Service closer towards the Woolf ideal of community prisons by arguing for a prison system that would be driven by regimes. Clusters of prisons, organized on a quite different basis from the managerial purposes served by the present division of the system into areas, would seek to enrich the prisoner's experience of custody through a sentence-planning process that would capitalize on the coherence of regime activities provided within each cluster. On the way to this conclusion the Inspectorate conducted research in sixty-four prison establishments but managed to throw little light on existing regime activities because its analysis was confined, for the most part, to target hours rather than achieved hours. Moreover, whilst it demonstrated the range of targets which varied quite widely both within and between institutions of different types, it failed to give any indication of central tendency within that range. As we and others have noted, regime-monitoring data does not always accurately reflect what actually happens on the ground, and the relationship between performance and targets often needs careful detective work to unravel. But the differences we found were trivial compared to what is cited in the Inspectorate report. Only one small section within the report (Table 4.10) addressed the question of actual performance against targets—and that included achieved performances which were said to exceed targets by in one case 112,746.5 per cent! Many other performance rates were several hundred per cent ahead of targets but no explanatory notes were provided to account for these quite extraordinary phenomena.

The inference has to be that the Inspectorate was more interested in the elaboration of an argument than in the careful presentation of research data. But the problem with the argument is that, however important the Woolf agenda on community prisons and rewarding regimes, and clearly we attach the highest priority to that, it is unrealistic to see any prison system as being regime-led because at bottom that is not what prison systems are primarily about. Not surprisingly the Home Secretary gave short shrift to this report. As things stand the service will have quite enough problems reaching its present targets. We turn to matters of community prisons and throughcare in our next chapter.

6
Helping Prisoners to Return to the Community

The fifth goal of the Prison Service is to help prisoners prepare for their return to the community (Prison Service 1993c, 5). A single key performance indicator is put forward as the basis for measuring success: the proportion of prisoners held in establishments where prisoners have the opportunity to exceed the minimum visiting entitlement (Key Performance Indicator 7). At the time the key performance indicator was set the minimum visiting requirements were as follows: convicted prisoners were entitled to one visit upon reception and then two visits every twenty-eight days, lasting at least thirty minutes; unconvicted prisoners were entitle either to a visit of at least fifteen minutes every day from Mondays to Saturdays, or to three visits a week which together amounted to at least 1.5 hours. The newly published *Operating Standards* (Prison Service 1994a), to which the service aspires, include provision for convicted prisoners such that one of the visits each month should be at a weekend and that visits should last not less than one hour (standard Q3); and for unconvicted prisoners the minimum visiting time is raised to thirty minutes up to a total of three hours a week, with at least one weekend visit.

In the *Business Plan 1993–94* the Service sets out its target that by 31 March 1994 at least 90 per cent of prisoners should have the opportunity to exceed the minimum requirements. On the basis of its claim that 84 per cent of the prison population was already held in such conditions, achieving this target required that a further four or more establishments exceed the statutory requirements in the course of the year (Prison Service 1993e, 9). Prisons might exceed the minimum entitlements by offering either longer, or more frequent, visits or both.

It turned out to be an easy enough target to achieve. In April 1994 it was reported that 99.4 per cent of prisoners were held in establishments which exceeded the minimum visiting entitlement (Prison Service 1994c). Indeed only one prison—Hindley—failed to meet the target, and that had promised faithfully to do so in 1994–5.[1] The next month Derek Lewis was able to claim that Hindley had met the target as well. If the 1993–4 target was disappointingly easy to achieve, it is even more disappointing that the target for 1994–5 only requires the service to maintain the status quo (*ibid* 4).

It is surprising that the fifth goal of the service is expressed in such a low-key manner and with such a limited key performance indicator. In this respect it contrasts sharply with the previous goal which, at least in theory if not in terms of its practical measurement, marked an advance over earlier formulations in that it stressed both purposeful activity and the need to address offending behaviour. Perhaps the best that can be said in relation to goal five is that the phrase 'where possible', which conditioned the commitment to assisting prisoners prepare for their return to the community in the former statement of the task of the Prison Service, has been removed (see Appendix I).

The importance of maintaining family contacts and preparing prisoners for release has increasingly been recognized in recent years. In their advocacy of the 'normalization of the prison system' King and Morgan (1980, 122–3) argued for the abolition of the distinction between local prisons and training prisons and the recommissioning of some twenty-one training prisons as multi-functional local prisons—an early formulation of what are now, post-Woolf, more commonly called community prisons. King and Morgan recognized that some prisoners would, for security or other reasons, always need to be kept in more specialist institutions which would be a regional or perhaps a national resource. However, they argued that normalization would involve as the first of its guidelines 'that prisoners should generally be held in the establishment closest to their community ties so as to maximize their opportunity to maintain family and other links' (*ibid.* 38–9) by minimizing 'the travelling time and expense of their most regular and important visitors' (King and Morgan 1979, para. 184).

King and Morgan gave detailed consideration to the reorganization of the existing prison estate because they wished at first to prevent and then, failing that, to reverse the massive building

---

[1] Personal communication from Philippa Drew.

programme which the May Committee advocated. They feared two things: that the new prisons would fill up and that the unjustifiable diversion of resources from the local prisons, where half of all prisoners then served the whole of their sentence, into new and largely ineffective training prisons would continue. The May Committee, on Home Office advice, roundly rejected King and Morgan's proposals for such a radical restructuring of the system because the redistribution of resources involved would damage 'some well-resourced and imaginatively run regimes in the training prisons' (Home Office 1979a, para. 6.54) and because of its commitment to 'positive custody'.

Things have moved on markedly since then. Circular Instruction 55 of 1984 made the maintenance of community links and preparations for release explicit tasks of the service and functions for all establishments. The Control Review Committee advocated the extension of home leave, the relaxation of censorship, and the use of telephones initially for category C and D establishments in order to make the progression of prisoners down through the security categories a more attractive proposition (Home Office 1984a, paras. 102–4). In 1986 Her Majesty's Chief Inspector of Prisons published an influential report on *The Preparation of Prisoners for Release* (Home Office 1986). Woolf, of course, not only presented powerful advocacy for community prisons (*ibid.*, para. 11.49) but also made many specific proposals for increasing the frequency of visits (*ibid.*, 14.229, 14.231 and 14.235), extending home leave (*ibid.*, para. 14.243–5), family visits (*ibid.*, paras. 14.249 and 14.250), the extension of the use of telephones (*ibid.*, paras. 14.259–62), and the abolition of remaining restrictions on correspondence (*ibid.*, para. 14.271).

In a variety of ways the service has responded to most, if not all, of these specific recommendations and we shall refer to these as appropriate in the subsequent discussion. With regard to community prisons, the service had already undertaken an estates review which had led to changing the functions of several prisons by the time of the disturbances at Strangeways; and since the publication of the Woolf Report consideration has been given to the clustering of prisons in ways that would facilitate sentence-planning and keep prisoners near to their homes. One such cluster already exists in Kent: another is planned for Humberside and the East Midlands in the near future. Furthermore, in a little-known development not apparently foreshadowed in Woolf, the Prison Service has developed Latchmere House and Kirklevington Grange as resettlement prisons for long-term prisoners at the end of their sentences. As we saw in the previous chapter the Inspectorate recently tried unsuccessfully to persuade the service into regime-led planning which would involve regrouping prisons from the present purely administrative areas into more meaningful clusters. However, the Penal Affairs Consortium has recently drawn attention to the way in which the rising prison population is hampering the further development of community prisons (Penal Affairs Consortium 1994).

King and Morgan based their arguments for the localization of custody and the preservation of family links primarily on the need to prevent, or at least minimize, further damage arising from a prison system which, nevertheless to some extent, still claimed to believe in the purposes of treatment, training, and rehabilitation of offenders. One of the present authors, however, on a number of public occasions and usually in answer to questions, has argued that ironically concentrating upon the family ties of offenders in custody might be the one, as yet untried, great hope of a treatment and training philosophy. In the light of the evidence to be presented in this chapter, we will develop just that argument, but without the sense of irony. In our view, the single most effective investment of resources in the prison system will be to maximize, and then to focus upon, all those points where prisoners and their families meet in custody, and through joint counselling confront not just offending behaviour but its consequences for families and victims.

Anticipating the argument to be developed, we should say now that we think that the performance indicator adopted by the Prison Service in respect of its expressed goals in this area is woefully inadequate as a serious measure of achievement in relation to the goals. However, it should also be acknowledged that the *Corporate Plan 1993–96* (Prison Service 1993d) seems to cover all of the ground that was included under the heading of community links and preparation for release in the former *Statement of Functions of Prison Department Establishments* (Appendix I). It also contains some valuable commitments in the course of its three-year programme, and we will return to these at the end of the chapter.

In this chapter we first set out hitherto unpublished data on the maintenance of family contacts and the preparation for release which prisoners received in our research prisons in 1986–7. In the second part of the chapter we look at these problems from a different stand-point by presenting materials from our later research on *Coping with Custody* in which we explored the different strategies for survival developed by families whilst one of their members was in custody. We then seek to update these materials, as we have done in earlier chapters, by reference to the subsequent inspections carried out by HM Chief Inspector of Prisons and the annual reports of prison governors. We also try to put our data in a wider context by comparing them with the findings from the national prison survey. Finally, in the light of our findings, we try to assess how far the present programmes of the Prison Service are likely to achieve their stated goals.

Maintaining Contact

There can be no question but that the single most important consideration in the minds of most prisoners in custody concerns their future domestic life, or what will remain of it, outside prison. While some prisoners have nothing outside prison to return to, for most their home and family provided some sense of personal history and future destiny: a 'real' identity beyond that of a numbered, docketed prisoner. Loss of a link to the outside world meant, above all, the danger of succumbing to the role of an 'inmate' for want of an alternative.

Of course, there are some prisoners who think of little else but returning to a more successful life of crime than they enjoyed in the past. Certainly this engages much of their conversation. It could hardly do otherwise in a culture which unites people whom the criminal justice system has brought together solely because of their criminal activity. Maintaining a front dictates that it is difficult for prisoners publicly to address private concerns, just as it is difficult for prison officers publicly to express positive and constructive concerns for prisoners except through a mouthing of authorized nostrums to visitors or in training sessions. This is not normally how they talk to each other, at least not without seeking refuge in irony or joking relationships. Kelsey Kauffman (1988, 248), in her excellent study of American prison officers, uses the term *pluralistic ignorance* to describe how, in a situation where colleagues depend on solidarity for their survival, even majority views can actually go unspoken, and thus unheard. The same is true of prisoners as Wheeler (1958) and others observed long ago. Most prisoners, locked in cells, may spend time fantasizing about their next crimes and 'getting even' with the police, the judge, their lawyers, or society: but most of them, to judge both from our questionnaire responses and our interviews, also dwell upon their health, as we noted in Chapter 4, and upon their families. All told, 81.5 per cent of our prisoners said that trying to preserve whatever family links they possessed—and they were sometimes tenuous—was very important to them, both for getting through this sentence and for their future. Another 11.7 per cent regarded maintaining those relationships as quite important. It is significant, in the meaningful sense, that there were no significant differences, in the statistical sense, between our prisons in this regard. Although, to judge from the differences in degrees of contact that were actually maintained, the strength of prisoners' family relationships varied widely, the vast majority of prisoners knew that it was important to hold on to what they had got.

It could, of course, be said that this often involved crocodile tears. After all, many prisoners had thought little enough about their families, not just at the time of their current offence but earlier offences as well, and had hardly been model fathers, husbands, or lovers—far from it, as many eventually admitted in our interviews with them. Perhaps it is not surprising that many who had themselves had an impoverished family upbringing spoke about their families in terms that sometimes sounded to us somewhat hollow, whilst others lacked any kind of vocabulary even to discuss the matter. However, we could not be other than moved by a number of prisoners whose eyes clouded with tears as we discussed with them the consequences of their conviction, and others who wished to show and share with us precious photographs or letters. Understandably some politicians, and even more understandably some victims, may take satisfaction from a punishment that 'really' hurts. But that is rather to miss the point that building and strengthening such ties rather than further weakening them might potentially have a much greater prophylactic effect.

It also has to be acknowledged that prisoners often take instrumental attitudes to their partners outside prison. Getting through the sentence may 'require' family support in the form of financial assistance to get decent training shoes, sweat shirts, and transistor radios, or in more extreme cases to pay off drug and gambling debts, or indeed to receive such pay-offs. It is nevertheless not hard to see, given the present realities of imprisonment, how prisoners come to take an instrumental approach. Certainly several prisoners also put to us the opposite side of that situation in expressing how frustrated they felt as a result of their inability to support their families outside or to participate in important family decisions.

Finally, some prisoners, though fewer than we had expected, either had no contacts to preserve or else had cut themselves off entirely from family contacts to get through their sentences more easily. Sometimes this was because they could not bear the anxiety of waiting for a 'dear John' letter, or of reading between the lines to find the things a letter failed to say, or of wondering what was really behind a missed visit. For such prisoners it was easier to do their time by saying the relationship was over whilst nevertheless being grateful that it might still exist once they got out. Sometimes prisoners cut themselves off from relationships because they thought it fairer to their partner outside, especially if they had a longish sentence; and sometimes because the relationship was of little consequence anyway and its break-up was seen by professional criminals as the inevitable price of a life of crime. Nevertheless, only 6.8 per cent of our prisoners had no relationship of any kind outside that they wished to preserve, or else said that they were indifferent to whether it survived or not.

Another, perhaps more extreme, measure of the importance of maintaining family links was that more than two-fifths (44.7 per cent) of our prisoners were concerned that they would not be able to cope at all upon release. There were significant differences between the prisons on this variable (chi-square 29.68246 p < .001). Not surprisingly, the highest proportion (53 per cent) was found amongst remand prisoners in Birmingham struggling to come to terms with the initial fact of custody. Thereafter the results followed the security gradient with 29.7 per cent in Ashwell, 40.4 per cent in Featherstone, 49.0 per cent in Nottingham, and 51.7 per cent in Gartree expressing these fears. These results were mediated, partly, by the length of time served which took its toll of family relationships as it became harder to discuss things in less frequent letters and visits.

The main methods available to prisoners for maintaining contacts with families at the time of our research were letters and visits; certain categories of prisoner were able also to use the telephone and were eligible for the home leave scheme. For convenience, before reporting our data on each of these matters we set out the current operating standards to which the service aspires.

Letters

Standard Q27 of the *Operating Standards* now provides that prisoners, other than those held in dispersal prisons, should be allowed to receive as many letters as they wish, without restriction on length, and that incoming mail should be distributed to prisoners within one working day of receipt at the prison. Under standard Q28 convicted prisoners may send one letter, and unconvicted prisoners two letters, a week at public expense and additional letters at their own expense. In dispersal prisons (Q29), where letters are still censored, restrictions may still be imposed and incoming mail has to be distributed within two working days (Prison Service 1994a).

At the beginning of our research all convicted prisoners were entitled to send out one letter per week for which the paper, envelope, and stamp were provided by the Prison Service. For remand prisoners the allowance was two letters per week. In addition they might be allowed 'canteen' letters, for which they could pay out of private cash or earnings at the discretion of the local governor. In Ashwell the allowance of canteen letters was limited to four per week, whereas the remaining three training prisons all allowed unlimited canteen letters, subject to the regulation that air mail letters must be paid for out of earnings rather than private cash. In Birmingham remand prisoners could send as many canteen letters as they wished, but convicted prisoners were restricted to three a week. All incoming and outgoing mail was recorded in prisoners' files and subject to censorship except in Ashwell where, in common with all open prisons, routine censorship was abolished on 1 April 1986. In fact, prior to that date Ashwell, again in keeping with other open prisons, had looked at only about 10 per cent of mail on a more or less random basis.

Some 19.3 per cent of prisoners claimed a daily contact by letter, and another 52.1 per cent weekly, so that 71.4 per cent of prisoners were in touch through correspondence at least once a week. The proportions of prisoners having this frequency of contact fell systematically with each increase in security of the training prisons, from 84 per cent in Ashwell, through 74.5 per cent in Featherstone, to 58.7 per cent in Nottingham, and only 53.8 per cent in Gartree. In Birmingham, 72.5 per cent of remand prisoners, who were also entitled to daily visits, claimed at least weekly contact by letter compared with 80.6 per cent of the convicted prisoners. At the other extreme, some 11 per cent had rather infrequent contacts, with 6.5 per cent receiving letters less often than once a month and 4.5 per cent who had no contact by letter at all. There was a concentration of these prisoners in the remand wing at Birmingham (16.5 per cent) although it is likely that many of them had been in custody for only a short period or did not need to write letters because they could avail themselves of visits. There were rather higher proportions of prisoners with either no contacts or contacts less often than once a month in Gartree (12.7 per cent) and Nottingham (12.2 per cent) than in Featherstone (8.8 per cent) and Ashwell (8.1 per cent) or amongst the convicted prisoners in Birmingham (8.8 per cent). Although the frequency of sending and receiving letters dropped gradually with the length of time served, there was a marked decline in the proportion maintaining weekly contact amongst prisoners who had already served four or more years.

Visits

We set out the current rules on visits, together with the new operating standards, at the beginning of this chapter when we outlined the key performance indicator of the service and its targets for 1993–4 in relation to its goal of helping prisoners to return to the community.

Under Prison Rule 34, as it applied throughout our research, a convicted prisoner was entitled to receive a visit once a month and an unconvicted prisoner to receive as many visits as he wished, subject to such conditions as the Secretary of State might direct. Standing Order 5, the first to be made public in October 1983, referred to the importance of maintaining outside contact and stated that convicted prisoners could be allowed visits as frequently as circumstances in establishments permitted, with a minimum of one visit after reception and thereafter one every four weeks. The minimum visiting time was thirty minutes, but where circumstances permitted governors should allow longer visits, and the visit should take place under 'the most humane conditions possible'. In practice Gartree, Nottingham, and Featherstone all allowed visits lasting between one and two hours every two weeks, and the visit could take place either during the week or at weekends. In Ashwell visiting arrangements were more restrictive: visits were allowed every three weeks and could take place on weekdays as well as at weekends, but only on Wednesdays and at weekends could the visits last for up to two hours, whereas visits at other times were restricted to just half an hour. In Birmingham remand prisoners could receive a fifteen-minute visit every day except Sundays, and convicted prisoners a visit of up to two hours every two weeks.

Although the take-up of visits naturally depended upon the personal situation and circumstances of individuals it is once again noteworthy that 81.8 per cent of all our prisoners regarded visits as very important to them, and that there were no significant differences between the prisons in this regard.

Some 36.5 per cent of the remand prisoners in Birmingham claimed that they had availed themselves of visits on a daily basis, and a further 31.8 per cent had been visited at least once a week. All told, some 33.5 per cent of remand and convicted prisoners had received visits on a fortnightly basis, 28.3 per cent monthly, 12.5 per cent less often than that, and 10.4 per cent not at all. There were statistically significant differences between the visiting patterns in the five prisons, with 37.2 per cent of prisoners in Gartree and 27.3 per cent of those in Nottingham being visited less often than once a month or not at all, compared with 21.1 per cent in Featherstone, 19.0 per cent in Ashwell, and only 16.9 per cent of the convicted prisoners in Birmingham. Many of those prisoners who were visited less frequently in Gartree and Nottingham, and indeed elsewhere, had served substantial parts of long sentences: as with letters, there was a gradual decline in the frequency of visits with time served, and a more marked decline after prisoners had served four or more years. Another factor accounting for the differences in visiting patterns, of course, was the role that each prison served within the prison system as a whole. Gartree, as a dispersal prison, was effectively a national as well as a regional resource, and for 14.9 per cent of its prisoners their most important visitor required an overnight stay when they came to visit. This was twice the proportion in Nottingham and three times the proportion in the other prisons. Indeed, in Gartree fewer than half of the prisoners reported that their most important visitor could get to the prison in under two hours, whereas this proportion ranged from three-fifths in Nottingham, through two-thirds in Featherstone and Ashwell, to three-quarters in Birmingham. For most prisoners' families facing a long and often difficult journey, the expense of visiting was an important, and often humiliating, additional impediment. At the time of our research the limited, means-tested, assisted visits scheme was operated by the DSS under which close relatives could get financial assistance in respect of one statutory visit per month for prisoners serving sentences of longer than three months.

Visiting conditions varied widely. In Birmingham visitors initially reported to a modern visitors' centre outside and across the street from the entrance to the main prison. It was run jointly by the probation service and volunteers and provided visitors with an opportunity to talk to probation staff and representatives from the Citizens Advice Bureau and other bodies. It had an air of normality to it, and it was possible for visitors to leave their children there under supervision while they visited the prisoner. Though the centre started the day clean and tidy, it did not take long to be reduced to a state of relatively cheerful disarray. Visitors were called over to the main prison in groups of about twenty, and only when they presented their credentials at the gate was the fact communicated to the prisoners concerned that they had a visitor. Everyone at the centre recognized that this involved needless waiting but it had thus far eluded the wit of the authorities to devise a more efficient system. The new operating standards suggest that visitors should wait no longer than thirty minutes between booking in and starting their visit (Prison Service 1994a, standard Q8). Nevertheless, the advent of the visitors' centre represented a marked advance over the previous arrangements which left visitors hanging around outside in all weathers. Remand visits took place in a room lined with tables and chairs, with a canteen at one end. With fifty people squeezed in at a time it was far too small for its purpose. There were no facilities for children, and the room was dark and drab. Prisoners wore uniform so that they could be easily identified at visits even though they theoretically could, and some actually did, wear their own clothes inside. There could be few more depressing sights than remand visits in Birmingham as people tried despairingly to blot out the conversations of others while they sought to get their own communication across to the intended recipient. Sometimes, given the delays, the visit itself was over in less than ten minutes. Virtually all the visitors we spoke to, as well as the volunteers at the centre, told us that even without considering the journey times they would prefer fewer remand visits that lasted longer. This view was not always shared by prisoners, however, most of whom wanted to be visited daily. Visits for convicted prisoners were only marginally more civilized: the room was slightly larger but equally drab, the visit lasted longer, but the general hubbub made it resemble a cattle market.

None of the training prisons had a visitors' centre and so waiting around outside or inside the gate before being taken across to the visiting room was the norm. The visiting conditions in Featherstone were much the best of those to be found in the training prisons. Visits there took place in a large room with small tables, well spaced apart, each with four chairs. Part of the room was partitioned off for legal and official visits. On the occasions we were there it was often full of children who had a climbing frame and other toys available at one end of the room. Prisoners were not routinely searched before and after visits and it was possible for them to kiss and hug visitors. In Ashwell visits took place in a large wooden hut opposite the administration building close to the gate. On Wednesdays and at weekends when the longer visits took place there was a supervised play group with toys and a television set, as well as an outside play area. It was reasonably decorated and, like the other prisons, it had a small canteen run by the WRVS.

In Nottingham the visits took place in an upstairs room across the yard from the main gate, but prisoners were searched before visits and this caused irritating delays. About a dozen visits went on at a time, and there was a small supervised crèche available. The visits accommodation in Gartree was situated inside the perimeter fence but outside the main area of the prison. Next to the visiting room was a small room where children could play during visits but it was unsupervised and contained no toys, and it became excessively noisy. The visiting room was poorly decorated. The visits facility was too small for the number of prisoners using it at any one time, and because the tables were too close together it was difficult to communicate.

We asked prisoners and staff to evaluate the visiting facilities provided and the results are given in Figure 6.1.

As can be seen from Figure 6.1 the evaluations of both staff and prisoners broadly followed the judgements made or implied in our descriptive account above. The differences between the prisons in each case were statistically significant (prisoners: chi-square 509.39248 $p < .0001$; staff: chi-square 118.47105 $p < .0001$). As on so many other matters it is remarkable how prisoners made their evaluations from within a context of what, given their experience, they could reasonably expect in prison and not against some more universal criteria of what is desirable. Staff were once again generally inclined to make judgements that were a good deal more favourable

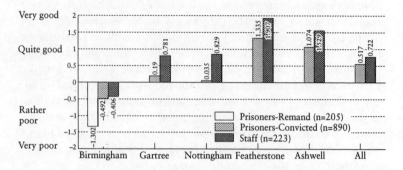

Fig. 6.1   Prisoner and staff ratings of visits facilities

than prisoners'. However, as on some other variables, it seemed that some staff in Birmingham felt compelled to step out of role and validate the judgements made by prisoners, whilst others regarded the visits facility negatively because of the ever-present potential for disorder.

We did not actually ask prisoners to rate their experience of visits as opposed to the facilities for visits, but it was clear from our interviews with prisoners that visits often created as much anxiety as they solved. Prisoners were frequently on tenterhooks before a visit, hoping that it would be 'good' but fearing that it might be a 'bad' one. As often as not it was neither one nor the other, and prisoners felt flat and listless afterwards; they then geared themselves for the next with much the same mixture of feelings as before.

Telephone Calls

Under standard Q19 telephones designated for use by prisoners should be provided in all establishments except Special Secure Units, in areas where they are readily accessible to prisoners. According to the annual report for 1992–3 all establishments had card telephones installed by the end of that year (Prison Service 1993g). Only calls by high-risk and exceptional-risk category A prisoners and escape-list prisoners should be monitored (Prison Service 1994a, standard Q22).

Card telephones were introduced for prisoners held in open prisons in April 1986 following recommendations from the Control Review Committee nearly two years earlier. At the time of our study, however, there was just one telephone installed in Ashwell to serve the needs of more than 350 prisoners; since it was only available for use during the evenings and at weekends there were always long lines of prisoners waiting to use it. Telephone calls were not monitored, but payment was, with special phone cards which could only be purchased in prison up to the value of £4 per month. However, it had long been possible for prisoners to apply to the governor to make a telephone call in place of a visit or in exceptional circumstances. Sometimes telephone calls could be made by arrangement with probation officers, and occasionally also through other members of staff, in cases where domestic crises required urgent consultation. In these cases the call was placed by a member of staff but, as so often with discretionary matters of this kind, whether or not a prisoner had his request granted depended upon due deference and demeanour. Amongst our prisoner contacts some were more successful in this regard than others. Just over half the prisoners in Ashwell (50.9 per cent) said that they used the telephone at least once a fortnight, although nearly a third (31.7 per cent) said they did not use it at all, primarily on grounds of expense. Elsewhere telephone use was much less frequent. Fewer than 5 per cent of prisoners in Birmingham had used the telephone, but 10.2 per cent in Featherstone, 26.1 per cent in Nottingham, and over 31.5 per cent in Gartree said that they had been allowed to use the telephone on at least one occasion. Even though card telephones were a relative novelty, and most prisoners had no chance of using them, 56.4 per cent of our prisoners thought them to be very important, and another 16.6 per cent thought them quite important as a way of keeping in touch. Somewhat surprisingly, the proportion thinking them important was no greater in Ashwell than elsewhere.

Home Leave and Temporary Release

The new operating standards X1 and X2 simply refer to the possibility of considering prisoners for temporary release or for home leave in accordance with nationally published criteria. Following the recommendations of the Woolf Inquiry which were largely accepted in the White Paper, *Custody, Care, and Justice*, more generous provisions were introduced, although new restrictions will come into force after the review ordered by Michael Howard.

Governors have long had discretionary powers to release prisoners temporarily under Rule 6 of the Prison Rules, but these powers have been used sparingly mainly to permit visits to dying relatives or to attend funerals and so on. Formal home leave schemes have been slow to develop in this country especially when compared with many European jurisdictions. Home leave can serve several functions: taken at intervals throughout a sentence it can keep relationships alive and help prisoners and their families get through difficult times and situations; taken towards the end of a sentence it can be a powerful tool in the preparation for release. The House of Commons Expenditure Committee (1978) noted that only a small proportion of prisoners got home leave and recommended that it should be given to more prisoners, more frequently and for longer periods. In 1986 the Home Office announced extensions in home leave, although it remained discretionary, to be granted on the recommendation of a home leave board in each prison. The board would take account of (usually) verbal reports from prison officers, probation officers, and other staff.

In practice during our research there were three possible forms which home leave might take: short home leaves of forty-eight hours' duration, excluding travel time, and normally to be taken at weekends; long home leaves, sometimes also called terminal home leaves, which last for five days, excluding travel time, and had to be taken during the last four months of sentence; and pre-parole home leaves, which could be granted usually, but not necessarily, on the recommendation of the Parole Board, between the announcement of a parole date and actual release. The intention behind terminal home leave and pre-parole home leave is clearly preparation for release, to enable prisoners to attend job interviews or seek employment and accommodation. Short home leaves potentially allow prisoners to maintain relationships with their families. Prisoners in category D prisons who were serving sentences of eighteen months or more could apply for short home leave, which could not be taken before their parole eligibility date, and thereafter at four-monthly intervals. Other prisoners were only permitted to apply for one short home leave to be taken within the last nine months of their sentence, and then only if they were serving three years or more. However, before our research was completed the scheme was relaxed to allow prisoners in category C establishments who were serving two years or more to apply for home leave at their parole eligibility date and thereafter at six-monthly intervals. All adult prisoners serving eighteen months or more were entitled to apply for long home leave.

Some 55.7 per cent of our prisoners thought that home leaves were

very important, and another 16.4 per cent thought them quite important, about the same proportions as regarded telephones as important. We did not ask prisoners how many of them had received home
leave—by definition most people eligible and who might have
received it would have been very close to their release date. All told,
however, there were 563 releases on home leave from our five prisons during the year 1986–7, of which 166 were short leaves, 118 were
long or terminal leaves, and 279 pre-parole leaves. Ashwell and
Featherstone accounted for 34 per cent each of the total, Nottingham
18 per cent, Gartree 9 per cent, and Birmingham 5 per cent. Only
thirty-one prisoners failed to return at the due time—a failure rate
of 5.5 per cent. The details are given in Table 6.1.

The data in Table 6.1 represented a modest increase of sixty-three
home leaves over the previous year, or 12.6 per cent. The pattern was
essentially the same in each prison and the overall failure rate was
virtually identical at 5.8 per cent.

When we asked prisoners and staff to evaluate the help given for
prisoners to maintain contact with their families there was a marked
split between the two groups. Prisoners were generally quite negative
in their ratings, with only a marginally positive outcome in Ashwell
in spite of the introduction of card telephones and the greater likelihood of home leave there. The differences between the prisons were
statistically significant (chi-quire 68.78544 p < .001). The staff, on the
other hand, were almost unanimous that these facilities were quite
good, even in Birmingham, and such differences as there were
between the prisons were not statistically significant. The details are
shown in Figure 6.2.

Preparing for Release

In addition to home leave the prison system has developed a number
of other schemes to assist prisoners in preparation for release: these
include pre-release courses in prisons, the pre-release employment
scheme (PRES), or the hostel scheme as it is more familiarly known,
and 'through care' operated by the probation service with the support of prison staff through social work in prison (SWIP) schemes.

As we have noted above, home leave potentially operates both as
a mechanism for maintaining contact with families outside and as a
preparation for release. If it were actually to serve those functions
prisoners arguably would need a great deal more counselling about

Table 6.1. Home leaves and failures to return: 1986–7

	Birmingham	Gartree	Nottingham	Featherstone	Ashwell	Total
Short Home Leave	0	23	27	57	59	166
Long Home Leave	9	15	25	53	16	118
Pre-parole Home Leave	17	14	50	81	117	279
Totals	26	52	102	191	192	563
Failures	2	0	10	10	9	31
% Failed	7.7	0	9.8	5.2	4.7	5.5

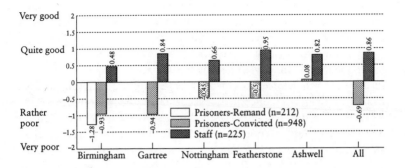

Fig. 6.2   Prisoner and staff ratings of encouragement to maintain contact

how best they might use it. All too often prisoners went out on home leave hopelessly ill-prepared and with quite unrealistic expectations. As one long-term prisoner put it to us when he returned from a disastrous home leave experience: 'In my head it was going to be a reunion of Robert Redford and Meryl Streep. It didn't turn out like that at all'. For fifteen years a supportive wife had stood by him. In letters and at visits they had sought and supplied superficial reassurance but had not really been able to address important things such as the way she had, as a result of that experience, necessarily become a much more independent woman. When their first attempt at lovemaking failed he could only retire to the local pub where at least he could make out with his mates. But neither had his wife received any support or advice. When a probation officer came to check whether she was prepared to have her husband back on a home leave he wanted only to know that a physical location existed and to have a yes or no answer.

Theoretically, 'through care' operated by the probation service and supported by the Prison Service is supposed to help bridge these transitions from community to custody and back again. It was talked about seriously by probation representatives on the Parole Board when one of us was a member as long ago as the late 1960s and it is regularly featured in a section of the annual reports of the Prison Service. It is, of course, possible that it was only the failures in through care that came to our attention; there may have been many unsung successes. Nevertheless, we have to say, both from the point of view of prisoners in this study and of families, as we shall be reporting shortly, our overriding impression was that they actually got very little or no constructive help in dealing with the processes of departure from, or return to, the community.

This is not to say that probation officers were held in poor regard by prisoners, for they were not. When we asked prisoners and staff to evaluate the service provided by probation we received positive responses from all concerned, except from the prison officers in Ashwell. The differences between the prisons were smaller than on most other variables reported in this study although they still reached statistical significance (prisoners: chi-square 25.89637 p < .05; staff: chi-square 54.87096 p < .0001). The results are presented in Figure 6.3.

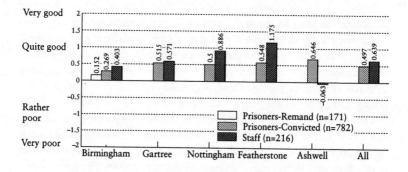

Fig. 6.3   Prisoner and staff ratings of probation

We suspect that both staff and prisoners put most other considerations on one side here and gave probation officers the benefit of any doubts. Prisoners were indeed grateful for the service they got from probation officers, particularly when it came to dealing with emergency situations which occurred whilst they were in custody. Thus probation officers would often make telephone calls on their behalf, or sometimes let prisoners make calls from their office, and could often obtain information that would reassure prisoners that a difficult situation was being managed. That this did not always happen was revealed in the incident which we described in Chapter 4 relating to the threats to a probation officer in Gartree. However, for the most part probation officers did try to respond, as best they could, to situations which they themselves saw as urgent. Nevertheless, prisoners were also suspicious of probation officers who they knew could exercise power in writing reports. Recognizing possible serious disjunctions between what was said to their face and what might be written behind their backs, prisoners sometimes withheld genuine respect. In many ways prison officers were even more suspicious of probation officers than prisoners. To many uniformed staff probation officers seemed often to take a soft line in meetings and even to argue a prisoner's case in ways that seemed to undermine their own position. It would seem from Figure 6.3 that uniformed staff mostly overcame these reservations and presented an authorized view of their colleagues, except in Ashwell where direct confrontations had occurred both within the probation team and between members of that team and other staff groups.

In any event we cannot see the above data as validating the role of probation staff in through care, not least because probation staff themselves told us too often that their role was largely reduced to one of purveyors of 'social sticking plaster'. They could deal with emergencies, but anything approaching sustained social work, particularly time-consuming counselling, was simply not possible, given the existing level of resources and the magnitude of the problems (cf. Shaw 1974; Holborn 1975).

It was partly to give prison officers the opportunity of a more meaningful role, and partly to relieve probation officers of routine matters so that they could concentrate on those for which they were professionally qualified, that SWIP schemes were introduced. We discussed the background to those developments when we considered the role of personal officers in Chapter 4. SWIP schemes existed in reality, in name or in prospect, in all of our prisons except Gartree. There the view seemed to be that most prisoners were sufficiently far from a release date, and would in all likelihood be released from another prison after transfer, that there was little point in developing through care or pre-release arrangements. In Birmingham SWIP officers on the remand side were seen as little more than useful messengers, although on the convicted side their knowledge of the prison was seen by the probation staff as helpful. However, both before and after Fresh Start they were constantly being taken away from SWIP duties to fill gaps elsewhere. This disappointingly, but accurately, reflected the sense of priorities in Birmingham. SWIP officers felt they had little support from senior management and were constrained to take most matters up the line of managerial authority rather than across divisions to their colleagues in probation. Indeed SWIP was still regarded very much as an experiment in Birmingham, where it was staffed by officers who had volunteered but who had little time and virtually no training for their tasks.

In Nottingham the SWIP scheme was regarded with some scepticism by most staff and seen as a fragile plant by those who sought to nurture it. Participating officers, who were known locally as WELOs (because the scheme was formally called the Welfare Liaison Scheme), were volunteers who were assigned to SWIP duties for two years, albeit for only sixteen hours a week. There was no training course for them as such, although as an induction they spent a week attached to a probation officer inside the prison and a week attached to the probation service outside. Whilst they were on duty the WELOs to whom we spoke seemed to enjoy their work, but they were frequently 'pulled' off and assigned to other duties. They felt that their future was very insecure and they pointed, as evidence for their fears, to the way in which group discussions had been curtailed and how the pre-release course, for which they were responsible, was largely on the back burner.

Featherstone had been one of the prisons operating the original experimental SWIP schemes reviewed by Jepson and Elliott (1984). It had, on paper at least, a more advanced scheme than any of our other prisons and included a training course for SWIP officers, which we attended. The training course was intended for eight officers, and much of the time was spent in trying to break down the macho image that prison officers often feel constrained to adopt. The formal sessions were sometimes rather heavy going, but during role-plays prison officers began to enter into the spirit of things and seemed to gain something from the experience. Although prison officers on the course found it hard to come to terms with the fact that they had previously been taught the importance of observation for maintaining security and control, and now were expected to observe to pick up emotional and welfare problems, at least they were confronting these issues. However, on the ground there was little evidence to suggest that SWIP had made much impact. Lack of continuity meant that prisoners had only a vague idea of the role of SWIP officers—just as they had not seen their group officer, if indeed they knew him, for several weeks. Nevertheless, the SWIP officers themselves believed in the value of the scheme, and Featherstone was the only one of our prisons that seriously committed resources to sustain it.

In Ashwell there had been real divisions between members of the probation team such that it scarcely made sense to speak of it as a team at all since they frequently pulled in different directions. SWIP in Ashwell was not so much practised as thought about, and it seemed to be the hope of the probation service there that Fresh Start would make it a reality. If it did, there would be barriers to break down, because probation staff tended to view uniformed staff as unhelpful and prison officers tended to see probation people as something of an appendage. Managerially there was an institutional lethargy about Ashwell which seemed unable to come to grips with this as an issue. Nevertheless, in spite of this, individual participants made real and worthwhile contributions to the pre-release course at Ashwell.

Only two of the prisons ran pre-release courses for prisoners. It was a surprise to us that Featherstone had not succeeded in getting an effective pre-release course off the ground. Officially this was said to be because prisoners would be transferred to a category D establishment before release, although it seemed to have more to do with internal politics within the education department. In Nottingham, as we have noted above, pre-release was regarded as being on the back burner during our research. In theory the course ran once a month for up to ten prisoners at a time, but lasted a mere two days. The course was run by the WELOs, but they were all too frequently called to other duties, and when they were available to run a course it was sometimes difficult to assemble a group of prisoners to take it. On the occasions we visited pre-release when a course was running it seemed to be operating at best in a rather low gear. In Ashwell there were difficulties about accommodation for the pre-release course, which the regional director had determined could not be resolved until Fresh Start was in operation. But there was, at least, an identifiable course comprising three core elements: communications, relationships, and life skills. The course ran ten times a year for ten prisoners at a time and lasted for three weeks, although it was planned to reduce it to two weeks in order to increase the throughput. We monitored one course during our research. The course was running below capacity because staff felt they had to get the right 'mix' of prisoners. It should have been operated by two officers, but one of them was called away for no fewer than five of the fifteen days. We were assured that this was better than had been the case in the past when sometimes both officers were called away and the course simply closed. Nevertheless, staff understandably wondered whether they had the requisite managerial support. It was viewed positively by prisoners who experienced it and it seemed to us that the course tackled real issues and broke down the usual barriers between discipline staff and prisoners.

Both Birmingham and Nottingham had pre-release employment scheme hostels attached to the prison. Since these were regional or national facilities, taking selected prisoners from far and wide, they could not sensibly be viewed for our purposes as part of their respective parent prisons. The Birmingham hostel was next to the visitors' centre and could house ten prisoners for the last six months of their sentence whilst they went to low-skilled and low-paid jobs in the local community. The Nottingham hostel occupied what was formerly the governor's quarter outside the prison. Potentially it was a fine building although somewhat run-down. We were surprised to find, however, that it was operating at little over half its real capacity of sixteen prisoners for which we could discover no good reason other than that there were insufficient candidates. We found that difficult to believe.

We asked prisoners and staff how they evaluated the help that was given to prepare prisoners for release. The results are given in Figure 6.4.

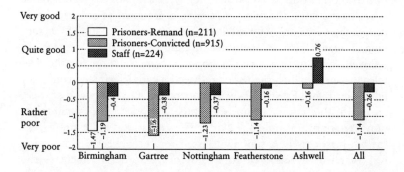

Fig. 6.4   Prisoner and staff ratings of preparations for release

The data presented in Figure 6.4 do not require a great deal of commentary, but we cannot sufficiently stress the importance of the findings. It was clear that this was one of the three or four items, in a vast array covered by our research, which was rated worst by prisoners and for the most part they were joined in this evaluation by staff. Only in Ashwell did staff give a positive rating. Everywhere else the preparation for release was regarded as poor by staff and very poor by prisoners. We believe they were absolutely right. We now examine some of these issues from the perspective of the families of prisoners.

Coping with Custody: Families and Prisoners

In our study of the ways in which the families of prisoners coped with custody we developed a 'snowball' sample starting with prisoners we knew well in the context of our existing research. Some twenty-six prisoners gave us permission to approach their families. We also accumulated a further fourteen prisoners and their families through our contacts at visitors' centres and in various voluntary organizations and support groups serving the needs of wives and partners of prisoners. All told we successfully maintained contact with forty families over a period of eighteen to thirty months.

A unique feature of this research, we think, was our attempt to focus on the relationship between prisoners and their families from *both* sides of the prison wall. We also wanted to see these relationships, as far as possible, within the contexts in which they currently existed. The mutual consent of all parties was sought for participation in the research. Questionnaires were ruled out for data collection purposes in favour of informal, loosely structured interviews in which interviewees had considerable scope to set the agenda. It was planned to interview prisoners not in the privileged circumstances usually accorded to researchers, but in the restricted situations usually experienced by families in the visiting rooms of prisons—even though this sometimes meant their giving up a visiting order to us for the sake of the research. Family members were mostly interviewed in their own homes, but also in a variety of other locations from cafés and car parks to play groups. In part this was because we decided, within time and resource constraints, to 'participate' in the situation in ways which provided opportunities for observation and verification of aspects of the relationship, and which would allow us to develop a more sympathetic and intuitive understanding of it.

For each of the families a main respondent (usually wife, partner, or mother) was initially interviewed in her own home. The interview lasted several hours. This was then followed up as necessary, in some cases over the telephone, in others by joining the respondent on a visit to a partner in prison, and in all cases by at least two further interviews. For those families who were themselves involved in support groups we had still more frequent contact at group meetings, get togethers, family outings, and so on. Most prisoners were interviewed either on a visit to the prison or at home during a home leave, although a few short-term prisoners had to be interviewed upon their release. We visited prisoners in fourteen prisons; we made long and difficult journeys to distant prisons (and some reasonably close and easy journeys) by public and private transport; we waited come rain or shine at the gate along with queues of other visitors; and we experienced short visits in dilapidated and crowded local prisons, longer and more relaxed visits in light and airy training prisons, and tense and closely observed high-security visits in dispersal prisons.

In the course of the research we developed close contacts with the Help and Advice Line for Offenders Wives (HALOW) at the visitors' centre at Birmingham and with the information and advice desk run by the Bourne Trust for remand prisoners' families at Wormwood Scrubs. Over a period of four months one of us (KMcD) spent a day a week at the information and advice desk. This provided an opportunity to demonstrate reciprocity for all the help given to the research, but it also provided a valuable source of data in its own right, particularly with regard to the kind of problems faced in the immediacy of the remand situation. Much of this material served to validate the reflections on these matters already given to us by our respondents.[2]

Our eventual sample was quite heavily weighted towards longer-term prisoners, with twenty-six serving sentences of imprisonment of four years or more. A further ten were serving sentences of less than four years; and four were in custody on remand. This arose partly because of the extraordinary delicacy of making contact with prisoners and their families during a remand or immediately upon sentence, and the sheer difficulty of making arrangements to visit prisoners who are only in custody for a short time. However, it also derived partly from our decision to include prisoners from our original study because there were important benefits flowing from this: in about half of the families we had known the prisoner—through

---

[2] For a more detailed account of the methodology of this part of the research see King and McDermott (1993).

the course of two research projects—for periods of up to five years. We were witness to some dramatic changes in their circumstances and prospects.

All of the prisoners in the sample were male. This was not so much a conscious choice as a product of the fact that the first research project was concerned with prisons for adult males and this project constituted a logical extension.[3] In twenty-eight of the cases the person in prison was the partner of our main interviewee on the outside, and in all but one of these families there were dependent children—a total of sixty-two children in all. In the remaining twelve cases the person in custody was either the son or the brother of the main interviewee outside. Ages of the prisoners ranged from 17 to 60 years, and of their most important visitors from 21 to 69 years. A quarter of the families involved at least one partner from an ethnic minority background.

Over four in ten of the men had never been in prison before, and for nearly six in ten of the families this constituted their first experience of having a relative in custody. Just over half the families lived in Greater London or the south east of England; the remainder were from Birmingham, Manchester, Liverpool, Peterborough, north and south Wales, and Belfast.

In an earlier paper on this research (McDermott and King 1992) we reported how the wives and partners of prisoners felt that the prison system relied upon them to 'stand by your man', expecting them to be there when needed but doing all too little to give them the appropriate support—indeed putting numerous difficulties in their way. Their experiences may, for present purposes, be considered under three phases: coming to terms with custody; doing the time apart; and anticipating and coming to terms with release.

Coming to Terms with Custody

After the upheaval of arrest, and through all the anxiety of a trial, the family may have difficulty in finding out exactly where a prisoner has been remanded in custody. Overcrowding and industrial relations problems in the local prisons of England and Wales sometimes create a 'game' of musical chairs for prisoners; some find themselves transferred from one prison to another or even from one police

---

[3] It goes without saying that female prisoners and their families are affected at least as much by penal policy and their needs and problems have been under-researched.

station to another (McDermott and King, 1988). As one of our respondents told us, 'You know, I was following him all over the bleeding country. First he went to Brixton, then to police cells in Lambeth, then to police cells in Norfolk, then to Ashford and then to the Scrubs. I never felt sure that I knew where he was especially after the first time I showed up in Brixton and they told me he wasn't there!' The remand phase is extremely stressful for all concerned. At a time when they felt their lives were 'turned upside down' or 'held in suspension' until the trial, many felt that essential information was difficult to obtain. Often partners felt that they were so busy going to the jail for visits and trying to arrange for solicitors that they had no time for anything else. Many prisoners had been on income support at the time of arrest and sometimes their partners, having failed immediately to inform the Department of Social Securty of the change in their circumstances as required, lost payments, and fell into debt. Relatives often did not know about the assisted prison visits scheme until after they had visited several times and then they learned that it would only pay for one visit a month. Visiting the prison frequently became a financial burden: 'I would go every day to see him at Risley. Sometimes I just didn't have any money left so I would hitch with my daughter. I . . . spent all my money on him. My little girl and I [went without so] he could have his magazines and stuff . . . I just felt so badly for him'.

It was sometimes a logistical nightmare as well, and one which brought few rewards. Having endured the journey and the waiting, in often inhospitable surroundings, families were marched in to take their places on one side of a long table while prisoners marched in on the other side, only to find themselves sitting closer to the stranger next to them than their relative across the table. It took on average three and a half hours for our families to accomplish their quarter of an hour of grossly restricted contact during remand visits—thirteen parts travel and waiting time to one part actually visiting. The following comment was typical: 'Going there every day with the kids and all was sheer hell. And all that hassle for fifteen minutes! Also the cost of it! It was getting there, feeding the kids to keep them happy, and supplying him inside'. The notices on display and the information handed out to visitors seemed designed more to intimidate than to inform and, given the pressure of numbers and the limited time, prison officers were often abrupt and impersonal. Their uniforms and their demeanour tended to exacerbate visitors' feelings of alienation. Children especially are distrustful of staff whom they may see as personally responsible for keeping their father inside. On our visits to prisoners we found that only one of the prisons provided really adequate and accessible information for visitors. It seemed to many of our families that the control of essential information was a mechanism for keeping them at a disadvantage. Could one hand in money at remand visits? they asked. 'Yes', they were told at Wormwood Scrubs, but 'no', at Winson Green, where it had to be sent in. Many felt bitter about the endlessly frustrating process of asking and being turned down.

Doing the Time Apart

The second phase, that of serving the sentence, is a time when both prisoners and families have to come to terms with being apart, and during which they find that the prison world completely permeates their lives. Sometimes families had not allowed themselves to contemplate a custodial outcome and certainly could not contemplate the prospect of an appeal: 'I didn't really talk about it with people before because I hoped it would all just be cleared up. It was all so confusing. A probation officer came up to me at court and said something but I could only see his lips moving, I had no idea what he was saying. The judge told the lawyers to appeal but I don't want to hear that he'll get his appeal'.

The length of a prisoner's sentence obviously limits the coping strategies that are possible and conditions the response of all parties. It is a commonplace of the prison literature that prisoners do their bird a day at a time: we found it was just as important for families.

I have to take it a day at a time . . . In the beginning I was in bad shape. I went down to six stone. The doctor had me on tranquillizers and all. But once he got sentenced I knew he was in for possibly a very long time and I knew I had to cope. It's been hard as I had to move with the kids, but now we have our routine and we're getting on with our lives.

Many prisoners serve the whole of their sentences in the local prison. But if they do not, then the most crucial decision made by the Prison Service, not only for the prisoner but for the family also, is the allocation to a training prison. Although the service tries to locate a prisoner near to his or her home this is not always achieved. Prisoners typically underestimated both the amount of time, and the amount of organization and planning, it took for their families to accomplish a visit. Their partners told us that a visit to the prison took up their whole day. The average round trip for families in our study took seven hours, of which not much more than a quarter was actually spent with their relative. The problem of initial location of prison can be compounded when a prisoner is transferred. Often this occurs without adequate notification to the family: sometimes this can be justified on grounds of security risk, but it is always a cause of stress to both families and prisoners. 'I didn't know he was moved until I got his letter from the new prison. He said it was very strange that for two or three days no one knew where he was. It was frightening because if anything had happened to him no one would know where he was'.

One mother in our study lived in Belfast and could only afford to travel by boat. She had to travel overnight in order to get to her son's prison in time for a visit.

I had called the prison three days before, saying that I was coming over and wanted to have a morning visit. They said that it was no problem. I then arrived at the gate only to find that he was transferred to Ashwell the day before! I then travelled another two hours to get there and then they weren't going to let me in to see him. I told them no one was going to stop me and in I went!

Some families have tried to have a relative transferred without either success or explanation.

My main problem is having my sons in different prisons. Why can't they both be in the same prison? I just can't afford to travel to both places. I hadn't seen either of them for four months when they had their inter-prison visit. And then they call giving me one day's notice. I drop everything and go because I'm their mother. I have petitioned to get them transferred for the past two years and still I get no answer. Both boys are model prisoners and don't cause any trouble. So why don't they transfer them?

The stress of not knowing why a prisoner is not being transferred is exceeded only when the family learns that a prisoner is being transferred, but on grounds of punishment. A prisoner who is considered a 'nuisance' to staff or labelled as a 'troublemaker' and a threat to good order and discipline (King and McDermott, 1990a) may find himself transferred to the opposite side of the country. While staff may view this as teaching a lesson to the prisoner, part of the tuition fee is paid through the effects on the family. Families of prisoners who have been 'ghosted' feel particularly vulnerable, that somehow

their relative is unsafe. The more frequent the moves the more victimized they feel:

My husband has been in thirteen prisons in seven years. I never feel settled
anymore because just when I think well, this is it and start feeling settled,
he gets moved again. I'm really worried about him as he is deteriorating.
You know, I have been fighting the prison system the whole time he's been
in to get him treated fairly. I could never have a job because I spend all my
time fighting for him or visiting him.

Transfers, including disciplinary transfers, are necessary from time
to time. But the effects on families make it still more important that
prisons should 'consume more of their own smoke'.

The prison staff constitutes the 'human face' of the prison to those
on the outside. Families gain their impression of what it must be like
inside in large part from the interaction they have with staff.
Sometimes this is reassuring and sometimes it is alienating, but either
way it is an impression of extraordinary power.

I hated Wandsworth, the prison was really hard on me and treated me like
I was a slag. It would take me two hours to get there, and they would only
give me fifteen minutes because they didn't like my husband. But Maidstone
is much better for him and for me. I've met his case officer. He's just an
ordinary bloke really who comes from Peckham and drinks in the pub across
the road. But he took the trouble to explain things. It really reassures me
that there is someone there I can trust and who cares.

Not all families ended up with such positive experiences. Several
recounted how staff had made rude remarks to them or refused to
help when asked questions. Perhaps the most sensitive interaction
between staff and families occurs during the search before a visit.
When we went as visitors we saw both good and bad practice: in a
difficult area some staff manage to treat families with dignity and
tact but others do not. Some of our families felt they were subjected
to unnecessary humiliation.

I went to Camp Hill to see my son and I was a bit late. There was a female
officer on and she did a body search on me not only in front of a male officer but also in front of my four-year-old grandson. I was so humiliated, I
had to fight back the tears. I felt that I was the one inside prison and I felt
dirty. I tried not to show anything when my son came in but he could tell I
was upset. Now he's all upset and who knows what he's going to do.

Families reported to us what a huge difference it made to their peace
of mind when they had a good rapport with staff.

Conditions inside prison can also be a source of either reassurance or distress for families. When prisoners are locked up for most of the day in unhygienic conditions with little to do, families feel understandably resentful that their son or partner is being treated inhumanely. They may genuinely fear that he will deteriorate mentally or physically, and that this will lead him to react with aggression directed either at themselves or the system. Many told us how powerless they felt as they watched their son or partner become increasingly bitter:

He's in Wandsworth waiting to be transferred to Downview, and I'm so worried about him. He's locked up for twenty-three hours a day. I went to see him on Saturday and he was really rough. I asked him if he could have at least shaved and he said that they had no water! He sat there during the visit just glaring with anger and couldn't even enjoy the children. I don't know what he'll do if he has to stay there much longer.

On the other hand, families can be exceedingly gratified when they find that a relative is in a prison that has a good regime: 'You know at least my son is doing something positive. He's not whining but getting on with his life. He is doing the OU and has won [an] award for [his] writing. I'm really proud of him and it shows that he has brains but has just used them the wrong way. Now when he gets out he knows that he can accomplish something'.

Even where the facilities of the prison regime are reasonably good, however, there can be few prisoners who find that their sense of self-responsibility is enhanced by the experience of imprisonment. A kind of wilful, childlike selfishness overtakes them and various 'wants' are seen as conditions of survival. It is often the families that bear the brunt of the cost. Given the low levels of prison pay it is hardly surprising that families are put under considerable pressure by prisoners both to send money in and to buy articles for them on the outside. This situation was not helped by the fact, as we discussed in Chapter 4, that in Birmingham, Gartree, and Nottingham the private cash limits were sometimes breached—a matter that has periodically caught the attention of the Chief Inspector of Prisons: 'It easily costs me £50 a month. I'm worse off now that he's inside because I have to support him in there. You can't really refuse him because all they really want are normal things. So he gets everything—he wants for nothing. But I have to pay the bills too. He and the kids get all my money. I'm the only one who goes without'.

We asked the families to itemize what they had bought for their imprisoned relative in the last year, how much money they sent in each week, and how much they spent on visits which was not covered by the Assisted Prisons Visits Scheme. On average it cost the families £545 a year (at 1989 prices) to keep their relative in prison. As most were already on income support, the effect of imprisonment was to impoverish them still more. In spite of this, partners of prisoners were allowed neither to claim single-parent allowance nor claim the prisoner as a dependent. This additional hardship could be eliminated or hugely alleviated if prisoners were paid a more sensible working wage.

It was characteristic of our families that they felt unable to tell their partners of the extent of the financial burden they were carrying, or the sacrifices that it entailed. But this was part of a broader problem of communication between those inside and those outside the walls. The fact is that families felt obliged to cope alone with almost whatever problem beset them, partly because they feared that to share it with their prisoner would only increase his sense of impotence, and partly because they were afraid he might blame them as uncaring or incompetent to have allowed it to occur without resolution. The introduction of pay telephones in low-security establishments was welcomed by many families but, as we have already seen with regard to Ashwell, the provision was parsimonious. Moreover, in a familiar 'catch 22', so long as prisoners' pay is so low the cost of this privilege will be passed on to the families. For most prisoners the only real time they have to talk over problems is on visits— an opportunity that arises, at best, twice a month. Throughout the visit the participants are watched, and they remain within the hearing of prison officers and other visitors. These circumstances are not conducive to any real sharing of experiences, and many families find that they dare not 'upset' their partner by broaching a difficult subject which they will not have time to resolve. Prisoners are especially concerned not to have a 'bad' visit. To avoid the worst, all parties may conspire to say as little as possible.

When I go on the visit I have to dress up and be cheerful for him no matter what is happening. He looks to me to lift his spirit. If I start to tell him some of my problems he get so wound up, and then the visit is ruined. A few times he was so upset that he argued with one of the officers afterwards and got nicked. It isn't worth it. There isn't enough time to go over everything, and besides he can't really do anything about it.

Sometimes in a situation of crisis, either the family or the prisoner may seek a 'welfare visit' which may offer the opportunity for a more extensive discussion in the more sympathetic presence of a probation officer or social worker. But welfare visits are not easy to obtain, and when they occur they often do no more than demonstrate how existing provisions have been inadequate to prevent the crisis from occurring in the first place:

I asked if we could have a welfare visit where the social worker comes up with me and we go into a private room and work out our problems. You just can't do that in the visits room with all these people around. How can you cry and yell with everybody watching? They told me we couldn't have one because I visit him every week. They seem to only go so far and don't recognize our needs.

It is not uncommon for an understanding probation officer, or even a wing principal officer, to allow a prisoner to use the office telephone to call home to deal with a crisis, but such thoughtfulness seems to occur in spite of, rather than because of, the system.

Some of the most difficult problems faced by prisoners and their partners, not surprisingly, concern their relationships with their children: imprisonment creates circumstances in which it is difficult to be either child or parent. One of the principal difficulties is the lack of co-ordination between bureaucratic rules of the system and the changing human needs of the people caught up in it. Perhaps one of the most important needs for children is the warmth of physical contact with fathers as well as mothers, and although this is now allowed in the maximum security prisons which we know, it is still the practice in many prisons to prohibit it: 'the visits are really hard on the little one. She always wants to sit on her father's knee but the staff get upset and tell her to get down. She just doesn't understand why she can't. He gave her a stuffed animal that is quite large and so she goes home and tries to sit on its lap'. Some of the women had asked if they could take a photograph inside the prison of the child with the father, only to have their request denied, apparently on security grounds. The mothers complained that their young children often did not realize that the person they visited was actually their father. A facility to take simple family photographs periodically would go a long way towards reinforcing and maintaining family identities for all parties. There is also a need for programmes whereby children can visit their fathers in prison for weekends in circumstances that are more children-friendly than anything we have seen in this country. As things stand at the moment one of the most pernicious and insidious aspects of the system is that the prospects for communication are so poor that virtually all of those we spoke to on the outside felt constrained to conceal the problems they had in bringing up the children from their partner inside, or else to give only the most sanitized account: 'he worships Paul and in his eyes his son can do no wrong. He has such an ideal picture of who Paul is. So whenever Paul got into trouble, I either didn't tell him or made it out less than it was. I'll tell you it's been hard having no one to share the hard time with'.

The only time when the prisoner and family feel that they have a real opportunity for communication is when the prisoner gets home leave—but by then so many unrealistic expectations have been built up that it is often too late.

Coming to Terms with Release

The first stage of preparing for release is the application for parole. It is a procedure that caused much distress to our families, partly because it was shrouded in so much secrecy and misunderstanding. Whatever anxieties many of our families felt about the eventual release of their relative, all seemed to hold out the hope that he would get parole as long as he behaved himself and had a home to go back to. Many families went to great lengths to secure him a job, believing this would also help ensure parole: 'I have got him a promise of a job if he gets parole. I can't understand why they would say no as he has a home to go to, a job, and a family who'll help him'. (He did not get parole.) The rejection of a parole application nevertheless might still leave a prisoner eligible for home leave. As the home leave policy then operated, it created high expectations and even higher disappointments. Imprisonment can be seen as a massive process of social de-skilling. All too often it takes away or severely damages the capacity to interact with people in a normal, open, give-and-take manner; the ability to share in the responsibility for self and others is largely replaced by a need to gratify selfish whims. It is not that they do not try; rather that by the time they get a chance to try the whole task is so daunting and so pressured that they are just ill-equipped to cope. Nowhere does the effect of this process reveal itself more than when the prisoner goes on home leave. We have already recounted how one prisoner thought it would be a case of

re-uniting Robert Redford and Meryl Streep. His wife found it
equally difficult: 'the kids had changed, they had grown up without
him. I had changed. He had not really made a contribution to our
lives for so long. He could not really face up to the fact that in an
important way we no longer really needed him. But that was difficult for me too, because I had dutifully supported him all these
years'.

The families are only drawn into the process of home leave when
a probation officer makes a home visit to see if the situation is appropriate for the prisoner to come home to. On the basis of our data
this contact is perfunctory; indeed so disproportionate was it to the
magnitude of the task that it could only be regarded as derisory. Not
one probation officer or prison official had asked any of the women
we interviewed if she had any problem with the prospect of a home
leave, or even the timing of the home leave. At no time did she
get any advice or preparation for the forthcoming event: 'first time I
see probation in over ten years is when they come to do a home
report. They were not at all interested in how I was or how I was
coping or whether this return was a problem for me. They just asked
me if I was willing to have him back. Once I said yes, they were
gone!'

The stress of home leave merely foreshadows the stress of release.
Release is, of course, the objective which sustains most prisoners
through their sentences. But the closer it comes the more anxious
they feel about it. Most are so badly prepared for it that its arrival
precipitates them into crisis. It is not just that they have to relearn
the skills they have lost while imprisoned: they have also to shake
off the very attitudes and behaviours that enabled them to survive on
the inside. And they have to do it all from day one: 'You know time
has stopped for me. I still think like I did when I went in and I'm
trying to make up for all the time that I lost, but I know I can't. I
also have this bitterness, this inner rage that I don't know how to let
go of. I've been treated as less than human for so long that I no
longer know what to expect or what is expected of me'.

However, release also creates a crisis for the family. During the
time of imprisonment the family has grown and changed as it has
had to adapt to a changing situation, a situation which excluded the
family member inside. The family now has to try and reintegrate
someone who has also changed, but changed in response to an environment that mostly excluded them:

I thought I was pretty well prepared for his coming home, but I wasn't. There was so much I resented about him, and we never got around to talking about it while he was inside. I guess also I did change. I stand up to him now and tell him what I think and he doesn't like that, but he's learning. I'm a lot more independent now. I've had to be. He hasn't been here to change the plugs at all. I've had to do it all.

Many prisoners, expecting their partners to continue in the more traditional and compliant roles they played before the sentence began, have difficulty in adapting to women who have become used to exercising their own independence and responsibilities. The situation is often made more difficult as a man seeks to come to terms with his anger about his treatment in prison while the woman has to deal with her anger at what he has put her through—an anger she could not express as she helped him through his sentence. 'When he came home, God it was hard! He just came barging into my life. I've made a life for myself here, and it's quiet and mine. He comes in and lies on the sofa and assumes that I'll do everything for him. I know this sounds petty, but it's the intrusion. I know a lot of this is prison, but I am the one who has to deal with the consequences'.

We could not but be impressed by the extraordinary tenacity with which most of our respondents—spouses, partners, and mothers,— 'stood by their man'. But most felt that at every turn they got no thanks and precious little help. Where there are no proper opportunities of maintaining civilized contacts with partners, problems are not discussed but put off, concealed, or glossed over until it is all but too late to do anything about them.

Strategies for Survival

How then do families cope in their efforts to come to terms with these problems? It first has to be said that some of them have faced these things before, and that for them a solution or solutions may come pre-figured. For those facing them for the first time, however, and for those who recalled their first experience for us, the length of sentence was an important factor. Broadly speaking, the shorter the time in custody the less one had to think about doing time apart and preparing for release: whatever emergency procedures one had put in place to cope with the fact of custody, no matter how rickety they were, seemed to serve well enough until it was all over. However, the longer the period of custody the more conscious all parties became of the need to develop survival strategies to get them through the sentence. It is vital, in trying to understand those strategies, to be clear about two things: first, that both prisoner and partner will bring to their situation, at least initially, their own previous coping mechanisms; and secondly, that their respective situations—the worlds in which they have to make out—are very different, with different pressures and constraints; only occasionally are they conjoined. Understanding the first proposition involves conceptualizing continuity as well as change. Understanding the second involves the recognition that mutual support is not easy, that potentially the strategies adopted by partners may conflict with one another and become catalysts for change. A repeated, but ironic, finding of our study was thus that the more aware people became of their own or their partners' survival strategy—particularly if the strategy was proving effective—the more anxious they became about all their prospects on release.

In some cases survival strategies were emerging, almost instinctively, from the very outset, so that a protective casing could be put in place from the moment that a custodial outcome was announced. Thus one of our sample told her partner: 'I have got to do this a day at a time. I cannot make any promises. If I am still here when you come out then we'll take it from there'. She in fact visited regularly throughout, coped with extraordinary resilience, and when we were last in touch was still there but very anxious about her partner's impending release. And a prisoner told us, what he could not say to his partner: 'If I even think about what is happening out there, I know I will never survive'.

In other cases the need for survival strategies emerged slowly as partners began to come to terms with radically changed circumstances: sometimes it was only after they found that they had come to terms with those circumstances that they realized they had in fact developed a survival strategy. As often as not what strategy they developed depended upon the kind of supportive relationships they had enjoyed in the past and how many of these were available to them now, although a surprising number began to develop new networks or degrees of independence, or both.

In the most basic sense virtually everyone survives because they have to. Although there are well-publicized cases of prison suicides, none of our prisoners seemed likely to take this option. No one knows how many of the family members of prisoners commit suicide: one member of our sample seemed to us potentially to present at least a possible risk. In what follows we attempt to characterize the strategies of those outside prison rather than those inside. Nevertheless, to judge from the relatively small group whom we were able to meet after release, what all prisoners had in common was a problem with the *very fact that their partners had survived*: they were at once both pleased and resentful—for no matter what strategy they had adopted for their own survival, life had moved on without them, and the relationship with partners, and especially children, would never the same again.

On the basis of our data it seemed possible to classify our sample of family members into four groups according to the networks of support upon which they could draw. They formed, in effect, a kind of hierarchy, with each succeeding level being able to draw upon new levels of resource in addition to those available to those below.

Vulnerable Families: Prisoner- and State-Dependent

At the bottom of the hierarchy were a group of eleven families who had no effective network upon which they could draw and who were heavily dependent for their survival on receiving benefits in cash or in kind from state, voluntary, or self-help agencies. These families were often in dire poverty. The relationship of partner to prisoner was typically one of dependence, but the prisoner upon whom they depended had given them little sustenance outside prison; indeed in almost all these cases there was a history of abuse to the partner, her children, or both. Moreover, the prisoner typically gave virtually no support from inside prison but instead often added to the burdens by making unrealistic requests. Most of the men were now in prison for some kind of violence or sexual abuse, and several did their time behind their doors or sometimes on Rule 43. In most cases where it had existed, the wider family network had effectively collapsed.

These women did not, for the most part, have jobs. What they did have was a disproportionate number of children. They were a highly vulnerable group, and many seemed so borne down by events that they found difficulty even in asking for what was due to them from the social security—they had just 'stood in too many queues' and were no longer able (if they ever were) to handle the constant hassles of dealing with authority. Without the support of voluntary agencies many of these women would not have got their state

benefits. They had all too little to look forward to when their partner came out.

Traditional: Family-Dependent

At the next level were a group of fourteen women who looked first
to their partner in prison for solutions to everyday problems as well
as life crises, but who could also draw on a fairly dependable network of close family for additional support. All but one of these
women (in fact all but one of our entire sample) were working class.
More importantly, more of this group than any other came from
Black, Asian, or Irish ethnic backgrounds. Nevertheless, all seemed
to operate within gender roles as traditionally defined within their
respective groupings. Often these women were poor and frequently
they were in debt, but they showed some initiative as they turned
from one source to another to pay off their debts. All of the women
were on state benefits, although some had little jobs on the side to
'eke things out'. At least one of them knew that she put her partner
'on a pedestal', but most tried to make sure they looked after their
partner while he was inside. The men seemed not to give a great deal
of support, and most tried to call all the shots in the relationship
from inside. Several of the women felt that they had no friends of
their own and suggested that 'our friends had mostly been his
friends'. Their men inside did not seem to have anything particularly
in common, either in terms of their offences or the way they did their
time. The women mostly looked forward to the return home of their
men, if a little uncertainly, hoping that things would return to normal: one was busy redecorating the whole flat so that it looked nice
for him and thus might help him to settle.

Traditional: Job-Centred

A third group of ten women had support networks of a more public kind. For the most part these women did have viable domestic
family networks, and some were partly dependent upon state benefits. However, they were also participants in wider groups of work
mates and friends to whom they could and did look to for advice
and help. Like those we have considered thus far, these women were
bounded by traditional gender roles within their social class, except
that these had already been moderated by the fact that they went out
to work. What may once have been an activity which generated 'pin

money' had become a more central focus to their lives, one which offered a real basis for survival and personal development. These women exhibited a degree of independence not found in the previous two groups and demonstrated an extraordinary capacity to survive and transcend often quite amazing problems and difficulties.

It was amongst this group that one felt the relationship between the prisoner and his partner might be most at risk on eventual release. We knew several women who had stood by their man for several years, in one case throughout a seventeen-year sentence, but who had felt constrained not to display to their partner how independent they had necessarily become as a result of his incarceration. The man inside often sensed this growing independence without being able to address it. In three or four cases we saw such prisoners acting up against the authorities, and doing much hard time. These men were able to describe both their anxieties about what was happening outside and their own behaviour in prison, but without being able to see a possible connection between them. The women sometimes wondered whether they would have anything left to give once their partners got out and, if they did, whether it would be appreciated. We have already described the home leave situation for one of these couples. On balance, whether or not the relationships survived, the women seemed more likely than their menfolk to cope on their own after release. In short, they had come to glimpse themselves as capable women. They had learned to deal with the social security system even though they resented the hassle this produced on a regular basis. They resented even more that they felt they had to learn to cope without any organized help. As one of them told us: 'I asked the probation officer why I never got any help and he said I was put down as a "capable woman". I would have liked to have been asked at least once if I needed help. Maybe I'd have said "no" but at least I would have had a choice'.

New Women: Campaigners

Finally, amongst our sample was a group of women whose network extended beyond family, friends, and colleagues to embrace a quasi-political dimension. All of them had become politicized as a result of their experience of the criminal justice system, and were now involved in campaigns of one kind or another. In some cases the object of the campaign was to overturn a conviction, or the sentence of the court; in others it was directed at bringing about remedies for some aspect of the way their relative had been treated by the authorities in the course of the sentence. In at least three instances the campaigns, led respectively by a mother, an aunt, and a wife, have since proved to be successful.

As might be expected, a sense of grievance, either that an innocent person has been convicted and sentenced or that someone has been unfairly treated with extremely damaging consequences, is a powerful driving force. It enables people to overcome all the initial obstacles and hardships, to learn from their experiences and to realize that if anything is to be done then organization and publicity will be required. Campaigns took over the lives of campaigners. Sometimes the campaign was highly personalized, relating to the injustice done to a specific individual or group, but sometimes the campaign took on a more general nature, dealing with whole classes of individuals or events. In one case a campaign started in relation to an individual case—the release of a husband and the quashing of a deportation order. When that was successfully accomplished, even though the marriage did not survive on quite other grounds, the campaigner turned her attention to the organization of a group to support the families of prisoners and to wider issues about immigration and deportation policies.

As this last example makes plain, there is nothing hard and fast about these categories of response to the problems of coping with custody. Some of the campaigners were probably always potentially formidable women, but it was the experience of custody that turned potential into reality. In the process of becoming new women they drew upon all the resources they could, expanding their own networks of support from family and friends through to a bewildering array of contacts, some of whom were drawn from very high places indeed.

Levels of Support

One important product, we think, of the analysis provided above is that it becomes more difficult to accept the common characterization in the literature of the wives and families of prisoners as overwhelmingly passive, dependent, and vulnerable. The picture is more complex than that, and the vulnerabilities take different forms. Some women in our study undoubtedly did fit the stereotype whilst their partner was in custody, and were left to flounder in extreme poverty with very little family or other support. However, although the fact of custody added considerably to their financial, practical, and emotional burdens, it seemed to us that they continued a pattern of dependence and vulnerability in their relationships which operated before their partners were imprisoned and in all probability would resume on their release. Others had derived at least enough support from family or friends to get by in their dealings with the prison and the official agencies, even if they experienced this as being against the odds. Still others developed a growing sense of independence through work or their commitment to a cause which changed the nature of their relationships with partners and their image of themselves. Such changes at one level were a direct response to the fact of custody, or the perception of injustice, although the changes might well have happened anyway in response to some other precipitating event. Although one consequence was that the process gave these women greater strength to survive, it seemed almost inevitably to bring in its wake a countervailing uncertainty in their partners inside about how they would cope on release. Many had to work through problems of guilt, and most had to some degree developed a sense of bitterness through the experience.

Much of that bitterness was directed to state agencies—the Prison Service, the probation service, and the social security service—and the officials who represented them. Amongst our respondents there was a near universal perception that the official services were inadequate to their needs. It was not just the limited financial help and other support services available, but the complex and off-putting way in which these were delivered. So off-putting and so complex were they that many of our respondents felt they needed *prior* help and support even to be able to make their request and then *more* help to cope with the feelings engendered once they had asked. The anxiety that one could not articulate one's need to officials in ways that could be made to fit any of the categories for which assistance was available left some of our respondents feeling desperately helpless, depressed, and alone.

It is perhaps not surprising that families often felt that they were but an appendage as far as the Prison Service was concerned—picked up when they became relevant in the maintenance of good order and discipline inside and put down again when they were not. One of the most extraordinary failings from the point of view of our respondents was the perfunctory help offered by the probation service—the official agency which ought to be best placed to give continuing advice and counselling to partners on what to expect in the various stages of custody and release, and how to handle the problems. Underlying the reactions of most of our respondents to dealing with officials of all kinds was the fear that frank discussion of their needs could prove double-edged, making them or their partner more vulnerable to, for example, an unhelpful plea bargain, a knock back on parole, or a sudden transfer to another establishment.

We cannot say how typical these results are from our small and unrepresentative sample. It was drawn from amongst those prisoners, primarily long-termers, who still had continuing relationships. In most cases that relationship was with a spouse or a partner. However, the feelings and fears described above were so pervasive among our respondents that we would be very surprised indeed if they were not part of the universal experience. If this sounds damning we should make it plain that it is not the case that there was no help from official agencies, no examples of personal kindnesses extended. Individual officials did sometimes manage to reach out in a human way either as part of their role or in spite of it. Most of our respondents eventually got their official entitlements, and most were able to report a human gesture at some point in the process. But it seemed on such occasions almost as though both the giver and receiver of such help and kindness recognized that these were small oases in an otherwise desert landscape in which most people had to find their own way to survive.

In so far as our respondents did in the end get their entitlements it was more often than not as a result of advice and support from voluntary organizations, such as the Bourne Trust,[4] or the burgeoning number of self-help groups, such as the Help and Advice Line for Offenders' Wives (HALOW) and Partners of Prisoners and Families Support Group (POPS),[5] which sought to fill the void. Many of our respondents said that these organizations had 'saved their lives' by listening to them, helping them to figure out what their needs were and how to get their entitlements from the welfare system. The voluntary groups typically employed professionally qualified or at least experienced staff, well-attuned to the needs of their constituents,

---

[4] Formerly the Catholic Social Services for Prisoners. Others which were influential at the time of our research were Save the Children—Prisoners' Families Policy Group, Prisoners' Families and Friends, and the Irish Commission for Prisoners Overseas.

[5] Others which were active amongst our respondents were Prisoners' Wives and Families Society, Birdwing, PRANG, and the Black Women Prisoners Support.

although there was sometimes a social gulf between helper and client that had to be overcome. The self-help groups had fewer problems of rapport between helper and client since all were in, or had been in, the same boat. But they were even less well funded than the voluntary groups and they often lacked structures that could assure continuity. Between them, however, these groups offered a clear statement that the needs of prisoners' families were important to someone and in 1989 they provided this ill-served constituency with an articulate voice through the foundation of the Federation of Prisoners' Families Support Groups.

The Present Situation and the Future

There can be little doubt that the establishment of the Federation of Prisoners' Families Support Groups helped to heighten awareness of the problems of maintaining community links and preparing prisoners and their families for release. Despite its fledgling status, the Federation managed to present united evidence on these matters to the Woolf Inquiry, for example in its proposal that the assisted visits scheme should be extended to two per month which Woolf endorsed (Home Office 1991a, para. 14.234) and the White Paper hinted at acceptance when resources permitted. Payment for the second monthly visit under the Assisted Visits Scheme was formally announced in March 1994 to take effect from the beginning of the new financial year. In the autumn of 1993 not only had this payment looked in doubt but so had the future of the assisted prison visits unit in Birmingham which was to be market tested. During much of our research assisted prison visits payments had been dealt with through the DSS and the transfer to the APVU in Birmingham was generally regarded as having provided a much better service.

As we pointed out at the start of this chapter, there have been a number of important changes since our research, and we have referred to some of them at appropriate points in the foregoing discussion. Before considering the extent of their possible contribution to meeting the goals of the Prison Service it will be helpful to see how far these changes had been introduced into our research prisons, and what impact they had made, on the basis of the information in governors' reports and those of the Inspectorate.

By the time of the Chief Inspector's visit to Birmingham in September 1989 the visiting accommodation above the new gate complex there was fully operational, but the prisoner still only learned of the visit after his visitor, having first waited at the visitors' centre, appeared at the gate (Home Office 1990b, para. 3.65). There is no doubt that the visiting conditions were a big improvement on what had operated earlier, although remand visits were still of fifteen minutes' duration, and convicted prisoners only became eligible for privilege visits after they had been in prison for more than three months. Plans were afoot to develop a pre-release social skills course for which three programmes had been piloted (*ibid.*, para. 3.55). After his visit in January 1992 the Chief Inspector was able to report that the pre-release course was timetabled for Tuesdays, Wednesdays, and Thursdays, that letters were no longer censored and that although no card telephones were yet available, six were due to be installed (Home Office 1992c).

In October 1989 the Chief Inspector suggested that a purpose-built visitors' centre should be provided outside the gate at Gartree and that better refreshment facilities for visitors and better ventilation should be provided to relieve the smoky atmosphere at visits (Home Office 1990c, paras. 5.102–4). Elsewhere in his report he recommended that consideration should be given to the installation of card telephones, even in a dispersal prison (*ibid.*, para. 3.31), and noted that although there were now three pre-release courses per year led by prison officers (*ibid.*, para. 3.49), through-care needed to be pursued much more vigorously (*ibid.*, para. 3.40). When the Chief Inspector returned, in September 1992, Gartree had already changed its role to a category B training prison, but there were a number of unfortunate hangovers from its days as a dispersal prison. The Inspectorate pointed out that closed-circuit television surveillance was no longer appropriate during visits and the policy of strip-searching prisoners afterwards should be reviewed (Home Office 1993e, para. 3.06). Card telephones had by then been installed although not with sufficient privacy (*ibid.*, para. 2.02), and the visiting arrangements were still unsatisfactory. A temporary visitors' centre was due to be opened in December 1992 but the Chief Inspector still wanted to see a new gate complex, new visiting accommodation, and a permanent visitors' centre remain a priority (*ibid.*, para. 3.06).

It is not really possible to say a great deal about the changes in Nottingham for neither the report of the short inspection carried out there in November 1992, nor the governor's annual report for that year, dwells upon any of these matters. However, the Chief Inspector was very complementary about the new prisoner support unit, which organized a number of offence-focused courses, as well as having taken over the pre-release course (Home Office 1993b, paras. 3.9–12). The Chief Inspector noted the good visiting arrangements in passing (*ibid.*, para. 3.26) but criticized the continuing under-use of the PRES hostel (*ibid.*, para. 3.8) and the fact that landing officers failed to open mail in front of inmates, thereby contributing to the belief that censorship continued (*ibid.*, para. 2.2e).

Just as we had been surprised that Featherstone did not operate a pre-release course, so was the Chief Inspector: at his inspection in June 1989 he complained that pre-release training should begin without further delay (Home Office 1989c, para. 3.48). The Chief Inspector noted that through-care was well established although the SWIP scheme had suffered as a result of Fresh Start. He was hopeful, however, that the scheme would be reinvigorated (*ibid.*, para. 3.29). That hope may have been in vain, because the senior probation officer, in his report for 1992, complained that the spirit of SWIP had been eroded and that probation staff were doing more rather than less of the traditional welfare tasks which, in theory, should have been taken up by prison officers. The governor's annual report for 1992 refers to the establishment of a pre-release course: however, it is not entirely clear from the report of the short inspection in July 1992 whether the course was still running, although it had clearly had accommodation problems (Home Office 1992b, para. 4.4). The Chief Inspector was impressed by the visiting arrangements, apart from the lack of a visitors' centre (*ibid.*, para. 2.6). In his commentary on the report the Home Secretary said that consideration was being given to providing a temporary visitors' centre on the prison car park, but that funds were unlikely to be available for a start on a permanent centre before 1996.

At the full inspection of Ashwell in May 1992 the Chief Inspector noted that although visits were available on a fortnightly basis many prisoners had been transferred from establishments where it was now possible to have three or more visits a month, and that this caused aggravation (Home Office 1993c, para. 5.01). He also expressed concern that only three of the four wings had card telephones: given that prisoners there could now buy two telephone cards a week from private cash and as many as they liked from earnings demand far outstripped supply (*ibid.*, para. 5.04). There continued to be problems with shared working, with some confusion of roles being apparent to the inspectors (*ibid.*, para. 5.10), but Ashwell's pre-release programme was praised (*ibid.*, para. 5.18). Indeed, Ashwell was now training staff for pre-release courses in other prisons, and the two-week course for prisoners was in the process of being broken down into smaller modules which could be staged throughout a prisoner's sentence (*ibid.*, para. 5.19).

One thing which has not changed is the importance that prisoners assign to these matters. As on so many variables it is sometimes difficult to make direct and detailed comparisons with the national prison survey, although the general picture is clear enough. Walmsley *et al.* (1992, 43) report that 81 per cent of their sample who had been in prison for three months or more had been visited during the last three months, although this proportion fell to 59 per cent for those who had been in custody for ten years or more. Moreover, 95 per cent of such prisons had received a letter during that time. Only 3 per cent of those who had been in custody for the three months prior to the interview had received neither a letter nor a visit during that time (*ibid.*, 48). When asked what improvements they wanted as far as visits were concerned, 72 per cent wanted more of them, 83 per cent wanted more privacy, 79 per cent better facilities for their visitors, 74 per cent longer visits and 73 per cent more help with travel costs (*ibid.* 46).

The national prison survey appears not to have asked how satisfied prisoners were with the help currently given to prepare them for release, but invited prisoners nearing their release dates to respond to a list of possible improvements: 87 per cent would like to be provided with money to tide them over, 64 per cent wanted more home leave, 60 per cent wanted improvements in the probation service, 54 per cent more training for employment, 43 per cent more training for life outside, and 33 per cent wanted help in finding accommodation.

Regime-monitoring data do not cover the maintenance of family links and preparations for release, and so it is difficult to make systematic comparisons in regard to performance in any of our prisons over the period since our research. However, the annual statistics attached to the reports of governors do provide details of the operation of the home leave scheme, and it is worth looking at the changes in home leave from 1987 to 1992, not least because the further extension of the scheme advocated by Woolf, accepted in the White Paper, *Custody, Care, and Justice,* and implemented in the following year, were recently put under threat by Michael Howard's expressed belief that home leave should not start so early in the sentence and his request for a review of policy. This change of heart, apparently, followed 'some spectacular cases of offending while on home leave' including at least one murder.[6]

In Table 6.1 we showed that in the five prisons in 1987 there were a total of 563 home leaves, of which 166 were short leaves, 118 terminal leaves, and 279 pre-parole leaves. With thirty-one prisoners failing to return, the failure rate was 5.5 per cent. In 1992 the same five prisons released some 1,253 prisoners on leaves, of which 248 were one-day temporary releases, 666 short leaves, 127 terminal leaves, and 212 were pre-parole leaves. Of these 132 failed to return so that the proportion of non-returnees had almost doubled to 10.5 per cent. The numbers getting home leave and the numbers who failed to return varied markedly from prison to prison in much the same way as they had in 1987. However, there were some differences: Birmingham accounted for 10 per cent of the home leaves in 1992 compared with just under 5 per cent five years earlier, whereas Gartree, which had accounted for 9 per cent in 1987, had fallen to less than 2 per cent in 1992. But it was Nottingham which appeared to present the worst problems in terms of selection. In 1987 it had accounted for 18 per cent of home leaves and 32 per cent of all the failures: in 1992 it accounted for less than 15 per cent of the home leaves but 37 per cent of all the failures. Clearly there are many delicate matters to weigh up in the use of home leaves, and decisions will always be a matter of fine judgement. Nevertheless, it has to be stressed, first, that an increase in failures to return has to be expected, as almost by definition any extension of the scheme is likely to include worse risks; and secondly that failure to return represents a breach of trust but does not necessarily put the public at risk.

At the time of the latest changes to Prison Service organization, following the retirement of Ian Dunbar, the outcome of Michael Howard's review of home leave was not known, although officials privately expressed confidence that they would be able to hold the line as far as essentials were concerned. No doubt their hopes were buttressed by the fact that failures to return from home leave and temporary release dropped by 19 per cent during 1993–4 compared with the previous year. At the Prison Service conference in October

[6] Para. 7 of the leaked memorandum of 30 July 1993.

1994, however, Michael Howard made it plain that some restrictions were to be placed upon the use of telephones, and that more rigorous risk assessments by the Probation Service would have to take account of the views of the police and of the victims of violent offenders before release decisions could be taken. Until the detailed guidance for prison governors becomes available it is not possible to predict the impact of these changes, although Brendon O'Friel, the former governor of Strangeways and Chairman of the Prison Governors' Association, expressed his misgivings to the conference (*Guardian*, 1 November 1994).

It would be idle to pretend that there have not been important improvements in the facilities provided to support the maintenance of family links, and to some degree to prepare prisoners for release. The annual report for 1991–2, for example, listed local initiatives to provide all-day visits by children at Styal, and family days which include visits to prisoners' living areas for life- and long-sentence prisoners at Aylesbury and Swinfen Hall, in addition to the general extension of twice-monthly visits announced in April 1991 (Home Office 1992a, paras. 223–5). Moreover the report noted that there were seventy crèches in visiting areas and thirty-one visitors' centres across the system as a whole (*ibid.*, paras. 226–7). The report for 1992–3 pointed out that in 1993–4 it was expected there would be support for thirty-six visitors' centres; that card telephones had been installed in all prisons; that eighty-two establishments provided pre-release courses and that it was hoped that all establishments would do so by 1996; that two prisons were functioning as resettlement prisons for long-sentence prisoners; that, in collaboration with the employment service, employment focus courses had been piloted in twenty-four establishments and five job clubs established with plans to double the numbers of both these in the coming year; and that it continued to fund NACRO's prison link unit (PLU) and expected to have PLU-trained staff in all establishments by 1996 (Prison Service 1993g). Compared to what had gone before, during the astonishing years of stagnation and decline in the Prison Service, they reflect not just a change of rhetoric but a major release of energy and resources which ought to have produced palpable improvements on the ground.

The *Corporate Plan 1993–96* foreshadowed the developments referred to above and also proposed closer links with the probation service to help prisoners find ways of coping on their return to the community without re-offending. To that end written agreements were introduced between prison governors and their local chief probation officers, which from April 1994 might become contracts, with the budget for probation services devolved to governors (*ibid.*, paras. 9.12–15).

In its discussion of the changing relationship to the probation service the *Corporate Plan* correctly states, 'a prisoner's needs must be identified at an early stage and met in the most effective way using resources from the prison and probation services and outside agencies' (Prison Service 1993d, para. 9.14).

Sentence-planning and through-care, in other words, need to work hand-in-hand: or rather one should be seen as part of the other. This is, unfortunately, much more easily said than done. Most of the other welcome improvements which have been made have involved the investment of money to improve facilities and the frequency with which they may be used. They are beginning to provide a structure within which positive linkages and preparations for release may take place. But it is important to remember that they do only constitute the *structure* and they do not guarantee that the *linkages and preparations for release will actually be made*. Of course much will be up to the prisoners and their families themselves. But the most striking of the findings reported in this chapter were the way in which both prisoners and staff thought that what was actually done to prepare prisoners for release was so pathetic; and that the families outside had such perfunctory and largely pointless contact with the probation service.

Our fear is that, unless some very dramatic improvements are made very quickly on this score, prisoners and their families will continue to flounder, dodging and glossing over many of the real issues which continue to confront them. It is our considered view that major additional resources are required so that probation and prison staff, working in conjunction with prisoners and their families, can identify as quickly as possible the consequences of offending behaviour upon the offender, his family, and his victims, and the relationship of family and domestic circumstances to initial and subsequent offending behaviour. This would require much more than an initial diagnosis and an eventual home leave or parole report: it would require systematic follow-up involving direct meetings between the prisoner, his family, and the probation officer throughout the sentence. This might in some circumstances be achieved in the course of normal visiting arrangements but would probably require special visits fully funded and programmed for just this purpose at regular intervals. Nothing remotely approaching that seemed to operate in 1987 in any of our prisons. Such a scheme could not be a panacea, because there are many other circumstances which may influence offending behaviour which are outside the scope of the family, the Prison Service, or the probation service. Nevertheless, we regard this as the best potential shot in the locker of the Prison Service if it is to make real progress towards its stated goals.

In 1994 the new *National Framework for the Throughcare of Offenders* was published (Prison and Probation Services 1994). It is an elaborate document which sets out the joint responsibilities of the Prison and Probation Services as well as what amounts to the kind of detailed job specification which would make any sane applicant have second and third thoughts. It covers a great deal of ground in a formalized way—but nowhere does it suggest that it would be a good idea if seconded probation officers, prisoners, and their families should sit down to talk things through in the way we have suggested, let alone require such things to take place. Nevertheless, it is important to record that in an area where the performance of the Prison Service has been least satisfactory, and its pretensions least credible, there have been welcome attempts at improvement. It is hoped that they will not be undermined by the changes currently in train, or overwhelmed by the growth in the prison population.

Postscript

At the proof-reading stage of this book it is necessary to add that it has now become clear that the changes to home leave and temporary release will be far more sweeping than officials had anticipated, perhaps amounting to a reduction of 40 per cent. The stringent new release criteria, coupled with the threat of criminal sanctions for late returners, send a radically different message to the one contained in the Woolf Report. Whatever slender hopes may so recently have been raised will now be considerably dashed.

7

Economy, Efficiency, and Effectiveness: Making Sense of the Prison System

Symmetry has dictated that we devote a chapter to the sixth and final goal of the Prison Service, namely, *to deliver prison services using the resources provided by Parliament with maximum efficiency* (Prison Service 1993c, 5). Necessity, however, dictates that we widen that discussion into one of effectiveness. We collected no systematic data about the use of resources in the establishments in our study, and although we have accumulated fragmentary materials on some relevant issues it would ill behove a sociologist and an anthropologist to try to spin these out into an economic analysis. We have no intention of doing so, although we do have some observations to make on the costs of imprisonment in general and Key Performance Indicator 8—*the average cost per prisoner*—in particular before we go on to consider issues about the effectiveness of the service. Extending the brief in this way conveniently makes it possible for us to allow the discussion in this chapter to serve also as our conclusions.

Economy and Efficiency

Economy is about keeping costs down and delivering services as cheaply as practicable. To judge from the evidence offered by the Prison Service to the May Committee, in which it presented itself as the Cinderella of the public sector, prisons might have been regarded as the perfect paragon in this regard. In their evidence to the May Committee King and Morgan (1979, para. 25) challenged that view, pointing out that it was not unambiguously the case that the Prison Service had been starved of resources, and argued that the proportion of post-war accommodation in prisons, for example, was only marginally lower than that in schools and rather higher than in hospitals. The May Committee conceded that 'prisons' current expenditure has done better than any of the other social services, including public expenditure as a whole and compares favourably on capital expenditure' (Home Office 1979a, para. 6.95). And it further acknowledged that between 1965 and 1978 staff had increased by 88 per cent whereas the prisoner population had increased by only 38 per cent. Nevertheless, the Committee took the view, in what amounts to an early version of Michael Howard's thesis, that *prison works*, that it would be irresponsible and dangerous not to increase the level of protection against terrorism and rising crime. It recommended, therefore, a major increase in prison building and accepted that this would lead to staff increases, although it hoped that these would be as economical as possible consistent with the need to phase out dependency on overtime. Thus did Cinderella acquire the wherewithal to go to the ball.

How have things developed since then? Perusal of the Central Statistical Office Blue Book shows that, in the analysis of general government total expenditures, the public order and safety budget had achieved rates of increase in excess of the growth in public expenditure as a whole throughout the 1980s, and into the 1990s. Indeed it has exceeded the increase in every one of the other main headings separately. Thus over the period 1982–92, standardized at 1990 prices, the public order and safety budget increased 2.85 times compared with its nearest rivals, health, which increased 2.48 times; recreational and cultural affairs, 2.34 times; social security 2.31 times; and education 2.29, times (CSO 1993, Table 9.4). Unlike the earlier period, however, the prime beneficiaries within public order and safety services, in terms of proportionate increase, were the law courts, which achieved an increase in budget of over 400 per cent. In 1982 the law courts' budget was only 30 per cent greater than the prisons budget, but by 1992 it was twice as large. Nevertheless, the prisons budget grew 2.72 times—more quickly than that for the police, which grew 2.56 times. In 1982 the police budget from central government sources was 7.6 times the size of the prisons budget; by 1992 it was only just over four times as big. It also has to be said that, contrary to the pattern of the previous decade (see CSO 1981), the prisons' vote did not rise inexorably year by year: there were major jumps in the budget of 29 per cent in 1986 and again in 1990 with more modest increases averaging 10 per cent for the years in between. The only exceptions were 1988 and 1992, which actually saw marginal falls over the preceding years.

By any standard there has been a very substantial increase in investment in prisons, so that the service will shortly be able to claim another twenty new prisons completed, providing over 8,000 additional places. Furthermore, new housing blocks in many existing prisons have added several thousand more cells to the penal estate. In 1979, and on a number of occasions since, King and Morgan have argued strenuously against the need for such a prison-building programme on the ground that many prisoners then in custody did not need to be there. They also feared that, once built, the prisons would simply be filled up. They claimed that building a way out of overcrowding in the prison system had been official policy since 1959, but that opening an average of two new prisons a year throughout the 1960s and early 1970s had made no inroads whatever into that problem. Whether or not the present building programme will turn out to have been a good investment, time will tell. Already there are unfortunate straws in the wind. Much of the accommodation in the new prisons is of very high quality—indeed of such high quality that some has been described as lavish. It has provoked a 'less eligibility' backlash in many quarters, which has in part been fed by Michael Howard during his tenure as Home Secretary. His assertion that 'prison works', apparently supported by the Prime Minister, John Major, and that henceforth the size of the prison population should not be a test of the success of prison policy, might suggest that the government may be looking to get full use from its enormous investment. Making sure that the prisons are full would at least reduce one measure of unit cost, although if that is the current intention it runs counter to what was envisaged at the time that the new plans for the Prison Service Agency were drawn up, as we indicate below.

Far more important than the new prisons, in terms of the real needs of the Prison Service and the prisoners it contains, has been the major programme of refurbishment in the old Victorian local prisons and elsewhere, which is providing not just integral sanitation but also improved visits, kitchen, and other facilities. There is also a sensible maintenance programme which should help prevent such prisons from falling into the kind of disrepair that the former Prison Department reported to the May Committee. There is, clearly, still a great deal to do in the refurbishment programme; but there is also

little doubt that physically the penal estate must now compare quite
favourably with what is to be found anywhere else in the world.
Certainly it will never again be possible for the Prison Service to
claim that it has been starved of resources. In our view, however, a
much greater proportion of those resources would have been better
spent on improving the programmes in the existing institutions and
upgrading their physical plant, rather than on more new prisons on
existing or green field sites.

Measuring Unit Costs

The target in relation to KPI 8 adopted by the Prison Service for
1993–4 is *to ensure that the cost per prisoner place does not exceed
£23,561 per annum.* The final cost per prisoner place for 1993–4 will
presumably be published in the *Annual Report and Accounts.*
Meanwhile, on the basis of the latest available information, the service claims this target has ben met. It is estimated that the cost per
place will be around £23,000, about 2 per cent below target and a
reduction of 1.9 per cent in real terms compared with 1992–3 (Prison
Service 1994c).

Very little detail has been publicly set out on how such a calculation is made. It is important to note that the target refers to cost per
prisoner *place* and not cost per *prisoner*, although official arguments
sometimes move confusingly from one to the other measure and back
again. The *Business Plan 1993–94* (Prison Service 1993e) indicates
that the target reflects current expenditure provision in the supply
estimates for 1993–4 and the agreed baseline certified normal accommodation or CNA. However, such an explanation needs some
unpacking. Baseline CNA is a completely new concept which differs
markedly from all hitherto-published CNA figures in the annual
reports of the Prison Service or the monthly statistics on prison occupancy. Whereas what we suppose we must now call 'actual' CNA
refers to accommodation which is currently available for use, *baseline* CNA includes all accommodation currently within the penal
estate which *could theoretically be brought into use* for prisoners. It
therefore includes not just the places out of use because of the refurbishment programme—which at times has been over 4,000 although
it averages some 2,500 places—but also the places in mothballed
prisons, although not those in prisons permanently closed,[1] as well

---

[1] Oxford Prison is not included in the 1993 figure because it was intended that it

as some other accommodation which is currently out of use for one reason or another. This explains why the figure of 52,864 for base-line CNA quoted in the *Business Plan* is some 6,653 larger than the 46,211 placed quoted for CNA at the time the *Plan* was published in April 1993, and remains much larger than the end of year CNA of 47,498.

To the extent that baseline CNA accurately reflects the real accommodation potentially available to the Prison Service, this is valuable material to have in the public domain for the first time. In 1979 King and Morgan struggled to establish what might be the true picture of CNA for the May Committee as they picked their way through unexplained fluctuations in annual reports. Later King (1987) pointed to the 'missing' 450 maximum-security cells—equivalent to a whole new prison—which were simply not used, apparently because of fears about maintaining order within the dispersal system. In fact the missing accommodation within the dispersal, and former dispersal, prisons continues to be missing because it is not included in the baseline CNA.[2] In spite of the apparent precision of the newly published baseline CNA figure, it turns out to be an estimate based in part upon the first stage of the census of accommodation referred to in the *Corporate Plan 1993–96* and in part upon the existing accommodation certificates completed by governors and area managers. The published figure for 1993–4 is in fact the mid-point between the estimate of CNA at the beginning of the year and what it was expected to be at the end of the year when further new prisons had come on stream.[3]

Although the baseline CNA purports to describe the potential uncrowded capacity of the system it is still not clear precisely what that means. At the time the census of accommodation was being carried out the standard for double-occupancy cells in the July 1993 draft code was, as we pointed out in Chapter 4, at least 1.5 times the minimum 5.5 square metres for single occupancy. In the long-awaited published version (Prison Service 1994a) this has been reduced to 1.3 times the single-occupancy figure, but that only

be permanently closed and returned to the local authority. The re-opening of Oxford had to be renegotiated in the light of prison population growth and thus accommodation in Oxford is now in the baseline CNA for 1994–5.

[2] Although Albany and Gartree are no longer part of the dispersal system the latest CNA figures suggest that they still operate at 167 and ninety places below their design capacities respectively.

[3] We are grateful to Linda Wilson for this clarification of baseline CNA.

applies to refurbished cells. Existing cells continue to be certified for use by the prison governor and his line manager in the time-honoured way.

According to the *Corporate Plan for 1993–96* (Prison Service 1993d, para. 7.17) the census was supposed also to develop a figure for the crowded state of the prisons. There have been a number of formulations for this over the years; during the worst years of overcrowding there were several thresholds which reflected different levels of discomfort before prisons reached what was then called the 'bust' figure, at which point everything broke down. Now it seems that 'operational capacity' constitutes a figure which the Prison Service regards as 'acceptable overcrowding'. So far as we have been able to ascertain, operational capacity was not determined on the basis of a census but calculated on a prison-by-prison basis by the governor in conjunction with the area manager. As far as we are aware, operational capacity figures have never been published, either for the system as a whole or for individual establishments. The difference between normal accommodation and operational capacity, however, was at the heart of the dispute between the POA and the Prison Service at Preston and other overcrowded prisons in the north west which led to court injunctions in October and November 1993.

Some agreed baseline is, of course, a useful addition to the repertoire of possible measures of the costs of imprisonment, if only because, once built, prisoner places are relatively permanent and should be accounted for. There thus now seem to be three possible divisors for the calculation of unit costs: average daily population, actual CNA and baseline CNA. Each produces a different answer and each has its own merits and deficiencies.

The most obvious measure involves dividing the total current expenditure by the average daily population to produce a cost per prisoner. This is a readily understandable measure, but it suffers from the immediate drawback that it would always be possible to reduce costs by crowding—that is, of course, why local prisons traditionally have always been so much cheaper per prisoner than closed training prisons. In 1992–3, however, when the population in local prisons more closely approximated to their actual accommodation, the weekly cost per prisoner in local prisons was £526, much less than in dispersal prisons at £816, but more than category B training (£518), and much more than category C (£387) and open prisons (£331). If prison populations were consistently below prison capacity, then using cost per prisoner would involve a different distortion because it would take no account of the need to maintain and service existing, but unused, spaces. Nevertheless, cost per prisoner is a familiar and useful index and has been published in the annual reports of the Prison Service for several years; it should not lightly be discarded. Thus the average annual cost per prisoner for 1990–1 was £21,112, for 1991–2 it was £22,472, and for 1992–3 it jumped to £25,688 as the prison population declined. For 1993–4 we estimate the cost per prisoner to be about £26,500 considerably above the cost per prisoner-place figure used as the key performance indicator.

The second measure of unit costs, published in all recent annual reports, is a cost per prisoner-place based on actual CNA. The virtue of this measure is that it reflects the accommodation actually available for use for prisoners, even though some of it may be used for more (or fewer) prisoners than was intended. In 1991–2 this produced a unit cost of £22,939 per place—higher than the cost per prisoner, just as it had been in most earlier years, because of the influence of overcrowding. However, in 1992–3 the cost per actual place was £24,232—less than the cost per prisoner because of the reduction in the prison population. We estimate that for 1993–4 the unit cost based on actual CNA would be about £25,500, once again considerably higher than the statistic actually used in the key performance indicator.

The use of an agreed baseline figure in the *Business Plan* perhaps reflects a post-Woolf recognition that costs should not simply be driven down at the expense of crowding and a worsening of conditions. If that is the case, then it represents a step away from a measure of economy towards a measure of effectiveness. It could be argued in that case that it may not actually matter what agreed baseline figure is used because, presumably, its main purpose would be to offer a more stable basis for the calculation of costs which would not be contaminated by a lowering of standards through overcrowding. Nevertheless. the fact is that the larger the divisor the smaller the unit cost will appear to be, and this cannot have been lost on the service when choosing its KPI. It is not possible to make comparisons on this indicator for earlier years because baseline CNA has not previously been published and recalculating it might be a hazardous business. However, it should be noted that future costs per place will in any case be further reduced because they will be calculated on the basis of an enlarged divisor—the newly projected baseline CNA for 1994–5 of 53,840—a figure which now includes the reclaimed Oxford. The target for 1994–5 is to ensure that costs per place do not exceed £24,500 (Prison Service 1994d). It would obviously make sense to keep an eye on all three of these unit cost measures rather than to rely on the single KPI which might appear to show performance in the best light.

In practice, it is clear that the public expenditure settlement for the Prison Service is driven by total historical costs, and so the cost per prisoner-place is a purely notional residual figure after dividing the current expenditure by a nominal number of prison places. However, if one accepts that it is not the government's intention to reduce costs through overcrowding, much will depend upon the greater powers vested in governors to control staffing and other budgets to force costs down. Over the period covered by the *Corporate Plane 1994–97* (Prison Service 1994b) there will be a drive to reduce unit costs by five per cent in real terms. It is said that this reflects ministerial concern at the difference between unit costs in the contracted-out prisons and those in the public sector. At this point the argument reverts to costs per prisoner. Thus it is said that average weekly costs per prisoner held in The Wolds have fallen to £350 during 1993–4 from £538 in its first year of operation. In 1992–3 costs at The Wolds were higher than the average cost of £494 a week for the service generally, but had been inflated because of the slow build-up of the population.[4] Costs as The Wolds will look even lower when compared with the costs in the now less crowded local prisons instead of the average costs over the system as a whole.

Some indication of the way in which costs per place work out in practice can be gained from looking at our research prisons. In Table 7.1 we present data on the average costs per prisoner based on ADP taken from the annual reports of the Prison Service for our five prisons for the year 1986–7, during the currency of our research, and for 1991–2. The year 1986–7, of course, was also the financial year immediately before the implementation of Fresh Start. It should be noted that during the interval Ashwell had changed its function from an open prison to a category C training prison, and that some increase in costs is attributable to that change. However, the change in role at Gartree from a dispersal to a category B training prison took place in the financial year 1992–3 and so does not affect the

---

[4] Personal communication from Philippa Drew.

comparison. We also present a cost per place figure which we have calculated on the basis of published CNA. We cannot, of course, calculate a figure for the cost per place based on baseline CNA because those figures are not published on a prison-by-prison basis. We have not made any adjustments for inflation.

Table 7.1. Cost per prisoner and cost per place in 1986–7 and 1991–2

		ADP	Cost per Prisoner	CNA	Cost per Place
Birmingham	1986–7	1,086	11,024	570	21,060
Birmingham	1991–2	927	17,264	567	29,744
Gartree	1986–7	307	24,284	315	23,764
Gartree	1991–2	251	45,240	245	46,332
Nottingham	1986–7	295	13,312	215	18,252
Nottingham	1991–2	212	28,548	218	27,768
Featherstone	1986–7	510	9,724	510	9,724
Featherstone	1991–2	580	12,948	599	12,532
Ashwell	1986–7	333	9,256	300	10,244
Ashwell	1991–2	388	16,536	404	15,860
Total System	1986–7	47,200	13,098	41,650	14,843
Total System	1991–2	46,472	22,470	45,527	22,936

Sources: Annual Reports of the Prison Service

It can be seen from Table 7.1 that cost per place is a somewhat more stable measure than cost per prisoner, even though it is affected by new building and refurbishment. Costs per prisoner in Birmingham and Nottingham in 1986–7 were significantly reduced by overcrowding, so that by 1991–2 average cost per prisoner had increased by 57 per cent and 115 per cent respectively. Nevertheless, the escalation in costs has been very dramatic even on a cost per place basis: 41 per cent in Birmingham and 52 per cent in Nottingham. The costs per place at Gartree are inflated by taking some accommodation out of use during installation of sanitation, which in part accounts for the phenomenal growth in costs of 95 per cent. However, even if CNA were standardized in Gartree at the 1986–7 level of 315 places the cost per place would still have increased by 51 per cent, whilst costs per prisoner increased by 86 per cent. It should be noted that, although there were cheaper dispersal prisons than Gartree it was by no means the most expensive. The increases, both in cost per prisoner and cost per place, at Ashwell may in part be accounted for by its change of role as well as growth in both ADP and CNA, and so it had best be excluded from consideration for current purposes. This leaves only Featherstone with relatively modest increases in costs of 33 per cent on a per-prisoner basis and 29 per cent in terms of costs per place.

The average increase in costs per prisoner for our five prisons from 1986–7 to 1991–2 was 73.8 per cent which compares with 71.5 per cent for the system as a whole. In terms of costs per place the increase in our prisons averaged 54.4 per cent compared with 54.5 per cent for the whole system.

Staff Costs

Prisons are very labour-intensive organizations, and one measure of efficiency might be the delivery of a given level of service by fewer staff. For several years manpower costs have been shown separately in the annual reports. In 1986–7 manpower accounted for 82.9 per cent of the net operating costs in establishments. By 1991–2 this appears to have fallen to 77.6 per cent, but this is largely an accounting artefact brought about by a change that year in the way in which rates and opportunity cost rents are applied. Assigning the same rateable and rental value that applied in the previous year produces a proportion of 81.2 per cent for manpower costs in 1991–2. In 1987–8, immediately after Fresh Start, the proportion had increased to 83.6 per cent, but there seems to have been marginal decreases in each year thereafter. It is possible, however, that this proportionate decrease has been achieved not by reduced manpower but by the transfer of tasks and contracting out of services from more expensive prison officers to less expensive custody officers and civilians.

Between 1 April 1987, the date on which Fresh Start was first implemented, and 6 April 1992 the number of permanent staff employed by the Prison Service increased by about 29 per cent from 28,200 to 36,500 (Home Office 1992a, para. 247). Over the same period the prison population declined from 49,000 to 47,746, a decrease of 2.5 per cent. In an earlier paper (King and McDermott 1989) we were able to show that between 1971 and 1986–7 the prison population increased by less than a fifth whilst the numbers of staff increased by more than two-thirds. In those days this was a fairly straightforward comparison because throughout the period the staff concerned were working ever-increasing hours of overtime. Since Fresh Start there has been an exchange—disputed at virtually every stage of the process—whereby additional staff were employed, but each of them was employed for fewer hours., Whereas in 1986–7 prison officers were paid on an hourly basis and worked an average of fifty-six hours a week, by April 1992 this had been reduced to thirty-nine hours a week, and they were paid on a monthly basis. If those figures can be taken at their face value, then the 28,200 staff working fifty-six hours a week would have been equivalent to 40,492 staff working thirty-nine hours a week today: the 1992 workforce of 36,500 would thus represent an effective reduction of almost 10 per cent.

However, the comparison is not as simple as that. Fresh Start effectively bought out prison officers' overtime by fixing salaries, for a forty-eight-hour week, reducing to thirty-nine hours, at around the pay levels they were earning with overtime. Reductions in hours are not, therefore, translated directly into reductions in staff costs. Nor is it obvious where the additional costs of overtime rates trade off against the additional national insurance and pension costs of extra staff. Moreover, it is clear that officers continue to work overtime seven years after Fresh Start was introduced; although they are supposed to have time off in lieu (TOIL) there are apparently considerable debts owing in many prisons. Finally, the Prison Service has progressively civilianized a number of posts which prison officers previously filled, and has contracted out a number of others. These jobs no longer appear in the records as being filled by Prison Service permanent staff. A decline in expensive officer hours may thus to some extent be balanced by an increase in cheaper civilian hours. How far these considerations complicate the picture it is probably not possible to say without significant research which would take us far beyond the scope of this volume. However, if the big picture is less than fully clear it is worth turning once again to our research prisons where there certainly does not seem to have been any decline in staffing.

As we have reported in earlier chapters we collected additional data on our prisons for November 1992 so that we might make comparisons with data we already had for November 1987. As a result it is possible for us to compare staff in post and staff ratios in our prisons at these dates. Because by November 1992 Gartree had ceased to be a dispersal prison, and Ashwell had long since become a category C training prison, we restrict this comparison to Nottingham, Featherstone, and Birmingham, whose functions in 1992 remained broadly as they had been during our research. In an

attempt to make the comparison more meaningful we have recalculated the numbers of officers in post in November 1987 in terms of
full-time equivalent staff working thirty-nine hours, by applying the
actual average overtime rates which applied in our prisons at that
date (fourteen hours in Nottingham, five hours in Featherstone, and
18.5 hours in Birmingham). We present the recalculated findings in
Table 7.2, with the original data that we presented in our paper
which drew attention to what we then called the ever-deepening crisis in the prison system (King and McDermott 1989) in brackets.

As can be seen from Table 7.2, the net effect of what seems to have
happened for the three prisons for which we can make reasonable
comparisons is that all have ended the period with an improved
staff:prisoner ratio, although this has largely been accounted for by
big increments in other, non-uniformed, staff. In Nottingham an
increase in the actual number of uniformed staff has been more than
offset by the loss of overtime hours but the reduction in the prison
population has nevertheless left them with substantially improved
staff:prisoner ratios across the board. In Featherstone the increase in
numbers of officers more than offset the relatively low levels of overtime that had been worked before Fresh Start, but an increase in the
numbers of prisoners effectively worsened the ratio with uniformed
staff. Indeed, Featherstone was the only prison to show substantial
problems with regard to TOIL in its staff-in-post returns, although
it may simply be that the other prisons did not fill in that section of
the form. Even so, the increase in other staff at Featherstone has been
sufficient to improve their overall staff:prisoner ratio, if more modestly than at Nottingham. Birmingham follows a similar pattern to
Nottingham with regard to uniformed officers except that the
smaller proportionate reduction in numbers of prisoners was not
enough to compensate for the reduction in full-time equivalent officers. However, a huge increase in other staff at Birmingham has
more than bridged the gap.

It would be idle to pretend that the foregoing amounts to a full-
blown economic analysis. It does not. Nevertheless, it does provide
food for thought. When other measures besides baseline CNA are
considered it is far from evident that the Prison Service operates at
lower cost now than in recent years. Nor is it evident that it deliv-
ers a service more efficiently than it did before, at least in terms of
staffing. Indeed, the probability is that staff have increased, although
the service may have made marginal proportionate savings in labour

Table 7.2. Staff:prisoner ratios in 1987 and 1992

	Date	ADP	Officers		Other Staff		All Staff	
			number	ratio	number	ratio	number	ratio
Nottingham	1987	295	142 (105)	2.08 (2.81)	70	4.21	212 (175)	1.39 (1.69)
Nottingham	1992	212	120	1.77	85.5	2.48	205.5	1.03
Featherstone	1987	512	151 (134)	3.39 (3.82)	104	4.92	255 (238)	2.01 (2.15)
Featherstone	1992	580	159	3.65	151	3.84	310	1.87
Birmingham	1987	1,091	549 (373)	1.99 (2.92)	122	8.94	671 (495)	1.63 (2.20)
Birmingham	1992	977	468	2.09	197	4.96	665	1.47

Notes: Numbers of staff for 1987 have been recalculated, allowing for average overtime, on the basis of full time equivalents at 39 hours per week. Figures in brackets are those previously published (King and McDermott 1989) costs through employing cheaper civilian labour and farming out some tasks and services to private contractors.

There have unquestionably been important improvements to the prisons estate. If we continue to reserve judgement about whether the vast programme of new building as distinct from the programme of refurbishment, was necessary, this is not to deny that many more prisoners are housed in more civilized circumstances of confinement than was the case a decade ago. There can be no doubt either that prison officers have better conditions in which to work, as well as more appropriate structures of pay and conditions of employment. Or that visitors to many prisons will find better facilities when they get there and may now have somewhere to leave the children while they visit. But these developments have been costly and not just in terms of capital expenditures. If our research prisons are any guide, operating costs continued to increase, and the ratios of staff to prisoners continued to grow, at least in the period until 1992.

However, the main questions which are raised by the research reported in this volume are not so much about economy and efficiency as about effectiveness—the extent to which the Service might realistically be said to approach or achieve its goals—and it is to these matters that we now turn.

Effectiveness

Most of our work was conducted against a backdrop of what became known as the statement of tasks and functions in Circular Instruction 55 of 1984. Our data showed that in important respects the service was moving further away from its goals rather than closer towards them. What for us constituted the 'ever-deepening crisis' of the prison system was the locking up of prisoners for longer hours in conditions of greater security than they needed, with more and more impoverished regimes: this seemed much more important than overcrowding or poor physical conditions as such. If the events at Strangeways in April 1990 represented a manifestation of that crisis to which the Woolf reforms in turn constituted a response, it has seemed important for us to try to update our work in an attempt to assess the extent to which the prison system has succeeded in turning itself around. Accordingly, we have organized our findings around the new statement of goals and performance indicators set out by the re-formed Prison Service Agency.

It may be necessary to acknowledge, and we readily do so, that we are here addressing only the publicly stated goals of the Prison Service. To the extent that it is possible to argue, for example, that it is a manifest goal, as distinct from a latent function, of the service to 'promise and deliver' 'deliberate and calibrated' 'state legitimated pain as punishment', as does Carlen (1994), we have not directly examined that. This is, in part, for want of an authoritative statement that such is the legitimated goal of the Service. It is also because in a general sense, although there will always be some people who look to increase the tariff or to bring back secondary punishments, there probably is not much room for doubt that prison, whatever else it does, has effectively proved itself as a distributor of pain—hence its survival. Nevertheless, in concentrating on the minutiae of certain aspects of prison performance it is important not to lose sight of the larger role which imprisonment can and does play, nor the processes which select some offenders but not others for incarceration, so that the unequal power struggles which are there played out often reflect social, economic, and power differentials in society at large. Tonry (1994), for example, has recently provided an impressive and sobering reminder of the even greater extent to which racial disproportion is to be found in British prisons than is the case in the United States.

Some writers, such as Sim (1994), have called into question the extent to which Woolf has restored legitimacy to he system. He has drawn attention, for example, to the incongruity of the social contract model within which prisoners' rights, expectations, and responsibilities were supposedly contained, given the realities of the distribution of power in prisons, or indeed in society. As one of us has observed elsewhere (King 1994b), it seems unlikely, even in a world conditioned to the anodyne platitudes of the Citizens' Charter, that the analogies sometimes drawn between prisoners and customers will ever be taken so far as to suggest that the customer is always right. However, most writers seem to have taken the view that Woolf undertook a sufficiently fundamental reconstruction of aims, policies, and procedures for the prison system to be re-legitimated, in a situation where its legitimacy could no longer be taken for granted. Thus Sparks (1994) has argued that the Woolf Report constituted a distinct conceptual development over previous official statements which merely regarded 'the maintenance of legitimate authority in prisons as *essentially* unproblematic, albeit *practically* difficult at times'. Indeed, the measure of how far Woolf went in these matters was the genuine surprise that most observers felt when the White Paper, *Custody, Care, and Justice*, actually adopted so much of his agenda, and thereby gave a green light to a service keen to embrace reform. Again, as Sparks noted, Joe Pilling's emphasis, in his Eve Saville Memorial Lecture, on resonant concepts like respect, fairness, individuality, care, and openness, did much to further the process of re-legitimating the work of the Prison Service.

Nevertheless, we would wish to suggest that there is a danger that the re-found legitimacy of the Prison Service could turn out to be largely programmatic or procedural rather than substantive. By this we mean that, with respect to many, if not all, of the expressed goals of the service, it is possible to point to programmes or procedures that are in place, the express objective of which is to contribute to the stated goals: but it is not at present possible to know whether, or how far, the programmes or procedures do actually contribute towards achieving those goals. In some cases this is because the key performance indicators, or other monitoring systems, measure whether or not programmes exist rather than whether or not they actually work. In others it is because the performance indicator, though it genuinely focuses on performance, is not adequate to the complexity of the task. In still others there is simply no attempt to measure performance at all. Unfortunately, there is also a danger that self-congratulation in the meeting of sometimes superficial annual targets could mean that a deeper testing of a more substantive legitimacy may simply not happen.

We stress that we are at present only pointing to possible dangers: but to the extent that our analysis is correct we should probably own up to some small share of the blame. In our 1989 Perrie Lecture we commented on the poverty of Prison Service management as 'operating without clear objectives and with short-sighted, contradictory, and self-defeating policies. Every closure of a workshop, every reduction in the working day, every additional restriction of activity has been authorized by prison governors, approved by regional directors and agreed by Prisons Board'. In order to prevent further decline and to provide some basis for ratcheting up performance in future we advocated the monitoring of performance in relation to properly specified standards. We did not anticipate the kind of 'management rampant' approach that has come to dominate not just the Prison Service but all our public (and former public) services during the

1990s. In the name of 'quality assurance' and other buzz words management becomes subverted from actually improving quality into a meticulous demonstration that it has ways of holding quality to account. We would entirely understand it if Prison Service managers now felt that they were 'damned if they do and damned if they don't'. If it is any consolation to them, those are feelings that are likely to be shared in the universities and elsewhere. Nevertheless, it is to be hoped that the pendulum may settle down, and the overemphasis on paper systems of accounting will soon give way to a real focus on the activities for which those systems are actually put in place.

We cannot categorically assign weights to the dangers we identify because without a major programme of further research it would not be possible to draw definitive conclusions on what is now happening on the ground. What we can try to do here is to draw out some inferences from our research with a view to assessing how far the service is likely to have been successful in turning things around. We do not seek to cover everything, indeed it would be tedious to attempt a recapitulation of all that has gone before. But it may be helpful if we go back through some of our findings to highlight the lessons as we see them to form a rather selective summary and conclusion. We do this in reverse order, and in the process we try also to indicate what kinds of information it will be necessary to have if we are to get behind the existing performance indicators to tackle the question of real effectiveness.

Sentence-Planning, Through-Care, and the Problem of Procedural Legitimacy

No clearer example of what we mean by the contentment with procedural legitimacy could be found than in relation to goal five, *helping prisoners prepare for their return to the community*. The key concept which ultimately targets this goal is through-care, involving the probation service and prison staff in a partnership, which by its very name makes plain that this should be a continuing process from the beginning of the sentence, not merely something tacked on at the end. Organizationally this is to be orchestrated through the process of sentence-planning. The procedures for sentence-planning are now in place for certain categories of offenders and are to be progressively extended to cover all who are in custody long enough to benefit. In some sense, then, sentence-planning exists. If questioned about the

legitimacy of this aspect of the activities of the service it will be possible for managers to point to those procedures and to the volumi-
nous documentation associated with them.

But what difference does it actually make to prisoners and their
families, for whom these procedures are designed? The real answer
is that we do not know, although we do know what was happening
just a short time ago. Nothing much. As we argued in Chapter 5, in
the face of the virtual absence of meaningful advice and counselling
received by any of our prisoners or their families at any vital stage
of their sentence, what is desperately needed is a commitment on the
part of probation and perhaps prison staff to sitting down regularly
with offenders and their families face-to-face to confront and work
through the consequences of offending behaviour for offenders, their
families, and their victims. Yet in the formal agreement drawn up for
the implementation of through-care there are no such provisions, nor
indeed anything pertaining to the *content* or *substance* of what has
to be done. Instead there is a catalogue of staff responsibilities setting out the *form* in which procedures are to be carried out and
recorded. If sentence-planning and through-care are not to degener-
ate, as similar and much smaller but well-meaning schemes have
degenerated in the past, into a system where staff are merely required
to make at least three entries into a file which is never looked at
again, let alone acted upon, then the allocation of more time and
resources will be essential. It would have been better to have got real
activities into place on the ground and then to have found ways of
recording them than to develop documentary systems which may
have little or nothing to record.

We are quite sure that everyone associated with the Prison Service
is perfectly well aware of the complexity of the task of organizing
through-care. We would be the first to acknowledge that developing
meaningful through-care along the lines we suggest would be costly.
Our point here is simply that being able to point to the existence of
a system offers no guarantee that it works or is effective. Time and
again, in the course of asking staff and prisoners to evaluate a service or a programme, we were impressed by how prisoners reached
their judgements by reference to some outcome or other whereas too
often staff seemed to reach theirs on the basis that if the service
existed it was probably a good thing. To some extent that may be
an understandable reaction from prison officers, but it would be
unpardonable if it were endorsed by those responsible for managing

the Prison Service. Viewed in that light, using the proportion of prisoners held in establishments where prisoners have the opportunity to exceed the minimum visiting entitlements as the key performance indicator for testing the success of the Service in helping prisoners to return to the community seems to us to be derisory.

That is not to say that improving the minimum visiting entitlements has not been important and welcome. However, since all establishments now meet the minimum entitlements, retaining this as the key target for 1994–5 does not provide the service with much to aim for when in fact there is a great deal to be done. By the same token it would be churlish in the extreme not to welcome the virtual abolition of censorship, the installation of card telephones in all establishments, the extension of the assisted visits scheme, the opening of more visitors' centres, and the establishment of many more pre-release courses as parts of a battery of measures, all of which can be expected to improve contact and thus contribute to an easing of the transition between prison and the community. We do not intend to discount their importance when we point to the fact that, once a service or facility is provided, it is inevitable that attention must then turn to questions about access and quality. In the course of our research, we noted that it was perfectly possible for a nominally existing pre-release course to be cancelled whenever staff were required elsewhere, and even when it did run for it to operate well below capacity. The recent issue of a new booklet gives important advice on the setting up and running of inmate development and pre-release courses and makes it plain that only the governing governor has authority to make the decision to cancel courses.[5] How he exercises that authority, however, will presumably still depend upon whether the staff are available.

Positive Regimes: Catching Up and the Problems of Involvement and Measurement

As we discussed in Chapter 5, it is important to recognize the fact that the Prison Service is now committed to providing positive regimes which address offending behaviour. It would be a pity if this

---

[5] We are grateful to Philippa Drew for drawing our attention to this booklet which sets out guidance on the content of such courses which cover communications, relationships, problem drinking, drugs, gambling, accommodation, money matters, practical information, work, and how to cope with having time on one's hands.

renewed concern with offending behaviour were to usher in either a full-blooded return to the treatment and training philosophies of the past or a determination to measure how far 'prison works' by reference to reconviction rates. But it is probably a victory for common sense, if nothing else, that somewhere in their prison experience prisoners might ask, or be asked, what in their own behaviour (apart from all the other contingencies, of course) might have led to their being there and what might be done about them.

Once again the main mechanism for focusing attention on these issues is sentence-planning, and we do not need to repeat what we have said above. However, there are two issues in relation to sentence-planning that do warrant further rehearsal here. The first is that it is a pity that the sentence-planning process in England and Wales appears to be much more top down than is the case in Scotland. This thus gives prisoners much less opportunity to become involved in the process and thereby to take some responsibility for their past, present, and future. That needs to be re-addressed. The second is that sentence-planning will stand or fall upon there being enough real programme choices sensibly available to prisoners in the prisons where they are likely to be. We made it plain that we did not accept the Inspectorate's view (Home Office 1993d) that somehow the prison system should be regime-led, although we do believe that everything should be done to provide as full a range of activities and programmes as quickly as possible on a community prison basis. Some modest progress seems to have been made in that regard, and perhaps for the first time in the history of the prison system in England and Wales there seems to be a serious attempt at providing sex offender, anger-management, and other programmes—though regrettably so far very little that pays attention to drug-taking. We accept that at present such programmes probably capture the time of rather few prisoners, but these are important features, and we find it puzzling that there appears to be no mechanism for including these activities in the performance indicators. They ought to be so included. There is a count of such programmes, at present, but that is not enough. There needs to be a full and systematic evaluation conducted by researchers who are independent of the programme-providers.

Elsewhere there is a commitment to providing prisoners with as full a life as possible in which they engage in purposeful activities. These are the subject of a performance indicator, based on regime-monitoring, but as we argued in Chapter 5 it is not so much a measure of purposeful activities as a measure of total activities. That is useful to some extent, but it would be pointless to be deluded into thinking that all activities provided in prisons are purposeful. In our experience that is manifestly not the case. We would strongly recommend that a measure of genuinely purposeful activities, based on a more limited range of regime-monitoring returns, also be used to assess performance in this area. We indicated what this might include in Chapter 5: workshops, VTCs, CITs, daytime and evening education, and physical education. There may be other possible items for inclusion, but we would not wish to see physical education excluded—however, reprehensible sporting activities might seem to Michael Howard—because of the relationship we were able to show between physical activity, time locked in cell, and prisoners' feelings of physical and emotional well being.

There are important methodological difficulties involved in regime-monitoring, to which we drew attention. Morgan (1992b) has suggested that one way of improving the methodology would be to give prisoners a role in reporting on the regimes they experience. Our data suggest that they would do this more reliably than managers might think. It would certainly involve them in taking a responsible approach to their situation in an innovative, and cost-effective, way.

In spite of, or perhaps because of, the methodological difficulties, and with a little bit of sleight of hand, the Prison Service was able to claim success in achieving one of its performance indicators on hours spent in 'purposeful' activities, but not the other, hours out-of-cell. The new levels of performance do seem to show that a halt has at last been called to the deterioration which we reported in 1989, and that the long climb back has begun. But in the euphoria of achieving, or nearly achieving, the targets set we cannot stress sufficiently that this level of performance remains significantly below what was achieved in the system a quarter of a century ago, when the *Prison Regimes Project* was being carried out. The new targets for 1994–5 of 25.5 hours of 'purposeful' activity and 36 per cent of prisoners in establishments where they can be out of cells for twelve hours will represent a further step towards what once was taken for granted. In case that sounds niggardly we should also recognize that there are now undoubtedly some prisons, of all types including perhaps some local prisons, which have genuinely high standards of performance.

Providing Decent Conditions: The Spectre Waits

There can be little doubt that the enormous investment in prisons has produced better conditions for a great many prisoners. It would be very surprising indeed if it had not. Whether or not such a costly programme was needed—and we expressed our doubts both in Chapter 4 and when we reviewed the prisons budget earlier in this chapter—there are important questions to be answered on how that investment will be used and how well it will be protected. Certainly Woolf LJ's hope that, once banished, overcrowding would not return was dashed when the government made clear that it would not proceed with new rules to limit the population in establishments to CNA. The census of accommodation has yielded not merely a revised CNA but a new figure of operational capacity, which seems to be the official view of acceptable overcrowding. Moreover, the published operating standards failed to deliver a basic space standard for prisoners, except in new and refurbished accommodation, and stepped back from the commitments to require social dining and to allow prisoners to wear their own clothes.

Overcrowding, after the briefest possible respite, is back. All the signs are that the government will allow it to continue. One initial consequence has been the failure to meet the advanced date for providing access to sanitation, although the fact that over 90 per cent of prisoners now have such access compared to only 50 per cent in 1989 is an impressive achievement by any standards. But overcrowding diverts attention from other targets. Unfortunately, the tactical management of the prison population, and the doubt about whether it is better to keep prisoners in police cells rather than shuttle them around the system and risk disruptions such as occurred at Wymott, is a prospect the Prison Service could well do without. It has other much more important things to do. But this is the spectre that looms over the service and will continue to do so unless there is a change of regime at the Home Office which allows more rational counsel to prevail on criminal justice policy.

Security, Safety, and Control: The Depth and Weight of Imprisonment

To a remarkable degree the determination of a prisoner's security categorization also determines the nature of his experiences in prison. From the point of view of prisoners at least, a great many of the findings throughout this study followed what we have called the security gradient. That is to say most situations were rated more favourably the lower the security category of the prison. It was for that reason that King and Morgan (1980) argued for their minimum use of security principle and the reduction of the size of the dispersal system or its replacement with an alternative policy of concentration for high-security-risk prisoners. We would continue to advocate that today, and indeed there have been some modest, but nevertheless welcome, reductions in the size of the dispersal system which have involved the redesignation of Gartree as a category B training prison. There has also been something of a shift towards the greater use of category C across the system as a whole following the advice of the Control Review Committee. We look forward, however tentatively, to further reductions in the security emphasis as and when the peace process gathers momentum following the Downing Street Declaration on Northern Ireland.

However, not everything followed the security gradient. As the study of Oak Park Heights showed, it was perfectly possible to operate deep-end custody and yet provide much higher degrees of safety for staff and prisoners whilst allowing prisoners longer time out of cells and greater involvement in purposeful activities than ever was achieved in Gartree or even for that matter in Featherstone. In a number of intriguing ways we found that the positions of Nottingham and Featherstone were reversed from what might have been predicted in security terms. This led us to draw a distinction between what we called the depth and weight of imprisonment in a development of Downes' (1988) formulation, allowing us to argue that, although Nottingham prisoners were 'deeper in' the system than their counterparts in Featherstone, they were nevertheless borne down to a lesser degree as a result of such matters as education, training, meals, and the canteen.

That reversal certainly did not apply in regard to matters of safety, or the concerns that prisoners had for their physical and emotional well-being. The level of fear of abuse by other prisoners and by staff, and the proportions of prisoners who claimed to have been victimized, were much higher in the higher-security prisons. We appear also to have uncovered higher levels of abuse than have so far been reported in the national prison survey. These matters are, however, very complicated to sort out. The Prison Service operates with a key performance indicator which requires it to reverse the rising numbers of assaults on both staff and prisoners. We suspect the Prison Service has set itself here a meaningless as well as an impossible task—like expecting the police to stop the tide of rising crime outside. In 1993–4 the numbers of assaults continued to rise—by 21 per cent expressed as a proportion of the population compared with the previous year. The Prison Service is aware that what is defined and acted on as an assault varies from prison to prison, and even recognizes that the apparent increase in assaults may paradoxically be a product of a greater determination to take action in cases of bullying. The Prison Service is committed to examining the reasons for the increase in assaults. One possibility it might explore is that prisoners may be exposed for a greater length of time, both to the risk and the temptation, as a result of more hours out of cells.

It would be a pity, in our view, if the over-zealous implementation of the recommendations in Sir John Woodcock's Report following the events at Whitemoor were to lead to an increase in the weight of imprisonment at the deepest end of the security system through the imposition of more rigorous, but usually pointless, searches of cells and visitors. It would be ironic if such measures were introduced largely for a population of Irish terrorists who were destined to disappear from the system.

Some Concluding Remarks

We cannot end without drawing together some other threads from the discussions we began in Chapter 1—in particular by commenting upon the drive towards contracting-out, and upon the impact of the first year of agency status, especially in regard to the extent to which the policies adumbrated by Michael Howard constitute a retreat from the Woolf agenda.

Contracting Out

Much of the public debate surrounding contracting out has been about issues of principle, although it has not always been well-informed. To judge from some discussions one could be forgiven for thinking that private companies were competing directly with the Prison Service in offering their services to the courts. Privatization of that kind has not yet been proposed for the United Kingdom. It is also ironic that, after more than two decades of trying to hold the state accountable for the deteriorating standards over which it has presided, the whiff of a profit motive has triggered a response which at times comes close to suggesting that the state is the only true defender of prisoners' rights. Nevertheless, there are many issues at a practical level which are also of genuine concern, but which so far have received too little attention. This is hardly the place for a detailed review, but the issues include the longer-term suitability of contracts as a means of delivering public services, the impact which the contracted-out institutions or services may have upon the integrity of the rest of the system, the extent to which contracted-out services could or should generate change or be expected to adapt to new conditions, and so on. Some of these issues have already begun to surface, the most celebrated being the problems arising from the Transfer of Undertakings (Protection of Employment) Regulations, known as TUPE, based on the European Community Acquired Rights Directive, to which we have referred in our discussion of prison education.

The 1994 Criminal Justice and Public Order Bill, now enacted, carefully sought to negotiate a way round unforeseen obstacles in this uncharted terrain—for example, giving private prison custody officers powers to search prisoners at magistrates' courts, as distinct from Crown Courts where they already have such powers, and to lay disciplinary charges (clauses 70 and 71); to permit the transfer of public sector prisons to private sector contractors on a gradual basis (clause 72); and to enable public sector prison staff and contracted-out prison staff to assist one another in emergencies (clauses 73 and 75). Nevertheless, we suppose that contracting-out is here to stay and, whether one likes it or not, it has certainly had an impact upon the system as we know it.

Agency Status

In the Prison Service *Briefing* which encouraged a wide-ranging debate on the question of agency status, its potential advantages were seen to be a stronger sense of corporate identity and the scope for more visible leadership from the Director General. But in a prophetic conclusion the key question was identified as 'how far, in practice, the Home Secretary would be able to stand back from the day-to-day business of the Service—given the strong Parliamentary interest in prisons and prisoners' (Prison Service 1989, 4).

How far any given Home Secretary would be able to stand back depends partly on politics and partly on personalities. It is inconceivable that Douglas Hurd or William Whitelaw, given their more serious and intellectually coherent criminal justice programmes, would have made the politically opportunist interventions so enthusiastically pursued by Michael Howard. When David Waddington memorably said that 'prison is an expensive way of making bad people worse' he confessed he was simply moving with the tide of informed and judicial opinion. Certainly Kenneth Clarke had no compunction in reversing some provisions of the Criminal Justice Act 1991 when it became clear that political supporters were the ones most at risk from the heavier financial penalties involved in unit fines (Ashworth 1993). Kenneth Clarke, of course, had set up the Prison Service Agency, and Derek Lewis was his choice for Director General, appointed in spite of the service's preference for the incumbent, Joe Pilling. It seems likely that, had he remained at the Home Office, Clarke would have been content to let well enough alone. But with Clarke's move to the Treasury and Howard's elevation to the Home Office the situation changed dramatically. With a cynical and wilful disregard of evidence and reasoned advice Howard has embarked on policies which promise to have more far reaching consequences as those of Leon Brittan a decade earlier. As one leading prison reformer has wryly observed, the irony is that during the first year of agency status the minister has exercised more direct control over what goes on in prisons than was ever the case when the Prison Department was part of the Home Office.[6]

There may yet be room for doubt about how far these policies constitute a full-blooded retreat from the Woolf agenda, or indeed how effective such a retreat would be. It may actually be quite hard for Michael Howard to go as far down the road as he might prefer when so much has already been argued so eloquently in *Custody, Care, and Justice* and enshrined in *Corporate* and *Business Plans* as goals and targets. To be sure there have been some significant changes. When it came to the question of appointing the ombudsman, Sir Peter Woodhead was not the professionals choice. His qualifications for the role do not, at first sight, inspire confidence. However, it should not be forgotten that much the same was said during the 1960s about Lord Mountbatten, although in the event the Admiral of the Fleet made a much better fist of analyzing the security problems of the Prison Service than did Radzinowicz, and there

---

[6] Stephen Shaw in conversation.

are already signs that Woodhead has won over many of his critics. There have also been some unfortunate changes to the published version of what are now called *operating standards*. However, anyone who attended the London seminar on standards in 1992 would have as many grounds for satisfaction that the operating standards have gone as far as they have as for disappointment that they did not go so far as they might.

Certainly the Home Secretary, backed by the Prime Minister (*Guardian*, 14 and 18 October 1993), has not shrunk from taking on Woolf LJ and other judges (*Observer*, 17 October 1993) in pursuit of his thesis, elaborated at the 1993 Conservative Party Conference on 6 October 1993, that 'prison works' and his belief that the size of the prison population should no longer be the test of the success of prison policy. When Woolf addressed the New Assembly of Churches on 12 October 1993 he made it plain that he saw his programme of reforms at risk, though this seemed more likely to result from talking up the prison population than from a frontal assault on policies and procedures. After all officials were usually adept at muting the impact of changes of which they did not approve. That was before the changes to home leave, the implementation of the Woodcock recommendations, and the introduction of compulsory drug testing.

It is impossible for us to conclude without recording a profound sense of *déjà vu*. The prisons are overcrowded. The service has been rocked by attempted escapes not just by dispersal prisoners from Parkhurst but by IRA terrorists from the SSU at Whitemoor. On Tuesday 31 January 1995—Fresh Start, privatization and the provisions of the Criminal Justice and Public Order Act banning industrial action notwithstanding—the POA has called simultaneous branch meetings in every prison to protest the contrast between their pay rise of 1.9 per cent and Derek Lewis's bonus of £35,000. So what else is new?

What is new is the extent to which the Prison Service has become a political plaything. The last word should fittingly reside with Woolf LJ: in the House of Lords on 25 January 1995 he criticized the knee-jerk reactions of ministers 'which are putting in jeopardy the reforms which have been made and could be made', and he argued that what is required is 'not more ministerial interference—but less'.

Appendix 1

Circular Instruction 55 of 1984: Tasks and Functions

Prisons Board Statement of the Task of the Prison Service

The task of the Prison Service is to use with maximum efficiency the resources of staff, money, buildings, and plant made available to it by Parliament in order to fulfil in accordance with the relevant provisions of the law, the following functions:

1. to keep in custody untried or unsentenced prisoners, and to present them to court for trial or sentence;

2. to keep in custody, with such degree of security as is appropriate, having regard to the nature of the individual prisoner and his offence, sentenced prisoners for the duration of their sentence or for such shorter time as the Secretary of State may determine in cases where he has discretion;

3. to provide for prisoners as full a life as is consistent with the facts of custody, in particular making available the physical necessities of life; care for their physical and mental health; advice and help with personal problems; work, education, training, physical exercise, and recreation; and opportunity to practise their religion; and

4. to enable prisoners to retain links with the community and where possible assist them to prepare for their return to it.

Prisons Board Statement of the Functions of Prison Department Establishments

Custody of Unsentenced Prisoners

1. To receive and keep in custody prisoners awaiting trial or sentence, civil prisoners, and any other person lawfully committed to custody.

2. To release such prisoners from custody on the directions of the court or other lawful authority or when the conditions of bail have been met.

The Court Commitment

3. To ensure that prisoners are produced at court as required.

4. To provide the requisite reports and documentation.

5. To provide staff required at the Crown Court and Court of Appeal (Criminal Division) and keep prisoners there in custody.

Custody of Sentenced Prisoners

6. To receive sentenced prisoners and keep them in custody.

7. To calculate and implement release dates.

8. To assess prisoners for the purpose of determining or recommending (a) an appropriate level of security and (b) an appropriate allocation.

9. To keep each prisoner's security category and allocation under regular review. In the case of life-sentence prisoners, to maintain regular formal Review Board procedures.

10. To give effect to the provisions relating to parole and release on life sentence.

Security, Safety, and Control

11. To maintain a level of security appropriate to the prisoners who are or may be held at the establishment.

12. To maintain good order in the interests of the operation of the prison, and take such steps as are necessary for the safety of its staff and inmates.

Services and Facilities for Prisoners

13. To provide in accordance with the statutory provisions and Departmental instructions: (a) accommodation, (b) meals, (c) facilities for personal hygiene and sanitation, (d) clothing, (e) opportunities for exercise, and (f) access to privileges.

14. To provide a service for the diagnosis, treatment, and prevention of physical and mental disorders and the promotion of health.

15. To provide help and advice with personal problems.

16. To enable prisoners to practise their religion.

17. To provide, with a view to occupying prisoners as fully as possible throughout the whole week, a balanced and integrated regime, which may include work, education, physical education, access to libraries, and individual and collective leisure activities.

18. To enable prisoners to spend the maximum possible time out of their cells.

Community Links and Preparation for Release

19. To enable prisoners to maintain contact with the outside world and in particular to communicate with their families, friends, and legal representatives.

20. To operate the home leave scheme.

21. To assist prisoners to prepare for release, which may include (a) providing such opportunities as are practicable for them to go out into the community on temporary release, (b) providing pre-release courses, and (c) putting prisoners in touch with the probation service and other external agencies.

22. To make arrangements as required for prisoners' after-care.

Appendix 2

Publications Arising From The Research Programmes

Dangerous Prisoners in Maximum Security Confinement in the USA

KING, ROY D. (1986), *Dangerous Prisoners in Maximum Security Confinement in the United States*, End of Award Report on Research Grant E00232030, British Library Document Supply Centre.
—— (1987), 'New Generation Prisons, the Prison Building Programme and the Future of the Dispersal System' in A. E. Bottoms and R. Light (eds.), *Problems of Long-Term Imprisonment*, Aldershot: Gower.
—— (1991a), 'Maximum Security Custody in Britain and the USA: A Study of Gartree and Oak Park Heights', *British Journal of Criminology*, 31/2: 126–52.

Security, Control and Humane Containment in the UK Prison System

BORLAND, J., KING, ROY D., and McDERMOTT K., 'The Irish in Prison: A Tighter Nick for the "Micks" ', *British Journal of Sociology*, 46/3, 371–94.
KING, ROY D. (1989), *Security, Control and Humane Containment*, End of Award Report on ESRC Research Grant YE06250020: British Library Document Supply Centre.
—— (1994b), 'Order, Disorder and Regimes in the Prison Services of Scotland, and England and Wales', in E. Player and M. Jenkins (eds.), *Prisons After Woolf: Reform through Riot*, London and New York: Routledge.
—— and McDERMOTT, K. (1989), 'British Prisons 1970–87: The Ever-deepening Crisis', *British Journal of Criminology*, 29/2: 107–28.
—— and —— (1990a), ' "My Geranium is Subversive": Notes on the Management of Trouble in Prisons', *British Journal of Sociology*, 41/4: 445–71.
—— and —— (1990b), 'As Full a Life' (Perrie Lecture 1989), *Prison Service Journal*, 77/Winter: 30–40.
—— and —— (1991), 'A Fresh Start: Managing the Prison Service' in R. Reiner and M. Cross (eds.), *Beyond Law and Order: Criminal Justice Policy and Politics into the 1990s*, London: Macmillan.

—— and —— (1992), 'Security, Control, and Humane Containment in the Prison System in England and Wales' in D. Downes (ed.), *Unravelling Criminal Justice*, London: Macmillan.

McDermott, K. (1990), 'We have no Problem: The Experience of Racism in Prison', *New Community*, 16/2: 213–28.

—— and King, Roy D. (1988), 'Mind Games: Where the Action is in Prisons', *British Journal of Criminology*, 28,3, 357–77.

—— and —— (1989), 'A Fresh Start: the Enhancement of Prison Regimes', *Howard Journal*, 28,3, 161–76.

Coping with Custody: Survival Strategies of Prisoners and their Families

King, Roy D., and McDermott, K. (1993), *Coping with Custody: A Study of Survival Strategies of Prisoners' Families*: End of Award Report on ESRC Research Grant R000231401: British Library Document Supply Centre.

McDermott, K., and King, Roy D. (1992), 'Prison Rule 102: "Stand by your Man": The Impact of Penal Policy on Families of Prisoners' in R. Shaw (ed.), *Prisoner's Children: What are the Issues?*, London and New York: Routledge.

Bibliography

ACPS (1968), *The Regime for Long-term Prisoners in Conditions of Maximum Security*, Report of the Advisory Council on the Penal System (Radzinowicz Report), London: HMSO.

ACTO (1961), *Work for Prisoners*, Report of the Advisory Council on the Treatment of Offenders on the Employment of Prisoners, London: HMSO.

—— (1964), *Organisation of Work for Prisoners*, Report of the Advisory Council on the Treatment of Offenders on the Employment of Prisoners, London: HMSO.

ADAM SMITH INSTITUTE (1984), *The Omega Justice Report*, London: Adam Smith Institute.

ADLER, J. (1994), *Fear in Prisons: A Discussion Paper*, London: Prison Reform Trust.

AMERICAN FRIENDS SERVICE COMMITTEE (1971), *Struggle for Justice: a Report on Crime and Punishment in America*, New York: Hill and Wang.

ASHWORTH, A. (1993), 'Sentencing by numbers', *Criminal Justice Matter*, 14/Winter 1993/4: 6–7.

BORLAND, J., KING, ROY D. and McDERMOTT, K. (1995), 'The Irish in Prison: A Tighter Nick for the "Micks" ', *British Journal of Sociology* 46/3, 371–94.

BOTTOMLEY, K., and HAY, W. (eds.) (1991), *Special Units for Difficult Prisoners*, papers presented at a Conference at the University of York, 2–3 April, 1990, Hull: Centre for Criminology and Criminal Justice.

BOTTOMS, A. E. (1977), 'Reflections on the Renaissance of Dangerousness', *Howard Journal*, 70–96.

—— (1990), 'The Aims of Imprisonment' in *Justice, Guilt and Forgiveness in the Penal System*, Edinburgh University Centre for Theology and Public Issues, Paper No. 18.

BOWKER, L. H. (1980), *Prison Victimization*, New York: Elsevier.

—— (1982), 'Victimizers and Victims in American Correctional Institutions' in H. Toch and R. Johnson (eds.), *The Pains of Imprisonment*, Beverley Hills and London: Sage.

BRODY, S. R. (1976), *The Effectiveness of Sentencing*, Home Office Research Study, no. 35, London: HMSO.

BROWN, A. (1994), 'Sex Offender Programme: A Suitable Case for Treatment', *Prison Report*, 26 spring 1994, 4–5, London: Prison Reform Trust.

CANTER, D. and AMBROSE, I. (1980), *Prison Design and Use Study*, Guildford: University of Surrey.

CARLEN, P. (1994), 'Why Study Women's Imprisonment? Or Anyone Else's?' in Roy King and Mike Maguire (eds.), *Prisons in Context*, Oxford: Oxford University Press.

CARLISLE, LORD (1988), *The Parole System in England and Wales* (The Carlisle Report) Cm 532, London: HMSO.

CASALE, S. (1984), *Minimum Standards for Prison Establishments*, London: NACRO.

—— (1985), 'A Practical Design for Standards' in M. Maguire, J. Vagg and R. Morgan (eds.), *Accountability and Prisons: Opening up a Closed World*, London and New York: Tavistock.

—— (1994), 'Conditions and Standards' in E. Player and M. Jenkins (eds.), *Prisons after Woolf: Reform through Riot*, London and New York: Routledge.

—— and PLOTNIKOFF, J. (1989), *Minimum Standards in Prisons: A Programme for Change*, London: NACRO.

CSO (1981), *National Income and Expenditure*, 1981 Edition, Central Statistical Office, London: HMSO.

CSO (1993), *United Kingdom National Accounts*, The CSO Blue Book 1993 Edition, Central Statistical Office, London: HMSO.

CHAPLIN, B. (1982), 'Accountable Regimes: Where Next?', *Prison Service Journal*, October, 3–5.

COGGAN, G., and WALKER, M. (1982), *Frightened for my Life: An Account of Deaths in British Prisons*, Glasgow: Fontana.

COUNCIL OF EUROPE (1973), *Standard Minimum Rules for the Treatment of Prisoners*, Committee of Ministers, Resolution 73/5, Strasbourg: Council of Europe.

—— (1987), *European Prison Rules*, Directorate of Legal Affairs, Committee on Crime Problems, February, Strasbourg: Council of Europe.

—— (1991a), *Report to the United Kingdom Government on the Visit to the United Kingdom carried out by the European Committee for the Prevention of Torture and Inhuman or Degrading Treatment or Punishment from 29 July 1990 to 10 August 1990*, Strasbourg: Council of Europe.

—— (1991b), *Response of the United Kingdom Government to the Report of the European Committee for the Prevention of Torture and Inhuman or Degrading Treatment or Punishment on its Visit to the United Kingdom from 29 July to 10 August 1990*, Strasbourg: Council of Europe.

DANTE, A. (1307), *Divine Comedy, Inferno, III*.

DITCHFIELD, J. (1990), *Control in Prisons: A Review of the Literature*, Home Office Research Study No. 118, London: HMSO.

DOWNES, D. (1988), *Contrasts in Tolerance: Post-war Penal Policy in the Netherlands and England and Wales*, Oxford: Clarendon Press.

DUNBAR, I. (1985), *A Sense of Direction*, London: Prison Department.

DUNBAR, I. (1989), *Report to the Secretary of State of the Inquiries into a Major Disturbance at HM Remand Centre, Risley, 30 April to 3 May 1989 and the Circumstances Surrounding the Disturbance—Summary*, London: Prison Department.

EVANS, R. (1987), 'Management, Performance and Information', *Prison Service Journal*, April, 9–12.

FITZGERALD, M., and SIM, J. (1980), 'Legitimating the Prison Crisis: A Critical Review of the May Report', *Howard Journal*, 19/2: 73–84.

GENDERS, E., and PLAYER, E. (1987), 'Women in Prison: The Treatment, the Control and the Experience' in P. Carlen and A. Worrall (eds.), *Gender, Crime and Justice*, Milton Keynes: Open University Press.

GUNN, J., MADEN, T., and SWINTON, M. (1991), *Mentally Disordered Offenders*, London: HMSO.

GUNN, J., ROBERTSON, G., DELL, S., and WAY, C. (1978), *Psychiatric Aspects of Imprisonment*, London: Academic Press.

HADFIELD, R., and LAKES, G. (1991), *Summary Report of an Audit of Custody Arrangements for Category A Prisoners and of an Inquiry into DOC 1 Division*, Home Office, HM Prison Service.

HOLBORN, J. (1975), *Casework with Short-term Prisoners*, Home Office Research Study 28, London: HMSO.

HOME AFFAIRS COMMITTEE (1987), *Contract Provision of Prisons, Fourth Report of the Home Affairs Committee*, HC 291, Report of the House of Commons Home Affairs Committee, London: HMSO.

HOME OFFICE (1959), *Penal Practice in a Changing Society*, Cmnd 645, London: HMSO.

—— (1966), *Report of the Inquiry into Prison Escapes and Security* (Mountbatten Report), Cmnd 3175, London: HMSO.

—— (1969), *People in Prison*, Cmnd 4214, London: HMSO.

—— (1977), *Prisons and the Prisoner*, London: HMSO.

—— (1979a), *Report of the Committee of Inquiry into the United Kingdom Prison Services* (The May Report), Cmnd 7673, London: HMSO.

—— (1979b), *Inquiry into the United Kingdom Prison Services*, i, Evidence by the Home Office, the Scottish Home and Health Department and the Northern Ireland Office, London: HMSO.

—— (1979c), *Inquiry into the United Kingdom Prison Services*, ii, Evidence by the Home Office, the Scottish Home and Health Department, and the Northern Ireland Office, Discussion Paper No. 13, 'The dispersal system: England and Wales', London: HMSO.

—— (1979d), *Inquiry into the United Kingdom Prison Services*, iii, Evidence by HM Treasury, the Civil Service Department, and the Central Policy Review Staff, London: HMSO.

—— (1982), *HM Prison Birmingham*, Report by Her Majesty's Chief Inspector of Prisons, London: Home Office.

—— (1984a), *Managing the Long-Term Prison System: the Report of the Control Review Committee*, London: HMSO.

—— (1984b), *Report on Prison Categorisation Procedures by HM Chief Inspector of Prisons*, London: Home Office.

—— (1984c), 'The Prison Disciplinary System: A Descriptive Memorandum': evidence to the Committee on the Prison Disciplinary System, London: Home Office.

—— (1985a), *New Directions in Prison Design: Report of a Home Office Working Party on American New Generation Prisons* (Platt Report), London: Home Office.

—— (1985b), *Report of the Committee on the Prison Disciplinary System* (Prior Report), Cmnd 9641-1, London: HMSO.

—— (1986), *The Preparation of Prisoners for Release*, Report by HM Chief Inspector of Prisons, London: Home Office.

—— (1987a), *Report of an Inquiry by HM Chief Inspector of Prisons for England and Wales into the Disturbances in Prison Service Establishments in England between 29 April–2 May 1986*, London: HMSO.

—— (1987b), *A Review of Prisoners' Complaints*, a Report by HM Chief Inspector of Prisons, London: HMSO.

—— (1987c), *Report on the Work of the Prison Service 1986/87*, Cm 246, London: HMSO.

—— (1987d), *Special Units for Long-Term Prisoners: Regimes, Management and Research*, A Report by the Research and Advisory Group on the Long-Term Prison System, London: HMSO.

—— (1989a), *Prison Sanitation: Proposals for the Ending of Slopping Out*, Report by HM Chief Inspector of Prisons, London: HMSO.

—— (1989b), *Report on the Work of the Prison Service, April 1988–March 1989*, Cm 835, London: HMSO.

—— (1989c), *Report on HM Prison Featherstone by HM Chief Inspector of Prisons*, London: Home Office.

—— (1990a), *Report on HM Prison Manchester by HM Chief Inspector of Prisons*, London: Home Office.

—— (1990b), *Report on HM Prison Birmingham by HM Chief Inspector of Prisons*, London: Home Office.

—— (1990c), *Report on HM Prison Gartree by HM Chief Inspector of Prisons*, London: HMSO.

—— (1990d), *Report on an Efficiency Scrutiny of the Prison Medical Service*, London: Home Office.

—— (1991a), *Prison Disturbances April 1990*, Report of an Inquiry by the Rt. Hon. Lord Justice Woolf (Parts I and II) and His Honour Judge Stephen Tumim (Part II), Cm. 1456, February, 1991, London: HMSO.

—— (1991b), *Custody, Care and Justice: The Way Ahead for the Prison Service in England and Wales*, Cm 1647, London: HMSO.

HOME OFFICE (1991c), *Tender Documents for the Operating Contract of Wolds Remand Prison*, London: Home Office.

—— (1991d), *Inquiry by HM Chief Inspector of Prisons into the Escape of Two Category A Prisoners from HM Prison Brixton on 7 July 1991*, Home Office, 5 August 1991.

—— (1992a), *Report on the Work of the Prison Service, April 1991–March 1992*, Cm 2087, London: HMSO.

—— (1992b), *HM Prison Featherstone, Report of an Unannounced Short Inspection by HM Inspectorate of Prisons*, London: Home Office.

—— (1992c), *HM Prison Birmingham, Report of an Unannounced Short Inspection by HM Inspectorate of Prisons*, London: Home Office.

—— (1992d), *Regimes*, Home Office, HM Prison Service.

—— (1992e), *Model Regime for Local Prisons and Remand Centres*, Home Office, HM Prison Service.

—— (1993a), *Report of an Inquiry by Her Majesty's Chief Inspector of Prisons for England and Wales into the Disturbance at HM Prison Wymott on 6 September 1993*, Cm 2371, London: HMSO.

—— (1993b), *HM Prison Nottingham, Report of an Unannounced Short Inspection by HM Inspectorate of Prisons*, London: Home Office.

—— (1993c), *HM Prison Ashwell, Report by HM Chief Inspector of Prisons*, London: Home Office.

—— (1993d), *Doing Time or Using Time*, Report of a Review by Her Majesty's Chief Inspector of Prisons for England and Wales of Regimes in Prison Service Establishments in England and Wales, Cm 2128, London: HMSO.

—— (1993e), *HM Prison Gartree, Report of an Unannounced Short Inspection by HM Inspectorate of Prisons*, London: Home Office.

—— (1993f), *Wolds Remand Prison, Report by HM Chief Inspector of Prisons*, London: Home Office.

HOUSE OF COMMONS EXPENDITURE COMMITTEE (1978), *The Reduction of Pressure on the Prison System*, Fifteenth Report of the Expenditure Committee, London: HMSO.

IRWIN, J. (1970), *The Felon*, Englewood Cliffs: Prentice Hall.

JACOBS, J. B. (1974), 'Street Gangs behind Bars', *Social Problems*, 21/3: 395–409.

JEPSON, N., and ELLIOTT, K. (1984), *Shared Working Between Prison and Probation Officers*, Report of the Working Group on the Review of the Role of the Probation Service in Adult Penal Establishments, Directorate of Regimes and Services Management Unit, London: Home Office.

JUSTICE (1983), *Justice in Prison*, London: Justice.

KANE, T., and SAYLOR, W. (1982), 'Security Designation System: Validation Study, Report to the Federal Prison System's Executive Staff', mimeograph.

KAUFFMAN, K. (1988), *Prison Officers and Their World*, Cambridge, Mass., and London: Harvard University Press.

KING, ROY D. (1972), *An Analysis of Prison Regimes*, Report to the Home Office, University of Southampton, unpublished.

—— (1979), *Dangerous Prisoners: Dispersal or Concentration*, Evidence to the May Committee, University of Southampton.

—— (1984), *Proposal for Research into Security, Control and Humane Containment in the Prison Service of England and Wales*, unpublished application to ESRC, Bangor: University of Wales.

—— (1985), 'Control in Prisons' in M. Maguire, J. Vagg and R. Morgan (eds.), *Accountability and Prisons: Opening up a Closed World*, London and New York: Tavistock Publications.

—— (1987), 'New Generation Prisons, the Prison Building Programme and the Future of the Dispersal System' in A. E. Bottoms and R. Light (eds.), *Problems of Long-Term Imprisonment*, Aldershot: Gower.

—— (1991a), 'Maximum Security Custody in Britain and the USA: A Study of Gartree and Oak Park Heights', *British Journal of Criminology*, 31/2: 126–52.

—— (1991b), 'The Woolf Report: An Agenda for Action', paper given to the Prison Reform Trust Conference, 18 July 1991, London.

—— (1994a), 'Russian Prisons after Perestroika: End of the Gulag?', *British Journal of Criminology*, 34, Special Issue.

—— (1994b), 'Order, Disorder and Regimes in the Prison Services of Scotland, and England and Wales' in E. Player and M. Jenkins (eds.), *Prisons after Woolf: Reform through Riot*, London and New York: Routledge.

—— (1994c) 'Breaking Down the Bars', *Guardian, Society*, 12 October 1994.

—— and ELLIOTT, K. W. (1978), *Albany: Birth of a Prison—End of an Era*, London: Routledge and Kegan Paul.

—— and MAGUIRE, M. (eds.) (1994), *Prisons in Context*, Oxford: Oxford University Press.

—— and McDERMOTT, K. (1989), 'British Prisons 1970–87: The Ever-deepening Crisis', *British Journal of Criminology*, 29/2: 107–28.

—— and —— (1990a), ' "My Geranium is Subversive": Notes on the Management of Trouble in Prisons', *British Journal of Sociology*, 41/4: 445–71.

—— and —— (1990b), 'As full a life' (Perrie Lecture 1989), *Prison Service Journal*, 77, Winter, 30–40.

—— and —— (1991), 'A Fresh Start: Managing the Prison Service', in R. Reiner and M. Cross (eds.), *Beyond Law and Order: Criminal Justice Policy and Politics into the 1990s*, London: Macmillan.

—— and —— (1993), *Coping with Custody: A Study of Survival Strategies of Prisoners' Families*, End of Award Report on ESRC Research Grant 000231401: British Library Document Supply centre.

KING, ROY D. and MORGAN, R. (1976) *A Taste of Prison: Custodial Conditions for Trial and Remand Prisoners*, London: Routledge and Kegan Paul.

—— and —— (1979), *Crisis in the Prison System*, evidence to the May Committee, University of Southampton.

—— and —— (1980), *The Future of the Prison System*, Farnborough: Gower.

LANE, LORD (1993), *Report of the Committee on the Penalty for Homicide* (The Lane Report), London: Prison Reform Trust.

LEE, B. (1983), 'On Standing Up and Being Counted', *The Lancet*, 4 June.

LEVINSON, R. B. (1980), 'Security Designation System: Preliminary Results', *Federal Probation*, September 1980, 26–30.

—— (1982a), 'The Federal Prison System's Security Designation/Custody Classification Approach' in L. Rans (ed.), *Classification as a Management Tool*, Baltimore: American Correctional Association.

—— (1982b), 'A Clarification of Classification', *Criminal Justice and Behaviour*, 9/2, June.

—— and WILLIAMS, J. D. (1979), 'Inmate Classification: Security/Custody Considerations', *Federal Probation*, March 1979, 37–43.

LIEBLING, A. (1992), *Suicides in Prison*, London: Routledge.

LIPTON, D., MARTINSON, R. and WILKS, J. (1975), *The Effectiveness of Correctional Treatment*, New York: Praeger.

LILLY, J. R., and KNEPPER, P. (1992), 'An International Perspective on the Privatisation of Corrections', *Howard Journal*, 31/3: 174–91.

LIVINGSTONE, S. (1994), 'The Changing Face of Prison Discipline' in E. Player and M. Jenkins (eds.), *Prisons after Woolf: Reform through Riot*, London: Routledge.

LLOYD, C. (1990), *Suicide and Self-Injury in Prison: a Literature Review*, Home Office Research Study 115, London: HMSO.

LOGAN, C. H. (1990), *Private Prisons: Cons and Pros*, New York: Oxford University Press.

McCONVILLE, S., and WILLIAMS, J. E. H. (1985), *Crime and Punishment: a Radical Rethink*, London: Tawney Society.

McDERMOTT, K. (1990), 'We Have No Problem: The Experience of Racism in Prison', *New Community*, 16/2: 213–28.

—— and KING, ROY D. (1988), 'Mind Games: Where the Action is in Prisons', *British Journal of Criminology*, 28/3: 357–77.

—— and —— (1989), 'A Fresh Start: the Enhancement of Prison Regimes', *Howard Journal*, 28/3: 161–76.

—— and —— (1992), 'Prison Rule 102: "Stand by your Man": The Impact of Penal Policy on Families of Prisoners' in Shaw (ed.), *Prisoner's Children: What are the Issues?* London and New York: Routledge.

McDONALD, D. C. (1994), 'Public Imprisonment by Private Means: The Re-emergence of Private Prisons and Jails in the United States, the United

Kingdom, and Australia' in R. D. King and M. Maguire (eds.), *Prisons in Context*, Oxford: Oxford University Press.

MAGUIRE, M., VAGG, J., and MORGAN, R. (eds.) (1985), *Accountability and Prisons: Opening up a Closed World*, London and New York: Tavistock.

MARRIAGE, H., and SELBY, M. (1983), 'Operational Assessment in the South East Region: A Fresh Approach to the Management of Institutions', *Prison Service Journal*, October, 11–13.

MARSDEN, D., and EVANS, R. (1985), 'Accountable Regimes at Featherstone Prison 1981–1984', *Prison Service Journal*, April, 4–6.

MARTIN, J. P. (1975), *Boards of Visitors of Penal Institutions* (Jellicoe Report), London: Barry Rose.

MATTHEWS, R. (ed.), *Privatising Criminal Justice*, London: Sage.

MIKHLIN, A. S., and KING, ROY D. (1994), 'Russian Prisons: Past, Present and Future', paper presented at *Prisons 2000*, An International Conference on the Present State and Future of Imprisonment, University of Leicester, 8--10 April 1994.

MORGAN, R. (1983), 'How Resources are Used in the Prison System', in *A Prison System for the 80s and Beyond* (The Noel Buxton Lectures, 1982–3) London: NACRO.

—— (1985), 'Her Majesty's Inspectorate of Prisons', in M. Maguire, J. Vagg, and R. Morgan (eds.), *Accountability and Prisons: Opening up a Closed World*, London and New York: Tavistock.

—— (1991), 'Woolf: In Retrospect and Prospect', *Modern Law Review*, 54/5: 713–25.

—— (1992a), 'Prisons: Managing for Change', *Public Money and Management*, 12/1, Jan.–March.

—— (1992b), 'Regime-monitoring with Prisoners', *Prison Report*, 18, Spring 1992, London: Prison Reform Trust.

—— (1994), 'An Awkward Anomaly: Remand Prisoners' in E. Player and M. Jenkins (eds.), *Prisons After Woolf: Reform Through Riot*, London and New York: Routledge.

—— and JONES, H. (1991), 'Prison Discipline: The Case for Implementing Woolf', *British Journal of Criminology*, 31/3: 280–91.

—— and KING, ROY D. (1987), 'Profiting from Prison', *New Society*, 23 October 1987.

NACRO (1987), *Women and the Prison Medical Service*, London: NACRO.

—— (1990), *The Prison Medical Service*, London: NACRO.

NATIONAL AUDIT OFFICE (1985), *Report by the Comptroller and Auditor General, Home Office and Property Services Agency: Programme for the Provision of Prison Places*, London: HMSO.

NAPO (1971), *Probation Officers in Prison*, Report of the Treatment of Offenders Committee, London: National Association of Probation Officers.

OWEN, T., and SIM, J. (1984), 'Drugs, Discipline and Prison Medicine' in P. Scraton and P. Gordon (eds.), *Causes for Concern*, London: Penguin Books.

PADEL, U. (1990), 'HIV and Prisoners' Rights', *Liverpool Law Review*, 12: 55–68.

PENAL AFFAIRS CONSORTIUM (1994), *The Path to Community Prisons*, London: Penal Affairs Consortium.

PILKINGTON, D. J. (1994), 'Sentence Planning: Designed to Fail?', paper presented at *Prisons 2000*, An International Conference on the Present State and Future of Imprisonment, University of Leicester, 8–10 April 1994.

PILLING, J. (1992), 'Back to Basics: Relationships in the Prison Service', Eve Saville Memorial Lecture to the Institute for the Study and Treatment of Delinquency, 11 June 1992 (reprinted in *Perspectives on Prison, A Collection of Views on Prison Life and Running Prisons*, Supplement to the Annual Report of the Prison Service for 1991–2, Cm 2087, London: HMSO).

PLATT, T. C. (1987), 'New Directions in Prison Design' in A. E. Bottoms and R. Light (eds.), *Problems of Long-term Imprisonment*, Aldershot: Gower.

PLAYER, E., and JENKINS, M. (eds.) (1994), *Prisons after Woolf: Reform through Riot*, London and New York: Routledge.

PLOTNIKOFF, S. (1986), *Prison Rules: A Working Guide*, London: Prison Reform Trust.

PRIESTLEY, P. (1985), *Victorian Prison Lives: English Prison Biography 1830–1914*, London: Routledge.

PRISON AND PROBATION SERVICES (1994), *National Framework for the Throughcare of Offenders in Custody to the Completion of Supervision in the Community*, London: HM Prison Service and the Probation Service.

PRISON DEPARTMENT (1981), *Working Party on Categorisation: Report*, P5 Division, August.

POA (1984), *The Prison Disciplinary System*, Submissions to the Home Office Departmental Committee on the Prison Disciplinary System, September 1984, London: Prison Officers Association.

PRISON REFORM TRUST (1985), *Prison Medicine: Ideas on Health Care in Penal Establishments*, London: Prison Reform Trust.

—— (1990), *Sex Offenders in Prison*, London: Prison Reform Trust.

—— (1992), *Implementing Woolf: The Prison System One Year On, Findings From a Questionnaire*, London: Prison Reform Trust.

—— (1993), *The Future of the Prison Education Service*, London: Prison Reform Trust.

PRISON SERVICE (1986), *HM Prison Service, Study of Prison Officers' Complementing and Shift Systems*, Joint Study by Prison Department and PA Management Consultants, Vol. I: Report, London: HM Prison Service.

—— (1987a), *Implementation of CI 55/1984: Regime-Monitoring*, London: HM Prison Service.

—— (1987b), *A Fresh Start: Bulletin 8*, London: HM Prison Service, 3 April.

—— (1989), *Briefing*, No. 12, HM Prison Service, Home Office, 10 August 1989.

—— (1990), *Briefing*, No. 25, HM Prison Service, Home Office, 25 September 1990.

—— (1991a), Prison Service News Release, 5 August 1991.

—— (1991b), *The Control Review Committee 1984: Implementation of the Committee's Recommendations*, Directorate of Custody, HM Prison Service, June 1991.

—— (1992), *Briefing*, No. 54, HM Prison Service, Home Office, 10 November 1992.

—— (1993a), 'In-house Team to Run Manchester Prison', News Release, 15 July 1993.

—— 1993b), 'Michael Howard Unveils Plan for More Private Sector Involvement in the Prison Service', News Release, 2 September.

—— (1993c), *HM Prison Service, April 1993, Framework Document*, London: HM Prison Service.

—— (1993d), *HM Prison Service, April 1993, Corporate Plan 1993–96*, London: HM Prison Service.

—— (1993e), *HM Prison Service, April 1993, Business Plan 1993–94*, London: HM Prison Service.

—— (1993f), *The Prison Service Code of Standards*, unpublished draft, July 1993.

—— (1993g), *Prison Service Annual Report and Accounts, April 1992–March 1993*, Cm 2385, London: HMSO.

—— (1994a), *HM Prison Service: Operating Standards*, April 1994, London: HM Prison Service.

—— (1994b), *HM Prison Service, April 1994, Corporate Plan 1994–97*, London: HM Prison Service.

—— (1994c), *Briefing*, No. 73, 11 May 1994, London: HM Prison Service.

—— (undated), 'The Regime-Monitoring System (RMS)—A Review', unpublished paper from the Regimes Research and Development Section, Prison Service.

REINER, R., and CROSS, M. (eds.) (1991), *Beyond Law and Order: Criminal Justice Policy and Politics into the 1990s*, London: Macmillan.

RICHARDSON, G. (1993), *Law, Process and Custody: Prisoners and Patients*, London: Weidenfeld and Nicolson.

RUTHERFORD, A. (1980), 'Report of the Inquiry into the United Kingdom Prison Services: Comments on the May Report', *British Journal of Criminology*, 30,2 166–71.

RYAN, M. 91993), 'Evaluating and Responding to Private Prisons in the United Kingdom', 21 *International Journal of the Sociology of Law* 319–33.

SAMPSON, A. (1992), 'The Unkindest Cut', *Prison Report*, 20, London: Prison Reform Trust.

SHAW, M. (1974), *Social Work in Prison*, Home Office Research Study 22, London: HMSO.

SHAW, R. (ed.) (1992), *Prisoners' Children: What are the Issues?*, London and New York: Routledge.

SHAW, S. (1985), 'Introduction: The Case for Change in Prison Medicine', in PRT (1985), *Prison Medicine: Ideas on Health Care in Penal Establishments*, London: Prison Reform Trust.

SIM, J. (1990), *Medical Power in Prisons: the Prison Medical Service in England 1774–1989*, Milton Keynes: Open University Press.

—— (1994), 'Reforming the Penal Wasteland? A Critical Review of the Woolf Report' in E. Player and M. Jenkins (eds.), *Prisons after Woolf: Reform through Riot*, London and New York: Routledge.

SMITH, R. (1984), *Prison Health Care*, London: British Medical Association.

—— (1985), 'A Comparison of Five Prison Health Services' in PRT (1985), *Prison Medicine: Ideas on Health Care in Penal Establishments*, London: Prison Reform Trust.

SOCIAL SERVICES COMMITTEE (1986), *Third Report from the House of Commons Social Services Committee Session 1985–86*, London: House of Commons.

SPARKS, R. (1994), 'Can Prisons be Legitimate? Penal Politics, Privatisation, and the Timeliness of an Old Idea' in Roy D. King and M. Maguire (eds.), *Prisons in Context*, Oxford: Oxford University Press.

SPARKS, R. F. (1971), *Local Prisons: The Crisis in the English Penal System*, London: Heinemann.

STERN, V. (1987, 1993), *Bricks of Shame: Britain's Prisons*, Harmondsworth: Penguin.

SYKES, G. M. (1966), *The Society of Captives*, New York: Atheneum.

TAYLOR, M., and PEASE, K. (1987), privately circulated paper later published in R. Matthews (ed.), *Privatising Criminal Justice*, London: Sage.

THOMAS, J., and POOLEY, R. (1980), *The Exploding Prison*, London: Junction Books.

THOMAS, P., and COSTIGAN, R. (1992), 'Health Care or Punishment? Prisoners with HIV/AIDS', *Howard Journal*, 31/4: 321–6.

TONRY, M. (1994), 'Racial Disproportion in US Prisons' in Roy King and Mike Maguire (eds.), *Prisons in Context*, Oxford: Oxford University Press.

TRAIN, C. (1985), 'Management Accountability in the Prison Service' in M. Maguire, J. Vagg, and R. Morgan (eds.), *Accountability and Prisons; Opening up a Closed World*, London and New York: Tavistock.

VON HIRSCH, A. (1976), *Doing Justice: the Choice of Punishments*, Report of the Committee for the Study of Incarceration, New York: Hill and Wang.
——, and ASHWORTH, A. (eds.) (1992), *Principled Sentencing*, Boston: Northeastern University Press; Edinburgh: Edinburgh University Press.

WALMSLEY, R., HOWARD, J., and WHITE, S. (1992), *The National Prison Survey 1991: Main Findings*, Home Office Research Study 128, London: HMSO.

WEILER, T. (1992), *Coping with a Crisis: The Introduction of Three and Two in a Cell*, London: Home Office Research and Planning Unit.

WHEELER, S. (1958), *Social Organization in a Correctional Community*, unpublished PhD Dissertation, Seattle: Department of Sociology, University of Washington.

WINDLESHAM, LORD (1993), *Responses to Crime Vol. 2: Penal Policy in the Making*, Oxford: Oxford University Press.

WORLD HEALTH ORGANISATION (1990), *Drug Abusers in Prison: Managing their Health Problems*, Report of a WHO meeting, The Hague, 16–18 May 1988, WHO Regional European Service, No. 27.

YOUNG, A., and MCHALE, J. (1992), 'The Dilemmas of the HIV Positive Prisoner', *Howard Journal*, 31/2: 89–104.

Index